Mutant Neoliberalism

Mutant Neoliberalism

Market Rule and Political Rupture

William Callison and
Zachary Manfredi, Editors

FORDHAM UNIVERSITY PRESS
NEW YORK 2020

Fordham University Press has no responsibility for the persis-
tence or accuracy of URLs for external or third-party Internet
websites referred to in this publication and does not guarantee
that any content on such websites is, or will remain, accurate or
appropriate.

Fordham University Press also publishes its books in a variety of
electronic formats. Some content that appears in print may not be
available in electronic books.

Visit us online at www.fordhampress.com.

Library of Congress Control Number: 2019945350

Printed in the United States of America
22 21 20 5 4 3 2 1
First edition

CONTENTS

Mutant Neoliberalism

Theorizing Mutant Neoliberalism

William Callison and Zachary Manfredi

To many observers, the present resembles Antonio Gramsci's depiction of crisis: a historical interregnum in which the old is dying and the new cannot be born.[1] In the wake of the 2008 global financial crisis, some scholars invoked the image of "zombie neoliberalism" to explain how the reigning form of political-economic governance could persist, as if undead, through the wreckage of its own making. Despite the economic devastation, more of the same neoliberal measures were implemented: liberalization, privatization, marketization, securitization, and austerity.[2] The zombie metaphor thus alluded to a seemingly consistent body of thought and practice while also figuring this body as a corpse. In *The Strange Non-Death of Neoliberalism*, for instance, Colin Crouch sought to understand how neoliberal theory and practice could survive a major financial crisis for which it was largely responsible.[3] Conjuring the image of an undead revenant, Jamie Peck also described "zombie neoliberalism" as the terminus of a once vital project: "The brain has apparently long since ceased functioning, but the limbs are still moving, and many of the defensive reflexes seem to be working too. The living dead of the free-market revolution continue to walk the earth, though with each resurrection their decidedly uncoordinated gait becomes even more erratic."[4] For some of the most insightful commentators, then, neoliberalism persisted through the crash, but only as a kind of corpse ideology.

Yet even the most incisive critics did not fully anticipate the explosion of reactionary forces boiling beneath the surface. Just a few short years after the initial devastation, far-right parties entered legislatures across Europe, and a cohort of authoritarian nationalists rose to power across the globe. Rodrigo Duterte declared a state of emergency for extralegal killings in the Philippines, Narendra Modi demonetized India's economy to the detriment of the country's poor, and Recep Erdoğan strengthened his grip on power in Turkey following a botched military coup by criminalizing the "terrorist" political opposition. Soon after Michel Temer's congressional putsch of Dilma Rousseff in Brazil, Jair Bolsonaro won the presidential election on a vow to marry market-friendly rule with morally infused repression of his political adversaries. Prime Minister Benjamin Netanyahu's coalition passed a constitutional amendment enshrining Israel as "the national home of the Jewish people," effectively denying non-Jewish citizens and Palestinian subjects the right to self-determination as well as other corporate, cultural, and linguistic rights. In the United States, Donald Trump cultivated anti-immigrant, misogynist, and white nationalist sentiment while delivering on long-sought libertarian goals of cutting tax rates and "deconstructing the administrative state."[5] Within and well beyond the Euro-Atlantic, then, right-wing authoritarians not only extended their reach through disruptive use of social media, but came to serve as members of parliament and heads of state. Still reeling from these shocks, the scholarly commentariat began to wonder again whether new political ruptures sounded the final death knell for "zombie" neoliberalism, or whether they rather portended an intensification of its signature forms of market rule.

Mutant Neoliberalism recasts debates about the fate of neoliberal governance and capitalism in the twenty-first century. Rather than treating neoliberalism as a monolithic ideology to be either vanquished once and for all or embraced and sustained *en toto*, the volume theorizes its multiple and mutating forms—as an intellectual and political project, a program of economic governance, a form of normative reason, and an order of material production. In doing so, the book opens up novel paths for understanding the relationship between neoliberalism and contemporary political ruptures. The chapters show how decades of neoliberal governance, policy, and depoliticization created the conditions for new social and political forces, while also reflecting on whether these actors will challenge, reconfigure, or extend neoliberalism's reach in diverse sites across the globe. Seen in this light, ascendant far-right, reactionary forces appear less as neoliberalism's gravediggers than as its own mutant progeny. Political ruptures may not amount to straightforward repudiations or affirmations of neoliberal programs, but rather catalyze new developments in the rationality of market rule.

Defined in biological terms, mutants are not simply physically abnormal or epigenetic specimens, but the result of changes at the level of an organism's genetic code. Though members of the species to which they belong, mutants also constitute a fundamental change in that species. Mutations thus play a critical role in the evolutionary process: when a mutation offers an advantage within the given environment, there is a greater likelihood that the mutant genes will be passed to future generations and thus become a dominant variant in the species. Though we only intend it as a metaphor, the figure of the "mutant" offers an adept analytics for conceptualizing the transformation of contemporary neoliberalism(s). For within the "species" of neoliberalism, new variants are emerging that are distinct but nevertheless members of the same cast.

Our diagnostic focus on "neoliberal mutations" not only calls into question initial responses to the 2008 financial crisis, but forces critical reflection on similar reactions to the Brexit referendum and the Trump election.[6] If neoliberalism was imagined as a zombie formation following the financial crisis, the events of 2016 yielded a renewed expectation of imminent or eventual death.[7] Though their individual analyses varied, critics such as Nancy Fraser,[8] Naomi Klein,[9] and Cornel West all viewed Trump's victory as a powerful rebuke of neoliberalism.[10] The way in which commentators interpreted neoliberalism's "death," however, reflected their respective assumptions and expectations about the nature of historical change. Whereas West saw Donald Trump's victory as "the end of neoliberalism with a neofascist bang," Nancy Fraser only believed that neoliberalism would be purged within the left. This she called the end of "progressive neoliberalism," as opposed to a "reactionary neoliberalism" retained by the right. In this sense, neoliberalism was understood as a stable core of "economic" tenets, albeit with some flexibility in their fusion with "progressive" social positions. Fraser further suggested that "reactionary" or "conservative" neoliberalism represents the revival of its more *original* version. This "return of the repressed" suggested a reinvigoration of Reagan and Thatcherite programs, which married a neoliberal economic platform with a socially conservative agenda. While these analyses were genuine attempts to grapple with the immediate aftermath of major political shocks, they tended to interpret new developments *within* neoliberalism through traditional ideological matrices. Just like the image of an undead ideology that came with the zombie imaginary, the binary of "progressive" and "conservative" neoliberalism relies on familiar heuristics of historical development—heuristics that seem increasingly out of place as the twenty-first century unfolds.

Deeply rooted in the Marxist schema, after all, is the idea that one regime of production births another. Traditional Marxist accounts show, for example, how feudalism bred an ascendant bourgeoisie or how the Fordist organization of industrial capitalism produced the conditions for a post-industrial economy of finance and services. Also found in the classical framework is the notion that revolutionary upheavals emerge when a social order has outlived the material conditions that gave rise to it. In turn, the discourse of an "undead" neoliberalism has, perhaps unwittingly, inherited certain strands of revolutionary political thought. For it imagines that a historical event like the financial crisis will finally reveal a regnant ideology as defunct. And when social and political forces failed to transform this historical "event" into a new order, an old Marxist question reemerged in a new form: "Why did the revolution fail to occur?" became "Why did neoliberalism not die?" The task was then to explain why an expected event never materialized. Underwriting these questions, however, is the quasi-teleological assumption that, once revealed as false or outmoded by historical events, hegemonic regimes are bound for crisis and will thus be replaced by wholly new paradigms of thought and practice.

The figure of "mutant neoliberalism" breaks with many underlying assumptions in contemporary accounts of neoliberalism. Unlike the image of an undead zombie, mutants are new life forms seeking to survive within changing environments. This alternative metaphor offers a nonteleological way of thinking change and continuity that requires greater attention to discursive, affective, and material dimensions of social transformations. For we cannot assume that blanket definitions or traditional expectations of neoliberalism's development will hold while its fundamental features (or its DNA, if you like) are also in flux. At the same time, we cannot simply rely on preexisting ideological categories to map changes within neoliberalism—for instance, by assuming that describing its "progressive" or "far-right" variations does the work of accounting for new historical formations. Indeed, among the central tasks of this volume is examining how the traditional political distinctions between left and right are themselves being unmoored in the context of neo-liberalism's mutations.

Rather than simply asking what neoliberalism "is," *Mutant Neoliberalism* explores a more complex and pressing set of questions: What historical forms has neoliberalism taken, and what are their various lineages in the present? How will past programs of institutional reform—such as privatization, marketization, and austerity—intersect with the ascendant agendas of racist and ethno-nationalist projects? What new forms of individual and collective identity are produced when xenophobic and libertarian logics are spliced together? How are gendered performances and hypermasculine discourses crystallizing in emergent popular and even "populist" formations? What "innovations" in financial technology and public policy paved the way for these mutations, and what new tools might they offer their own opponents? What regimes of value are being created, contested, and reconfigured as free-market stalwarts forge alliances with right-wing projects of alter-globalization? How, too, might left political forces splinter and regroup in the wake of recent right-wing victories?

Proceeding from diverse intellectual and disciplinary traditions, the following chapters interrogate these and related questions while challenging dominant and lasting assumptions about neoliberalism. To set the stage for these contributions, this introduction first provides a brief account of neoliberalism's historical mutations from its early twentieth-century birth to its more recent developments vis-à-vis financialization. It then provides a comparative examination of (Marxist, Foucauldian, and anthropological) theoretical approaches to conceptualizing these mutations. Finally, we discuss and draw out some of the most profound, if also less explicit, political and theoretical connections among the individual chapters.

Neoliberal Mutations

In common parlance, "neoliberalism" tends to serve as shorthand for "free market" principles and policies: free trade agreements between states, free flow of capital across borders, deregulation of private enterprise, privatization of public services, and the rollback of the welfare state. Recent scholarship, however, has challenged the common equation of neoliberalism with "laissez-faire capitalism" or "market fundamentalism" by revealing its distinct intellectual, political, and historical trajectories. Neoliberalism emerged neither by necessity nor all at once, but rather developed through a series of local and global projects that induced particular mutations—the earliest case of which could be seen as the birth of *neo*liberalism out of liberalism itself.

Recent historical work on neoliberalism has illuminated the scientific writings and ideological strategies of specific individuals and schools, including Ludwig von Mises, Friedrich von Hayek, and others in the Austrian School; Walter Eucken, Franz Böhm, Wilhelm Röpke, Alexander Rüstow, Ludwig Erhard, and others in the Freiburg School; Milton Friedman, Aaron Director, George Stigler, Gary Becker, and others in the Chicago School; and James Buchanan, Gordon Tullock, and others in the Virginia School—as well as Michael Polanyi and Lionel Robbins of Great Britain and Louis Rougier and Jacques Rueff of France. Historians have recast our understanding of neoliberalism's origins by tracing the development of its different currents before they affected major institutional transformations. Whereas the birth of neoliberalism is commonly dated to the 1947 founding of the Mont Pèlerin Society in Switzerland or the 1938 Colloque Walter Lippmann in Paris,[11] the category itself is often attributed to a 1932 speech by Alexander Rüstow,[12] though even earlier cases can be found, including in a 1927 treatise by Ludwig von Mises.[13]

Its contested birthdate notwithstanding, the like-minded economic, social, political, and legal theorists of early neoliberalism pursued a coherent if multivalent mission. Propelled by intellectual battles with rival ideologies between WWI and WWII, all of these actors sought to revise and reinvent the beleaguered doctrine of classical liberalism, to resolve the crises of interwar capitalism, and to counter the increasing influence of socialist thought and practice. To facilitate this triple enterprise, they realized, both scientific interventions and political organizations were necessary. Hayek and Röpke thus secured funding for the Mont Pèlerin Society, an indispensable forum for the development of neoliberal ideas that remains a central site of networked organizing to this day.

Importantly, the Mont Pèlerin Society's original goals included developing a "practical alternative" to the "state ascendancy and Marxist or Keynesian planning [that was] sweeping the globe."[14] The neoliberals' strategy aimed at recasting collective values, workers' consciousness, and social movements as both categorically "irrational" and tendentially "totalitarian."[15] Only the "price system," they argued, could secure economic liberty for private individuals engaging in market exchange. This alone, however, did not constitute a radical break with classical liberalism. It was rather the re-embedding of these ideas in a radical constructivist epistemology and a revised political framework that constituted neoliberalism's novelty.[16] Much like their socialist and Keynesian colleagues, the neoliberals did not consider markets "natural" in the classical sense, but saw them as "artificial" constructions in need of occasional buttressing by political (and, ideally, technocratic) agencies. In order to function properly, in other words, markets needed to be produced and sustained by constraining laws and institutions that set "the rules of the game."[17] In this sense, it is important to underscore that neoliberalism began and evolved as a constructivist project to reinvent liberalism, delegitimize "collectivism," and depoliticize market rule.

Animated by a shared hostility to democratic dynamics and state planning, neoliberalism is best understood as a family tree with different branches consisting of their own idiosyncratic philosophies and commitments. These included the Austrian School's "catallactic" model of market dynamics in which exchange is superior to value-laden "social engineering"; the Freiburg School's conviction that only an independent "strong state" can prevent democratic and corporate powers from destabilizing the competitive market order; the Chicago School's belief that almost all forms of state intervention and public ownership produce worse outcomes, disrupt market rule, and infringe upon individual liberty; the Virginia School's claim that all government officials use power to self-interested, inefficient, and wasteful ends, and thus require strict constitutional limitations like "debt brakes"; and the Geneva School's strategy of international institutional design to lock in market-friendly policies and legally delimit state sovereignty over capital flows.[18]

Historical and institutionalist approaches to the study of neoliberalism generally understand it as a set of political, economic, and legal prescriptions. Structural accounts in this genre tend to begin with the stagflation crisis of Keynesianism in the 1970s or the Reagan and Thatcher "revolutions" in the 1980s, which introduced an agenda whose effects can be seen everywhere today: the subsumption of full employment to monetarist or anti-inflationist monetary policies; the imperative of "supply side" or "trickle down" tax cuts for corporations and the wealthy; the privatization of publicly owned industries and goods; the empowerment of shareholders, creditors, and financial markets; and the disempowerment of labor unions. Stuart Hall aptly diagnosed the "authoritarian populism" behind these political programs at the moment of their ascent. But Sören Brandes's groundbreaking contribution to this volume reveals how the neoliberal intellectuals also used mass media to construct a peculiar neoliberal brand of "neoliberal populism" that recast "the people" with *the market* and against "the enemy" of *the government*.

Importantly, however, neoliberal actors not only sought to alter political and economic structures at the domestic level, but also to transform international institutions and postcolonial governance on a global scale. Some materialist and institutionalist scholars focusing on the "Washington Consensus" of the 1980s overlook the extent to which these reforms were, in large part, first formulated far earlier. For instance, Ludwig Erhard's 1948 economic and monetary reforms in war-torn West Germany "set prices free" from state rationing and price fixing amidst material deprivation and extreme hunger;[19] Augusto Pinochet led a 1973 coup against Salvador Allende's democratic socialist government in Chile, which set the stage for the IMF's "structural adjustment" across Latin America and the global South;[20] and in 1980 a violent military coup in Turkey facilitated market-friendly reforms, integration in the world market, and suppression of Left opposition.[21] All the while, as Quinn Slobodian's adept history of the movement has demonstrated, the neoliberals were focused on the design and influence of supranational entities like the International Monetary Fund, the World Trade Organization, and the World Bank over and against the laws and powers of democratic nation states.[22] And as Dieter Plehwe's meticulous mapping of neoliberal ideas reveals, they subsequently spread through diffuse networks of governmental and corporate bodies, nongovernmental organizations, lobby groups, and think tanks.[23]

By the turn of the millennium, neoliberal rationality was inscribed into governmental and common sense, constructing a bridge across the "right" and "left" political spectrum. Most consequential in this respect was arguably the "Third Way" transformation of politics led by figures like Tony Blair, Bill Clinton, and Gerhard Schröder. Each of these "center left" politicians, like many others of their ilk, seamlessly introduced neoliberal programs once too controversial for the right to implement itself.[24] In the same era, the European Union created the single currency and sought to lock in permanent austerity—the neoliberal dream—through constitutional balanced-budget amendments.[25] Despite critics' warnings of a "race to the bottom," the EU also insulated the European Central Bank from democratic influence—the ordoliberal dream—while consecrating price stability, competition, and growth as its technocratic raison d'être.[26]

Across the Euro-Atlantic, center-left governments put their own twist on privatization, marketization, and austerity through "welfare to workfare" programs. Specifically, they pursued "innovation" and "entrepreneurialization" by tightening social spending, "flexibilizing" labor markets, "responsibilizing" individuals, investing in the creditworthiness of some bearers of human capital while disciplining others deemed "discredited." In turn, such measures helped usher in a new "speculative age" of financial market hegemony.[27] At the end of his long tenure as chairman of the Federal Reserve, Alan Greenspan could thus offer the following, wholly unironic lesson just one year before the financial crisis struck: "It hardly makes a difference who will be the next president. The world is governed by market forces."[28]

Unleashing financial markets, empowering creditors, and expanding private debt had become the modus operandi of "left" and "right" parties alike. "Financialization" generally refers to the expansion of financial services and technologies,[29] and many of neoliberalism's mutations developed in tandem with this expansion. For example, it was through "the restructurings of the 1980s and 1990s," Gerald Davis explains, that "the corporation was again transformed from a social institution to a mere contractual fiction oriented toward shareholder value."[30] A central tenet of financialization—maximizing shareholder value—became the organizing principle of post-industrial economies. According to the financialized rationality of mutant neoliberalism, individuals should not rely on governments or corporations for their welfare; they should rely on themselves and their families, as well as the value of their human capital, social network, and real estate. In turn, banks and financial markets should both gauge and facilitate individuals' ability to maximize their creditworthiness. For failing to enhance one's ratings and rankings entails devaluation and discreditation—financially, morally, and emotionally.[31]

In analyzing such mutations, it is essential to recognize that there are multiple and often diffuse processes that neoliberalism put into motion but to which it cannot be reduced. Financialization is a prime example. For despite their many overlaps, financialization was more the unintended consequence than the original design of neoliberal reforms.[32] Among its wide-ranging effects are a shift from the "tax state" to the "debt state"; the empowerment of shareholders and bondholders on corporate and governmental policy; the increasing centrality of sovereign debt for policy decisions; and the speculative logic of ratings and rankings that traverse diverse spheres from financial markets and rating agencies to social media and universities.[33] While neoliberalism and financialization constitute distinct referents, in other words, the latter has arguably been the most significant catalyst for the ongoing mutations of the former.

Three Paradigms of Theorizing

Historical work on neoliberalism has revealed deeper and more complex mutations than are usually permitted by "definitional" debates over what, if anything, makes neoliberalism a legitimate object of scholarly investigation.[34]

More importantly still, historical or genealogical perspectives on neoliberal transformations—including many of the chapters in this volume—complicate efforts at articulating any singular, all-encompassing definition. Yet despite its historical variability and inherent mutability, neoliberalism is more than a mere "empty signifier." As an evolving political and economic theory, set of governmental techniques, and discourse interwoven with everyday life, neoliberalism also carries a discernable core of attributes. And the most illuminating theoretical perspectives on neoliberalism have sought to grasp this mutability while still providing analytic clarity as to its distinguishing features.

In this section we examine three of the most influential approaches to theorizing neoliberalism: Marxist, Foucauldian, and anthropological (or "situated") paradigms of theoretical inquiry. Our analysis draws on the contributions of particular theorists and acknowledges that insights from these different approaches are increasingly amalgamated; occasionally we exaggerate differences between them to draw out their respective virtues and weaknesses. Our discussion should thus be understood as providing a *conceptual heuristics* rather than a comprehensive account of particular thinkers or schools of thought. The aim is to show the panorama that emerges when different forms of analysis are deployed alongside, rather than against, one another.

Importantly, we feature Marxist, Foucauldian, and anthropological approaches because each seeks to grasp the particular, material, historical, and practical *constitution* of neoliberalism. Among their shared commitments is an understanding of historical reflection as a vital element of theoretical activity itself. History confronts thought with changing powers and experiences that cannot be conceptualized in the abstract; in turn, theory is embedded in and partially produced by this "movement of history." Overly formalistic definitions—of neoliberalism, capitalism, socialism, communism, or otherwise—are thus irreconcilable with these theoretical paradigms. At the same time, however, these approaches also diverge from one another in some of their foundational assumptions. As the following chapters make clear, such differences do not make the approaches mutually exclusive. Instead, they require us to mark their respective blind spots and to harness their unique resources—not due to the alleged "truths" they possess, but because of their adequacy as tools to analyze particular objects. At stake in this theoretical comparison is not which paradigm provides a definitive answer to what neoliberalism "is," but how they differently contribute to the intellectual and political task of grasping the mutations of our historical present.

Marxist theorists have largely understood neoliberalism as the most recent phase, and often as a kind of acceleration or intensification, of capitalist development. The tradition of Marxist theory, including a range of recent neo- and post-Marxist theory, contains countless currents, each with its own set of modified philosophical commitments. Taken together, however, this variegated tradition has shown how capitalism operates through capital accumulation, profit maximization, class domination, surplus value extraction, and intertwined processes of exploitation, alienation, and ideological mystification.

For example, Marxist scholars of political economy and human geography—from Giovanni Arrighi and Immanuel Wallerstein to David Harvey and David Kotz—have suggested that neoliberalism is best understood as the latest phase of capitalist restructuring, albeit one driven by a top-down ideological revolution on behalf of international capital and its search for new sites and techniques of accumulation by dispossession.[35] Writing in the tradition of Marxist state theory, thinkers like Nicos Poulantzas and Bob Jessop sought to rework materialist analysis at the beginning of the "neoliberal era" by focusing on interrelated dynamics of political and economic power. After cofounding the Marxist-inflected school of Cultural Studies, Stuart Hall was among the first to identify neoliberalism as the centerpiece of Margaret Thatcher's project of market rule and "authoritarian populism."[36] Étienne Balibar has also been one of the most persistent and influential theorists in the Marxist tradition to analyze the shifting terrain of neoliberal governance; in his contribution to this volume, for the first time, he frames his reflections on neoliberalism in the context of a new theory of "Absolute Capitalism." Proceeding from an internal critique of this tradition, theorists like Achille Mbembe and Gargi Bhattacharyya have interpreted neoliberalism as the latest phase in the history of "racial capitalism" whose technological and global organization has shifted over time.[37] According to these and related Marxist-inspired critiques of (racial) capitalism, neoliberalism carries essential continuities with the primitive accumulation and structural exploitation of earlier periods of Western imperialism and colonialism. At the same time, however, the scholars suggest that "neoliberalism" does in fact name a distinct era characterized by new technologies for oppressing and racializing "surplus" populations from laborers and migrants of color to residents of global slums.[38] What unites various Marxist-inspired critiques, then, is their designation of neoliberalism as a distinct "stage" or "phase" within a longer historical arc of capitalist expansion.

While Marxist thinkers have understood neoliberalism as a period in the capitalist mode of production, entailing new ideological categories and an entrenchment of class power, theorists relying on Michel Foucault's analysis have emphasized the dispersed character of its political rationality, its shifting discursive patterns, and its signature forms of governmentality. Defined as "the conduct of conduct" or "action at a distance," governmentality refers to indirect techniques of rule articulated both through and well beyond the state.[39] Whereas Foucault's formulation of governmentality inspired new interdisciplinary fields,[40] contemporary theorists have deployed related categories and methods from Foucault to understand "neoliberalism in practice," or what Michel Feher describes in this volume as "actually existing neoliberalism." Such analyses have illuminated a range of processes from the discursive reconfiguration of *homo œconomicus* as "human capital" to the financialization of institutional governance and of subjectivity itself.

Several theorists in this volume have shed light on neoliberalism in precisely these ways. Combining historical, sociological, and theoretical insights, Melinda Cooper's research has revealed the consequential marriage of neoliberalism and social conservatism. Michel Feher has worked to disentangle neoliberalism from financialization and to track how the logic of the latter (that is, creditworthiness) is remaking the subjects and the world produced by the former. Examining innovation as a core neoliberal economic strategy whose privileged site of incubation is the research university, Christopher Newfield has combined Arrighi's world-systems theory with his own pathbreaking work in Critical University Studies. And Wendy Brown has updated her own influential critique of neoliberalism's subversion of democracy with an account of its weaponization of traditional morality and its nihilistic enshrinement of a disinhibited libertarianism.[41]

What distinguishes these and other theorists who have made creative use of Foucault is arguably a nimble, historically informed analytics of power focusing on the reconfiguration of state, economy, and subjectivity.[42] Foucauldians have thus conceptualized neoliberalism as a political rationality, a mode of subjectification qua human capital, and as a differential practice of market rule. In the Foucauldian view, power is relational and omnipresent; it does not transcend economic relations of production, but importantly exceeds (and incorporates) them within larger discursive arrangements and dispositives. Yet if Foucauldian approaches have perhaps illuminated subtler transformations of neoliberalism than conventional Marxist accounts, the latter have also offered important correctives to the former—above all, in their attentiveness to the unique operations and plutocratic effects of finance capital. Though the Foucauldian perspective carries a new set of assumptions, it represents less a "paradigm shift" away from the Marxist paradigm than an important supplement to it. And each dovetails with a third, "anthropological" or "situated" approach to neoliberalism.

Anthropological and ethnographic approaches to neoliberalism often hybridize Marxist, Foucauldian, and other modes of theorizing. The same can be said of sociocultural inquiry into neoliberalism spanning legal, literary, gender, performance, critical race, critical university, and science and technology studies, among others.[43] In what follows, however, we will use "anthropological" and "situated" as modifiers to characterize a paradigm that is both distinctive vis-à-vis Marxist and Foucauldian approaches and representative of several contributions in this volume.[44] At stake is not merely identifying a disciplinary hybrid, then, but a qualitatively different procedure of theorizing.

This approach to neoliberalism often features greater attunement to regional histories and local contexts, deeper engagement with affective and psychic investments, and sustained analyses of cultural economies, tacit knowledges, and inherited practices. Yet its central point of departure is arguably the encounter with difference. Ethnographically rooted analysis allows for modes of conceptualization that do not generalize or universalize difference in theoretical form, as if "from above," but account for difference in embedded sites, concepts, and practices that often challenge general theories "from below." By blending historical, Marxist, feminist, ethnographic, and activist work, for example, theorists like Silvia Federici and Verónica Gago have provided "situated" accounts of neoliberalism without dispensing with larger-scale modes of critical analysis.[45]

Anthropologists who take neoliberalism as their primary object of investigation have pioneered situated approaches to theory that also incorporate systematic analysis. Sociocultural anthropologist Elizabeth Povinelli, for example, has written that, "whatever neoliberalism is, what it refers to is not an event but a set of uneven social struggles within the liberal diaspora. . . . Conceptualizing neoliberalism as a series of struggles across an uneven social terrain allows us to see how heterogeneous spaces provide the conditions for new forms of sociality and for new kinds of markets and market instruments (or 'products')."[46] From a different angle than many Marxist or Foucauldian approaches, pathbreaking anthropologies of neoliberalism have illuminated the emergence of new concepts, affects, and identities.[47] If neoliberalism produces the conditions from which new practices emerge, "situated" modes of theorizing are necessary to grasp the movement of such complex and mobile phenomena.

The cultural and anthropological theorists in this volume—including Julia Elyachar, Megan Moodie, Lisa Rofel, and Leslie Salzinger—deploy situated modes of theory to recast the different temporal, regional, and political valences of neoliberalism.[48] Drawing from fieldwork in Egypt, India, China, and Mexico, respectively, these thinkers chart how oft-overlooked neoliberal mutations have differentially constructed new techniques and subjects of market rule. What unites Elyachar, Moodie, Rofel, and Salzinger with other "situated" theorists of neoliberalism, then, is an effort to illuminate how race, class, gender, and sexuality have been reconfigured by neoliberalism's (post-) colonial and (post-)socialist transpositions. Given its dynamic relation to local concepts and situated practices, anthropological theory offers one of the most adept approaches to grasp how neoliberalism both coexists with and mutates through diverse spaces and paradigms of governmental and market rule.

New Mutants, Open Futures

In this final section, we develop some of the chapters' overlapping insights and offer a guide to the complexities of neoliberalism's past, present, and future. Our analysis does not provide a full overview of the individual contributions, but rather opens the intellectual dialogue they occasion. To this end, we consider how the relationship between mutant neoliberalism and new political forms is blurring traditional left–right ideological boundaries; how new subjectivities are emerging in response to neoliberal governance; and how the legacies of socialist and fascist political forms bear on neoliberalism's uncertain future.

LEFT AND RIGHT UNMOORED

The ideological grid of left–right politics inherited from the past half century appears increasingly inadequate to map the relationship between neoliberalism and new political forces. After Third Way social democrats became the executors of austerity measures across the Euro-Atlantic and the Pink Tide washed ashore in Latin America, new parties won electoral victories across the globe by openly attacking the platforms of these earlier reformers.

Consider, for example, some ostensible paradoxes in the relationship between "far-right" politics and neoliberalism. While imposing some of the most restrictive import tariffs in postwar history and providing subsidies to domestic industries harmed by ensuing trade wars, the Trump administration simultaneously passed a massive corporate tax cut and embraced a "neoliberal" agenda of underfunding, understaffing, and "deconstructing" the administrative state.[49] Across the Atlantic, the scrambling of familiar coordinates had long been underway. After winning a major election in Italy, the Five Star movement formed a governmental coalition with neo-fascists from the Lega and implemented a mix of anti-immigrant, anti-austerity, and basic income policies.[50] In Brazil, Jair Bolsonaro rode a wave of racist, misogynistic, homophobic, anti-indigenous, anti-socialist, and anti-corruption sentiment into the presidency. Championing nostalgia for an era of military dictatorship and promising security to the middle classes, he was also galvanized by support from the business community sympathetic to neoliberal reforms. In turn, he appointed Paulo Guedes, a Chicago School economist trained under Milton Friedman, as head of a new "super-agency of finance" with an explicit agenda to "privatize everything."[51] Far from zombie neoliberalism, these are new, brutal specimens.

The complex amalgamation of ideological positions has not, however, been confined to parties labeled right-wing. After the "centrist" candidate Emmanuel Macron defeated far-right leader Marine Le Pen in the French election, the mass mobilization of *gilets jaunes* ("yellow vests") undercut the reform agenda of this new "neoliberal president of the rich."[52] The social movement showcased the multivalent character of many current anti-establishment forces. Catalyzed by Macron's gas tax, the protests initially targeted a "progressive" reform package, pitched as a liberal initiative to curb the devastating effects of climate change.[53] At the same time, however, they also successfully recast the reforms as yet another attempt to pass the negative effects of globalization and the responsibility for climate change onto the working classes while exempting the wealthy and corporations. The protests contained elements of radical class politics reminiscent of left labor uprisings of the twentieth century and harbored some anti-immigrant and regressive fiscal policy perspectives.[54] They consisted of multiple, even mutant strains of political identification—opposed to some legacies of neoliberalism, yet compatible with others. Something similar could be said of the German "left gathering movement," *Aufstehen* ("Stand Up"), which launched in fall 2018 as a bid to "win back" the "left behind" who had turned to the far-right AfD (Alternative for Germany) party.[55] While embracing features of ordoliberalism—the "strong state" and the "social market economy"—*Aufstehen* fused leftist, nationalist, and anti-immigrant tropes, calling for a class-centered politics and tightly regulated borders.[56]

What to make of these hybrid formations? Can they be considered "for" or "against" neoliberalism in any straightforward way? And if certain elements of neoliberalism live on in new "right" and "left" formations, do "left" and "right" remain distinctive ideological categories, advocating for fundamentally opposed political, social, and economic orders? While the contributors to this volume offer no simple formula to address these questions, they provide critical lessons for those seeking to grasp neoliberalism's complex legacies in a shifting political landscape.

Melinda Cooper, Quinn Slobodian, and Dieter Plehwe's contributions provide important historical context and analytical clarity in this regard. Cooper begins her study of the European far right's anti-austerity programs with a provocative observation: among Europe's new political formations, genuine challenges to neoliberal monetary and fiscal policies have more frequently and forcefully come from right-wing than from left-wing parties. To better analyze the programs of the emergent far right, her chapter examines the emergence of Nazi central banking policies in response to an inflexible gold standard, austerity measures, and war debt payments imposed on Germany after WWI. In turn, Cooper offers extensive documentation of how contemporary far-right parties have developed similar alternatives to the austerity imposed by the EU and international financial institutions—from Viktor Orbán's unilateral cancellation of foreign exchange debt and nationalization of private pension assets in Hungary to Marine Le Pen's proposal to revoke the 1973 Pompidou-Giscard law that limited the Bank of France's ability to increase public spending through the purchase of treasury debt.

By comparison, Slobodian and Plehwe's contribution challenges standard narratives of the European Union as an inherently neoliberal institution by examining the changing responses to it from secessionist neoliberal actors. Their chapter traces how Hayek-inspired neoliberals mobilized against the democratic and "post-national" character of the EU due to concerns about its "social" and "leftward" tilt in the 1990s. Hostile to potentially redistributive policies, these neoliberals created Euroskeptic think tanks like the Bruges Group and the Center for the New Europe. Initially, they fought to secure neoliberal policies like capital mobility and free trade within EU institutions. Over time, however, they became increasingly critical of the EU and built new alliances with nationalist, far-right, and anti-immigrant forces—a line of flight that culminated in the campaign for Brexit and in Euroskeptic parties such as the German AfD. Accordingly, Slobodian and Plehwe argue that the "closed-border libertarianism of nationalist neoliberals like the German AfD" does not represent a "rejection of globalism" but rather a mutant "variety of it." While Cooper suggests we take seriously how genuine anti-austerity fiscal and monetary strategies are coming from the far right, Slobodian and Plehwe reveal how neoliberals have themselves joined (ethno-)nationalist, identitarian, and Alt-Right alliances in order to better achieve their programmatic aims.[57]

The widespread dispersion of neoliberal rationality has also made possible radically disparate responses to major political and economic events. Consider, for instance, how the anti-austerity far right studied by Cooper and the anti-EU neoliberals discussed by Slobodian and Plehwe reacted to the 2008 financial crisis differently than did members of the "cyberlibertarian" community. Cyberlibertarian cryptocurrency advocates, for example, were inspired to reinvent the gold standard by promoting the global adoption of Bitcoin as the new international reserve currency.[58] On the one hand, the cryptocurrency community contains diverse ideological positions and supports divergent theories of political economy: cryptocurrency advocates discuss neo-Keynesian and Hayekian theories side by side with John Nash's late work on "Ideal Money" and Ludwig von Mises's paeans to the gold standard.[59] Unlike anti-austerity far-right parties or anti-EU neoliberal think tanks, however, some cryptocurrency advocates would prefer to abolish central banking altogether. Rather than seeking to reassert national control over fiscal and monetary policy through nation-state authority, like some neoliberals and some on the far right, these cyberlibertarians aimed to reinvigorate the neoliberal dream of placing monetary policy "beyond politics" through novel technological means.[60] Bitcoin, in this sense, offered some advocates a technologically superior version of Mises's ideal gold standard: a reserve currency with a finite supply (designed to induce deflationary monetary policy in the long run) that, thanks to the innovation of blockchain technology, would remain impervious to any government's attempts to manipulate its value.[61]

Beyond these scenes of political contestation over fiscal and monetary policy, mutations *within* neoliberalism are also underway in major social and educational institutions. Christopher Newfield's chapter in this volume investigates how "innovation" became the neoliberal discourse par excellence governing global research universities. Importantly, in this context, the discourse of innovation traverses left and right trajectories and dominates administrative priorities within higher education. Newfield shows that innovation has a narrow, though mutable, definition in the business community: "putting a novel idea into a use that creates value." And when implemented as a rationale of neoliberal governance, "innovation translates thought, or intellectual capital, into returns, which become financial capital." Newfield's study centers on Clayton Christensen, "the dean of innovation theory" who shifted the corporate understanding of technical innovation from "steady, incremental improvement" to a market function aimed at disruption. By the 1990s, innovation signified an engine for disrupting and downsizing *everything* to produce new goods and economic growth. "By the late 2010s," Newfield observes, "corporate America, health care, manufacturing, and the contemporary university have all tied their reputations to the delivery of innovation." After being translated into university management, however, the imperative to innovate did not, by and large, produce the economic or educational results its prophets had promised: tuition exploded, salaries plummeted, and the tech industry took higher education for granted "as innovation's archaic resource."

Yet even in light of these failures, university leadership doubled down on its commitment to innovation. Newfield thus asks the perennial question: "Why does the failure of neoliberalism produce more neoliberalism?" And why, in particular, has the response been more neoliberal "innovation" rather than some kind of "left" alternative to it? To answer this question, Newfield analyzes how innovation has been less about increasing productivity and more about *demobilizing* professional knowledge workers whose empowerment threatens the authority of administrators and managers. The imperative to "innovate" monopolizes the time and ambition of academic workers and limits their political response to the failures of this managerial system. To counter this demobilizing strategy, Newfield exposes the ideological functions of innovation strategies in higher education and urges collective action as well as structural reforms centering on the organization of intellectual and skilled labor for a post-neoliberal economy. He also notes that, as a term of political contestation, innovation is mutable, with important family resemblances to "creativity" and "invention" that resonate with left projects to remake the university in accord with *public* and *democratic* values. In this sense, Newfield suggests that left political forces can perhaps challenge the trajectory of mutant neoliberalism by strategically working within its discursive frame.

Four critical lessons can be gleaned from these studies of the evolving relationship between neoliberalism and new political forces. First, Cooper's exhortation to take seriously anti-austerity policies on the far right shows that opposition to neoliberal economic and fiscal policies may come from actors without commitments to social equality or redistribution; indeed, her research reveals a longer history of anti-austerity politics arising out of ethnonationalist projects designed to mobilize state support to some populations through the exploitation and exclusion of others. Second, Slobodian and Plehwe make clear that, though new political forces may mobilize against policies and institutions historically associated with neoliberalism, this does preclude them from constituting a new species of neoliberalism themselves. Third, these contributions remind us that neoliberal responses to major events may take a variety of forms—potentially opposed to one another, but nevertheless deeply rooted in neoliberalism's core premises and practices. Indeed, the long history of neoliberal mutations indicates that opposing political positions can emerge from, or work within, an immanent relation to neoliberalism. While the far-right forces that Cooper, Slobodian, and Plehwe discuss saw the global financial crisis as an opportunity to experiment with nationalist control over financial imperatives, techno-futurists championing Bitcoin instead sought to revitalize an old neoliberal dream of "encasing" markets and money beyond democratic state control.

Fourth, building on insights from Newfield's chapter, we see that left responses to neoliberalized institutions may nevertheless themselves rely on specific forms of neoliberal rationality to achieve their own ends. Like Feher, discussed later, Newfield shows that creative strategies centering on labor can transform the economic practice of creative destruction into activities of learning and forms of creativity in service of the public good. Newfield's work therefore shows that left responses to mutant neoliberal discourse can make strategic use of those discourses, even as they aspire to political alternatives beyond the rationality of neoliberalism.

NEW SUBJECTS OF NEOLIBERALISM

In addition to defying classical ideological categorizations, neoliberal mutations have engendered novel forms of subjectivity. From Reagan's imperative to "be your own boss" to Clinton's agenda to "help you help yourself," neoliberal discursive, governmental, and structural changes have reconfigured social and economic life in the name of enhanced entrepreneurial "freedom." It is important to understand how different managerial discourses of "innovation" and professional imperatives of "entrepreneurialization" became objects of *psychic* and *affective* investment in the first place—forms of investment that, as the following contributors suggest, have developed in divergent and unanticipated ways.

Both Étienne Balibar and Michel Feher's contributions explore the ways in which neoliberalism produces new forms of subjectivity. Feher begins his piece with an analytic distinction that examines divergences between the normative proposals espoused by neoliberal theorists and the world produced by attempts to instantiate their visions. Riffing on rhetoric once used to indicate the gap between socialist theory and socialist regimes, Feher speaks of the "actually existing neoliberalism" that financialization has wrought. He specifically explains how the corporate focus on increasing shareholder value at all costs rose within a new speculative era dominated by finance capital. While neoliberal reforms—first the conservative programs of Reagan and Thatcher and then the Third Way model of Blair, Schroder, and Clinton—sought to produce a world of efficient entrepreneurial profit maximization, in reality, their efforts led to rising collateralized debt obligations, financial speculation, and a universal focus on *creditworthiness*. In Feher's words, while "pro-market reforms purported to create a world where capital owners, wage earners, and even the unemployed would envision their lives as a profit-seeking business, calculating the cost and benefit of every decision. . . . [What] financialized capitalism has actually bred are credit-seeking portfolio managers primarily concerned with the appraisal of their assets in the form of both material and human capital." Feher shows how the logic of financialization has driven governmental techniques of "discarding the discredited"—that is, of disposing of refugees, migrants, the Roma, the homeless, and others deemed uncreditworthy. He also offers a broader perspective on how such processes have recircuited subjects' self-esteem through the digital technologies of algorithms, derivatives, and big data.[62]

Balibar observes that "the name 'neo-liberalism' itself oscillates between an ideological discourse and actual transformations of economic institutions and practices," though he agrees that the "real effects" of neoliberalism are most apparent in the "production" and "destruction" of subjectivities. He specifically points to the "emergence of 'negative individualities' in the French *banlieues* and other places that increasingly host *precarious work*, or alternate between massive joblessness and unstable employment." At work in the production of new subjectivities, Balibar argues, is the logic of social contradiction as well as the systematic dismantling of conditions for "positive individualism" or "propriety in one's person." The (post-)Marxist analysis advanced by Balibar could thus be seen as recasting Feher's gap between neoliberal theory and "actually existing neoliberalism" as an instance of dialectical contradiction. While neoliberalism demands that subjects conduct themselves as entrepreneurial individuals, producing value and profit through the optimization of their human capital, it also creates political and social practices that systematically destroy the material conditions necessary to support this kind of individualism.

Leslie Salzinger adds depth to theories of neoliberal subjectivity by tracing how both the "idealized" neoliberal subject (qua *homo œconomicus*) and "actually existing" subjects of neoliberalism are deeply entwined with "discourses and enactments of masculinity." For Salzinger, neoliberal economic theory presupposes gendered labor as the background condition for its rationally self-interested and calculating subject. Even when the theory incorporates familial relations through mother figures, Salzinger observes, it still relies on a gendered exception to its theory of self-interest: mothers subordinate maximizing their own human capital in order to enhance the value of their children. Drawing from Cooper's account in *Family Values*, Salzinger argues that welfare-state dismantling also works through gendered constructions that effectively reassign care work to the private sphere as it "unburdens" the state from tasks of collective care. Moreover, Salzinger shows how, in practice, gendered enactments of neoliberal subjectivity rely on masculinist tropes to sustain the fiction of purely rational self-interested actors. Her ethnography tracks how financial traders in Mexico City and New York City engage in hypermasculine performances in order to achieve dominance in currency-trading markets. Yet she also cautions against the naïve assumption that a new form of "neoliberal feminism" can provide an antidote to the excesses of market rule. Recent calls for the creation of "Lehman Sisters" and "women-centric" financial institutions, Salzinger argues, effectively erase the gendered entailments of the hyperrational, self-interested *homo œconomicus* they were intended to cure, while often serving as an excuse for financial institutions to continue their risky speculative investments.

Salzinger's account of gendered neoliberal subjectivities intersects with Wendy Brown's diagnosis of the "wounded white masculinity" that has propelled authoritarian figures to power. In the context of Donald Trump's presidency and the rise of far-right parties across Europe, Brown draws attention to the historically specific scene of psychic life animating disinhibited and enraged (primarily white male) subjects whose fatalism and nihilism grew out of neoliberal social, political, and economic transformations. Brown traces how these effects, along with the gendered and racialized psychic formations they foster, have crafted a form of subjectivity particularly susceptible to the pull of authoritarianism.

Taken together, these contributions reveal how new forms of (gendered and racialized) subjectivity have emerged from within a world of uncertainty, displacement, and precarity. Some wounded subjects may react to devalued human capital or perceived loss of status by embracing far-right politics, whereas others may double down on neoliberal logics by re-gendering market relations as a project of "feminist empowerment." Years of neoliberal market rule, coupled with near-impossible expectations for the subjects governed by it, have created mutant hybrids: subjects born of neoliberalism, often deeply attached to its core tenets and practices, and yet also reacting against its effects.

NEOLIBERALISM'S SOCIALIST AND FASCIST REMAINDERS

The contributors also reveal that neoliberalism's new mutations cannot be adequately understood without reference to its old, original rival: socialism. Looking back from this centenary year, Julia Elyachar's chapter offers a novel reading of the twisted paths this battle has taken since its origins in the Versailles Peace of 1919. In the aftermath of WWI, Ludwig von Mises, Friedrich von Hayek, and other "reactionary liberals" sought to attribute the "irrationality" and "savagery" of the Great War not to the West itself, but to socialism and its allegedly disastrous attacks on the free market. By intervening in intellectual and political debates about the purported rationality of different economic systems, Elyachar explains the early neoliberals sought to place socialism in the "Savage Slot," a concept she borrows from the Haitian anthropologist Michel-Rolph Trouillot.

Alongside her study of Mises and Hayek, Elyachar also illuminates the historical intersections between economics and anthropology, two nascent disciplines that participated in the same debates over rationality, markets, and planning. During the same period that Mises and Hayek led the charge against socialist economics, anthropologist Bronisław Malinowski completed his influential ethnographic studies of the people on the Trobriand Islands. According to Malinowski, the ritual modes of exchange on the Trobriands were not "irrational," but rather constituted a different (nonmarket) economic form of rationality—thus contradicting central claims of the early neoliberals. Elyachar argues that these early debates shaped the legacies of neoliberal practice to this day. Her chapter specifically follows Hayek's notion of "tacit knowledge" from interwar debates about psychology and economics into post–Cold War organizational and management theory in corporate America. After the fall of the Soviet Union, anthropologists like Jean Lave "rediscovered" tacit knowledge in embodied learning practices "outside of the market" and identified it as a potential source of market value in the age of Big Data. Tracing the long shadow of these debates not only reveals how neoliberal intellectuals cast their own project as a "civilized" antidote to leftist "savagery," it also sheds light on how neoliberalism's shifting representations of "irrationality" were used to justify free market programs as socialist planning fell in defeat—supposedly, once and for all.

Since neoliberalism began as a project to discredit socialism in the early twentieth century, most commentators have assumed that its rise to power from the late 1970s onward was directly correlated with socialism's waning influence. Lisa Rofel and Megan Moodie's chapter complicates this narrative. In the context of ostensibly "post-socialist" states of China and India, they show how neoliberal governance both relied on and radically reshaped socialist dynamics of political economy. They examine firms that use state-sponsored subsidies to take control over formerly nationalized industries; once in control, these firms enact neoliberal policies of "flexibilized labor" and terminate, or radically amend, union contracts. Even though many firms rely on ostensibly "public" funds through their state partnerships, they also impose reforms on workers that parallel processes described as "privatization." Moodie and Rofel draw on the insights of feminist theory to contest the notion of "privatization" as a unidirectional process of making once-public things private. By contrast, they encourage us to identify the arrangements of power and expropriation that attend efforts to increase "profits" in hybrid economic ventures. Neoliberal strategies, in other words, have learned to incorporate certain aspects of "socialist planning" or "public subsidies" to maximize capitalist profit and labor exploitation.

Importantly, Moodie and Rofel also reject "post-socialism" as a temporal designation for the period after which socialism exited the world stage. Alternatively, they suggest we conceptualize the legacy of socialism in much the same way this volume encourages readers to understand neoliberalism: as a plural and variable set of ideas and practices with disparate remainders in the present. In this spirit, their ethnographies document the ways socialism continues to animate notions of the public good for workers in India and

China subjected to conditions of flexibilized labor. Their research suggests that workers may desire a return to shared ownership of the production process, public welfare benefits, and collective bargaining rights. Moodie and Rofel reveal that subjects of human capital may harbor socialist dreams to be other than what neoliberalism would make of them.

The relationship between neoliberalism and socialism also features prominently in Balibar's analysis of Absolute Capitalism. For Balibar, neoliberalism is a historically specific capitalist form of political and economic reason that rests on a fundamental contradiction. Neoliberalism seeks to "overcome" all socialist legacies (including the last vestiges of the postwar "class compromise") by subjecting all forms of life to market logic. By its nature, however, the latter part of this project needs the former as its constitutive "outside"— that is, neoliberalism requires the existence of socialist remainders to be available for its incorporation. For Balibar, neoliberalism is animated by the desire to destroy socialism—as its necessary and perennial antagonist—and yet necessitates a socialist enemy in order to justify its own existence. In this dynamic Balibar sees a self-defeating contradiction that leaves neoliberalism necessarily open to socialist reversals. Wherever neoliberalism exists, it must posit a "socialist" alternative; and, in so doing, it opens up the possibility that political forces will demand its overthrow in the name of socialism.

If socialism constitutes one irradicable alternative that haunts neoliberal capitalism,[63] many observers suggest that another twentieth-century force has been revived: fascism. Indeed, some commentators have described new far-right parties as a fusion of neoliberalism and fascism—a hybrid "neoliberal-fascism."[64] However, the authors in this volume suggest a more complicated relationship between new movements and different neoliberal and fascist legacies. Melinda Cooper, for example, shows how Nazi economic policy figured the national body-politic as a gendered and racialized mechanism for social reproduction. Cooper offers a "minimal definition" of fascism as a heterodox economic formation that "attempt[s] to overcome the threat of deflation without substantially threatening the existing distribution of wealth and income." Fascist programs, she argues, continually exploit and exclude the "surplus" elements of the population from redistributive benefits. Her analysis reveals that fascist political economy may be formally "opposed" to certain elements of neoliberalism—that is, to the "encasing" of certain market mechanisms and monetary policies beyond political regulation—while nevertheless converging with neoliberalism's disposal of "unproductive" minority populations. Building on these observations, Cooper suggests that we understand fascism as a distinct form of political economy with its own internal logics. In some circumstances, fascism may develop in parallel with neoliberalism; at other times, they may be opposed.

By comparison, Wendy Brown examines new, perhaps unexpected, convergences between neoliberalism and authoritarian politics. In *Undoing the Demos*, Brown initially marked neoliberalism's limited conjunction with fascism in "the valorization of a national economic project and sacrifice to the greater good," along with "growing devaluation of politics, intellectuals, educated citizenship, and all collective purposes apart from economy and security."[65] In her contribution to this volume, she updates her analysis by charting neoliberalism's assault on "the social." Brown traces how neoliberal reforms appealed to "traditional morality" and promulgated patriarchal values of authority, hierarchy, and sexual control. In this sense, neoliberalism laid the groundwork for the rise of new authoritarian political impulses, even if the sudden explosion of these authoritarian sentiments caught many avowed neoliberals by surprise. In Brown's account, the economization of political democracy ultimately unleashed a libertarian variant of neoliberalism as its own nihilistic nightmare. For if libertarianism often imagines itself to be the opposite of authoritarian politics (both fascist and totalitarian), Brown reveals how new anti-democratic forms of authoritarian politics were themselves born of neoliberalism. The authoritarian "Frankenstein" she describes may be a political creation of neoliberalism but, ironically, it is also a monstrous form of anti-politics shorn of any commitment to the public or to truth. For Brown, this new political form is both susceptible and attached to certain fascistic tendencies, from disinhibited hate speech to racialized and sexualized social oppression.

For many, the individualistic and anti-political valences of the neoliberal mutants discussed earlier have been difficult to reconcile with the alleged status of "populist" political uprisings. Indeed, because neoliberalism long presented itself as a thoroughly "individualist" and "anti-collectivist" philosophy, it was widely seen as a natural enemy of all forms of "populism." However, Sören Brandes's chapter reveals that neoliberalism is neither a complete stranger to nor an inherent enemy of populism, broadly understood. Drawing on Ernesto Laclau, Brandes argues that neoliberalism's political ascent relied on "populist" discursive devices to implant itself in the popular imagination. The chapter specifically explores the overlooked role of mass media (television, print, and radio) in the dissemination of neoliberal ideas to the public. Focusing on Milton Friedman's television series "Free to Choose," Brandes shows how neoliberal intellectuals intervened in public discourse and recast their economic theories through a populist veneer. In turn, he argues that the entrepreneurial individual of the market was represented as the antagonist to the "cold, impersonal forces" of the welfare state and government bureaucrats. Through television, journalism, electoral campaigns, and lobbying groups, neoliberal advocates created a distinct vision around a new figure: the "market's people" whose enemy is "the government." Crucially, Brandes calls into question narratives that portray neoliberalism as either merely a "stealth" or an "elite" form of governance imposed by economic liberals. By contrast, he reveals how its wide-ranging critique of government was founded upon "anti-elite" and "anti-establishment" sentiment. From Friedman's aerial overview of Washington, D.C., to Steve Bannon's rhetoric of "the swamp," Brandes exposes the longer history of twisted entanglements between neoliberalism and mass politics.

While fascism and socialism may represent neoliberalism's constitutive "others," both political forms can potentially present neoliberal rationality with new vehicles for its own reinvention. Rather than depending on traditional frames of reference to grasp transformations within neoliberalism, critical theorists would do well to recognize that heterodox approaches to political economy may lend themselves to widely divergent political programs.

Nearly four decades ago, Stuart Hall, a prescient critic of neoliberalism, urged the left to recognize the ways in which Thatcherism had succeeded by channeling the desires of contemporary subjects. Neoliberalism did not win political victories primarily because of its policy proposals or as a result of changing economic conditions. Rather, Hall argued, neoliberalism was an attempt to shape to "some of the core and root social ideas in the population."[66] To challenge the "populist" dimensions of neoliberal politics, he called for a *"socialism which is without guarantees*, that is to say a socialism which does not believe that the motor of history is inevitably on its side. One has to fasten one's mind, as Gramsci said, 'violently' on to things as they are: including, if things are not good, to the fact that they are not too good."[67] Political actors who wish to confront neoliberalism with the alternatives it declares impossible would need to reach "the root values, the root concepts, the root images and ideas in popular consciousness without which no popular socialism can be constructed."[68] This task seems all the more demanding, but also all the more necessary, in our own time.

Neoliberalism is not on its deathbed, but is instead splintering and mutating to survive in changing circumstances—with potentially devastating effects for human and planetary life.[69] As political ruptures yield unexpected lines of alliance and enmity, prevailing strategies of market rule are also being reprogrammed. The analyses gathered here caution against treating such transformations as a double movement or dialectical turn that will slay "zombie" neoliberalism once and for all. In times when resistance must be as radical and adaptable as the world it seeks to change, the "mutant" seems a more adept metaphor. Challenging neoliberalism's mutant progeny will require critical interventions rooted in robust visions of political freedom—interventions that, after Hall, take no guarantees from past orthodoxies and yet seek to construct radically different futures.

Notes

1. Gramsci's famous note reads, "The crisis consists precisely in the fact that the old is dying but the new cannot be born; in this interregnum a great variety of morbid symptoms appear." Antonio Gramsci, *Selections from the Prison Notebooks of Antonio Gramsci*, ed. and trans. Quintin Hoare and Geoffrey Nowell-Smith (London: Lawrence & Wishart, 1971), 276. Following the financial crisis, Slavoj Žižek popularized a "free translation" of the same passage: "This is the time of monsters." Ever since Marx invoked the image of capital as a blood-sucking vampire feeding off of living labor, Gothic tropes have formed prominent undercurrents in Marxist discourse. From specters and vampires to zombies and monsters, the tropes retain analytic and aesthetic power to this day. Nonetheless, as we argue later, the imaginative horizons that come with these metaphors also demand our critical scrutiny.

2. Other significant works that responded to the financial crisis include Gerard Dumenil and Dominique Levy, *The Crisis of Neoliberalism* (Cambridge, Mass.: Harvard University Press, 2011), and Philip Mirowski, *Never Let a Serious Crisis Go to Waste: How Neoliberalism Survived the Financial Meltdown* (London: Verso, 2014).

3. Colin Crouch, *The Strange Non-Death of Neoliberalism* (London: Polity, 2011). In the years that followed, Crouch came to ask, "Can capitalism be reshaped so that it is fit for society, or must we acquiesce to the neoliberal view that society will be at its best when markets are given free rein in all areas of life?"; Crouch, *Making Capitalism Fit for Society* (London: Polity, 2013). His latest work seeks to rehabilitate the "positive contributions of neoliberalism"; see Crouch, *Can Neoliberalism Be Saved from Itself?* (London: Social Europe Edition, 2017).

4. Given that Peck qualifies his account of the "zombie," his approach is likely best understood as straddling this and the former approach: "Crises themselves need not be fatal for this mutable, mongrel model of governance,

for to some degree or another neoliberalism has always been a creature of crisis. But selectively exploiting the crises of Keynesian-welfarist, developmental, or state-socialist systems is one thing, responding to crises of neoliberalism's own making is quite another"; Jamie Peck, "Zombie Neoliberalism and the Ambidextrous State," *Theoretical Criminology* 14, no. 1 (2010): 104–10; see also Peck, Nik Theodore, and Neil Brenner, "Neoliberal Urbanism: Models, Moments, Mutations," *SAIS Review* 29, no. 1 (Winter–Spring 2009); and the excellent case studies in Peck, *Constructions of Neoliberal Reason* (Oxford: Oxford University Press, 2010). For a related metaphor of the neoliberal "centaur state" and an influential study of the prison as a political institution, see Loïc Wacquant, *Punishing the Poor: The Neoliberal Government of Social Insecurity* (Durham, N.C.: Duke University Press, 2009).

5. These are Steve Bannon's words at the 2017 meeting of CPAC, the annual convention of conservatives that just one year prior had shunned Bannon and his colleagues from attending as audience members, much less as center-stage speakers. Now the headliner, Bannon added, "The way the progressive left runs is that if they can't get it passed, they're just going to put it in some sort of regulation in an agency. That's all going to be deconstructed." Beyond the expected praise from his own white nationalist site *Breitbart*, other neoliberal and neoconservative outlets like *National Review* approved of Trump and Bannon's shared mission; see David French, "Trump Wants to Deconstruct the Regulatory State? Good. Here's How You Start," *National Review*, February 24, 2017; see also Philip Rucker and Robert Costa, "Bannon Vows a Daily Fight for 'Deconstruction of the Administrative State,'" *Washington Post*, February 23, 2017.

6. See David Kotz, *The Rise and Fall of Neoliberal Capitalism* (Cambridge, Mass.: Harvard University Press, 2015; and Kotz, "End of the Neoliberal Era? Crisis and Restructuring in American Capitalism," *New Left Review* 113 (September–October 2018): 29–55.

7. Perhaps most committed to both the zombie metaphor and the concept of postneoliberalism is Simon Springer: "The implication is that postneoliberalism is akin to a zombie apocalypse, where the horror we are exposed to is characterized by the mutations, deformity, and insatiable hunger of a living dead idea"; Springer, "No More Room in Hell: Neoliberalism as Living Dead," in *The Sage Handbook of Neoliberalism*, ed. Damien Cahill, Melinda Cooper, Martijn Konings, and David Primrose (Thousand Oaks, Calif.: Sage, 2018).

8. For Fraser, it was more specifically the death of "progressive neoliberalism," defined as "an alliance of mainstream currents of new social movements (feminism, anti-racism, multiculturalism, and LGBTQ rights), on the one side, and high-end "symbolic" and service-based business sectors (Wall Street, Silicon Valley, and Hollywood), on the other"; Nancy Fraser, "The End of Progressive Neoliberalism," *Dissent*, January 2, 2017. Fraser subsequently developed and clarified her position, explaining that she sees Trump's rise to power as evidence of a "hyper-reactionary neoliberalism," which, in a Gramscian sense, proved an effective "counter-hegemonic" force to "progressive neoliberalism";

Fraser, "From Progressive Neoliberalism to Trump—and Beyond," *American Affairs Journal* 1, no. 4 (Winter 2017). While still cursory in its treatment of neoliberalism's historical and ideological mutability, Fraser's revised thesis better approximates the crucial relationship between neoliberal rationality and far-right formations.

9. The day after the U.S. presidential election, Naomi Klein pointed to "the force most responsible for creating the nightmare in which we now find ourselves wide awake: neoliberalism. That worldview—fully embodied by Hillary Clinton and her machine—is no match for Trump-style extremism. The decision to run one against the other is what sealed our fate. If we learn nothing else, can we please learn from that mistake?"; Klein, "It Was the Democrats' Embrace of Neoliberalism That Won It for Trump," *Guardian*, November 9, 2016.

10. Cornel West, "Goodbye, American Neoliberalism: A New Era is Here," *Guardian*, November 17, 2016; see also Martin Jacques, "The Death of Neoliberalism and the Crisis in Western Politics," *Guardian*, August 21, 2016.

11. Transcriptions of the 1938 meeting can be found in Jurgen Reinhoudt and Serge Audier, eds., *The Walter Lippmann Colloquium: The Birth of Neo-Liberalism* (New York: Springer, 2018). For an overview of the society's different lineages, see Mirowski and Dieter Plehwe, eds., *The Road from Mont Pelerin: The Making of the Neoliberal Thought Collective* (Cambridge, Mass.: Harvard University Press, 2009). For other influential studies, see Daniel Stedman Jones, *Masters of the Universe: Hayek, Friedman, and the Birth of Neoliberalism* (Princeton, N.J.: Princeton University Press, 2013); Angus Burgin, *The Great Persuasion: Reinventing Free Markets since the Depression* (Cambridge, Mass.: Harvard University Press, 2015); and Quinn Slobodian, *Globalists: The End of Empire and the Birth of Neoliberalism* (Cambridge, Mass.: Harvard University Press, 2018).

12. See Alexander Rüstow, "Freie Wirtschaft—Starker Staat (Die staatspolitischen Voraussetzungen des wirtschaftspolitischen Liberalismus)," in *Deutschland und die Weltkrise*, ed. Franz Boese (Dresden: Schriften des Vereins für Sozialpolitik, 1932); Rüstow, "State Policy and the Necessary Conditions for Economic Liberalism," in *The Birth of Austerity: German Ordoliberalism and Contemporary Neoliberalism*, ed. Thomas Biebricher and Frieder Vogelmann (London: Rowman & Littlefield International, 2017); see also the following autobiographical note penned by Albert Hunold, cofounder and former secretary of the Mont Pelerin Society, which highlights the intersecting roles of Mises, Hayek, Röpke, Rüstow, and others in establishing neoliberalism well before the Paris and Mont Pelerin meetings: "I became fed up with the socialist philosophy, killing all initiative and spontaneous action. After *Liberalismus*, I soon started studying *Die Gemeinwirtschaft* which Mises had first published in 1922, a comprehensive critique of socialism which was then considered to be his main work. Owing to the influence of these books I changed my mind completely. Although I could not attend the two subsequent meetings of 'Verein für Sozialpolitik' in 1930 and 1932, I followed closely what was said at these meetings and what was published in the 'Schriften des Vereins für Sozialpolitik' such as the

writings of Wilhelm Röpke and Alexander Rüstow, the latter having delivered at the conference of Dresden in 1932 a paper which can be regarded as the founding speech of neo-liberalism"; Albert Hunold, "How Mises Changed My Mind," *Mont Pelerin Quarterly* 3, no. 3 (October 1961): 16.

13. See Ludwig von Mises's early distinction between liberalism and neo-liberalism: "Nowhere is the difference between the reasoning of the older liberalism and that of neoliberalism clearer and easier to demonstrate than in their treatment of the problem of equality. . . . Nothing is as ill-founded as the assertion of the alleged equality of all members of the human race. Men are altogether unequal"; Mises, *Liberalismus* (Jena: Verlag von Gustav Fischer, 1927). For other examples of early self-identification with neoliberalism, see Louis Rougier, "L'offensive du néo-libéralisme," *Le Figaro*, October 29, 1938; a letter from Umberto Ricci to Rougier in June 1939: "Röpke . . . has told me of your political triumphs (for this is what they must be called), because not only have you founded a neoliberal movement . . . but you have also worked with Paul Reynaud"; cited in François Denord, "The Origins of Neoliberalism in France: Louis Rougier and the 1938 Walter Lippmann Conference," *Le Mouvement Social*, no. 195 (2001–2): 9–34; and Milton Friedman, "Neo-Liberalism and Its Prospects," *Farmand*, February 17, 1951. On the earliest use(s) of "neoliberalism" (*Neoliberalismus*), see Bernhard Walpen, "Von Igeln und Hasen oder: Ein Blick auf den Neoliberalismus," *Utopie Kreativ*, no. 121–22 (November–December 2000).

14. Friedrich A. von Hayek, in "Mont Pelerin Society Inventory of the General Meeting Files (1947–1998)" (Ghent: Liberaal Archief, 2005), cited in Ronald Max Hartwell, *A History of the Mont Pelerin Society* (Indianapolis: Liberty Fund, 1995).

15. See William Callison, "Political Deficits: The Dawn of Neoliberal Rationality and the Eclipse of Critical Theory" (Ph.D. diss., University of California, Berkeley, 2019); and Julia Elyachar's chapter in this volume.

16. See Callison, "Political Deficits"; Slobodian, *Globalists*; and Thomas Biebricher, *The Political Theory of Neoliberalism* (Stanford, Calif.: Stanford University Press, 2019).

17. See, for example, Wilhelm Röpke, *Social Crisis of Our Time* (1942; repr. Chicago: University of Chicago Press, 1950); Hayek, *The Constitution of Liberty* (Chicago: University of Chicago Press, 1960); and Milton Friedman, *Capitalism and Freedom* (Chicago: University of Chicago Press, 1962).

18. The concept of the "Geneva School" was coined in Slobodian, *Globalists*.

19. See Callison, "Ordoliberalism's Trans-Atlantic (Un)Intelligibility: From Friedman and Eucken to Geithner and Schäuble," in *Ordoliberalism, Law and the Rule of Economics*, ed. Josef Hien and Christian Joerges (Portland, Ore., and Oxford: Hart and Bloomsbury, 2018).

20. Juan Gabriel Valdés, *Pinochet's Economists: The Chicago School of Economics in Chile* (Cambridge: Cambridge University Press, 1995); Klein, *The Shock Doctrine* (New York: Random House, 2007).

21. Each of these instances introduced liberalization measures at a rapid pace, overturning social-democratic policies from price fixing to state provisioning. On Turkey, see Zeynep Gambetti, "'I'm no Terrorist, I'm a Kurd': Societal Violence, the State, and the Neoliberal Order," in *Rhetorics of Insecurity: Belonging and Violence in the Neoliberal Era*, ed. Zeynep Gambetti and Marcial Godoy-Anativia (New York: NYU Press, 2013), 127–28, and Cihan Tugal, *Passive Revolution: Absorbing the Islamic Challenge to Capitalism* (Stanford, Calif.: Stanford University Press, 2009).

22. See Slobodian, *Globalists*.

23. Plehwe, Moritz Neujeffski, and Werner Krämer, "Saving the Dangerous Idea: Austerity Think Tank Networks in the European Union," *Policy and Society* (2018); Plehwe and Karin Fischer, "Neoliberal Think Tank Networks in Latin America and Europe: Strategic Replication and Cross-National Organizing," in *Think Tanks and Global Politics: Key Spaces in the Structure of Power*, ed. Alejandra Salas-Porras and Georgina Murray (New York: Palgrave, 2017); Plehwe, "Neoliberal Think Tanks and the Crisis," in *Liberalism and the Welfare State: Economists and Arguments for the Welfare State*, ed. Roger E. Backhouse, Bradley W. Bateman, Tamotsu Nishizawa, and Plehwe (New York: Oxford University Press, 2017); and Plehwe and Matthias Schmelzer, "Marketing Marketization: The Power of Neoliberal Expert, Consulting, and Lobby Networks," in *Zeithistorische Forschungen* 3 (2015). See also pieces by Fischer, Plehwe, Elaine McKewon, Hernán Ramírez, and Matthias Kipping, in "Neoliberal Think Tanks," *Global Dialogue Magazine*, August 2018.

24. On the neoliberalization of social democracy, see Stephanie L. Mudge, *Leftism Reinvented: Western Parties from Socialism to Neoliberalism* (Cambridge, Mass.: Harvard University Press, 2018); Andrew Hindmoor, *What's Left Now? The History and Future of Social Democracy* (Oxford and New York: Oxford University Press, 2018); and the pieces by David Bailey, Fabian Escalona, Jean-Michel de Waele, Jeremy Gilbert, César Rendueles, Jorge Sola, Ludovic Lamant, and Jordi Mir Garcia in "Europe at a Crossroads," *Near Futures Online* 1 (March 2016).

25. See Biebricher, *The Political Theory of Neoliberalism*; Biebricher, "Neoliberalism and Law: The Case of the Constitutional Balanced-Budget Amendment," in *Democracy and Financial Order: Legal Perspectives*, ed. Matthias Goldmann and Sylvia Steininger (Berlin: Springer, 2018); Biebricher and Frieder Vogelmann, eds., *The Birth of Austerity: German Ordoliberalism and Contemporary Neoliberalism* (London: Rowman and Littlefield International, 2017); Nancy MacLean, *Democracy in Chains: The Deep History of the Radical Right's Stealth Plan for America* (New York: Viking, 2017); Markus K. Brunnermeier, Harold James, and Jean-Pierre Landau, *The Euro and the Battle of Ideas* (Princeton, N.J.: Princeton University Press, 2017); and Mark Blyth, *Austerity: The History of a Dangerous Idea* (Oxford and New York: Oxford University Press, 2013).

26. See William Davies, *The Limits of Neoliberalism: Authority, Sovereignty and the Logic of Competition* (London: Sage, 2014).

27. See Feher, *Rated Agency: Investee Politics in a Speculative Age* (New York: Zone Books, 2018).

28. Alan Greenspan in 2007, as quoted and discussed in Adam Tooze, *Crashed: How a Decade of Financial Crises Changed the World* (New York: Penguin, 2018).

29. Davis, *Managed by the Markets*; Greta Krippner, *Capitalizing on Crisis: The Political Origins of Finance* (Cambridge, Mass.: Harvard University Press, 2012); Martijn Konings, *The Development of American Finance* (Cambridge: Cambridge University Press, 2011); Randy Martin, *The Financialization of Everyday Life* (Philadelphia: Temple University Press, 2002); Joseph Vogl, *The Ascendancy of Finance* (London: Polity, 2017); Ivan Ascher, *Portfolio Society: On the Capitalist Mode of Prediction* (New York: Zone Books, 2016).

30. "What emerged can be called a portfolio society, in which the investment idiom becomes a dominant way of understanding the individual's place in society. Personality and talent become 'human capital,' homes, families, and communities become 'social capital,' and the guiding principles of financial investment spread by analogy far beyond their original application"; Gerald Davis, *Managed by the Markets: How Finance Reshaped America* (Oxford: Oxford University Press, 2009), 6; see also Abraham A. Singer, *The Form of the Firm: A Normative Political Theory of the Corporation* (Oxford: Oxford University Press, 2018).

31. See Michel Feher's chapter in this volume; see also Josh Lauer, "Your Credit Score Isn't a Reflection of Your Moral Character. But the Department of Homeland Security Seems to Think It Is," *Slate*, November 23, 2018.

32. See Feher, *Rated Agency*; Vogl, *The Specter of Capital* (Stanford, Calif.: Stanford University Press, 2010); Konings, *Capital and Time: For a New Critique of Neoliberal Reason* (Stanford, Calif.: Stanford University Press, 2018).

33. See Wolfgang Streeck, *Buying Time: The Delayed Crisis of Democratic Capitalism* (London: Verso, 2014); Claus Offe, *Europe Entrapped* (Cambridge and Malden, Mass.: Polity, 2015); Benjamin Lemoine, "The Politics of Public Debt Structures: How Uneven Claims on the State Colonize the Future," at "Europe at a Crossroads: Perennial Austerity," *Near Futures Online*, March 2016, http://nearfuturesonline.org/the-politics-of-public-debt-structures-how-uneven-claims-on-the-state-colonize-the-future/; Martha Poon, "Rating Agencies," in *The Oxford Handbook of the Sociology of Finance*, ed. Karin Knorr Cetina and Alex Preda (Oxford: Oxford University Press, 2012); and Feher, *Rated Agency*.

34. For critical perspectives, see Rajesh Venugopal, "Neoliberalism as Concept," *Economy and Society* 44, no. 2 (2015): 165–87; Bill Dunn, "Against Neoliberalism as a Concept," *Capital & Class* (2016); and pieces by Daniel Rodgers, N. D. B. Connolly, Mike Konczal, Julia Ott, and Timothy Shenk in the forum on "Debating the Uses and Abuses of 'Neoliberalism,'" *Dissent* (January 22, 2018). For lucid defenses of the concept, see Biebricher, "Introduction," in *The Political Theory of Neoliberalism*; Slobodian, "Against the Neoliberalism Taboo," *Verso Blog*, January 23, 2018, https://www.versobooks.com/blogs/3583-against-the-neoliberalism-taboo.

35. See Giovanni Arrighi, *Adam Smith in Beijing: Lineages of the 21st Century* (London: Verso, 2009); Immanuel Wallerstein, *The Essential Wallerstein* (New York: New Press, 2000); David Harvey, *A Brief History of Neoliberalism* (Oxford: Oxford University Press, 2007); and Kotz, *Rise and Fall of Neoliberal Capitalism*.

36. Stuart Hall, *The Hard Road to Renewal: Thatcherism and the Crisis of the Left* (London: Verso, 1988).

37. Achille Mbembe, *Critique of Black Reason*, trans. Laurent Dubois (Durham, N.C.: Duke University Press, 2017), 3; and Gargi Bhattacharyya, *Rethinking Racial Capitalism: Questions of Reproduction and Survival* (London: Rowman and Littlefield International, 2018). For another pathbreaking account of state power and embodied resistance as biopolitics and necropolitics, see Banu Bargu, *Starve and Immolate: The Politics of Human Weapons* (New York: Columbia University Press, 2014). For the original formulation of "racial capitalism," see Cedrick J. Robinson, *Black Marxism: The Making of the Black Radical Tradition* (Chapel Hill: University of North Carolina Press, 1983); for what remains one of the most remarkable analyses of racial capitalism in practice, see W. E. B. Du Bois, *Black Reconstruction in America, 1860–1880* (1935; repr. New York: Free Press, 1998); and for select recent works within this expanding tradition of critique, see Nikhil Pal Singh, *Black Is a Country: Race and the Unfinished Struggle for Democracy* (Cambridge, Mass.: Harvard University Press, 2004); and Michael C. Dawson and Megan Ming Francis, "Black Politics and the Neoliberal Racial Order," *Public Culture* 28, no. 1 (2016): 23–62.

38. On the latter, see Mike Davis, *Planet of the Slums* (London: Verso, 2005).

39. See Michel Foucault, *The Birth of Biopolitics: Lectures at the Collège de France, 1978–79*, ed. Michel Senellart, trans. Graham Burchell (New York: Picador, 2008).

40. See Mitchell Dean, *Governmentality: Power and Rule in Modern Society* (Los Angeles and London: Sage, 1999); Nikolas Rose and Peter Miller, *Governing the Present: Administering Economic, Social and Personal Life* (Cambridge and Malden, Mass.: Polity, 2008); and Thomas Lemke, *A Critique of Political Reason: Foucault's Analysis of Modern Governmentality* (London: Verso, 2019).

41. See Cooper, *Family Values: Between Neoliberalism and the New Social Conservatism* (New York: Zone Books, 2017); Feher, *Rated Agency*; Wendy Brown, *Undoing the Demos: Neoliberalism's Stealth Revolution* (New York: Zone Books, 2015); Brown, *In the Ruins of Neoliberalism: The Rise of Antidemocratic Politics in the West* (New York: Columbia University Press, 2019); and Christopher Newfield's chapter in this volume.

42. See Lemke, "Foucault, Governmentality, and Critique," *Rethinking Marxism: A Journal of Economics, Culture & Society* 14, no. 3 (2002); Brown, *Undoing the Demos*; Feher, "Self-Appreciation; or, The Aspirations of Human Capital," trans. Ivan Ascher, *Public Culture* 21, no. 1 (2009); Jason Read, "A Genealogy of Homo Economicus: Neoliberalism and the Production of Subjectivity," *Foucault Studies*, no. 6 (2009); Luc Boltanski and Eve Chiapello, *The New Spirit of Capitalism*, trans. Gregory Elliott (London: Verso, 2007); Pierre Dardot and Christian

Laval, *The New Way of the World: On Neoliberal Society* (London: Verso, 2013);
Imre Szeman, "Entrepreneurship as the New Common Sense," *South Atlantic
Quarterly* 114, no. 3 (July 2015): 471–90; Maurizio Lazzarato, "The Making of
the Indebted Man: An Essay on the Neoliberal Condition," *Semiotext(e)* (2012);
and Vanessa Lemm and Miguel Vatter, eds., *The Government of Life: Foucault,
Biopolitics, and Neoliberalism* (New York: Fordham University Press, 2014).

43. For a mere sampling from these literatures, see Zachary Manfredi, "An
Unlikely Resonance? Subjects of Human Rights and Subjects of Human Capital
Reconsidered," in *The Politics of Legality in a Neoliberal Age*, ed. Ben Golder and
Daniel McLoughlin (London: Routledge, 2017); Samuel Moyn, *Not Enough:
Human Rights in an Unequal World Book* (Cambridge, Mass.: Harvard University
Press, 2018); Annie McClanahan, *Dead Pledges: Debt, Crisis, and Twenty-First-
Century Culture* (Stanford, Calif.: Stanford University Press, 2017); Mitchum
Huehls and Rachel Greenwald Smith, eds., *Neoliberalism and Contemporary
Literary Culture* (Baltimore: Johns Hopkins University Press, 2017); Michelle
Murphy, *The Economization of Life* (Durham, N.C.: Duke University Press,
2017); Christian Riley Nagler, "Performing Labour's (Non)Futures," *Per-
formance Research* 23, no. 6 (2018); David Theo Goldberg, *The Threat of Race:
Reflections on Racial Neoliberalism* (Malden, Mass.: Wiley-Blackwell, 2008); Grace
Kyungwon Hong, "Neoliberalism," and Jodi Melamed, "Racial Capitalism,"
Journal of Critical Ethnic Studies 1, no. 1 (Spring 2015); Christopher Newfield,
Unmaking the Public University: The Forty-Year Assault on the Middle Class (Cam-
bridge, Mass.: Harvard University Press, 2011); Newfield, *The Great Mistake:
How We Wrecked Public Universities and How We Can Fix Them* (Baltimore: Johns
Hopkins University Press, 2016); James Vernon, "The Making of the Neolib-
eral University in Britain," *Critical Historical Studies* 5, no. 2 (Fall 2018); Donald
MacKenzie, Fabian Muniesa, and Lucia Siu, eds., *Do Economists Make Markets?
On the Performativity of Economics* (Princeton, N.J.: Princeton University Press,
2007); Charis Thompson, "Race Science," *Theory, Culture & Society* (Special
Issue on Problematizing Global Knowledge) 23, nos. 2–3 (2006); and Melinda
Cooper, *Life as Surplus: Biotechnology and Capitalism in the Neoliberal Era* (Seattle:
University of Washington Press, 2008).

44. In the expansive literature on situated and standpoint feminist theory,
Donna Haraway formulated the notion of situated knowledges as follows: "Even
the simplest matters in feminist analysis require contradictory moments and a
wariness of their resolution, dialectically or otherwise. 'Situated knowledges' is
a shorthand term for this insistence. . . . We do not seek partiality for its own
sake, but for the sake of the connections and unexpected openings situated
knowledges make possible. The only way to find a larger vision is to be somewhere in particular"; Haraway, *Simians, Cyborgs and Women: The Reinvention
of Nature* (New York: Routledge, 1991), 110–11, 196. We would like to thank
Andrea Sempertegui for insightful feedback on this section.

45. See Silvia Federici, *Revolution at Point Zero: Housework, Reproduction, and
Feminist Struggle* (Oakland, Calif.: PM Press, 2012); and Verónica Gago, *Neo-*

liberalism from Below: Popular Pragmatics and Baroque Economies (Durham, N.C.: Duke University Press, 2017).

46. To this Povinelli adds, "What does seem clear is that neoliberalism is not a thing but a pragmatic concept—a tool—in a field of multiple maneuvers among those who support and benefit from it, those who support it and suffer from it, and those who oppose it and benefit from it nevertheless—each action changing if only slightly the field of maneuver itself"; Elizabeth Povinelli, *Economies of Abandonment: Social Belonging and Endurance in Late Liberalism* (Durham, N.C.: Duke University Press, 2001), 17, 19.

47. For a noncomprehensive list of excellent examples, in addition to the works cited in the following footnote, see Anne Allison and Charles Piot, eds., "Futures of Neoliberalism" (Special Issue), *Cultural Anthropology* 29, no. 1 (February 2014); Stephen J. Collier, *Post-Soviet Social: Neoliberalism, Social Modernity, Biopolitics* (Princeton, N.J.: Princeton University Press, 2011); John L. Comaroff and Jean Comaroff, eds., *Millennial Capitalism and the Culture of Neoliberalism* (Durham, N.C.: Duke University Press, 2001); Comaroff and Comaroff, *Ethnicity, Inc.* (Chicago: University of Chicago Press, 2009); Arturo Escobar, *Territories of Difference: Place, Movements, Life, Redes* (Durham, N.C.: Duke University Press, 2008); Karen Ho, *Liquidated: An Ethnography of Wall Street* (Durham, N.C.: Duke University Press, 2009); Aihwa Ong, *Neoliberalism as Exception: Mutations in Citizenship and Sovereignty* (Durham, N.C.: Duke University Press, 2006); Timothy Mitchell, "How Neoliberalism Makes Its World: The Urban Property Rights Project in Peru," in Mirowski and Plehwe, *The Road from Mont Pèlerin*; Annelise Riles, *Collateral Knowledge: Legal Reasoning in the Global Financial Markets* (Chicago: University of Chicago Press, 2011); and Anna Tsing, *The Mushroom at the End of the World* (Princeton, N.J.: Princeton University Press, 2015).

48. See Julia Elyachar, *Markets of Dispossession: NGOs, Economic Development, and the State in Cairo* (Durham, N.C.: Duke University Press, 2005); Megan C Moodie, *We Were Adivasis: Aspiration in an Indian Scheduled Tribe* (Chicago: University of Chicago Press, 2015); Lisa Rofel, *Desiring China: Experiments in Neoliberalism, Sexuality, and Public Culture* (Durham, N.C.: Duke University Press, 2007); and Leslie Salzinger, *Genders in Production: Making Workers in Mexico's Global Factories* (Berkeley: University of California Press, 2003).

49. For a discussion of Trump's trade policies' complex tensions with other free-trade globalization advocates, see Ashley Smith, "Trump and the Crisis of the Neoliberal World Order," *International Socialist Review* 105 (Summer 2017); for an account that explains Trump's trade policy as ultimately compatible with programs to increase mobility of capital and goods, but not people, see Slobodian, "Trump, Populists and the Rise of Right-Wing Globalization," *New York Times*, October 22, 2018.

50. For an example of how the coalition between Five Star and Lega was perceived as a complicated threat to elite financial investors, see Wolfgang Munchau, "Italy's Political Threat to the EU and to Investors," *Financial Times*, January 28, 2018.

51. Guedes promised to implement in Brazil the same shock-and-awe reforms from Pinochet's dictatorship in Chile. Bolsonaro gave him sweeping powers to privatize state-owned industries and to accelerate natural resource extraction, deforestation, and climate devastation in indigenous territories in the Amazon; see David Biller and Raymond Colitt, "Milton Friedman's Brazil Moment: Band of Disciples Takes Charge," *Bloomberg*, December 12, 2018.

52. Cole Stangler, "'Yellow Vests' against the 'President of the Rich,'" *Jacobin*, November 21, 2018.

53. Rokhaya Diallo, "Why Are the 'Yellow Vests' Protesting in France?" *Al Jazeera*, December 10, 2018.

54. Andrew Higgins, "France's Far Right Sees Gold in Yellow Vest Movement," *New York Times*, December 16, 2018.

55. Heather Horn, "The Voters who Want Islam Out of Germany," *Atlantic*, May 27, 2016.

56. Slobodian and Callison, "Pop-Up Populism: The Failure of Left-Wing Nationalism in Germany," *Dissent* (Summer 2019); and Richard Seymour, "Reinventing the Anti-Immigrant Wheel," *Patreon*, September 3, 2018, https://www.patreon.com/posts/reinventing-anti-20945069.

57. See also Slobodian, "Neoliberalism's Populist Bastards," *Public Seminar* (Spring 2018).

58. See Nathaniel Popper, *Digital Gold: Bitcoin and the Inside Story of the Misfits and Millionaires Trying to Reinvent Money* (New York: Harper, 2015).

59. While Bitcoin's protocol might be an easy fit for (cyber-)libertarian political projects, the diverse set of actors vying to shape the future of new technologies makes it a contested site for future political struggles. For the view that Bitcoin is an inherently right-wing political project, see David Golumbia, *The Politics of Bitcoin: Software as Right-Wing Extremism* (Minneapolis: University of Minnesota Press, 2016).

60. See Saifedean Ammous, *The Bitcoin Standard: The Decentralized Alternative to Central Banking* (Hoboken, N.J.: John Wiley & Sons, 2018). The book jacket perfectly encapsulates this view: "As it challenges the most sacred of government monopolies, Bitcoin shifts the pendulum of sovereignty away from governments in favor of individuals, offering us the tantalizing possibility of a world where money is fully extricated from politics and unrestrained by borders."

61. Ibid., 200–215.

62. See Feher, *Rated Agency*, and Feher, "The Political Ascendancy of Creditworthiness," *Public Books*, January 9, 2019. See also Evgeny Morozov, *The Net Delusion: The Dark Side of Internet Freedom* (New York: Public Affairs, 2012); Bernard Harcourt, *Exposed: Desire and Disobedience in the Digital Age* (Cambridge, Mass.: Harvard University Press, 2015); Jacob Silverman, *Terms of Service: Social Media and the Price of Constant Connection* (New York: Harper Collins, 2015); Frank Pasquale, *The Black Box Society: The Secret Algorithms That Control Money and Information* (Cambridge, Mass.: Harvard University Press, 2016); Edward LiPuma, *The Social Life of Financial Derivatives: Markets, Risk, and Time* (Dur-

ham, N.C.: Duke University Press, 2017); and Cathy O'Neil, *Weapons of Math Destruction: How Big Data Increases Inequality and Threatens Democracy* (New York: Crown, 2016).

63. After Augusto Pinochet's coup d'état in 1973, the Chilean dictator defined his enemy as a specter: "Marxism is like a ghost. It's very difficult to catch— even impossible to trap." At his inauguration in January 2019, Brazilian president Jair Bolsonaro used the same tactic in declaring, "This is the beginning of Brazil's liberation from socialism, inverted values, political correctness, and a bloated state." From the start, the Bolsonaro administration promised to eradicate "Cultural Marxism" and "gender ideology" from schools and universities.

64. Among the many excellent scholars currently working on this relationship are Zeynep Gambetti and Enzo Traverso.

65. Brown, *Undoing the Demos*, 219.

66. Stuart Hall, "The Battle for Socialist Ideas in the 1980s," in *The Hard Road to Renewal: Thatcherism and the Crisis of the Left* (London: Verso, 1981), 190.

67. Ibid., 195.

68. Ibid.

69. Adrian Parr, *The Wrath of Capital: Neoliberalism and Climate Change Politics* (New York: Columbia University Press, 2014).

Neoliberalism's Scorpion Tail

Wendy Brown

Taking even themselves by surprise, hard-right forces have shot into power in liberal democracies across the globe. Every election brings a new shock: neo-Nazis in the German and Austrian parliaments, neo-fascists in the Italian one, Brexit ushered in by tabloid-fueled xenophobia, the rise of white nationalism in Sweden and other parts of Scandinavia, authoritarian regimes taking shape in Turkey and Eastern Europe, and, of course, Trumpism. Racist, anti-Islamic, misogynist, and anti-Semitic bellicosity has taken to the streets, the Internet and the voting booths, and newly coalesced far-right groups have burst boldly into public after years of lurking mostly in the shadows. Politicians and political victories embolden far-right movements, which in turn acquire sophistication and legitimacy as political handlers and social media experts craft the message. As recruits grow, centrists, mainstream neoliberals, liberals, and leftists are spinning. We even have trouble with the naming—is this authoritarianism, fascism, populism, illiberal democracy, undemocratic liberalism, rightwing plutocracy? Or something else?

Failure to predict, understand, or effectively contest these developments is due partly to blinding assumptions about perduring Western values and institutions, especially progress, Enlightenment, and liberal democracy, and partly to the unfamiliar agglomeration of elements in the rising right. These new forces conjoin familiar planks of neoliberalism (licensing capital, leashing labor, demonizing the social state, attacking equality, promulgating freedom) with their seeming opposites (nationalism, enforcement of traditional morality, populist anti-elitism, and demands for state solutions to economic and social problems). They combine moral righteousness with nearly celebratory amoral and uncivil conduct. They endorse authority while featuring unprecedented public social disinhibition and aggression. They rage against relativism but also against science and reason, spurning evidence-based claims, rational argumentation, credibility, and accountability. They disdain politicians and politics while evincing a ferocious will to power and political ambition. They condemn elites and worship wealth. Where are we?

A composite Left account, with a focus on the United States, goes roughly like this: In the global North, neoliberal economic policy devastated rural and suburban regions, emptying them of decent jobs, pensions, schools, services, and infrastructure as social spending dried up and capital chased the cheap labor and tax havens of the global South.[1] Meanwhile, a consequential cultural and religious chasm deepened as hip, educated, slender, secular, multicultural, globetrotting urbanites built a different moral-cultural universe from the midlanders, whose economic woes were salted with estrangement from those who ignored, ridiculed, or disdained them. More than hard up and frustrated, they were alienated and humiliated, left out and left behind—"strangers in their own land," in Arlie Hochschild's phrase. Then there was enduring racism, fueled as new immigrants transformed suburban neighborhoods and as policies of "equity and inclusion" appeared to the uneducated white male to favor everyone over him. Thus, liberal political agendas, neoliberal economic ones, and cosmopolitan cultural ones generated a growing sense of abandonment, betrayal, and rage on the part of the new dispossessed, the white working- and middle-class populations of the first and second world. If their dark-skinned counterparts were harder hit by neoliberal decimations of union-protected jobs and public goods, they did not suffer lost pride of place in America or the West.

As this phenomenon first took shape, the story goes, plutocrats manipulated it brilliantly: the dispossessed were thrown under the economic bus at every turn while being played a political symphony of Christian family values along with paeans to their whiteness and their young sacrificed in senseless, endless wars.[2] Patriotism-as-militarism, Christianity, family, racist dog whistles, and unbridled capitalism made up the successful recipe of conservative neoliberals until the 2008 finance capital crisis devastated incomes, retirements, and home ownership for its working- and middle-class white base.[3] With even the economists muttering that they had been wrong about unchecked debt financing and globalization, serious discursive displacement was now required. This meant screaming about ISIS, undocumented immigrants, and affirmative action myths and, above all, demonizing government and the social state for the economic catastrophe—slyly shifting the blame from Wall Street to Washington because it rescued the banks while hanging the little people out to dry. Thus was a second wave of reaction to neoliberalism born, this one more unruly, populist, and ugly. Already galled by an elegant black family in the White House, disgruntled American whites were also fed a steady diet of right-wing commentary on radio, TV, and social media, inflected from the fringes as a potpourri of previously isolated movements—white nationalist, libertarian, anti-government, and fascist—connected with each other via the Internet.[4] Family values and militaristic patriotism were no longer enough. Rather, the new hard-right populism was bled directly from the wound of dethroned privilege that whiteness, Christianity, and maleness granted to those who were otherwise nothing and no one.

The dethronement was easy enough to blame on job-stealing immigrants and minorities, along with other imagined undeserving beneficiaries of liberal inclusion (most outrageously those of terrorist religions and races) courted by elites and globalists.[5] Thus were casualties of neoliberal deracination mobilized by the figure of their own losses mirrored in a nation lost: this figure drew on a mythical past when families were happy, whole, and heterosexual, when women and racial minorities knew their place, when neighborhoods were orderly, secure, and homogeneous, when terrorism was outside the homeland, heroin was a black problem, and a hegemonic Christianity and whiteness constituted the manifest identity, power, and pride of the nation and the West.[6] Against invasions by other peoples, ideas, laws, cultures, and religions, this was the fairytale world right-wing populist leaders promised to protect and restore. The campaign slogans tell it all: "Make America Great Again" (Trump), "France for the French" (Le Pen), "Take Back Control" (Brexit)," "Our Culture, Our Home, Our Germany" (Alternative for Germany), "White Europe/Pure Poland" (Law and Justice Party).

The accent marks in this story vary. Sometimes they are on neoliberal policy, sometimes on left liberal absorption with multiculturalism and identity politics, sometimes on the growing political importance of evangelicals and Christian nationalists, sometimes on the vulnerability of the uneducated to lies and conspiracies and increasingly siloed media, sometimes on the existential need for horizons and inherent unattractiveness of a globalist worldview for all but elites, and sometimes on the enduring racism of an old white working class or the new racism cleaved to by younger uneducated whites. Some stress powerful right-wing think tanks and political money. Most agree that neoliberal intensification of inequality *within* the global North was a tinderbox and that mass migration from South to North was a match to the fire.

With its various inflections, this has become the Left common sense since the political earthquake of November 2016. The narrative is not wrong but incomplete. It does not register the forces shaping the profoundly antidemocratic form of the rebellion and thus tends to align it with fascisms of old. It does not consider the demonized status of the social and the political in neoliberal governmentality or the valorization of traditional morality and markets in their place. It does not reflect how the neoliberal mobilization of traditional values and brutal attack on social equality could turn up the heat on *and* legitimate long-simmering racisms and misogyny. It does not register the intensifying nihilism that challenges truth and transforms traditional morality into weapons of political battle. The account does not identify how assaults on constitutional democracy, equality, public education, and a civil, nonviolent public sphere have been carried out in the name of freedom *and* traditional morality. It does not grasp how neoliberal rationality generated the hard right and disoriented the left with an ordinary discourse in which social justice is at once trivialized and monsterized as tyrannical "political correctness" or what right-wing media star Jonah Goldberg termed the left's Gramscian *Kulturkampf* aimed at overthrowing liberty and morality.[7]

If these are some of the legacies of neoliberalism fomenting the present, theorizing them requires thinking beyond *Undoing the Demos*, where I characterized neoliberalism's world-making powers as economizing all features of existence.[8] It requires revising formulations of neoliberal and neoconservative rationalities as distinct, as I also did in previous work and many others have done as well. Both moves miss crucial features of the Reagan-Thatcher neoliberal revolution, features that took their bearings not only from America's more familiar Chicago boys, but from the Austrian philosopher Friedrich Hayek and the Freiburg School of ordoliberalism. This revolution aimed at releasing markets *and* traditional morality to govern and discipline individuals while maximizing freedom and de-democratizing the state.

That markets have this role in neoliberalism is a commonplace; not so with traditional morality. Its concrete place in the neoliberal revolutions of the 1980s and '90s is the subject of Melinda Cooper's invaluable 2017 book *Family Values*. However, only a careful rereading of Hayek reveals the architecture of reason that binds traditional morality to neoliberal economics and casts all political challenges to gender, racial, and sexual hierarchies and to class extremes as assaults on freedom and moral order. For Hayek, markets and morals together are the foundation of freedom, order, and the development of civilization. Markets can only do their work if states secure and support them but do not encroach on or intervene in them. Traditional morals can only do theirs when states are likewise restrained from usurping them with justice precepts and when expanding their reach beyond what Hayek calls "the personal protected sphere" gives them more legitimacy in public and commercial life than secular social democracies ordinarily permit. Thus, more than a project of "economizing everything," as I argued in *Undoing the Demos*, Hayekian neoliberalism is a moral-political project aimed at protecting traditional hierarchies by negating the social as a domain of justice and radically restricting democratic claims on states.[9]

Put another way, the attack on society and social justice in the name of market freedom and moral traditionalism is an emanation of neoliberal rationality, hardly the invention of political conservatives. Of course, hard-right parties have made a steady drumbeat of appeals to traditional morality paired with homilies to the free market, together wrapped in nativism, Christianity, and patriotism. And it is easy enough to see how white and male superordination and nativist exclusions are tucked into the markets-and-morals project. On the one hand, deregulated markets tend to reproduce rather than ameliorate historically generated social powers and stratification. On the other hand, traditional morality repels challenges to inequalities and links patriotism not just with love of country but love of the way things *were*, tarring objections to those ways as unpatriotic. Yet, as I shall suggest in the essay's final turn, this nostalgia also blends with unique forms of nihilism, fatalism, and *ressentiment* animated in turn by a panoply of forces including economization, rapture Christianity, climate change, and above all what we might call the end of the Cretaceous period for white male supremacists. These dinosaurs, of course, may burn down the planet rather than adapt. We will get to that problem later. First, we need to consider in more depth the anti-democratic markets-and-morals project of neoliberalism, forwarded largely through attacks on the social and the political.

Attack on the Social

Democracy, especially in large capitalist nation-states, requires explicit effort to bring into being a citizenry capable of self-rule. Neither markets themselves nor winners within them can be permitted to dominate democratic life; both must be contained to generate political equality, democracy's fundament. Democracy also requires a robust cultivation of society as the place where we experience a linked fate, where we are more than private individuals or families, more than economic producers, consumers, or investors, more than mere members of a nation, and more than our differences. Situated conceptually and practically between state and personal life, society is where we are brought together and thought together, politically enfranchised and gathered (not merely cared for) through public goods and care for the public interest. It is also where historically produced inequalities are manifest as differentiated political access, voice, and treatment and where they can be redressed. Social justice, then, more than an intrinsic good, is the antidote to otherwise depoliticized stratifications, exclusions, abjections, and inequalities shrouded by liberal privatism and undermining political equality.[10]

Tellingly, society—its intelligibility, harboring of stratifying powers, and standing as a site of justice and the commonweal—is precisely what neoliberalism set out to destroy conceptually, normatively, and practically. Social regulation and redistribution were discursively delinked from democracy's dependence on political equality and inverted into tyranny, democracy's opposite. Hayek deemed the very notion of the social false and dangerous, meaningless and hollow, destructive and dishonest, a "semantic fraud." Concern with the social was the signature of all misbegotten efforts at controlling collective existence, the token of tyranny. Social justice he called a dangerous "mirage," attraction to it "the gravest threat to most other values of a free civilization."[11]

Why such over-the-top hostility toward the social, society, and social justice? Complex interdependence in modernity does not, Hayek says, arise from organized common pursuit but from individuals "freely" following rules of conduct emerging from markets and moral traditions. To call this society wrongly conflates "such completely different formations as the companionship of individuals in constant personal contact [on the one hand] and the structure formed by millions connected only by . . . infinitely ramified chains of trade [on the other]."[12] More than merely wrong, this conflation reveals the "concealed desire" of social justice or planning advocates to model modern orders on intentional, organized notions of the good—the stuff of totalitarianism. The idea of society, he says, is based on a false personification of what is only a collection of individuals and a false animism, in which "what has been brought about by the impersonal and spontaneous processes of the extended order is [imagined to be] . . . the result of deliberate human creation."[13] Both the personification and the animism lead to the delusion that society is the product of design, hence improvable by a more rational design. And they lead to the delusion that justice pertains to the Good rather than the universal application of known rules.

Social justice, then, is an overdetermined object of opprobrium for Hayek. It draws on the "fatal conceit" of society and attempts to replace the hierarchy and freedom of market and moral conduct with designs imposed by states. It submits morality to rational standards and confuses justice with outcomes rather than rules. It destroys the spontaneous order, justice, freedom, and civilizational development secured by markets and morals with a totalitarian statism. If the care for society takes us down this road, society must be dismantled.

In actually existing neoliberalism, this dismantling has many fronts. Epistemologically, dismantling society involves denying its existence, as Thatcher infamously did in the 1980s, or dismissing concern with inequality as "the politics of envy," as Republican presidential candidate Mitt Romney did thirty years later. Politically, it involves dismantling and delegitimizing the social state—public funding of welfare, education, parks, health, and services of all kinds. Legally, it involves wielding liberty claims to challenge equality and secularism mandates along with environmental, health, safety, labor, and consumer protections. Culturally, dismantling society entails what the ordoliberals termed "de-massification"—shoring up individuals and families against their weakening first by capitalism and then by the social state. Entrepreneurializing and responsibilizing the subject and retasking families with shouldering everything previously provided by the social state (from the cost of education to the cost of dependent young, old, and infirm) disintegrates society to revitalize both individual and family at a moment of their historical waning. Ethically, dismantling society involves challenging social justice with the natural authority of traditional values.

It is obvious yet perhaps worth underscoring that if there is no such thing as society, but only free individuals and families oriented by markets and morals, then there is no such thing as social power generating domination, exclusion, or subjectivity at the site of class, gender, or race. If these social powers do not exist, then complaints rooted in them are baseless whining. Rather, there is only he said/she said, only "whom do you believe"—no social powers of gender, class, and race orchestrating conduct, framing utterances, constituting intelligibility and acceptable norms. Moreover, as it disavows social

powers, neoliberalism's exclusive identification of power with coercion spot-
lights forces of conformism and censorship. Thus, we have a liberalism today
that denies social powers of subject production and intelligibility, denies social obligation or responsibility, and foregrounds powers of coercion said to
distort relations properly ordered by markets and morals.[14]

There is more. The neoliberal fetish of freedom without society destroys
the lexicon and practices by which freedom itself is made democratic, paired
with social consciousness and nested in political equality. As neoliberal reason
demonizes the social, it unleashes freedom and traditional morality *against*
democracy, licensing both as claims against democratically determined principles and practices of social justice, especially against the equality that is
both required by democracy *and* is one of its proper objects of justice. Freedom becomes entitlement to refuse democratic principles and accountability; traditional morality becomes a legitimate usurper of democratic social
norms. Thus *undemocratic* liberal governments, even (as we shall see shortly)
authoritarian ones, are legitimated—this is what neoliberalism bore to the
world. And, when this formation is also energized by the rancor of wounded
whiteness—wounds generated by neoliberal *economic* effects—it can become
freedom and traditional morality with a fascist glint in its eye.

The neoliberal attack on the social is key to generating an *anti-democratic
culture from below* while building and legitimating *anti-democratic forms of state
power from above*. The synergy between them means that an increasingly anti-
democratic citizenry is ever more willing to authorize an anti-democratic state.
As the attack on the social vanquishes an understanding of society tended by
a diverse people equally entitled to share in self-rule, politics becomes a field
of extreme and uncompromised positioning, and liberty becomes a right of
appropriation, disruption, and destruction of the social—its enemy.

Assault on the Democratic Political

The power-sharing entailed in democracy is a uniquely political project requiring cultivation, renewal, and institutional support. Democracy's legitimacy is drawn from exclusively political vocabularies and the affirmation of
political life as a crucial site of human freedom. Yet, as with the social, the
founding neoliberal intellectuals and policymakers were at best wary of the
political and at worst, hostile to it, especially its sovereign and engorged democratic variant. Politics, Hayek declared forthrightly, must be dethroned.[15]

But what did he mean? The neoliberal objection to robust democracy had both ontological and practical-historical dimensions. Ontological: writing in the shadow of fascism, neoliberal intellectuals understood political power to be auto-inflating and inherently overreaching, thus in need of tight constraints. Destructive of the spontaneous and organic orders of markets and morals, coercive by nature, political power uncaged would destroy freedom. This was an argument against sovereignty *tout court*, including popular sovereignty. Practical-historical: universal suffrage would yield representation controlled by the numerically largest class, making social democracy, with its inherently totalitarian trajectory, inevitable. Unless workers and the poor are tricked, trained, or effectively disenfranchised (each of which has been an element of neoliberal governance in recent decades) they will always fight markets as unfair in distributing opportunities and rewards. In addition, democratic energies will inherently bloat the domain of the political, mass activism inherently challenges authority and disrupts order, and even too much ordinary democratic decision-making inherently yields a redistributive, bureaucratic, and overreaching state.[16]

The answer to the dangers of robust democracy and ballooning political power, the neoliberals believed, was to eliminate political sovereignty (about which more in a minute) and dissolve democracy into the most anemic form imaginable—love of private liberty tempered by respect for authority. The neoliberals thus aimed to depoliticize democracy and de-democratize the state by attenuating democratic energies in civil society, prizing apart the state and democratic practices and expectations, and expanding the claims of private liberty and traditional morality. Put the other way around, the democracy that neoliberalism endorses (for facilitating the peaceful transfer of power) is detached from political freedom and equality and divested of political power-sharing by citizens as well as legislation aimed at the public interest.[17]

If leashing democracy and dethroning politics formed a vital part of the neoliberal reprogramming of liberalism, no neoliberal intellectual sought a weak state. Rather, the aim was to delimit its purview, focus it on protecting and supporting economic competition, and insulate it from interests, pluralist compromise, and the demands of the masses.[18] This focus and containment would also build the authority of the state, an authority that could even become legitimately authoritarian as long as it respected personal freedoms and traditional morality.[19]

The neoliberal critique of democracy is packaged as a brief for individual liberty, especially by Hayek and Friedman, but key to reformulating the state in the required fashion was the rejection of popular sovereignty. Popular sovereignty, like society, was another "nonsense notion" for Hayek. Democracy based on it threatens individual liberty and permits legislative power to exceed its narrow task of formulating universal rules of justice.[20] Under its auspice, legislatures take their mandate to be advancing the public interest, yet another "nonsense notion" that expands and corrupts the state. An avalanche then: popular sovereignty unbinds the legislature from limits and its single task of making "equal law for all," hence unbinds legislation from justice, which expands state power.[21]

Thus Hayek attempts to pull liberalism and democracy apart, strengthening the legitimacy of liberalism, radically diminishing democracy and depleting it of sovereign power. He achieves this in part by distinguishing the two and allowing liberalism to limit democracy— "democracy is a method of government" while "liberalism concerns its scope and purpose."[22] Most important, however, is Hayek's formulation of their different opposites. Democracy's opposite is authoritarianism, concentrated rather than shared exercise of political power. Liberalism's opposite is totalitarianism, complete control of every aspect of life. This makes nonsovereign authoritarianism perfectly compatible with a liberal order of personal freedom, traditional morals, and protected private sphere. It also makes totalitarianism something democratic majorities can generate unless their power is constitutionally limited. This is a limit Hayek sought from general principles and one the ordoliberals sought to secure with what they called an "economic constitution" to guarantee a liberal economic order. (This guarantee is essentially what the European Union established with its 2011 MIP reforms.)[23]

In addition to authoritarian liberalism, these two sets of opposites—democracy vs. authoritarianism and liberalism vs. totalitarianism—generate the notion of "excesses of democracy." All of the neoliberals used this phrase to decry 1960s social movements along with efforts to enlarge "the scope of state action guided by democratic decision."[24] However, it was the 1975 Trilateral Commission Report that would make the "excess of democracy" charge infamous. The report's claim that democracy was in crisis *because* of its unbounded reach and energies was straight out of the neoliberal playbook, linking increased demands on the social state with decreased respect for autonomous state functions and authority.[25] Too much democracy meant too much social state and too little respect for law and state power, a problem ramified by the social state's usurpation of family authority and discipline with welfarism and its usurpation of moral authority with social justice. Too much democracy yields too much of the wrong kind of statism and too little of the right kind, exactly the problem Steve Bannon aimed to target with his infamous call to "deconstruct the administrative state."[26]

We are familiar with how free markets and market conduct are meant to function as limits on democratic legislation, but what kind of bulwark against democratic demands does Hayek draw from traditional morality? One strategy, already alluded to, is expanding what he calls the "personal protected sphere" into the place where society once was; this is the strategy advanced by the Alliance for Freedom, the leading evangelical Christian legal organization, and that is also endorsed in a number of Supreme Court decisions permitting conservative Christian claims of conscience to trump federal mandates of equality and inclusion. However, a second strategy involves the limit on state action set by established social norms. Here is Hayek's formulation:

> It is the acceptance of common principles that makes a collection of people a community. A group of men . . . become a society not by giving themselves laws but by obeying the same rules of conduct. *This means that the power of the majority is limited by those commonly held principles and there is no legitimate power beyond them.*[27]

"No legitimate power beyond them." With this phrase, Hayek aims to make "commonly held principles" (the mores emanating from tradition) constitute a limit on the state—restricting the reach of democracy and dethroning the political. These are the principles that make a cohesive people and that they "freely" abide.

Now we have before us the schema of the entire neoliberal logic that simultaneously aims to shore up individual liberties, expand the reach of traditional values into the public sphere, *and* push back against democratic norms, energies, and social justice. These nest compatibly in Hayekian neoliberalism and in European ordoliberalism. Where personal freedom and "commonly held principles" (think racial segregation, gender norms and hierarchies, or hegemonic religions, but also ecologically savage production and consumption practices) constitute the limit on the political and challenge democratic notions of society, markets and traditional morality are easily conjoined. This is how the state is at once limited, detached from democracy and the public interest, and wholly removed from the equality business.

Many scholars have detailed the concrete unfolding of this rationality in legislative and court attacks on civil rights and equality law, capital regulations, and other democratic norms. It is generally framed, however, as a "conservative" assault on "progressive" mid-century policy, a framing that misses the deep neoliberal transformations achieved by wielding market freedom and moral traditionalism against democracy. The conservative framing also occludes the ways in which a multifaceted hostility to democracy has generated in neoliberalized populations at best widespread disorientation about democracy's value and at worst opprobrium toward it. And it misses the extent to which neoliberal reason has rendered thinkable and legitimate authoritarian plutocratic liberalism—perhaps the most apt descriptor of our current regime.

And yet, we are not living the neoliberal dream today. The point of dismantling society, choking democracy, and reprogramming and leashing the state was to eliminate a panoply of political forces—powerful market actors, egalitarians, social engineers, and ignorant, myth-mongering masses. But things went awry in actually existing neoliberalism, as they did in the Marxist revolutions of the last century, which is one reason there is such confusion about what neoliberalism is and whose fault the economic and political disasters are. Democracy has been throttled and demeaned, yes. But angry right-wing mobilizations and their demagogues in power are at odds with neoliberal dreams of pacified, orderly citizenries, denationalized economies, and lean strong states and international institutions dedicated to facilitating global competition and capital accumulation.[28] Instead of insulated from and thus capable of steering the economy, the state has been openly politicized as an instrument serving big capital and at the same time broken off from democratic representativeness, accountability, and the common good. And instead of spontaneously ordering and disciplining populations, traditional morality has become a battle cry, often emptied of substance as it is instrumentalized for other ends. As anti-democratic political powers and energies in constitutional democracies have swollen in magnitude and intensity, they have yielded a monstrous form of political life—one dominated by the financial markets, yanked by powerful economic interests and popular zeal, one without democratic or even constitutional coordinates, spirit, or accountability, hence, perversely, one without limits or limitability. In the absence of the robust notions of the social and the political required to nourish political equality, the public good, and a citizenry committed to both, *Realpolitik* rules, and its raw maneuvering, deal-making, branding, spinning, and indifference to facts, argument, and truth all further disorient populations about democracy's meaning or value. And the more it is loosened from standards of truthfulness, accountability, and negotiating difference to achieve the public good, the more discredited democracy becomes.

But neoliberalism suffering from its internal deficits and contingent developments only partly explains the raging racist, sexist, authoritarian pique trammeling both democracy and the anti-democratic markets-and-morals project. There is also the acid river of nihilism, wounded entitlement, and apocalypticism coursing through the twenty-first century in the global North, a river widened by globalization and neoliberalism, but fed from other tributaries, too. In a final turn, let us briefly consider these contributions to shaping our perilous times.

Nihilism begins, Nietzsche insists, when reason and science challenge God and other forms of authority, a challenge that ungrounds all meaning, revealing it to be humanly invented rather than intrinsic or divine. Weber calls it disenchantment, Tolstoy desacralization; their different angles converge in agreement that intrinsic value flees the world. However, for Nietzsche, as Hans Sluga reminds us, nihilism heralds not the end of values but a world in which "the highest values devaluate themselves" as they are unmoored.[29] The Christian virtues along with democracy and equality—but also truth, reason, and accountability—all lose their value as they lose their fundaments. They do not vanish or even become devitalized but rather fungible, trivial, superficial, and easily instrumentalized. This trivialization and instrumentalization, ubiquitous in commercial, political, and even religious life today, further degrades the values of values, which further abets the nihilism . . . an unending spiral infusing culture, public life, and subjectivity. When a Martin Luther King speech about public service is used to advertise Dodge trucks during the Super Bowl, when the Catholic church hierarchy is revealed to have thrown thousands of babes to men, when conservative religious or political leaders are exposed for adultery, abortion payments, or sexual assault, it brings not shock but a knowing grimace.

The economizing side of neoliberalism added force to the nihilism of the age, first leaving nothing untouched by entrepreneurialization and then, with financialization, submitting everything to investor calculations about its future value. As we become human capital all the way down and all the way in, neoliberalism makes selling one's soul *de rigueur* rather than scandalous. But economization, with its effect on values, is not the only problem here. Nihilism also has its way with the moral dimension of neoliberalization as it desublimates the will to power in morality. Here is how this goes.

As it devalues values, nihilism weakens conscience, itself both formed by and bound to values and unable to withstand their devaluation. But more than simply making subjects less conscience-bound, there is a cascading set of effects here, including desublimation of the will to power out of which conscience is formed. In Nietzsche's account, the sublimation of the will to power required by Judeo-Christian morality involves turning the will to power inward, unleashing it on the subject as its object. This interiorization is what Nietzsche (and Freud, though differently) place at the seat of conscience and is why both treat conscience as self-cruelty, not just self-containment. Conscience is the specifically human formation through which we internally berate or attack and not only restrain ourselves.

As the nihilistic devaluation of values lightens the force of conscience, it desublimates the will to power, freeing us from its containment, self-blame, and self-abuse. Desublimation sends the will to power outward again, releasing the subject from the lash and restraint of conscience. Hans Sluga puts it this way: "With nihilism, there is a falling back and collapse of the will to power into its own elementary form . . . even religion and the appeal to religious values become cynical instruments for the unrestrained use of power."[30] If this desublimated force, tinged by the pain of something like wounded whiteness and masculinity, is what courses through traditional values politics today, we could not be further from the order of freely accepted rules of conduct that the neoliberal intellectuals counted on moral tradition to provide. Wielded as a political cudgel, revenge, or last stand of supremacism, that morality has turned into something else.

The historically specific formation of desublimated freedom animated by woundedness helps account for the unprecedented aggression and viciousness emanating from the Alt-Right as well as more mainstream right-wing news sites, blogs, tweets, talk radio, and even Fox News today. Such aggression issues not just from the neoliberal valorization of libertarian freedom, not just from wounded white maleness, not just from new disinhibitions of expression facilitated by social and interactive media, but from nihilism's radical depression of conscience and hence social responsiveness and obligation. This desublimated will to power, aggrieved by its wound, emancipated by neoliberal reason from social responsiveness and democratic precepts of equality and power-sharing, spirited by valorization of individual freedom, turns its back or worse on the predicaments and vulnerabilities of other humans, other species, the planet. It may merely assert its right not to care, as Arlie Hochschild's red-state interlocutors do with regard to refugees, global warming, or racialized police brutality. Or it may, as Nietzsche puts it, "wreak one's will" on others and the world for the sheer pleasure of it, unbound from the superego for a drunken festival of laughter and indulgence.[31] Or it may become vengeful apocalypticism, scorching everything as it feels its own place and future to be scorched, in Nietzsche's words, "making others suffer as it has suffered."[32]

In this consequential turn, freedom is torn from its habitus in tradition and shorn of the disciplining by market and moral values by which it was to be restrained in the original neoliberal formulation. Instead, nihilistic devaluation of values, combined with neoliberalism's denigration of the political and the social and with wounded whiteness, generates a disinhibited freedom, one symptomizing ethical destitution even as it often dresses in religious righteousness or conservative melancholy for a phantasmatic past. This is freedom paradoxically expressed as nihilism and against nihilism, attacking and destroying while faulting its objects of derision for the ruin of a rightly ordered world. It is the freedom of "I will because I can, because the world has become nothing and I am nothing apart from my wounds and fury."[33] One extreme expression is the so-called "incel" movement, comprising men whose wrath at being spurned or ignored by women is unleashed on the women themselves through online trolling and Gamergate but also in murderous terror attacks such as those in Isla Vista and Toronto.[34] Here, desublimation permits what was formerly the material of shame, misery, and self-loathing—being a "loser" in the heterosexual dating world—to be acted out as murderous rage. The movement also draws on a nihilistic version of moral traditionalism, "before feminism," in which male sexual access to women was a matter of right.

Attention to the desublimated will to power in subjects and in morality itself would explain another feature of the present—namely, how the Right, with its values agenda, routinely survives moral scandals enveloping its religious and political leaders, indeed survives them better than the Left. Why were Clinton's blowjobs from an intern more damaging to his presidency than Trump's pussy grabbing, assault allegations, peeing prostitutes, and affairs with porn actresses and Playboy bunnies have been to his—especially given their respective constituencies? How does a right-wing Supreme Court justice nominee survive allegations that would have taken down a Democratic nominee in a nanosecond? One answer is that nihilism reduces the importance of conduct, consistency, and truth: one no longer need be moral, only shout about it and line up with others who shout about it. Another is that nihilism makes everything contractual, even religious values: Trump's evangelical base doesn't care about his personal conduct as long as he delivers on Jerusalem, abortion, traditional marriage, the trans-ban in the military, prayer in schools, and the rights of Christian businesses and individuals. Both sides understand this deal. As Ralph Reed, chairman of the Faith and Freedom Coalition and leader in the evangelicals' campaign for Kavanaugh, put it, "Jimmy Carter sat in the pew with us. But he never fought for us. Donald Trump fights. And he fights for us."[35]

But neither the contractualism nor the decreased importance of consistency taps the most important feature of nihilism here. Nihilism releases the will to power not just in subjects but in traditional values themselves, baldly revealing their raw power purposes, and the privilege and entitlement they encode. Thus morality itself "falls back" to its elementary form, its will to power, as nihilism shatters its foundations. Pussy grabbing, prostitutes, and assault, as well as scamming contractors and undocumented workers—these are rights of the powerful that traditional values implicitly license as they explicitly prohibit, encode as they disavow.[36] If the power purposes in traditional morality are enormous, they are what remain when nihilism de-grounds and devalues it. Boorishness, rule-breaking, and of course raging at those who object to it, far from being at odds with traditional values, consecrate the white male supremacism at their heart, whose waning spurs its hard-right insurgent base.

Ressentiment

In addition to nihilism, Nietzsche is the master theorist of the force of *ressentiment* in battles born of unmetabolized wounds and rage. Judeo-Christian morality, he suggests in *On the Genealogy of Morals*, emerged as the revenge of the weak against a value system affirming strength, power, and action. The weak resented not their own weakness, but the strong, whom they (mistakenly) blamed for their suffering. And so they invented a new value system, in which strength was reproached as evil and weakness lofted as good. This invention, Nietzsche says, occurs when *ressentiment* stops seething long enough to "become creative and give birth to values."[37] The weak cannot act, only react; this is what their moralizing critique is, but because it is all they have, they will pursue it relentlessly until they triumph. Thus does a Judeo-Christian valorization of meekness, humility, self-abnegation, and asceticism, but also of equality and democracy, emanate from the wound of weakness and take down the strong and the powerful, whom this new morality attacks, constrains, punishes. The creature of *ressentiment*, with no capacity to make the world, reproaches the world it holds responsible for its suffering, thereby anesthetizing the sting. This means the moral system it builds has rancor, reproach, negation, and even revenge at its heart.

Ressentiment, rancor, rage, reaction to humiliation and suffering—certainly all of these are at play in hard-right mobilizations today. However, this politics of *ressentiment* emerges from the historically dominant as they feel that dominance ebbing—as whiteness and masculinity seemingly fail to prevent the displacements and losses that decades of neoliberalism yielded for the working and middle classes. This *ressentiment* varies importantly from Nietzschean logics rooted in the psychic vicissitudes of what he called weakness. The frustrations of weakness (existential or historical) and of aggrieved power are worlds apart, obvious enough in the racially disparate response to declining standards of living neoliberalism delivered to the working and middle classes.

What happens when *ressentiment* is born of dethronement, displacement— lost entitlement rather than weakness? I want to conclude with just two speculations.

First possibility: the rancor and rage are not developed into a refined moral system but remain rancor and rage. They are not sublimated into the Christian self-abnegation and love of thy neighbor that Nietzsche treats as the apex (or nadir) of the process he recounts in *On the Genealogy of Morals*. Suffering and humiliation, *ressentiment* unsublimated, become a permanent politics of revenge, of attacking those blamed for dethroned white maleness— feminists, multiculturalists, globalists who both unseat *and* disdain them. The unstaunched wound and unsublimated rage, combined with a nihilism that mocks in advance all values, means that high levels of affect, not developed moral systems, not what Nietzsche called "unprecedented cleverness" building whole systems of critique, animate populations mobilized by them. This is raw *ressentiment* without the turn toward discipline, creativity, and intellectual mastery that Nietzsche tracks as slave morality in building Judeo-Christian civilization. This is *ressentiment* stuck in its rancor and rage, unable to "become creative" and build a new table of values. It has only revenge, no way out, no futurity.

It is significant that Trump himself openly identifies revenge as his sole philosophy of life.[38] Beyond efforts to destroy disloyalists and opponents and overturn every Obama-era achievement, revenge is the motive that scorches everything from climate accords to the Iran Deal and all that these policies aimed at protecting or preserving: the earth, the most vulnerable species and populations, a future. It is also significant that many Trump supporters, when interviewed about his flouting of truth, law, marital fidelity, or basic protocols of the office, echo some version of this one: "I don't care. I'm tired of the disrespect his opponents have for him and for me."[39] What kind of defense of your man is this? Insofar as it eschews reasons *and* values, it expresses nihilism; insofar as it identifies a wound as the basis of attachment, it expresses *ressentiment*. Indeed, it confesses that Trump both embodies their pain and a retort to it, that spiting their humiliators is all that matters. Again, his abuses of power and office are vital to this desire, not at cross purposes with it, as his own will to power is condensed into aggressive vengeance. Indifferent to matters of political competence, moral rectitude, or even betterment of their own condition, the desire is for an anointing of their wound of nothingness as he lashes out at the world from his own. This is *ressentiment* in a nasty stew with nihilism.

Second possibility: There *is* a table of values that emerges from the wellspring of *ressentiment* for those suffering the lost entitlements of historically conferred supremacism. If Nietzsche is right that *ressentiment* of the weak redeems its predicament by naming "evil" what it holds responsible for its pain and naming itself "good," then wounded supremacism would denounce equality and even merit to affirm its supremacy based only on traditional entitlement. In this move, it performs a historic reversal of values to close out three centuries of modern experiments with democracy. It attacks the very Judeo-Christian morality whose course Nietzsche charted, completing what nihilism began and what neoliberalism's attack on equality, social justice, and democracy put on steroids. The white male supremacism in contemporary traditional values politics becomes explicit, then, not only because nihilism de-grounds it, devalues it, and reduces it to supremacist reaction but because the supremacism has been wounded without being destroyed. Its subject reviles the democracy it holds responsible for its wounds, seeking to pull democracy down as it goes down.

This may be how nihilism goes when futurity itself is in doubt, its form shaped by the waning of a type of social dominance or the waning social dominance of a historical type. As this type finds itself in a world increasingly emptied of meaning *and* of its own place, far from going gently into the night, it turns toward apocalypse.[40] If white men cannot own democracy, there will be no democracy. If white men cannot rule the planet, there will be no planet. Nietzsche was immensely curious about what would come after the two centuries of growing nihilism he forecast. But what if there is no "after"? What if supremacy is the rosary held tight as white civilization appears finished and takes with it all futurity? What if this is how it ends?

Neoliberalism, nihilism, and a murderous *ressentiment* about dethroned entitlement, with no democracy left to contain it: we have never been here before. We probably have to be humbled by this newness before attempting a different order of the new, one that might finally redeem the outsized powers of the species we call human and not only be conquered by their most destructive face and force. The struggle for this alternative requires a vision singularly appropriate to the complex powers and dangers of the age. This vision must reckon with neoliberalism's multiple damages to democratic institutions, expectations, and souls. It must reckon with the rage and pain of those permanently dethroned from privilege by neoliberal policy. It must reckon with technological platforms for "communication" that enshrine ignorance and enable public invective. It must reckon with the impossibility of return to a time before values lost their foundations, and rely instead on building enthusiasm for what is manifestly invented. It must affirm difference *and* equality, freedom *as* emancipation, and feature human beings as but one particularly powerful, destructive, and creative species on the planet, not especially entitled but alone capable of repairing the destruction it has wrought.

Notes

1. Quinn Slobodian, *Globalists: The End of Empire and the Birth of Neoliberalism* (Cambridge, Mass.: Harvard University Press, 2018).

2. Thomas Frank, *What's the Matter with Kansas?* (New York: Metropolitan, 2004).

3. For thoughtful treatments of the long tail of 2008 crisis as *the* precipitating cause of the hard-right turn, see Yanis Varoufakis, "Our New International Movement Will Fight Rising Fascism and Globalists," *Guardian*, September 13, 2018, and David Leonhardt, "We're Measuring the Economy All Wrong: The Official Statistics Say That the Financial Crisis Is Behind Us. It's Not," *New York Times*, September 14, 2018.

4. David Neiwert, *Alt-America: The Rise of the Radical Right in the Age of Trump* (London: Verso, 2017).

5. In *Strangers in Their Own Land* (New York: New Press, 2016), Arlie Hochschild narrates this displacement as if it were factual. White men, however, have rarely been displaced from anything anywhere. What they have faced, however, is new competition from women and minorities, and this alone is enough to gall the racists. But far more important still is the inequality that has generated their dethronement.

6. See James Kirchick, *The End of Europe: Dictators, Demagogues, and the Coming Dark Age* (New Haven, Conn.: Yale University Press, 2017); Douglas Murray, *The Strange Death of Europe* (London: Bloomsbury Continuum, 2017); and Walter Laqueur, *After the Fall* (New York: Thomas Dunne, 2011).

7. Jonah Goldberg, *Liberal Fascism* (New York: Doubleday, 2007).

8. Wendy Brown, *Undoing the Demos: Neoliberalism's Stealth Revolution* (New York: Zone Books, 2015).

9. Quinn Slobodian argues that neoliberalism was a *global political project* from the beginning and thus fundamentally entailed limiting national sovereignties, especially in the economic domain, and radically constricting democracy. See especially the Introduction and Chapter 1 in Slobodian, *Globalists*.

10. In the Preface to *Fugitive Democracy*, one of the last things he wrote, Sheldon Wolin offers an eloquent discussion of the importance of modifying social extremes to generate the very possibility of the political equality required for democracy. He also discusses how social democracy fosters a sense of commonality and shared fate; Wolin, *Fugitive Democracy and Other Essays*, ed. Nicholas Xenos (Princeton, N.J.: Princeton University Press, 2016).

11. Friedrich A. von Hayek, *Law, Legislation and Liberty* (Chicago: University of Chicago Press, 1973), 2:66–68.

12. Hayek, *The Fatal Conceit: The Errors of Socialism* (Chicago: University of Chicago Press, 1989), 113.

13. Hayek, *Fatal Conceit*, 116.

14. The logical consistency rests in the assumption that power is only coercive and that freedom is the absence of coercion. Coercive social power, for a neoliberal, rests in (illegitimate) dictates, rules, enforcement, and punishments—not in what Marx identified as relations of exploitation and domination, what Foucault identified as forces of subjectification, or what critical race theorists and feminists identify in grammars of subordination and abjection. All of these Hayek would call animistic and nonsensical.

15. See Hayek, *Law, Legislation and Liberty*, vol. 3, chap. 18.

16. Several fine intellectual and political histories of neoliberalism have recently revealed its many strategies for retrenching democratic institutions and energies. See, among others, Melinda Cooper, *Family Values* (New York: Zone Books, 2017), especially chap. 6 on the relationship between choking democratic "excess" and privatizing higher education; Nancy MacLean, *Democracy in Chains: The Deep History of the Radical Right's Stealth Plan for America* (New York: Viking, 2017); Thomas Biebricher, *The Political Theory of Neoliberalism* (Stanford, Calif.: Stanford University Press, 2019); and Slobodian, *Globalists*.

17. The neoliberal intellectuals differed in their degree of wariness about the domain of the political as well as in their programs for resetting the state-economy relation and limiting democracy. Hayek and Friedman were most direct in treating the entire domain of the political as a self-expanding force that needed to be caged. The ordoliberals drew closer to Schmitt and sought to build the strong state required for economic order and stability while giving it a technocratic cast and insulating it from democratic demands. However, all regarded individual liberties and markets as endangered by the coercive, unruly, and arbitrary interests and power harbored by the political in its sovereign and democratic form. Hayek and Friedman especially objected to its disruption and deformation of organic developments and spontaneous order. The Ordos

objected to its irrational, unscientific character, its failure to hew to technical expertise and mechanisms. See Biebricher, *Political Theory of Neoliberalism*;
William Callison, "Political Deficits: The Dawn of Neoliberal Rationality and
the Eclipse of Critical Theory" (Ph.D. diss., University of California, Berkeley,
2019); and my discussion in Wendy Brown, *In the Ruins of Neoliberalism: The Rise
of Antidemocratic Politics in the West* (New York: Columbia University Press, 2019).

18. This form of state, as Thomas Biebricher has argued, required a new
form of political theory and practice in which states were legitimated but not
saturated by democracy (now limited to universal suffrage and equality under
the law) and in which state action was relentlessly tied to the well-being of the
market order. See Biebricher, *Political Theory of Neoliberalism*.

19. This authority was, paradoxically only to a social democratic ear, premised on liberal freedom and on the basis of the state's guarantee of that freedom. Only if the state could be insulated from mass democratic demands could
the freedom of the individual, and of capital, be secured.

20. Hayek, *Law, Legislation and Liberty*, 40.

21. The unboundedness can be offset to some degree by vigilant separation
of powers in which legislative, judicial, and executive functions are assiduously
confined to their tasks and kept apart from one another.

22. Repeatedly, Hayek declares that democracy is a method for making
decisions, "not a good in itself" or a principle with general application: "While
the dogmatic democrat regards it as desirable that as many issues as possible be
decided by majority vote, the liberal believes that there are definite limits to the
range of questions which should thus be decided." The crucial conception of the
dogmatic democrat? "Popular sovereignty"; Hayek, *The Constitution of Liberty*
(Chicago: University of Chicago Press, 1960), 170–71.

23. See Biebricher, "Disciplining Europe: The Production of Economic De-
linquency," *Foucault Studies*, no. 23 (August 2017): especially 70–76.

24. Hayek, *Constitution of Liberty*, 170; see also MacLean, *Democracy in
Chains*, 151.

25. Slobodian, *Globalists*, 92. See also Samuel Huntington on the "excess
of democracy" in the infamous Trilateral Commission Report of 1975: "The
vitality of democracy in the United States in the 1960s produced a substantial
increase in governmental activity and a substantial decrease in governmental authority"; Trilateral Commission, *The Crisis of Democracy* (New York: New York
University Press, 1975).

26. Philip Rucker and Robert Costa, "Bannon Vows a Daily Fight for 'Deconstruction of the Administrative State,'" *Washington Post*, February 23, 2017.

27. Hayek, *Constitution of Liberty*, 171.

28. Financial, economic, and security crises have added fuel to the fires of
constitutional democracies, auguring their transformation or replacement with
novel, twenty-first-century regimes.

29. Hans Sluga drew my attention to this in "Donald Trump: Between
Populist Rhetoric and Plutocratic Rule," a paper presented at the UC Berkeley

Critical Theory symposium on the election, February 2017. I rely heavily on his reading of Nietzsche in the ensuing paragraphs. The paper is part of his larger work in progress: Sluga, *The Empire of Disorientation: Politics in the Age of Donald Trump* (forthcoming).

30. Sluga, "Donald Trump," 17. Yet more is at stake in this collapse than a will to power unbridled by humility or ethics. Rather, Sluga writes, "What also goes by the way in this unrestrained will to power is any concern for others . . . in particular the compact between generations on which our entire social order has rested so far."

31. Friedrich Nietzsche, *On the Genealogy of Morals*, trans. W. Kaufmann (New York: Vintage, 1989), 64–67.

32. Ibid., 64–67.

33. There are countless variations on this. One of Trump's voters accounted for her support like this: "It doesn't seem like it makes any difference which party gets in there. Whatever they say they'll do when they get in there, they can't really do it. . . . I just want [Trump] to annoy the hell out of everybody, and he's done that"; cited in Steven Rosenfeld, "Trump's Support Falling among Swing-State Voters Who Elected Him, Recent Polls Find," *Salon*, July 23, 2017.

34. Jessica Valenti, "When Misogynists Become Terrorists," *New York Times*, April 26, 2018.

35. Tim Alberta, "Trump and the Religious Right: A Match Made in Heaven," *Politico*, June 13, 2017.

36. Karl Marx and Alexandra Kollontai were hardly alone in depicting prostitution and adultery as the handmaidens of bourgeois morality.

37. Nietzsche, *Genealogy of Morals*, 33–40.

38. See Chauncey DeVega, "Pulitzer-Winning Reporter David Cay Johnston: 'The Evidence Suggests Trump Is a Traitor,'" *Salon*, April 23, 2018, and Alexander Nazaryan, "Trump's Revenge: How the Assault on Obama's Legacy Explains the President's Priorities," *Newsweek*, September 6, 2017.

39. See James Hohmann, "Trump Voters Stay Loyal Because They Feel Disrespected," *Washington Post*, May 14, 2018, and Paul Waldman, "Why Democrats Can't Win the 'Respect' of Trump Voters," *Washington Post*, May 15, 2018.

40. Rapture Christianity is one version of this. That the vice president and former attorney general of the United States, along with the secretaries (and former secretaries) of housing, education, labor, energy, and environment, subscribe to this creed may help explain the administration's manifest indifference to climate change and willingness to gamble with nuclear war. See Heather Timmons, "Trump's Foreign Policy Looks a Lot Like Rapture Christians' Plan to Welcome the Apocalypse," *Quartz*, May 15, 2018.

The Market's People:
Milton Friedman and the Making of Neoliberal Populism

Sören Brandes

In a narrow, stuffy basement room somewhere in Rochester, New York, the phones are ringing. There is a lot to do; multiple orders are rolling into the small firm, P. H. Brennan Hand Delivery. Pat Brennan—a small woman determinedly facing the camera—is the small company's founder. The camera shows her carrying letters in front of a menacing neo-classical high-rise in downtown Rochester, one of many huge government-owned properties to appear in this series. In their sheer massiveness, the buildings visualize what Milton Friedman, narrating the scene, calls "big government." And soon enough, big government indeed crushes Pat Brennan's prosperous little enterprise. In 1978, the U.S. Postal Service is still a state monopoly protected by law. Thus, after a prolonged struggle with the government, Brennan Hand Delivery is forced to close. The last shot of the sequence shows the basement in which the firm was based—now quiet, empty, and deserted. In *this* fight against Goliath, David has lost.[1]

This little story from Milton Friedman's TV series *Free to Choose* (1980) illustrates some of the central considerations of this chapter. Departing from familiar histories of neoliberalism, which have often focused on the neoliberals' role in academic circles or on their connections to businesses and think tanks,[2] this chapter tracks neoliberal engagements with mass publics. By reconsidering how the movement made its mark on the collective imagination, it explores the seemingly paradoxical construction of a "neoliberal populism" that, like all populisms,[3] rests on the imaginary of a collective—what I call "the market's people." Contrary to its self-positioning as the nemesis of "collectivism," neoliberalism, too, advanced visions of the "public good." It likewise cultivated the notion of a collective "people" whose enemy is "the government" and whose common interests converge in the marketplace. Such a populist form of neoliberalism emerged through interactions between organized neoliberals, the mass media industry, and mass politics around the 1970s.

To make this argument, the chapter follows Milton Friedman through his engagements with mass media and politics during this period and analyzes his TV series *Free to Choose*.[4] As will become apparent, such an approach gives us an important perspective on the current conjuncture in which a right-wing populist discourse is not so much defying as *transforming* an earlier neoliberal one. But let us first consider some ways in which this account may challenge or complement current constructions of neoliberalism itself.

Stealth Revolutionaries? Constructions of Neoliberal Politics

Recent histories of neoliberalism tend to approach their subject through two interconnected narratives: one is a story of "stealth" and secrecy, the other a story of undermining. Wendy Brown describes neoliberalism as a "Stealth Revolution," and Nancy MacLean speaks of neoliberalism's "Stealth Plan."[5] Secrecy, or at least operating under the radar of public scrutiny, is often thought to be one of neoliberalism's hallmarks. Philip Mirowski charges that the neoliberals even sought to obscure the very term "neoliberalism" to "cover their tracks."[6] Mirowski has also written on what he calls the "double truth" of neoliberalism: the side-by-side existence of exoteric and esoteric doctrines. Whereas the former are presented to the public, the latter are the outcome of internal debates among closed groups like the Mont Pèlerin Society—and only the latter make up the "real" neoliberalism, as uncovered by Mirowski and other intellectual historians.[7]

Recent scholarship has also examined neoliberalism's relationship to democracy and to democratic politics as a project of undermining. In this view, rather than a shrinking or retreat of the state, neoliberalism attempted and achieved a reinstitutionalization of policy, law, and governance to protect markets and the freedom of capital rather than reign in their excesses. This necessitated an institutional isolation of state power from majoritarian, democratic institutions like parliaments and national governments, which were now restricted and controlled by constitutional amendments, technocratic bodies, international institutions, and free trade agreements. The state, as enshrined by neoliberal institutions, became a mechanism to reign in rather than to empower popular democracy. Thus, politics in the sense of an institutionalized enactment of a collective will was muted. In William Davies's phrasing, the technocratic side of this power grab amounted to "the disenchantment of politics by economics."[8]

This story provides important insights for understanding both the history and the present of neoliberalism. Not only has there indeed been "a deep strain of elitism and contempt for the masses"[9] and a notable preoccupation with the dangers of popular sovereignty among many neoliberal intellectuals and experts, there is also a curious convergence between these neoliberal visions and important features of "actually existing" neoliberalism since the 1970s. It is not for nothing that analyses and complaints about "post-democracy" and the "post-political," describing a political world in which collective power is stifled and elections reduced to acclamations of already existing power structures, have been so persuasive and influential in the last decades.[10]

By and large, this literature has centered on very specific parts of the neoliberal networks and histories, focusing either on their intellectual and academic legacies or on the enactment of neoliberal policy and political economy. But there is something missing from these accounts: an engagement with the problem of popular legitimacy. Looking only at attempts to undermine and encase democracy can make it seem as if the neoliberal project were inherently unpopular.[11] This, however, may dangerously underestimate the "moral force and affective charge" of neoliberalism as a political project.[12] It also ignores the ways in which policies like lower taxes and increased access to consumer credit initially expanded opportunities for people even at the long-term expense of social service provision and personal debt.[13] If neoliberal hegemony has been established, we need to account for how it obtained and preserved its mass legitimacy, especially in democratic contexts where seizing power depended on winning elections.

From this vantage point, it becomes visible that neoliberalism, rather than (or in addition to) circumventing democracy, directly engaged in and worked with the mechanisms of democratic politics. Current literature, with its interest in the "stealth" elements of neoliberalism, is often pervaded by a tendency to overlook or underestimate neoliberal encounters with broad publics, with mass media and mass politics, sometimes going so far as to paint any neoliberal interactions with the public as only an attempt at "knowledge manipulation" and "bamboozlement."[14] While it is certainly true that public pronouncements are communicative acts operating according to different logics than internal lectures and discussions, it seems all the more important to analyze and discuss these logics rather than shunting them aside as insincere or unsophisticated.

To do so necessitates a dual shift: first a redirection of attention toward those instances in which neoliberal actors and networks engaged directly with broad publics, as in journalism, press, or television appearances and political campaigns. Second, it means a theoretical reorientation toward theories of mass media (and methods of media analysis) and theories of the political. Theories of mass media have pointed out, most notably in the works of Marshall McLuhan and Friedrich Kittler, that media are not neutral tools for dissemination but actively shape and change the messages they convey and the societal fields they represent. They thus play a fundamental role in every political activity. To understand the political, in turn, I rely on a nonessentialist approach, taking a special interest in Ernesto Laclau's theory of populism and in Stuart Hall's penetrating analyses of Thatcherism.[15]

Milton Friedman, Free to Choose, *and the Making of Market Populism*

In 1980, Milton Friedman was at the pinnacle of his career. While his academic success could not exceed the Nobel Memorial Prize in Economics he received in 1976, his star as a media celebrity was still rising. Ever since his participation in Barry Goldwater's 1964 presidential run and his subsequent hiring as one of *Newsweek*'s regular economic columnists, he had appeared in national newspapers and magazines and on television with ever-increasing frequency.[16] During the late '60s and '70s, he had emerged as one of the most well-known economists in the United States and even throughout the world. But now, even compared to this high point, his public recognition was reaching an entirely different level.

On the evening of January 11, 1980, PBS stations around the country aired the first episode of *Free to Choose,* a documentary miniseries that Friedman and a group of television professionals had been working on since 1977.[17] The series originally consisted of ten episodes, though an eleventh was filmed in 1990 in Eastern Europe to feast on the failure of "real socialism." Each hour-long episode featured a half-hour documentary with Friedman (on- and off-scene) introducing his free-market thinking, and a second half-hour of debate between Friedman and notable scientists and publicists, politicians and government officials, unionists and businessmen—some agreeing, others disagreeing to varying degrees with Friedman's views.[18]

Paradoxically, the history of *Free to Choose*, a series markedly opposed to many forms of government intervention, was inextricably linked to that of government-funded public television broadcasting. It was part of a new documentary format that BBC 2 had invented in the latter years of the 1960s, which produced a number of highly successful series like *Civilisation*, with Kenneth Clark (1969), *The Ascent of Man*, with Jacob Bronowski (1973), and *The Age of Uncertainty*, with John Kenneth Galbraith (1976). They all featured a talking-head expert who traveled the world and provided the viewer with his "personal view" (hence the full titles, *Civilisation: A Personal View by Kenneth Clark*, etc.) on the history of the arts, humanity, and science and economics, respectively.[19] In what became the best-known example of the format, David Attenborough later starred in the *Life* series. Though inspired and influenced by this format, Friedman's series diverged from it in significant ways.

In the American market, the "Personal View" series were aired by PBS. This included Galbraith's series *Age of Uncertainty*, which presented a market-critical overview of the history of economics and the economy in the last 200 years. This is where Robert Chitester comes in. Chitester was the ambitious head of a regional public broadcasting station in Erie, Pennsylvania, which was part of the PBS network. He took offense at the thirteen hours of prime airtime given to what he thought of as Galbraith's "socialist tract."[20] Fortunately for him, he met Allen Wallis, a member of the Mont Pèlerin Society involved with public broadcasting at the time. Wallis shared his outrage at the Galbraith series, and together they birthed the idea of countering it with a neoliberal TV project. Wallis put Chitester into contact with Milton Friedman, whom he knew well from his time as a student and later as a professor at the University of Chicago.[21] Not until the beginning of 1977 were Chitester and Rose Friedman, Milton's wife, successful in convincing him to undertake the project. It took three years of work until the series was finally broadcast.

While I cannot reproduce the entire story of the production of the series here,[22] there are some notable takeaways. First, the initiative for the series did not come from Friedman, but from people deeply involved with the television industry. Second, its production was not a one-way process in which television professionals simply created images and narratives around a text Friedman provided (as had been mostly the case with Galbraith's series).[23] Rather, highly skilled and experienced staff from the British company Video Arts were involved in the series' conception and execution from the very beginning, and they took an active part in a fundamental rewriting of the material. Friedman did serve as the speaker of the on- and off-screen commentary, and he provided the text, most of which he came up with on the spot. (One of "four essential requirements" Friedman determined at the beginning of the venture was "I am going to speak my own words and noone's elses [sic]."')[24] However, all the detailed work of filming—mise en scène, filming sites, camera work, montage, sound design—and thus also large parts of the narrative (of the whole series as well as single episodes) were created by the television professionals, even as they collaborated closely with the Friedmans.[25] In this manner, the structure of the series' argument was broadly shaped by those who knew the medium of television. Rather than a top-down "popularization" process in which Friedman's propositions were merely "translated" for television, the argument had to be remade.[26]

This process built on earlier rearrangements in the way that Friedman, who had been deeply involved with mass media ventures since the '6os, spoke to the public. In 1966, Friedman had been endowed with a tri-weekly economics column at *Newsweek* magazine. Alongside Paul Samuelson and Henry Wallich, whose columns alternated with his, Friedman had started out as an expert handing out economic advice to policymakers—largely following the pattern set by postwar representations of economics as an arcane, technocratic art to help steer the economy.[27] As Tiago Mata has observed, "In this imagined relationship of influence the public was merely a witness."[28] In the course of the '7os, however, Friedman increasingly represented himself as someone speaking up for the public rather than as an advisor of elites. In one notable example, he ended one of his columns by paraphrasing the call of the *Internationale*: "Arise ye prisoners of taxation, you have nothing to lose but the IRS."[29]

This shift was connected to his growing involvement both with the realm of media and that of politics. His appearances on TV, radio, and in popular print outlets like *Playboy* became ever-more frequent, requiring him to talk much less about his academic research and more about his easy-to-grasp political stances. His constant correspondence with his *Newsweek* readers gave him an opportunity to consider reactions to different ways of presenting arguments and to readjust them accordingly.[30] He also had to adapt his rhetoric to audiences at university lectures around the country, which since the '60s were increasingly attended by left-wing students whom he tried to win over by presenting himself as an idealist like them.[31]

Another important juncture was his participation, in 1973, in California Governor Ronald Reagan's campaign for Proposition 1—a statewide ballot initiative to cut and limit income and property taxes. In mid-February of 1973, Friedman, who was in Palm Springs reconvalescing from an open-heart surgery, was picked up to join Reagan for a whole day of press conferences on the proposition, flying from place to place on a private plane with the governor.[32] The Prop. 1 campaign, posing as speaking up for a taxpayer poised to become "the pawn in a deadly-game of government monopoly whose only purpose is to serve the confiscatory appetites of runaway government spending," used a populist language decrying the "vast special interest-oriented government bureaucracy."[33] As a sample speech put it, "It's your money. Make them give it back."[34] While Proposition 1 failed in 1973, in the coming years Friedman and Reagan both played prominent roles in various proposals along the same political and rhetorical lines as the Prop. 1 campaign. Although Reagan himself often flattered Friedman by indicating his intellectual debts to him,[35] the relationship of influence can and should also be seen in the reverse: Friedman's direct involvement in and advocacy for professional political campaigns such as these, side by side with an experienced major politician, certainly helped the economist to strike a different, more populist chord and to imagine his audience as voters rather than academic colleagues or policymakers.

With television, this narrative style found its complement medium. There were several features that set the TV documentary *Free to Choose* apart from other media projects Friedman had previously been engaged in. The most obvious is that television works with images. This already partly accounts for a predilection for the concrete over the abstract and philosophical. Whereas the latter had largely characterized *Capitalism and Freedom*, Friedman's 1962 book-length treatise in political philosophy, the former dominated *Free to Choose*.[36] Another feature is the striking degree to which everyday stories of "normal people" were used to give substance to seemingly abstract claims. The series portrayed and interviewed these people in surroundings that were presented as their everyday habitat.

The program was structured around a series of visual sequences, which together provided a narrative that should, as one of the producers explained to Friedman, "not merely carry the argument, but illustrate and reinforce it as well."[37] The necessity for visuals meant that abstract concepts like "the market," "government," or "inflation" had to be visualized. And these visual-izations necessitated—and enabled—significant choices. Thus, "the market" was constantly depicted as a street market where everyday people bargained with one another on the same (street) level by exchanging vegetables, trou-sers, and other mundane things. By contrast, "government"—the state—was continuously represented by images of massive grey high-rise buildings, indi-cating not only the vastness of modern government that Friedman criticized throughout the series, but also its distance and unapproachability vis-à-vis the "little guy" who inhabited the street markets. According to these images, government had sealed itself off in these buildings, literally looking down on the people it allegedly served. The market, by contrast, was the site and savior of the everyday, hard-working American.

This general narrative was built and reinforced by the stories and witnesses the series employed. Every episode told at least two or three of these sto-ries and introduced new, everyday characters from the "real world." While these people were indeed real, the reenactment of their stories in front of the cameras contained highly artificial elements. Brennan Hand Delivery, for example, the mail delivery firm challenging the government's post monopoly, was already closed at the time of filming.[38]

A social typology of the characters who, like Pat Brennan, were introduced in these visual and narrative sequences while also speaking into the camera, reveals a great deal about the series' intended audience.[39] These protagonists comprise three recognizable groups. The first is the white suburban middle class: "fairly average American families" who, like the Vasellis, exemplify the upward mobility of immigrants in American capitalism; or whose real income is diminished by inflation, like that of the Crawfords; or who want to send their son to a school of their own choice, like the Waltons.[40] The closing sequence of the series is located in Ottumwa, Iowa, the "All-American city" of 1978 (the year *Free to Choose* was filmed), "where ordinary, hard-working American people live," as Friedman's voiceover explains. The stories of these families are aided by a visual language and soundscape that underline how ordinariness is conceptualized as a well-off, middle-class white suburb.[41]

So far, this choice of protagonists is hardly surprising. Recent research on the social history of the conservative turnaround in this era has pointed to the importance of the white, suburban middle class as a core constitu-ency of the then-ascendant conservative movement.[42] However, in *Free to*

Street markets from episode 1 of *Free to Choose*

Massive government buildings in *Free to Choose*

Choose, those (or some of those) who have not yet climbed the social ladder figure prominently as well. One such group consists of small businessmen and -women—entrepreneurs like Pat Brennan, who often resemble founders of what we now call "start-ups." A third group is, significantly, the worker. A notable example is a group of black workers in the South Bronx calling themselves "Sweat Equity," who decided to renovate the vacant buildings on their blocks. It is interesting to observe how Friedman engages with them: He asks questions and listens to what they have to say, reaffirms it ("sure," he says twice), and, when he starts to talk himself, alludes to their local situation first before making general statements about "the government bureaucracy."[43] The contrast with J. K. Galbraith in his *Age of Uncertainty* series could not be greater. Galbraith was only shown conversing with other intellectuals and political leaders and thus seemed, as Angus Burgin notes, "wholly alien to the people whose interests he was ostensibly defending."[44]

In contrast to earlier neoliberal attempts at using mass media to convince a broader public, such as in the 1950s,[45] *Free to Choose* positioned the worker prominently. He (workers were mostly represented as male) was even the subject of a whole episode in the series, entitled "Who Protects the Worker?" (episode 8). This program works in a similar vein as "Who Protects the Consumer?" (episode 7). In both cases, the notion that the government "protects" workers or consumers—that is, the "ordinary, hard-working American," the "little guy"—is deconstructed through the arguments of public choice theory: despite their initial good intentions, bureaucracies and unions get caught up in the dynamics of their self-interests and thus end up harming rather than helping ordinary people, especially the most disadvantaged.

The tactic of turning arguments previously employed *in favor* of government intervention into arguments *against* the welfare state entered the show's debates as well. When consumer advocate Kathleen O'Reilly accuses Friedman of being a defender of big industry, he replies, "I am not pro-industry, I am pro-consumer. I'm like you!"[46] And in a discussion with Michael Harrington, a socialist author, he explains:

> I will agree in part with what [Michael Harrington] just said: I do not believe it's proper to put the situation in terms of industrialists versus government. On the contrary—one of the reasons why *I* am in favor of less government is because when you have more government, industrialists take it over [Harrington nods approvingly], and the two together form a coalition [Harrington nods faster] against the ordinary worker and the ordinary consumer. I think business [gestures admonitorily toward Robert Galvin, the businessman in the group] is a

wonderful institution *provided* it has to face competition in the market place
. . . and that's why I don't want government to step in and help the business
community.[47]

The treatment of Robert Galvin leads us to a further observation: *big* business—private power—is strikingly absent from the visual language of the
series. There are no images to represent huge trusts or monopolies (whose
headquarters often resemble the large government buildings that *are* depicted), and there are no personalized stories about powerful executives or
"robber barons." In one of the five discussions produced for a new and partly
updated run of *Free to Choose* in 1990, left-wing economist Samuel Bowles
commented on this lopsided representation:

> When I read your stuff, Milton, when I watch you on TV, I think: . . . Milton
> has this idea of, you know, Charlie Brown and Linus are gonna have a lemonade
> stand, and Lucy's gonna have another lemonade stand and *that's* your idea of
> capitalism. But that's a myth, that's not what capitalism is, we don't have thou-
> sands and millions of little firms competing on a level playing field. We have giant
> industrial corporations that use their power to their own advantage and to the dis-
> advantage of others. And *that's* what you have to be able to deal with if you wanna
> be relevant to the modern world . . . : dealing with the problem of economic
> power so that the power of those institutions can be used by and large for public
> good. If you ignore them with this lemonade stand capitalism myth you're simply
> giving those powerful standers of wealth and affluence free reign.[48]

While this description captures an important element of the series' narrative, it ignores what Friedman said in response to Michael Harrington. Even
though big business is purposefully excluded from visual representation, it is
not wholly absent from the argument of the series: "How to Stay Free," the
last episode of the 1980 version of the series, introduces Warren Richardson,
a lobbyist employed by big firms to represent their interests in Washington.
The camera shows him walking, seemingly problem-free, through the doors
of government buildings. The message of these images appears clear: government always provides an open door for the special interests of big business.[49]
Thus, big government figures as an *ally* of big business, as another reason the
government's power should be constrained. Big business has enough money
and power to influence governmental policy—unlike the "little guy." Far from
restraining private power, government ends up sustaining and enlarging it.

These stories and arguments tie in with an argumentative direction that
the Video Arts staff had emphasized from the start and that already appeared

in early outlines—an emphasis with which Friedman himself was not entirely happy. In response to an early outline of the series by Video Arts executive Antony Jay, Friedman complained that

> there is too much of a tendency to state the matter as if the issue were one of material prosperity either through or versus freedom. The real issue we want to stress is freedom vs coercion; free choice vs bureacratic [sic] control; not affluence vs poverty. The basic case for freedom is moral not prudential.[50]

This controversy points to a central tension in the representation of the neoliberal project: Is neoliberalism about morality or about prudence? Why "free" markets—because they are morally superior, or simply because they work better than government planning? What is worse—that the government interferes with our freedom or that it makes us poorer than we otherwise would be? At the core of Friedman's earlier book, *Capitalism and Freedom*, had been the argument that capitalism was ethically superior because it was the only economic system consistent with freedom. In post-Sputnik America, this was an important point, since it was no longer self-evident to contemporaries whether capitalism was functionally superior—another, more fundamental argument was needed. Now, in the letter to Jay, Friedman went on to explain that, "fortunately," there was no need to make a choice between freedom and abundance "because freedom also yields greater abundance."[51] He struggled to keep the issue of freedom at the forefront of the series, sensing that the economic argument was gaining greater prominence than had originally been his intention. In the case of immigration to the United States, a central storyline of the first episode of the series, Friedman complained about Jay's outline:

> The stress is wholly on material wellbeing. Yet the waves of immigration to the US were not primarily for material benefit but to avoid oppression—a striking case of why I object to the overemphasis on material wellbeing. . . . And what is the shame of our welfare state and non-free government with its immigration restrictions? That the US did not offer a haven to the Jews fleeing the Nazis, the Viet Namese fleeing the communists. . . . That is far more important both as a virtue of freedom and as a vice of the present system than the gain in material wellbeing from the free society or today's unemployment.[52]

Despite Friedman's protest, in the final product the almost sole emphasis was on material gains for immigrants escaping poverty rather than escaping political persecution and oppression.[53]

This problem was directly related to the new medium he was now engaging. "Freedom" is an abstract concept not easily put into images. It is a philosophical, intellectual term. Although Friedman made it clear time and again that he wanted the series to be an "openly and unashamedly" intellectual program,[54] that he wanted "dedication to ideas, to logical, intellectual argument,"[55] and that he was willing to "sacrifice numbers for thoughtfulness,"[56] Video Arts was anxious to ensure the series would have as broad an audience as possible. Jay suggested that the aim of the programs should be "to make a whole new audience, hundreds of thousands—perhaps millions—of reasonably intelligent laymen, suddenly think in a new way about their old assumptions."[57]

Friedman did succeed in inserting much of his more abstract talk about freedom into the series, especially in his on-site commentary. But the stories about individual people the programs told and the visuals they employed were often geared toward supporting the claim that government takes from the poor and gives to the well-to-do—an early title of the episode "Who Protects the Worker?" was "The Robin Hood Myth."[58] In the process of producing the series, the argument became more "economic" in the sense that the series was often concerned with the everyday financial problems—and successes—of "ordinary people" rather than with abstract claims about their freedom or lack thereof. And when it did engage with these more abstract questions, it had to substantiate the abstract idea of freedom by showing concrete, intelligible cases of oppressed economic freedom—like the story of Pat Brennan and her mail delivery firm, closed down by the government.

Taken together, what emerges through all of the visuals, stories, and arguments is a *market populist* notion in which government is always "up there," while the market represents us, the (average, small) people "down here." The market is on our side—it is our site, the place where our interests are served. It is our savior, whereas the government is our menace—it conspires with the rich to deprive us of what we have and what we want.[59] Back in 1962, *Capitalism and Freedom* had been based on an ethical consideration: How can freedom, understood mostly as economic freedom, be preserved? Compared to the TV series *Free to Choose*, this issue was as abstract as was the language in which it was discussed. By contrast, the focus of *Free to Choose* shifted from the abstract concept of freedom toward a populism that concerned itself directly with the economic woes and needs of the "little guy."

But in what sense are we dealing with "populism" here, and what are its specific attributes? Contrary to earlier understandings of the term, Ernesto

Laclau conceptualizes populism *not* as "a *type* of movement—identifiable with either a special social [socioeconomic] base or a particular ideological orientation"—but rather as a "*political logic*."[60] The antagonistic relationship at the core of a populist political logic is not preexistent (as if dependent, for example, on an "objective" economic relationship), but is construed in the discursive process of naming it. This construction "requires the dichotomic division of society into two camps,"[61] positing an enemy ("the elite") as the antagonist of a collective identity ("the people") that is based on what Laclau calls an "equivalential chain" of demands.

This is where this conception of populism becomes particularly pertinent. Laclau contrasts the equivalential logic on which populism operates with a "logic of difference" that stresses the particularity of different demands. Equivalence implies that a group of demands, as contrasted with an antagonistic force, has something in common, whereas the logic of difference denies that commonality.[62] The "logic of difference" corresponds to liberalism's methodological and ethical individualism—ever since "the construction of a bourgeois hegemony in the second half of the nineteenth century," Laclau asserts, "the long-term line is unmistakable: the primacy of a differential logic over equivalential ruptures."[63] In liberal capitalism, it seems, differential particularism has generally been on the upswing, although parsed by periodic crises of legitimacy in which populism became particularly visible.

However, as Laclau notes in passing, liberal ideologies—even one as seemingly differentialist as neoliberalism—can build equivalential chains and therefore construct a populist politics, too:

> A society which postulates the welfare state as its ultimate horizon is one in which only the differential logic would be accepted as a legitimate way of constructing the social. In this society, conceived as a continuously expanding system, any social need should be met differentially; and there would be no basis for creating an internal [antagonistic] frontier. Since it would be unable to differentiate itself from anything else, that society could not totalize itself, could not create a "people." What actually happens is that the obstacles identified during the establishment of that society—private entrepreneurial greed, entrenched interests, and so on—force their very proponents to identify enemies and to reintroduce a discourse of social division grounded in equivalential logics. In that way, collective subjects constituted around the defense of the welfare state can emerge. The same can be said about neo-liberalism: it also presents itself as a panacea for a fissureless society—with the difference that in this case, the trick is performed by the market, not by the state.[64]

Following Laclau, we can see that the populist discourse created during the era of the New Deal helped constitute an underlying popular legitimacy for Fordist social democracy throughout the West. Like neoliberal populism, it centered on a particular, though radically different concept of government. Dorothea Lange's famous photograph from the Great Depression, *Migrant Mother, Nipomo, California, 1936*, captured this emerging narrative early on: the starving mother and her children lack the protection of a father, without whom they sit alone, ravaged by the forces of capitalist crisis. So another provider and guardian has to step in—the government.[65] In the United States especially, the idea of government as guardian of the people became fused with the idea of democracy. It helped form the concept that "we, the people" *are* the government.[66] While "the people" thus formed a seamless relationship with government, the "elite" against which government had to guard "us" was constructed as the forces of private greed and powerful corporations, as in consumer advocate Ralph Nader's books.[67] *Free to Choose* tackled the postwar era's underlying populist discourse head-on by creating its own neoliberal populism, which effectively reversed the relationship: now, "we" were the market, while the government was the elite.

This process of chaining together a logic of equivalence, however, did not unfold without serious tensions.[68] In a 1975 collection of his *Newsweek* columns, Friedman commented on a view that was popular among contemporary adherents of the New Left—namely, that

> there is a "ruling class" that runs the government and through the government the society. . . . Fortunately . . . [this view] is false. True enough, we have a mass of special-interest legislation and of regulating agencies dominated by the industries that they are supposed to regulate. True enough, the apparent beneficiaries of each such piece of legislation or of such regulating bodies are generally in the upper income groups, or at least in groups above the average. However—and here is the fallacy in the "ruling class" view—the special interests that are served are fragmented and each gets its benefits largely at the expense of other special interests. It is likely that the special-interest groups as a whole and possibly each one separately would benefit if the special-interest legislation as a whole were abolished.[69]

The tension is palpable: even as he finds some truth in a narrative that is clearly structured around a simple populist antagonism—the "ruling class" versus "the people"—Friedman denies its accuracy, maintaining his methodological individualism. But in doing so, he once again speaks of "the special-interest groups *as a whole*" who could benefit from abolishing government intervention, thereby construing an equivalential chain between these groups.

Dorothea Lange, *Migrant Mother, Nipomo, California, 1936* (retouched, Library of Congress, LC-USF34-9058-C)

The chain's "common denominator," to pick up another of Laclau's terms,[70] is the market. A whole bouquet of interests or demands that originally seemed differential from one another come together in an idealized space, imagined as a street market. It is the site where the interests of the consumer, the worker, the poor, the middle class, the entrepreneur, and ultimately even the businessman come together as one to construe a new kind of *Volk*: the market's people. Whatever their differences, they have one interest in common: that the market be as free as possible. But the constitution of this equivalence is impossible to achieve without an antagonist lurking around the corner. This function is fulfilled by the government. Consequently, one of the captions under which Friedman's *Newsweek* columns are presented is "Government vs. the People."[71]

It is noteworthy that this constitutes a relatively—or even largely—depersonalized populism. It is a populism that still deals in abstractions— "the market" vs. "the government"—and that does not, at this point, need charismatic populist elites to take over. When Jan-Werner Müller asserts that populists reveal themselves in claiming that "we—and only we—represent the people,"[72] it is important to note that this kind of neoliberal populism does not necessarily posit a "we," or an "I," a charismatic leader, as the people's representative, but an "it"—the market. (In a private letter during an emotional exchange with John Kenneth Galbraith, however, Friedman even crossed this line, revealing that "I regard myself if anything as leading a revolt of the poor against the rich.")[73] Even so, neoliberals themselves, and especially their popular media ventures, had an important function. In putting together the *Free to Choose* episode "Who Protects the Consumer?," Friedman explained to his collaborators that it was important to show

> that the fundamental values of *the people* are in conflict with the fundamental
> objectives of the consumer advocates and that *when the issue is perfectly clear and*
> *open and above board* the public at large will reject the pressure of the consumer
> advocates. Therefore the consumer advocates, although they proclaim that
> they are democrats, are not really democrats; they are trying in indirect ways
> to impose on the public restrictions which the public would never knowingly
> accept.[74]

At this point, the circle is complete: the public simply needed widely distributed mass media primers like *Free to Choose* to make the issue "perfectly clear and open." And the broader the audience was that neoliberal media ventures envisioned, the more intelligible their language and, more importantly, the more populist their message had to become. The public needed to understand that the government was not a father protecting them from the hazards of the market (as New Deal populism would have it), but just the opposite: the market protected them—the market's people—from the thieving hands of government.

Laclau describes populism as "the royal road to understanding something about the ontological constitution of the political as such."[75] The political is unthinkable, he holds, without collective identities. Strikingly, this holds true even for an ideology as seemingly individualist as neoliberalism. To construct a populist antagonism, neoliberalism, too, had to rely on collective imaginaries in the form of ideas of "the people" and even "the public good."[76] Collective identities cannot be established without constructing the kind of antagonistic relationships for which populism is so notable—that is, without constructing friends and foes. With its arrival in popular mass media and its construction of a collective, populist imaginary, then, neoliberalism truly entered the site of the political.

From Friedman to Trump: Learning from Neoliberalism

Let's talk about the swamp. The swamp is a business model. . . . It's a donor, consultant, K Street lobbyist, politician . . . 7 of the 9 wealthiest counties in America ring Washington, DC. . . . [The swamp] is the permanent political class as represented by both parties.[77]

When political analyst Thomas Frank heard these words, spoken by Steve Bannon in a CBS interview with Charlie Rose shortly after Bannon's stint at the White House had ended, he was shocked.[78] Bannon's stories about the kleptocratic Washington elite sounded all too familiar: Frank, a decidedly left-wing author, had written about those same wealthy counties ringing D.C. in his 2008 book *The Wrecking Crew*, and now asked himself "Are those my words coming out of Steve Bannon's mouth?"[79]

Bannon, however, could rely on a distinctly non-left tradition in painting Washington as a "swamp." For example, a sequence in the *Free to Choose* episode "Who Protects the Worker?" tells the same story. In a voiceover to images of mansions with pools and tennis courts, Friedman explains:

Half an hour drive out of Washington you come to Montgomery County, where many *very* senior civil servants live. It has the highest average family income of *any* county in the United States. Of the people who live here who are employed, one out of every four works for the federal government. Like all civil servants, they have job security, salaries linked to the cost of living, a fine retirement plan, also linked to the cost of living, and many manage to qualify for Social Security as well, becoming double dippers. Many of their neighbors are also here because of the federal government: Congressmen, lobbyists, top executives of corporations with government contracts. As government expands, so does this neighborhood. Government protects its workers just as trade unions protect their members, but both do it at someone else's expense.[80]

As we can see here, the trope of the Washington "swamp" is already as present in neoliberal populism as it is in today's Trumpian propaganda. It is a way of narrating class conflict by pointing at government intervention not as a possible source of *relief* from, but rather as the *cause* of exploitation. These continuities open up an avenue to understand today's right-wing populism as a continuation and reinvigoration of neoliberalism rather than an antithetical reaction to it. If we understand neoliberalism primarily as a technocratic mode of governance without paying attention to its popular, legitimizing strands, we might conclude, as William Davies does, that the new right-wing populism of Trump and Brexit, because it is directed against expert elites, is also "fervently anti-neoliberal."[81] Davies thereby wholly identifies neoliberalism with its technocratic incarnation as a rarely questioned ideology of governance in the decades leading up to the popular revolts of the 2010s. But this risks underestimating the continuities between the neoliberal era and whatever we might currently be entering. Upon closer observation, these continuities are obvious not only on the level of its personnel and infrastructure,[82] or on the level of ideology,[83] but also on that of the corresponding popular imaginaries—at least in part.

For conspicuously absent from current reinventions of populism is this very figure: the market. Apparently, after it continuously failed to live up to its promises of "protecting the worker" and alleviating the common man, the market, while still easy to find in party programs and policy proposals, no longer captures enough popular appeal to be at the forefront of right-wing populist discourse. What in Friedman's case was still a largely depersonalized populism now depends on the figure of the populist leader. The role of the positive abstraction is now being played by the nation, inseparable as it is from racialized constructions of the "other." Even so, now, as then, the anti-elitist critique expressed by neoliberal as much as right-wing populism might well be the more effective part of its messaging.

I have argued that neoliberalism, in the process of actively engaging mass media and mass politics, articulated its own version of populism, challenging the underlying discourse legitimizing mid-century versions of social democracy. Focusing on the popular strands of neoliberal discourse reveals those instances in which neoliberals, rather than trying to curb democratic sovereignty, actively made their own use of it. Only if we concern ourselves with "neoliberalism's distinctive sources of legitimacy"[84] can we take full account of neoliberal rule and develop strategic ways to engage with it. It might turn out that rather than seeking to establish "something like its own Mont Pèlerin,"[85] or merely replacing neoliberal technocratic elites with more "capable," nonneoliberal ones, the left has to challenge neoliberalism's popular engagements—both discursively and structurally. Learning from neoliberalism, in this sense, entails understanding how it brought about a realignment of popular sentiment[86]— and which tensions in this alignment could be used as cracks and wedges to contest it. Finally, taking neoliberal populism seriously should make us aware that democracy—including its potential for voicing popular discontent and for creating fundamental transformation—is not only still alive, but our only way out of the neoliberal condition.

Notes

1. *Free to Choose*, episode 10, "How to Stay Free," 21:01–23:56; Pat Brennan in front of the building: 21:05; deserted basement room: 23:45.
2. With the terms "neoliberalism" and "neoliberals," I refer to a political movement that has been built up since the 1930s and 1940s. It has worked through a network of people and organizations that has been, since 1947, centered on the Mont Pèlerin Society. Although often led by economists, it has also featured other scholars, businessmen, politicians, and (notably) journalists and media professionals as prominent members. Through links to political parties, it had gained considerable power in several countries by the 1970s and 1980s (notably through connections with the Reagan and Thatcher governments). To get a grasp of the scale of the network and the state of current research, cf. esp. Philip Mirowski and Dieter Plehwe, eds., *The Road from Mont Pèlerin: The Making of the Neoliberal Thought Collective* (Cambridge, Mass.: Harvard University Press, 2009); Quinn Slobodian, *Globalists: The End of Empire and the Birth of Neoliberalism* (Cambridge, Mass.: Harvard University Press, 2018); Daniel Stedman Jones, *Masters of the Universe: Hayek, Friedman, and the Birth of Neoliberal Politics* (Princeton, N.J.: Princeton University Press, 2012); Angus Burgin, *The Great Persuasion: Reinventing Free Markets since the Depression* (Cambridge, Mass.: Harvard University Press, 2012). Also, among others: Richard Cockett, *Thinking the Unthinkable: Think Tanks and the Economic Counter-Revolution, 1931–1983* (New York: HarperCollins, 1994); Bernhard Walpen, *Die offenen Feinde und ihre Gesellschaft: Eine hegemonietheoretische Studie zur Mont Pèlerin Society* (Hamburg: VSA, 2004); Philip Plickert, *Wandlungen des Neoliberalismus: Eine Studie zu Entwicklung*

und Ausstrahlung der Mont Pèlerin Society (Stuttgart: Lucius und Lucius, 2008); Matthias Schmelzer, *Freiheit für Wechselkurse und Kapital: Die Ursprünge neoliberaler Währungspolitik und die Mont Pèlerin Society* (Marburg: Metropolis, 2010); Kim Phillips-Fein, *Invisible Hands: The Businessmen's Crusade against the New Deal* (New York: W. W. Norton, 2009).

3. My conception of populism, detailed later, draws heavily from Ernesto Laclau, *On Populist Reason* (London: Verso, 2005).

4. A full layout of my argument, relying on a much larger variety of sources, beginning in the 1930s and leading up to the 1980s, is currently underway in Sören Brandes, "The Market's People: Mass Media and the Making of Neoliberal Populism in the US and UK, 1930s–1980s" (Ph.D. diss., Free University Berlin).

5. Wendy Brown, *Undoing the Demos: Neoliberalism's Stealth Revolution* (New York: Zone Books, 2015); Nancy MacLean, *Democracy in Chains: The Deep History of the Radical Right's Stealth Plan for America* (New York: Viking, 2017).

6. Philip Mirowski, "The Political Movement That Dared Not Speak Its Own Name: The Neoliberal Thought Collective Under Erasure," Institute for New Economic Thinking Working Paper no. 23, September 2014, https://ssrn.com/abstract=2682892, quote on p. 11. Chastising historical actors for failing to use our analytic categories remains an odd way of engaging with history. It also seems wholly unnecessary considering that a concept's analytic utility does not depend on its usage by the actors in question, as David Engel rightly argues in "Away from a Definition of Antisemitism: An Essay in the Semantics of Historical Description," in *Rethinking European Jewish History*, ed. Jeremy Cohen and Moshe Rosman (Oxford: Littman Library, 2009), 30–53.

7. Mirowski, *Never Let a Serious Crisis Go to Waste: How Neoliberalism Survived the Financial Meltdown* (London: Verso, 2013), 68–83, esp. 68. Note the typical juxtaposition of Friedman's "most superficial response" to this problem with Hayek's "richer and more complex answer," 74.

8. William Davies, *The Limits of Neoliberalism: Authority, Sovereignty and the Logic of Competition*, rev. ed. (London: Sage, 2016). Cf. Mirowski and Plehwe, *Road from Mont Pèlerin*; Brown, *Undoing the Demos*; Mirowski, *Never Let a Serious Crisis Go to Waste*; Jamie Peck, *Constructions of Neoliberal Reason* (Oxford: Oxford University Press, 2010); Wolfgang Streeck, *Gekaufte Zeit: Die vertagte Krise des demokratischen Kapitalismus* (Berlin: Suhrkamp, 2013); MacLean, *Democracy in Chains*. Slobodian, *Globalists*, adds a much-needed consideration of scale to this narrative.

9. Mirowski, "Author's Response," *Antipode: A Radical Journal of Geography*, Book Review Symposium (November 2013), https://radicalantipode.files.wordpress.com/2013/11/mirowski-reviews_authors-response.pdf (accessed December 12, 2018), 4.

10. Colin Crouch, *Post-Democracy* (London: Polity, 2004); Chantal Mouffe, *On the Political* (London: Routledge, 2005).

11. See, for example, MacLean, *Democracy in Chains*, xxiv.

12. Martijn Konings, "Imagined Double Movements: Progressive Thought and the Specter of Neoliberal Populism," *Globalizations* 9, no. 4 (2012): 609–22, h. 609. Apart from Konings's great work, others have traced these questions of neoliberal legitimization as well. See, among others, Melinda Cooper, *Family Values: Between Neoliberalism and the New Social Conservatism* (New York: Zone Books, 2017); Roberto Romani, "Varieties of Neoliberalism: On the Populism of Laissez-faire in America, 1960–1985," *Global Intellectual History* (2019) [this has not yet appeared in print, only online].

13. Greta Krippner, *Capitalizing on Crisis: The Political Origins of the Rise of Finance* (Cambridge, Mass.: Harvard University Press, 2012); Monica Prasad, "The Popular Origins of Neoliberalism in the Reagan Tax Cut of 1981," *Journal of Policy History* 24, no. 3 (2012): 351–83; Kieran Heinemann, "Aktien für alle? Kleinanleger und die Börse in der Ära Thatcher," *Vierteljahrshefte für Zeitgeschichte* 64, no. 4 (2016): 637–64.

14. Mirowski and Plehwe, "Preface," in *Road from Mont Pèlerin: The Making of the Neoliberal Thought Collective*, with a new preface, ed. Mirowski and Plehwe (Cambridge, Mass.: Harvard University Press, 2015), xvii. Cf. Mirowski, "The Political Movement That Dared Not Speak Its Own Name," 9, where he blames Friedman's public appearances for the "distortions" he finds in current accounts of neoliberalism.

15. Stuart Hall, "The Great Moving Right Show," *Marxism Today*, January 1979, 14–20; Hall, "Authoritarian Populism: A Reply," *New Left Review* 151, May/June 1985, 115–24; Hall, "The State—Socialism's Old Caretaker," *Marxism Today*, November 1984, 24–29.

16. See "The Making of 'Milton Friedman,'" Chapter 4 of Brandes, "Market's People."

17. For a more thorough analysis, see Brandes, "Free to Choose: Die Popularisierung des Neoliberalismus in Milton Friedmans Fernsehserie (1980/90)," *Zeithistorische Forschungen/Studies in Contemporary History* 12, no. 3 ("Marketization"), (December 2015): 526–33, http://www.zeithistorische-forschungen .de/2015-3/id=5284; Brandes, "Free to Choose Friedman: Die Popularisierung neoliberalen Wissens in Milton Friedmans Fernsehserie 'Free to Choose'" (M.A. thesis, Humboldt University Berlin, April 2015). Other accounts include Burgin, "Age of Certainty: Galbraith, Friedman, and the Public Life of Economic Ideas," in *The Economist as Public Intellectual*, ed. Tiago Mata and Steven G. Medema, *History of Political Economy*, annual supplement 45 (2013): 191–219; Caroline Jack, "Producing Milton Friedman's Free to Choose: How Libertarian Ideology Became Broadcasting Balance," *Journal of Broadcasting & Electronic Media* 62, no. 3 (2018): 514–30; Daniel J. Flynn, *Blue Collar Intellectuals: When the Enlightened and the Everyman Elevated America* (Wilmington, Del.: ISI, 2011), 87–97; and Laurence Jarvik, *PBS: Behind the Screen* (Rocklin, Calif.: Forum, 1997), 275–87. The complete series is online at http://www.freeto choose.tv/broadcasts/ftc80.php; accessed October 29, 2018.

18. The debates were carefully prepared in order to achieve a balance and not just let Friedman, who was a very able discussant, win; see Milton Friedman and Rose Friedman, *Two Lucky People: Memoirs* (Chicago: Chicago University Press, 1998), 492–95. The *New York Times* concluded accordingly, "Nobody wins or loses in the give or take of the discussion. Impressive points are scored on all sides. In the end, the viewer should be left with a valuable sense of the sheer complexity of the subject"; John J. O'Connor, "TV: Milton Friedman Economics Series in Rerun," *New York Times*, July 14, 1981. Consequently, the discussions stood in stark contrast to the documentary parts.

19. See Brandes, "Free to Choose Friedman," 15–20, 24.

20. Jarvik, *PBS*, 278.

21. Ibid., 277–79; Brandes, "Free to Choose Friedman," 21.

22. The "making of" this series is detailed in Brandes, "Free to Choose Friedman," 20–28; on Chitester's funding efforts, see Jack, "Producing Milton Friedman's Free to Choose."

23. Catherine Atwater Galbraith, "The Professor as TV Star," *American Film*, February 1977, 6–11, h.

24. Milton Friedman to Antony Jay and Michael Peacock, December 18, 1977, 1 (Milton Friedman papers, Hoover Institution Archives, Stanford, Calif., box 224, folder 3).

25. See especially Friedman's correspondence with Antony Jay, Michael Peacock, and Robert Reid of Video Arts (Friedman papers, box 224, folder 3, and box 225, folders 2 and 4), as well as the several meetings mentioned in Friedman and Friedman, *Two Lucky People*, 476, 479, 484f.

26. For the interactionist model of the popularization of knowledge I am following here, see Carsten Kretschmann, "Einleitung: Wissenspopularisierung—ein altes, neues Forschungsfeld," in *Wissenspopularisierung: Konzepte der Wissensverbreitung im Wandel*, ed. Carsten Kretschmann (Berlin: Akademie, 2003), 7–21.

27. See especially Tiago Mata, "Trust in Independence: The Identities of Economists in Business Magazines, 1945–1970," *Journal of the History of the Behavioral Sciences* 47, no. 4 (2011): 359–79; Michael Bernstein, *A Perilous Progress: Economists and Public Purpose in Twentieth-Century America* (Princeton, N.J.: Princeton University Press, 2001).

28. Tiago Mata, "'Arise Ye Prisoners of Taxation,' the Work of the Imagination in the Media Writings of Economists," 2016, https://www.fea.usp.br/sites/default/files/anexo-evento/mata-newsweek-usp2016.pdf, 18.

29. Milton Friedman, "After the Elections," *Newsweek*, November 15, 1976, 100. See also Mata, "'Arise Ye Prisoners of Taxation.'"

30. See Friedman papers, boxes 228–31. Cf. Milton Friedman to Madeleine Edmonson, at *Newsweek*, July 15, 1971, Friedman papers, box 228, folder 1: "I find that letters from readers, while they do raise problems of handling, give me an insight that I would not otherwise have on what the reactions to the columns are." Cf. Mata, "'Arise Ye Prisoners of Taxation,'" 18.

31. Friedman and Friedman, *Two Lucky People*, 342.

32. Ibid., 389. Cf. Milton Friedman to Ronald Reagan, December 4, 1984, and July 13, 1988, Friedman papers, box 174, folder 1.

33. Governor Ronald Reagan to the Members of the California Legislature on "Revenue Control and Tax Reduction," March 12, 1973, 3, 6, Deaver & Hannaford Collection, Hoover Institution Archives, Stanford, Calif., box 15, folder 1.

34. "It's Your Money. Make Them Give It Back," 25-minute sample speech on Proposition 1, prepared by Californians for Lower Taxes, Deaver & Hannaford Collection, box 15, folder 1.

35. For example, Reagan to Friedman, October 25, 1976, and May 23, 1977, Friedman papers, box 174, folder 1.

36. This partly also applies to the book of the same name, written by Rose and Milton Friedman based on a transcript of Milton's commentary in the series; Friedman and Friedman, *Two Lucky People*, 496. The basis in spoken English and in the narrative and argumentative arch of the series led to a narrative driven by reliance on concrete images and examples rather than abstract principles when compared to the earlier book. Published to accompany the TV series, it went on to become one of the most successful nonfiction books in the United States in 1980; Milton Friedman and Rose Friedman, *Free to Choose: A Personal Statement* (New York and London: Harcourt Brace Jovanovich, 1979).

37. Antony Jay to Milton Friedman, January 6, 1978, 4, Friedman papers, box 224, folder 3.

38. *Free to Choose*, episode 10, "How to Stay Free," 21:01–23:56. Cf. Brandes, "Free to Choose Friedman," 41f.

39. I adapt this theoretical concept from literary studies. See Erwin Wolff, "Der intendierte Leser: Überlegungen und Beispiele zur Einführung eines literaturwissenschaftlichen Begriffs," *Poetica* 4 (1971): 141–66.

40. *Free to Choose*, episode 1, "The Power of the Market," 05:48–07:56 (Vaselli); episode 9, "How to Cure Inflation," 08:50–11:00 (Crawford, "fairly average American family" quote at 09:16); episode 6, "What's Wrong with Our Schools," 15:11–17:30 (Walton).

41. *Free to Choose*, episode 10, "How to Stay Free," 29:53–30:30, quote at 30:05.

42. See esp. Lisa McGirr, *Suburban Warriors: The Origins of the New American Right* (Princeton, N.J.: Princeton University Press, 2001); Matthew Lassiter, *The Silent Majority: Suburban Politics in the Sunbelt South* (Princeton, N.J.: Princeton University Press, 2006).

43. *Free to Choose*, episode 4, "From Cradle to Grave," 22:01–24:46; the conversation is at 22:18–23:09, 24:13–24:45.

44. Burgin, "Age of Certainty," 203.

45. Cf. Tiago Mata, "The Battle over the Public: American Neoliberal Journalism in the 1950s," paper presented at the More Roads from Mont Pèlerin conference, convened by Dieter Plehwe, Quinn Slobodian, Philip Mirowski, and

Hagen Schulz-Vorberg at Wissenschaftszentrum Berlin, March 20–22, 2016; Brandes, "Shooting Santa: Early Neoliberal Journalism in the US," in Chapter 3 of "Market's People."

46. *Free to Choose*, episode 7, "Who Protects the Consumer?," 33:40.

47. *Free to Choose*, episode 1, "The Power of the Market," 35:58–36:30, emphasis in the original.

48. *Free to Choose*, episode 3 (1990), "Freedom and Prosperity," 41:27–42:15, emphasis in the original. Bowles might have gotten the idea of "lemonade stand capitalism" from one of the drawings used to promote the series; see ad for *Free to Choose*, episode 2, "The Tyranny of Control," prepared by ad agency Foote, Cone & Belding; Free to Choose Collection, Hoover Institution Archives, Stanford, Calif., box 5, folder 6.

49. *Free to Choose*, episode 10, "How to Stay Free," 01:08–04:15, open doors: 02:57, 04:14.

50. Milton Friedman to Antony Jay and Michael Peacock, December 18, 1977, Friedman papers, box 224, folder 3, 1. The drafts by Jay to which Friedman reacts here are in Free to Choose Collection, box 1, folder 1.

51. Friedman to Antony Jay and Michael Peacock, December 18, 1977, Friedman papers, box 224, folder 3, 1.

52. Cf. ibid., 3.

53. *Free to Choose*, episode 1, "The Power of the Market," 1:45–7:51.

54. Friedman to Antony Jay and Michael Peacock, December 18, 1977, Friedman papers, box 224, folder 3, 1.

55. Ibid., 2.

56. Ibid., 1.

57. Antony Jay to Milton Friedman, January 6, 1978, ibid., 4.

58. Michael Peacock to Milton Friedman, January 17, 1978, ibid., 4.

59. I take the concept of market populism from Thomas Frank, who defines it as the belief that "markets expressed the popular will more articulately and meaningfully than did mere elections. Markets conferred democratic legitimacy; markets were a friend of the little guy; markets brought down the pompous and the snooty; markets gave us what we wanted; markets looked out for our interests"; Frank, *One Market under God: Extreme Capitalism, Market Populism, and the End of Economic Democracy* (London: Secker & Warburg, 2000), xiv.

60. Laclau, *On Populist Reason*, 117, emphasis in original.

61. Ibid., 83.

62. Cf. esp. ibid., 77f.

63. Ibid., 93.

64. Ibid., 78f.

65. See, for example, Thomas Hertfelder, "Unterwegs im Universum der Deutungen: Dorothea Langes Fotozyklus. Migrant Mother,'" *Zeithistorische Forschungen* 4, no. 1–2 (2007): 11–39, http://www.zeithistorische-forschungen .de/1-2-2007/id=4520; Helmut Lethen, *Der Schatten des Fotografen: Bilder und ihre Wirklichkeit* (Berlin: Rowohlt, 2014), 129–34.

66. Thus presented, for instance, in a textbook brochure from 1945: Mary Elting, in collaboration with Margaret Gossett, *We Are the Government* (Garden City, N.Y.: Doubleday, 1945).

67. See especially Ralph Nader, *Unsafe at Any Speed: The Designed-In Dangers of the American Automobile* (New York: Grossman 1965). *Free to Choose* explicitly dealt with Ralph Nader at the outset of the episode on consumer protection: episode 7, "Who Protects the Consumer?," 1:05–1:30.

68. Laclau notes repeatedly that these kinds of internal tensions between equivalential and differential logics never disappear, but form one of the important core elements of populist politics. See, for example, Laclau, *On Populist Reason*, 120–23.

69. Friedman, *There's No Such Thing as a Free Lunch* (LaSalle, Ill.: Open Court, 1975), 234.

70. See Laclau, *On Populist Reason*, 95, where the market is also mentioned as one example.

71. Rose Friedman, *There's No Such Thing as a Free Lunch*, 208.

72. Jan-Werner Müller, *Was ist Populismus? Ein Essay* (Frankfurt am Main: Suhrkamp, 2016), 19.

73. Since this book (although published under Milton's name) was put together by Rose Friedman, this heading should probably be attributed to her. Rose generally had less qualms about simplifications for political effectiveness and played an important role in transforming her husband into the populist figure I describe here. Friedman to John Kenneth Galbraith, February 4, 1980, John Kenneth Galbraith Personal Papers, John F. Kennedy Presidential Library, Boston, Mass., box 200, folder "Friedman, Milton, 1984–1978."

74. Milton Friedman to Antony Jay and Michael Peacock, Video Arts, December 14, 1977, Friedman papers, box 224, folder 3, 3, emphasis added.

75. Laclau, *On Populist Reason*, 67.

76. See, for instance, memorandum from Michael Peacock to Antony Jay, Robert Reid, Michael Latham, February 14, 1978, on "Notes of Conversation with MF and RF [Milton and Rose Friedman], 13th February," 1, Friedman papers, box 225, folder 2. But see Davies's claim that neoliberalism's "disenchantment of politics by economics involves a deconstruction of the language of the 'common good' or the 'public,' which is accused of a potentially dangerous mysticism"; Davies, *Limits of Neoliberalism*, 6.

77. Charlie Rose, Interview with Steve Bannon, Part 2, CBS, aired September 12, 2017, https://charlierose.com/videos/30956 (accessed December 10, 2018), minutes 25:45–26:13.

78. Thomas Frank, "Are Those My Words Coming out of Steve Bannon's Mouth?," *Guardian*, October 6, 2017.

79. Frank, *The Wrecking Crew: How Conservatives Rule* (New York: Henry Holt, 2008), 11.

80. *Free to Choose*, episode 8, "Who Protects the Worker?," 16:53–18:00, emphasis in the original.

81. Davies, *Limits of Neoliberalism*, xiii.

82. See, for example, Dieter Plehwe's and Quinn Slobodian's chapter in this volume.

83. Slobodian, "Neoliberalism's Populist Bastards: A New Political Divide between National Economies," *Public Seminar*, February 15, 2018, www.public seminar.org/2018/02/neoliberalisms-populist-bastards.

84. Martijn Konings, "From Hayek to Trump: The Logic of Neoliberal Democracy," *Socialist Register* 54 (2018): 48–73, h.

85. Mirowski, "Author's Reply," 5.

86. Texts that serve as important points of departure are Stuart Hall, "Thatcher's Lessons," *Marxism Today*, March 1988, 20–27, and Chantal Mouffe, *For a Left Populism* (London: Verso, 2018), 25–38.

THREE

Neoliberals against Europe

Quinn Slobodian and Dieter Plehwe

> We have not successfully rolled back the frontiers of the state in Britain,
> only to see them re-imposed at a European level with a European super-
> state exercising a new dominance from Brussels.
>
> — MARGARET THATCHER, The Bruges Speech, 1988

Since the advent of the European debt crisis in 2009, it has become common
to hear descriptions of the European Union as a neoliberal machine hardwired
to enforce austerity and to block projects of redistribution or solidarity. In
some cases, such arguments have been used to support the case for exit from
the EU. Credit for inspiring neoliberal Europe has often been given to the
British-Austrian economist F. A. Hayek, whose writings from the 1930s have
been described as blueprints for the EU.[1] One historian places him among
"the founding fathers of the new era" despite the absence of any connection between Hayek and the treaties of European integration.[2] Bearing more
evidence are those who point to the role of German ordoliberals in helping
shape European competition policy and pushing for the "four freedoms" of
goods, capital, labor, and services as an axis for the union.[3] With Germany's
finance ministry and Bundesbank playing key roles in the scrum of the Eurozone crisis, especially in the all-important case of Greece, it became routine
to see Europe as "Germany's iron cage," as one article dubbed it.[4]

Such descriptions have migrated to the mainstream. "Those who say the
European Union is a neoliberal plot," observed the *Wall Street Journal* in

October 2017, "are, of course, largely right. Any single market that allows free movement of capital and people by its very nature pits country against country, region against region and town against town in a competition to attract investment and productive people."[5] Leaving aside the reality of the national and international redistribution mechanisms of the welfare state as well as the EU's structural and regional funds so disliked by neoliberals, the statement expresses a logical fallacy.[6] To say that the EU has been neoliberal in its outcome does not imply ipso facto that neoliberal actors were responsible for its genesis. Scholars have rightly emphasized the need to distinguish between the use of the category of neoliberalism as a description of a historical period or variety of capitalism, on the one hand, and an organized intellectual and political movement rooted in the Mont Pèlerin Society, on the other.[7] Failure to keep the levels of analysis distinct can lead to empirical confusion, at best, and conspiratorial thinking at worst.

The problems with a straightforward compound of "neoliberal Europe" became starkly evident with the success of the "leave" vote in the Brexit referendum in 2016. If the EU was neoliberal, were those who called to abandon it the opponents of neoliberalism? A widely circulated photo showed the two victors of 2016, Donald Trump and UKIP leader Nigel Farage, smiling in front of the golden elevator of Trump Tower. This was an unlikely vanguard for neoliberalism's opposition. Yet by adopting an explanatory framework associating neoliberalism with supranational organizations like the EU, NAFTA, and the WTO against the so-called populism of its right-wing opponents, many observers had painted themselves into a corner. If the EU was indeed the "neoliberalism express," as one scholar dubbed it, then to disembark was by definition a gesture of refusal against neoliberalism.[8] Anti-European neoliberalism had no interpretive home.

This chapter offers an exit from the explanatory impasse by way of an overlooked fact. Notwithstanding the many descriptions of the EU as a neoliberal plot, the intellectuals, think tankers, and policy entrepreneurs in the actual existing neoliberal movement since the early 1990s have more often been the EU's critics than its champions. While the Left has seen the EU as an austerity machine, the most engaged neoliberals have seen it as a framework for socialist expansion. Threatened by what they saw as the leftward tilt of Jacques Delors as European Commission president in the early 1990s, neoliberals formed Euroskeptic think tanks, including the Bruges Group (1989), the European Constitutional Group (1992), and the Center for the New Europe (1993). To oppose expanding European environmental and climate policies, they also organized the European Science and Environment Forum (1994).

Even as they kept a sharp eye on left-leaning "federalism," most Euroskeptic neoliberals in the early 1990s maintained faith that European institutions could be reformed to serve their vision of free trade, total mobility of capital and services, and, ideally, competing currencies. A change emerged in the years after the Maastricht Treaty (1992) and the move to the introduction of the Euro in 1999. While some Euroskeptic neoliberals retained hope for a re-formed union, others began forging alliances with cultural nationalist parties. In the process, their opposition to Europe became more absolute, culminating in calls like the Brexit campaign for secession from the EU itself.

While laboring on the political margins for much of the 1990s and the early 2000s, Euroskeptic neoliberals experienced a breakthrough following the backlash against, first, the European "rescue operations" of the debt crisis after 2009, and, second, the arrival of over one million refugees to Central Europe in 2015. Building on alliances with anti-immigrant politicians and political blocs, Euroskeptic neoliberals have given political form to a novel hybrid of libertarianism and anti-migrant xenophobia. Prime examples are the Alternative for Germany party (AfD) and the Austrian Freedom Party. At the European level, the New Right Euroskeptic parties have created the Alliance of European Conservatives and Reformers (AECR) (2009) (as of 2016 renamed ACRE) with its affiliated European party foundation and think tank, New Direction (2010).

The neoliberal roots of many of Europe's right-wing parties have barely been explored.[9] The backlash literature about Euroskepticism has largely focused on the national frame. Yet right-wing populism cannot be explained only as a nationalist category. The formation of a new European Right relies paradoxically on a postnational politics, which swears by the national state while forging ahead with economic globalization. Public debate consistently overlooks the neoliberal, postnational, and transnational dimensions of the nationalist right. Understanding the rightward shift in domestic politics in Europe requires attention to the activity of right-wing parties at the European level. The most obvious amalgam of nationalist and neoliberal perspectives in a contemporary right wing "populist" party is the AfD, formed in 2013 in protest against the official German conduct in the Eurozone crisis. AfD leaders voice concerns about European integration and trade policies that are considered harmful to German interests and about restrictions against freedom of ownership resulting from social and environmental regulation. Rather than dismissing neoliberal economic policies altogether, the AfD recommends carrying them out at the nation-state level without the cumbersome need for coordination and compromise with partners in the EU. To make sense of the resurgent phenomenon of the far right in European politics, we must track such continuities over time and avoid misleading dichotomies that pit neoliberal globalism—and neoliberal Europeanism—against an atavistic national populism. The closed-borders libertarianism of nationalist neoliberals like the AfD is not a rejection of globalism but a variety of it.

The Bruges Group: The Origins of the Neoliberal Euroskeptics

The European integration of the 1990s shattered the relatively pro-Europe position held by neoliberals in the 1980s. At that time, insofar as national sovereignty was infringed on, it appeared to be more often in the causes favored by neoliberals themselves. Beyond the well-known case of competition law, the laudatory moves in the eyes of neoliberals included the liberalization of internal capital movements and the expansion of majority decisions in the European Council when the Single European Act went into force in 1987.[10] The most consistent point of criticism was European trade policy, especially the protectionist Common Agricultural Policy, which was a special focus of the London-based Trade Policy Research Centre with key publications by Swiss economists and Mont Pèlerin Society (MPS) members Gerard Curzon and Victoria Curzon-Price (MPS president 2004–6).[11] The situation changed with the Maastricht Treaty when it appeared that the French socialist Delors, commission president from 1985 to 1995, might take Europe in a more social democratic and redistributive direction. The Single Market won support from trade unions because of a considerable compensation package that included increases in structural and regional funds and a new emphasis on "social union" with the promise of measures such as common employment policy. Beyond the "social" shift, the agreement on movement to a single currency under control of a European Central Bank was also a special concern for neoliberals.

A signal moment for the new neoliberal opposition took place in September 1988 when British prime minister Margaret Thatcher spoke in Bruges, Belgium. In her speech, Thatcher acknowledged the bonds that Britain shared with Europe, placing a special emphasis on "Christendom . . . with its recognition of the unique and spiritual nature of the individual." She declared that "our destiny is in Europe, as part of the Community" but also expressed concern about tendencies toward centralization and protectionism in the process of integration. "We have not successfully rolled back the frontiers of the state in Britain," she announced, "only to see them re-imposed at a European level with a European super-state exercising a new dominance from Brussels." In conclusion, she voiced the demand that would be taken up by many neoliberal Euroskeptics in the decades that followed. She called for Europe as a "family of nations."[12]

Taking both inspiration and their name from Thatcher's speech, the Bruges Group was formed the following year as the first Euroskeptic neoliberal think tank. The leader was Ralph Harris, a veteran of the Institute of Economic Affairs and long-time secretary of the MPS as well as its president from 1982 to 1984, whom Thatcher made "Baron Harris of High Cross" a lifetime peer in her first year in office. The organization was formed in February 1989 and held its first meeting in Bruges itself in April. In an invitation to be part of the new organization sent to MPS members, Harris explained that Thatcher was not "anti-European" but was simply opposed to "the enforcement of unnecessary harmonization from Brussels, followed by spreading European dirigisme."[13] Calling for "a Europe of sovereign states," the Bruges Group contended that "European economic prosperity is served best by encouraging as much free competition and diversity between the differing national systems as possible."[14] Echoing the ordoliberal language of the "strong state and the free market," the Bruges Group stated in its purposes and aims that "the freedom and safety of Europe relies upon strong—but not necessarily big—government for our defense and security, and this strength is, in our view, best preserved by the independent nation state and by the promotion of a healthy, natural patriotism that the citizen feels toward the state."[15]

The Bruges Group trod a narrow line in calling for the relinquishing of some aspects of national policymaking to central European authorities while preserving the principle of the sovereign nation-state anchored in an affective foundation of "healthy, natural patriotism." Their primary fear was that the balance would be upended by the seizure of power by left-leaning European bureaucrats. In one of the first pamphlets published by the Bruges Group, Chicago-trained LSE professor and future cochair of the organization Brian Hindley wrote that "the real issue . . . is whether there should be an effort to move toward a United States of Europe" complete with a "social charter" granting minimum rights to workers along with worker participation in management.[16]

Mobilizing against the specter of a "social Europe," the Bruges Group brought in allies old and new. One of their distinctive moves was to incorporate partners from Eastern Europe. In early 1989, months before the fall of the Berlin Wall, they held events with members of Polish Solidarity calling for a broader conception of Europe.[17] They also showcased economists who had long engaged with alternative proposals of European integration, especially related to currency policy. At a press conference in London in June 1989, four Mont Pèlerin Society members criticized Delors with a focus on the proposed monetary union, leading to one of the Bruges Group's first publications, *A Citizen's Charter for European Monetary Union*.[18] One of the speakers was the sitting MPS president, Antonio Martino, who played a coordinating role in the Bruges Group and would become a founding member of the Forza Italia political party in 1994 and hold cabinet positions in two of Silvio Berlusconi's governments. Also speaking were Pascal Salin, who would be MPS president from 1994 to 1996, and the German economist Roland Vaubel.

Both Salin and Vaubel had been involved with European monetary policy since the 1970s. They were core members of a long-standing group of neoliberals that advocated competing or parallel currencies as an alternative to a single, common currency as the basis of the European monetary union. As early as November 1975, Salin published the All-Saints Day Declaration in the *Economist* along with the German economist Herbert Giersch (MPS president from 1986 to 1988) and seven other economists, calling for the introduction of a parallel European currency called the Europa to compete with national currencies. As part of a group of experts assembled by the European Commission, Salin coauthored another report making similar recommendations the same year.[19] Vaubel, who finished his Ph.D. in Kiel under Giersch's direction, also served as an expert drafted by the commission (while still in his mid-twenties) and published his first book on the idea of "currency competition and the case for a European parallel currency" in 1978.[20] Both Salin and Vaubel were in conversation with Hayek, who was writing about the idea of competing currencies at the same time, including two texts published in 1976 that would become touchstones in the cryptocurrency debates of the 2010s.[21]

The specifically European context of Hayek's proposals is often overlooked.[22] Salin retroactively dubbed Hayek "the real inspiration" behind the work of neoliberal economists on parallel currencies.[23] Yet in light of the fact that Hayek's two texts followed research and proposals already underway by Giersch, Vaubel, and Salin himself, one can infer that the inspiration went both ways. Giersch had published two formal proposals for competing currencies in Europe by the time of Hayek's signature texts.[24] Giersch and Hayek had known each other since the late 1940s, and Hayek invited Giersch to apply for a position at Freiburg University in 1963.[25] Further testifying to the influence of the Kiel group, Hayek called Vaubel's work "to a great extent, the departure point" for his continuing work on competing currencies and predicted that Vaubel would be the first German economist to receive the Nobel Prize.[26]

It was a sore point for neoliberals in the 1990s that their most developed proposal for Europe—that of "currency choice"—lost out to the common currency of the Euro.[27] In 1992, Giersch led fifty-nine other economists in publishing an open letter critical of the proposed monetary union.[28] While the chief economists of major banks felt that centralized monetary policy was necessary to prevent the collapse into competing national policies, Giersch and others feared that the agreement did not include sufficient sanctioning power to keep the individual state budgets in line. A dividing line was created between those neoliberals who felt supranational governance was necessary to defend overall economic order and right-wing neoliberals who felt that such an order must be anchored more soundly in national states. Neither were opposed to an active role for the state per se. The disagreement was about whether a central European bank or national central banks were the most effective site for monetary management.

At the turn of the 1990s, there was a meaningful divide between the neoliberals of the Bruges Group who emphasized the importance of the nation-state as an ongoing locus of sovereignty and others who saw the very merit of European institutions in its ability to pickpocket national sovereignty for the sake of locked-in market freedoms at the supranational level. The contrast is best illustrated in a contribution from an unlikely quarter: the American economist James M. Buchanan, MPS president from 1984 to 1986 and recipient of the Nobel Memorial Prize in Economics in 1986, who otherwise engaged little with European or international questions.[29] At the first MPS general meeting after the fall of the Berlin Wall, held in Munich in September 1990, Buchanan led off with an "American perspective on Europe's constitutional opportunity." The respondents were the German-Swiss economist Peter Bernholz and Harris. The published version of the talk appeared in French and German as well as in English and in both the United States and the United Kingdom, suggesting its centrality to the discussion at the time.[30]

In a provocative departure from the right-wing neoliberals, Buchanan diagnosed a waning of the very sentiments of nationalism and patriotism to which Harris, Thatcher, and the Bruges Group appealed. Far from seeing nationalism as "healthy" or "natural," Buchanan saw it as one of many "artificial" "dependency-induced loyalties" concocted by intellectuals to shape collectives to their own self-interested ends.[31] By the end of "the socialist-collectivist century," he wrote, "political entrepreneurs can no longer exploit the Hegelian sublimation of the individual to a collective zeitgeist or the Marxian dialectic of class conflict."[32] He saw the belief in the need for a culturally homogeneous nation inhabiting a single territory as part of a "romantic myth . . . substantially displaced in the public consciousness of the 1990s."[33]

Evidently convinced by contemporary arguments about the eclipse of the nation in an era of globalization, Buchanan believed that the waning of nationalism created an opening for constitutional design. "Europe waits for its own James Madison," he wrote, "who understands the constitutional economics of competition."[34] Because, as he put it elsewhere, "socialism is dead but Leviathan lives on," there would have to be checks to prevent the expansion of the remit of power by rent-seeking private interests.[35] The European constitutional mandate must be limited to the guarantee of "competition among producers and consumers of goods and resources across the territory that encompasses the several nation-states."[36] Significantly, he also emphasized that a European constitution would need the right of secession. Without an exit option, the temptation of elite-led leftward mission creep would be too great.

Buchanan's plan harked back to the proposals of Hayek and Lionel Robbins from the 1930s, when they sought consciously to harmonize and lock in free-trade policies through supranational federation.[37] Yet Buchanan recalled his proposal being met with hostility:

> I was attacked by the right mostly by Britishers who at that time had formed
> what they called the Bruges Group. There were a few European members in that
> group, but basically it was dominated by the British. I was a vicious man because I
> was proposing the possibility that Europe was moving toward some sort of federal
> structure. "Federal" is a black word in their lexicon; the idea of federalism or
> federation or anything like that they consider outrageous. They were essentially
> refusing to agree to have England or Britain give up even one jot of what they
> thought was their national sovereignty.[38]

The early 1990s neoliberal discourse on Europe is captured well by the opposing stances of Buchanan and the Bruges Group. There was a faction within the MPS, including Curzon-Price, who believed similarly that "tying the hands" of sovereign governments was precisely the goal of supranational monetary order, either through binding rules or a central authority.[39] In 1989, she referred positively to the "Ferrari model" of integration in the wake of European Court of Justice decisions securing competition over European borders and, most importantly, the freeing of capital movements between member states, which she believed would lead organically to the disciplining of national governments and the narrowing of their space of policy discretion.[40] Martino himself followed Buchanan in the argument that what was essential was the institution of rules binding national governments and central banks and that the content of the rule itself could change with time.[41]

Following Buchanan's prompt, the European Constitutional Group was formed in 1992 by German public choice economist Christian Kirchner. The ECG drafted a proposed European constitution in 1993 outlining a narrow set of supranational political capacities for the EU. Following Buchanan, they included the right of secession. Among the ten original participants in the ECG, seven were Mont Pèlerin Society members, including Bernholz (the original respondent to Buchanan at the 1990 MPS meeting), Francisco Cabrillo, and Salin.[42] In 1997, the ECG drew up another counterproposal to the proposed constitution of the Amsterdam Treaty, adding Vaubel and German think tanker and MPS member Detmar Doering, among others, to their ranks.[43] The core group remained active in the ECG into the 2010s, demanding reform while also stating that "the ultimate protection against a breakdown of the rule of law is the right to withdraw. There ought to be more room for opt-outs."[44]

If the constitutionalist contingent of Euroskeptic neoliberals, with a preponderance of German-speaking and Southern European participants, leaned toward internal reform, the British members of the Bruges Group edged toward rejection of the EU through the 1990s. In 1996, the organization's co-chair, Brian Hindley coauthored a paper titled *Better Off Out? The Benefits or Costs of EU Membership.* The paper set out to dispel the idea that leaving the EU would be economically devastating, concluding that "the idea that dire economic consequences make UK departure from the EU unthinkable has no evident foundation."[45] In the introduction to a 1997 Bruges Group publication titled *A Euro-Sceptical Dictionary*, Chris R. Tame, the founder of the UK's Libertarian Alliance, captured the development of the second half of the decade when he wrote that "there has been an increasing shift in 'Euroskeptic' opinion from the hope that the increasingly statist and illiberal character of the EU could be reformed, to the view that the European-project is now irrevocably flawed and inherently statist, and that total withdrawal is the only feasible option."[46] The Bruges Group promoted this line in an online web magazine called *eurocritic* as well as a publication titled *Critical Journal.*

By 1999, the die seemed cast. The campaign director of the Bruges Group promised publicly that "the EU will break-up because of its contradictions. Just in the way that the USSR broke-up then the EU will suffer a similar fate."[47] From the hope of internal reform, the British neoliberal Euroskeptics had moved to the prediction of dissolution.

Centre for the New Europe: The Opening to the Right, or the Meaning of the Mole

The Bruges Group was joined on its path of Euroskeptic radicalization by an affiliated think tank, Centre for the New Europe, founded in Brussels in 1993 by the Belgian lawyer Fernand Keuleneer and the Belgian jurist and journalist Paul Belien, who presented the new organization at the MPS meeting in Cannes in 1994.[48] Belien paid homage to Hayek's last book in the same year in an article titled "The Fatal Conceit of Europe."[49] Keuleneer and Belien had already launched a magazine together, *Nucleus*, in 1990. Keuleneer acted as president of the CNE with the French economist Paul Fabra as director general and Belien as research director. Ralph Harris helped secure funding, which came through the Roularta Media Group and the pharmaceutical company, Pfizer.[50] The links to the pharmaceutical company were intimate, as CNE's vice president into the 2000s, Catherine Windels, retained a parallel position there as a marketing executive.[51] The center's publications reflected the interests of their patron with an emphasis on health care and environmental regulation.[52] Belien contributed treatments of the European health care regulation to the broader neoliberal network, including Vancouver, British Columbia's Fraser Institute, to which Windels was an international advisor.[53]

The CNE was designed as a Brussels outpost for the Euroskeptic neoliberal position. Its mandate was comparable to the Bruges Group in its self-description as promoting "a pro-market, yet pro-Community viewpoint."[54] It emphasized the need to return to the primary European function of encouraging competition and preventing "over-regulation" and centralization. At the same time, it included explicit attention to traditionally socially conservative positions, arguing that "the backbone of a community is its ethical, moral and cultural framework."[55] The organization insisted that "the concept of community depends upon commonly held systems of values: criteria to distinguish good from evil, right from wrong. Pluralism, civilised debate, personal freedom and human dignity cannot survive in a cultural climate that denies either the existence of truth (nihilism) or the importance of truth (relativism)."[56] According to Belien, the attention to socially conservative themes reflected their goal to cast the CNE in the mold of American think tanks like the Heritage Foundation and American Enterprise Institute, which combined themes of free markets with traditional morality and thereby, in his metaphor, "walk[ed] on two legs" instead of only one.[57]

The mixture of conservative and market themes also reflected the approach of the Social Affairs Unit (SAU), an offshoot of the IEA, overseen by MPS member Digby Anderson, who sat on the board of directors of the CNE. In the 1990s, the SAU published books suggesting that the loosening of sexual norms since the 1960s had eroded the conditions for reproducing the free market order. The title of one of Anderson's edited SAU volumes illustrated the approach starkly: *This Will Hurt: The Restoration of Virtue and Civic Order*.[58] Belien's own investment in socially conservative themes was reflected in his engaged activism in support of homeschooling as well as a polemical text opposing abortion, published by the Roularta Media Group, which hosted the CNE offices in their early years.[59]

Belien wrote the CNE's first publication in 1994 and became an MPS member in 1996.[60] Toward the end of the decade, his politics shifted further rightward. In 1995, his wife, Alexandra Colen, who had suggested the names for both *Nucleus* and CNE, entered Belgian parliament with the far-right Flemish separatist party Vlaams Blok. During her time in parliament, the couple published a "quarterly journal for the study of secession and direct democracy" titled *Secession* (*Secessie*). The journal's website offered links to the Bruges Group and the CNE alongside right-wing libertarian Lewrockwell.com and the anti-immigration site VDare, run by the former *National Review* journalist and forerunner of the Alt-Right Peter Brimelow.[61] After Colen's party was outlawed as racist in 2004, Belien wrote for VDare that a new party would arise that would spell the end of Belgium through the partition he desired and "will bury mass immigration too."[62] Since 2006, Belien has directed the think tank Islamist Watch and published articles warning of Muslims as "predators" who "starting when they're small, learn at their yearly offerings how to cut the throats of warm-blooded livestock." "We get sick at the sight of blood," he warned, "but they don't. They're trained and they're armed."[63]

Belien's swing from reformist Euroskeptic to separatist xenophobic nationalist is an extreme case of a trajectory taken by others. A case in point is Belien's successor as research director at CNE, the German philosopher Hardy Bouillon, who also established a branch office of CNE in Trier, where he taught and lived in the late 1990s. Bouillon was an MPS member, and the CNE's advisory board was heavily stacked with others. MPS members accounted for twenty-two of twenty-four advisors, including those involved with the Bruges Group like Harris, Salin, Vaubel, and Martino and the ECG like Bernholz, Jiri Schwarz, and Angelo Petroni.[64] Martino's wife, Carol Erickson, was a member of the five-person board. During his tenure at CNE, Bouillon became actively involved with the libertarian magazine *Eigentümlich Frei* founded in 1998, writing articles on libertarianism and sitting on its editorial board.[65] According to the mandate of its publisher, André Lichtschlag, the goal of the journal was to create an alliance between libertarians and the New Right.[66] He followed the model set by American libertarian Murray Rothbard in the famous "paleo alliance" he formed in the late 1980s between the paleoconservatives of the Right, including Samuel Francis and others around the Rockford Institute, and the paleolibertarians centered on the Ludwig von Mises Institute in Auburn, Alabama.[67] The latter regularly promoted topics of "race realism" as well as secession, neo-confederacy and the need for increased regulation of immigration.[68] In 1992, Rothbard laid out a strategy of "right-wing populism" returned to innumerable times since by right-wing libertarians. The goal, he wrote, was to oppose Hayek's approach of "trickle-down educationism" that targeted elites with a style that was "exciting, dynamic, tough, and confrontational, rousing" and that appealed to the masses.[69] Also known as the "redneck strategy," the goal was to transform people's natural dislike of politicians into a dislike for politics as such, thereby paving the way to a stateless society.

A connection between U.S. paleolibertarians and German neoliberals existed via the most forceful proponent of the "closed borders libertarian" position after Rothbard's death in 1995, his protégé, the German economist Hans-Hermann Hoppe. Rothbard brought Hoppe to the United States on a scholarship from the Center for Libertarian Studies and eventually found him a position at the University of Nevada–Las Vegas, where Rothbard himself worked. In the 1990s, Hoppe wrote about immigration as "forced integration" and spoke positively about the neo-nationalist secession groups sweeping Europe.[70] His most famous book, published in 2001, was titled *Democracy: The God That Failed* and called for a shift to a nondemocratic "private law society."[71] Following his mentor, Rothbard, Hoppe referred to his philosophy as anarcho-capitalism.

Bouillon met Hoppe in 1991. Having grown dissatisfied with "Hayek's concept of individual freedom," Bouillon recalls finding Hoppe "refreshing."[72] It is likely through Bouillon that Hoppe was hosted at the Center for the New Europe in 2001.[73] Hoppe also joined Bouillon as a member of the advisory board of *Eigentümlich Frei* in 2006. At an event where Hoppe spoke in front of a gathering of libertarians and German liberals of the FDP in 2005, Bouillon brandished the mascot of Krtek, a stuffed cartoon mole, calling "for a combination of adapting to and subverting the system."[74] The spirit of the meeting was that of Rothbard and Lichtschlag—the search for a viable union between right-wing populism and libertarianism. The Swiss rightist Christoph Blocher was named as one candidate for such a politics at the meeting, and the examples of the AfD and the Austrian Freedom Party would follow.[75]

Bouillon counted Rothbard as one of his favorite authors.[76] As director of academic affairs, he held the same position as Rothbard had at the Mises Institute in Alabama. Under Bouillon's direction, the CNE took a similar route to the Bruges Group but with a bent toward radical-right libertarianism, where the Bruges Group tended to a more staid Toryism. The CNE enjoyed what they saw as tweaking the noses of the European bureaucrats, hosting a "Capitalist Ball" in 2003 where Bouillon gave the CNE's F. A. Hayek Award to his coauthor and mentor, the MPS member and philosopher of science Gerard Radnitzky, who used his talk to skewer the European Commissioner Frits Bolkestein.[77] Radnitzky's perspective resembled Hoppe's. He questioned the necessity of democracy for a functioning market order, wrote extensively on the importance of Western values for the success of capitalism, and denounced the EU as "the forerunner to a global tax cartel."[78]

The CNE's perspective overlapped substantially with that of Lichtschlag's *Eigentümlich Frei*. Another of the magazine's advisors, the MPS member Detmar Doering, published a report for CNE on the need for a right of secession from the EU a few years after an article in *Eigentümlich Frei* attempting to recuperate the reputation of social Darwinism.[79] Climate denial became another focus as the CNE published a report refuting "the scientific foundations of the global warming scare" and Bouillon claimed that the belief in climate change was based on "falsification."[80] By the first decade of the 2000s, the CNE had established itself as the wild sibling of neoliberal Euroskepticism, flirting with anti-democratic strains of right-wing libertarianism and seeking a basis for an effective neoliberal populism. The breakthrough would come with the Eurozone crisis.

New Direction: The Breakthrough of Neoliberal Secessionism

Throughout the 1990s, a Euroskeptic Right formed at the European level with little effect on the individual national political landscape. In a painful irony, the directly elected members of European parliament, originally intended to help bridge the so-called democratic deficit and legitimate Europe-wide governance, ended up offering a stage to those suspicious of the European project as such. Although there was already a robust transnational network of Euroskeptic right-wing parties by 1994, few scholars paid attention or took them seriously as part of the system of national and transnational European civil society. The fact that the hurdle for a seat in the European parliament is only 3 percent (as opposed to 5 percent in the German Bundestag) lowered the barriers to entry for protest parties.

The opening for neoliberal populist parties came after the financial and economic crisis of 2008. A so-called critical realignment took place as the existing party system could no longer channel the economic and social problems produced by the global financial crisis. The formation of the Alliance of European Conservatives and Reformers (AECR) in 2009 was a clear expression of the increased confidence of the European New Right.[81] The decision of the British Conservative Party, along with that of the Czech ODS and the Polish PiS to end their traditional cooperation with the majority conservatives and social democrats in the European Parliament, marked a break with the integration policy of the past. The new formation introduced a conservative perspective with no ties to the previous policy of integration. The AECR became the counterpart party of the new cross-European party grouping of the European Conservatives and Reformers (ECR) that contained Tories, ODS, PiS, and others.

The AECR was formally launched in March 2009 with the ten-point Prague Declaration, spearheaded by the British Tories and the ODS, founded by MPS member Vaclav Klaus. The Prague Declaration linked neoliberal and conservative thinking. The manifesto opened with the demand for economic rather than political freedom as the basis of personal freedom and national welfare. "Free enterprise, free and fair trade and competition, minimal regulation, lower taxation, and small government," it declared, were "the ultimate catalysts for individual freedom and personal and national prosperity." The declaration also demanded more individual freedom and responsibility, clean energy, and energy security and emphasized the family as the basis of society, national sovereignty against European federalism, and the significance of NATO, especially for the younger democracies in Eastern Europe. It called for a stricter control of immigration and greater transparency for the expenditure of European funds.

In 2010, the AECR launched its own think tank, titled New Direction—the Foundation of European Reform (ND). Expressing continuity with the genesis of neoliberal Euroskepticism in the late 1980s, Thatcher was the patron of the foundation until her death in 2013. The foundation was directed by Tom Miers and erstwhile Polish Solidarity activist Krzysztof Grzelczyk as the East European coordinator. Its deputy director from 2011 to 2015 was none other than Hardy Bouillon, formerly of the CNE. The *Alternative für Deutschland*, or AfD, was formed as a protest party in 2013 against the German government's conduct in the Eurozone crisis. Although some AfD politicians were part of ECR, they were not part of the affiliated AECR. Nonetheless, there was overlap with New Direction. Hans-Olaf Henkel, one of the founders of the AfD, who later left to join the splinter Liberal Conservative Reformers (LKR), was New Direction's vice president.[82] In 2015 he edited the first issue of its magazine, titled *That Sinking Feeling*, which pictured the symbol of the Euro descending into a dark sea as a shark's fin approached. The magazine included an article by the veteran neoliberal Euroskeptic Roland Vaubel calling the banking union a "breach of faith" and another by MPS member (and founding AfD member) Joachim Starbatty questioning the positive impact of the Euro on the German economy.[83] The participation of neoliberal Euroskeptics in New Direction and the AECR represents the culmination of the arc beginning in 1988 from internal reform to a call for dissolution. Once considered salvageable, neoliberals now pictured the EU in the process of drowning.

Conclusion

When the Institute of Economic Affairs held a debate in March 2016 about how Hayek would have voted in the referendum on British EU membership, the think tank's head of public policy concluded that "Hayek would have been a Brexiteer."[84] This chapter has narrated the shift in neoliberal Euroskeptic organization from 1988 to the 2010s as a passage from reform to radicalism, from demands for conservative reconstruction to separatism and secession. The recent far-right parties must be understood within this backdrop. Ironically the new right-wing neoliberalism profits from the dislocations of the neoliberal project (free trade, free capital movements, deregulation, and liberalization) and the inadequate protection offered by the ever-shrinking welfare state. The transformation of welfare capitalism has effected changes that have boomeranged on the neoliberal camp itself. Neoliberals may not like it, but the logic of the competition state and locational competition inevitably frees up centrifugal dynamics, both in Europe and in the nation state, because competition requires a free hand in influencing local conditions. Nation-state building and the construction of Europe is premised to a large degree on regulating and even limiting certain conditions of competition. Europe and even some of the member states are at a critical juncture, because cross-regional cohesion and competition ultimately cannot be easily reconciled by going in one direction only. Because right-wing neoliberalism embodies a culturally and socially conservative variant of neoliberalism, it offers its own kind of regressive politics: exclusionary social romanticism takes the place of egalitarian social policy. An adherence to the ideology of family and competition replaces the spirit of equality of opportunity and social mobility.

At the MPS meeting in South Korea in 2017, Václav Klaus expressed the spirit of neoliberal nationalism. The biggest problem was that of migration, accelerated in his opinion by the inducements of the welfare state along with a "post-modern ideological confusion connected with the ideas of multiculturalism, cultural relativism, continentalism (as opposed to the idea of nation-state), human-rightism and political correctness." "Mass migration into Europe," he said, "threatens to destroy European society and to create a new Europe which would be very different from the past as well as from MPS way of thinking." He defended the right-wing populist parties in France, Austria, Germany, the Netherlands, and Italy as "powerless people who try to oppose the arrogant European (or American) political elites." The solution was to ground "continental or planetary thinking" back in the nation-state.[85] The neoliberal nationalist position rebukes the legalist constitutionalism of thinkers like Buchanan and places questions of affect and psychology front and center. Far from a proposition of one-dimensional homo œconomicus, it is a vision of human nature, social order, and political subjectivity grounded in extra-economic factories of morality and emotion.

The relationship of neoliberal nationalism to the wider world is highly selective. In the programs of two of these parties—the AfD and the Austrian Freedom Party—we find that the rejection of Europe does not mean a blanket rejection of economic globalization, as suggested by the frequent conjoining of populism, political isolationism, and economic protectionism. While the parties condemn the EU, the language demanding increased trade and competitiveness is entirely mainstream. The AfD calls for trade agreements to be settled through the WTO and the lifting of barriers for exports from developing countries in the place of foreign aid transfers. Fiscal conservatism is raised to an absurd degree with criminal charges demanded for policymakers who overspend. Both parties call for school choice and an end to inheritance tax and burdensome regulations, even as they make new promises for social spending.

In the right-wing neoliberal imaginary, free-market capitalism is not displaced but anchored ever more deeply in conservative family structures and a group identity defined against an Islamic threat from the East. Aware of the resonances with the West German social market economy of the 1950s, the AfD self-consciously employs the same slogan in its party program as the country's first economics minister and MPS member Ludwig Erhard: "Prosperity for all!" Rather than contrasting a neoliberal Europe against its populist critics, this chapter has shown that the anti-European neoliberal nationalism must be seen as a political position with its own cast of characters and a clear pedigree. Any future description of Europe as a neoliberal plot must acknowledge the neoliberals who have plotted against it too.

Tracking the history of neoliberal Euroskepticism offers important information in its own right—as a revision, or at least complication, of the commonly circulated assertion about the European Union's essential neoliberalism. It also provides evidence of the need for careful genealogy in tracking the "mutations of neoliberalism."[86] It is ill-advised, in most cases, to seek a kind of "pure" neoliberal doctrine from which one can draw conclusions about the world. Neoliberal thought—like all genres of political thought—is subject to processes of constant bifurcation and recombination. Following the trajectories of specific intellectuals and the organs of their expression, such as think tanks and political parties, offers one methodology for seeing how ideas are both formed and serve as the basis for new political platforms and idioms of claim-making. In the case of the recent backlash against supranational legal institutions like the WTO and treaty bodies like the EU, following strains of mutant neoliberalism helps us better understand what scholars call the "supply side" of right-wing populist movements, or the political entrepreneurs who provide the storyline and narrative: "Here is what is happening, this is why, and these are the people doing it to you," as Dani Rodrik describes it.[87] If we understand neoliberalism as embodying less a credo than an injunction—to defend capitalism against democracy—then mutations should be expected. Prescriptions change with the threat. Following the form they take at any given time requires scholarly vigilance and attention to detail.

Notes

1. Wolfgang Streeck, *Buying Time: The Delayed Crisis of Democratic Capitalism* (New York: Verso, 2014).

2. John Gillingham, *European Integration, 1950-2003: Superstate or New Market Economy?* (New York: Cambridge University Press, 2003), 6. A more insightful version comes from Perry Anderson, who points out that Hayek's proposal of supranational federation could potentially be diverted toward a social-democratic program. He speculates that this was Delors's own hope; see Anderson, "The Europe to Come," *London Review of Books*, January 25, 1996.

3. See Pierre Dardot and Christian Laval, *The New Way of the World: On Neoliberal Society* (New York: Verso, 2014); Fritz W. Scharpf, "The Asymmetry of European Integration, or Why the EU Cannot Be a 'Social Market Economy,'" *Socio-Economic Review* 8 (2010): 211–50; Laurent Warlouzet and Tobias Witschke, "The Difficult Path to an Economic Rule of Law: European Competition Policy, 1950–91," *Contemporary European History* 21, no. 3 (2012): 437–55. For an overview of these debates, see Slobodian, *Globalists: The End of Empire and the Birth of Neoliberalism* (Cambridge, Mass.: Harvard University Press, 2018), Chapter 6.

4. François Denord, Rachel Knaebel, and Pierre Rimbert, "Germany's Iron Cage," *Le Monde Diplomatique*, August 10–16, 2015.

5. Simon Nixon, "The European Union's Neoliberal Dilemma," *Wall Street Journal*, October 4, 2017. See also Alan Johnson, "Why Brexit Is Best for Britain: The Left-Wing Case," *New York Times*, March 28, 2017.

6. On the intellectual genealogy of locational competition or *Standortwettbewerb* see Dieter Plehwe and Quinn Slobodian, "Landscapes of Unrest: Herbert Giersch and the Origins of Neoliberal Economic Geography," *Modern Intellectual History* 16, no. 1 (Apr 2019): 185–215.

7. See, e.g. Mitchell Dean, "Rethinking Neoliberalism," *Journal of Sociology* 50, no. 2 (2012): 150; Joshua Rahtz, "Laissez-Faire's Reinventions," *New Left Review*, no. 89 (September–October, 2014): 137. On the MPS, see Philip Mirowski and Plehwe, eds., *The Road from Mont Pèlerin: The Making of the Neoliberal Thought Collective* (Cambridge, Mass.: Harvard University Press, 2009).

8. Philipp Ther, "Europe's Ride on the Neoliberalism Express," *Bloomberg View*, September 8, 2016.

9. For exceptions, see David Bebnowski, *Die Alternative für Deutschland: Aufstieg und gesellschaftliche Repräsentanz einer rechten populistischen Partei* (Wiesbaden: Springer VS, 2015); Herbert Schui, Ralf Ptak, Stephanie Blankenburg, Günter Bachmann, and Dirk Kotzur, *Wollt ihr den totalen Markt? Der Neoliberalismus und die extreme Rechte* (Munich: Knaur, 1997). For previous publications by one author, see Plehwe and Matthias Schlögl, "Europäische und zivilgesellschaftliche Hintergründe der euro(pa)skeptischen Partei Alternative für Deutschland (AfD)," *WZB Discussion Paper*, November 2014; Plehwe, "Alternative für Deutschland, Alternativen für Europa?," in *Europäische Identität in der Krise? Europäische Identitätsforschung und Rechtspopulismusforschung im Dialog*, ed. Gudrun Hentges, Kristina Nottbohm, and Hans-Wolfgang Platzer (Wiesbaden: Springer VS, 2017).

10. On the former, see Rawi Abdelal, *Capital Rules: The Construction of Global Finance* (Cambridge, Mass.: Harvard University Press, 2007).

11. The TPRC was founded by Australian Hugh Corbet in 1968. It closed in the late 1980s to be reborn as the Cordell Hull Institute. For key publications, see Gerard Curzon Price and Virginia Curzon-Price, *Hidden Barriers to International Trade*, Thames essay (London: Trade Policy Research Centre, 1970); Victoria Curzon-Price, *The Essentials of Economic Integration: Lessons of EFTA Experience* (New York: St. Martin's Press for the Trade Policy Research Centre, 1974); *Industrial Policies in the European Community*, World Economic Issues (London: Macmillan for the Trade Policy Research Centre, 1981); and André Bénard, *A Europe Open to the World* (London: Trade Policy Research Centre, 1984).

12. "The Bruges Speech," https://www.margaretthatcher.org/document/107332.

13. Harris, IEA to Hayek, March 22, 1989, Duke Archive, Hayek papers, box 97, folder 10.

14. The Bruges Group, "A Campaign for a Europe of Sovereign States" pamphlet, Duke Archive, Hayek papers, box 97, folder 10.

15. Ibid.

16. Brian Hindley, "Europe: Fortress or Freedom?," the Bruges Group, Occasional Paper 2, Duke Archive, Hayek papers, box 97, folder 10.

17. Patrick Robertson to Hayek, September 5, 1989, Duke Archive, Hayek papers, box 97, folder 10.

18. Roland Vaubel, Antonio Martino, Francisco Cabrillo, and Pascal Salin, *A Citizen's Charter for European Monetary Union*, Occasional Papers (Brussels: Bruges Group, 1989).

19. Emmanuel Mourlon-Druol, *A Europe Made of Money: The Emergence of the European Monetary System*, Cornell Studies in Money (Ithaca, N.Y.: Cornell University Press, 2012), 87.

20. Vaubel to Hayek, April 12, 1976. Duke Archive, Hayek papers, box 56, folder 6; Vaubel, *Strategies for Currency Unification: The Economics of Currency Competition and the Case for a European Parallel Currency* (Tübingen: Mohr, 1978). See also Vaubel, "Plans for a European Parallel Currency and SDR Reform: The Choice of Value-Maintenance Provisions and 'Gresham's Law,'" *Weltwirtschaftliches Archiv* 110, no. 2 (June 1974).

21. See Hayek, *Denationalisation of Money: An Analysis of the Theory and Practice of Concurrent Currencies* (London: Institute of Economic Affairs, 1976), and Hayek, *Choice in Currency: A Way to Stop Inflation* (London: Institute of Economic Affairs, 1976). On cryptocurrency, see David Golumbia, *The Politics of Bitcoin: Software as Right-Wing Extremism* (Minneapolis: University of Minnesota Press, 2016).

22. For an exception see Anderson, "Europe to Come."

23. Pascal Salin, "General Introduction," in *Currency Competition and Monetary Union*, ed. Pascal Salin (The Hague: Martinus Nijhoff, 1984), 1.

24. The Kiel Report was published in December 1974 and the Marjolin Report in March 1975. For details, see Mourlon-Druol, *A Europe Made of Money*, 35.

25. Plehwe and Slobodian, "Landscapes of Unrest," 15, 21.

26. Hayek to Klaus Dellmann, December 22, 1983, and Hayek to Klaus Dellmann, Kiel University, November 17, 1983, both at Duke Archive, Hayek papers, box 56, folder 6.

27. Charles P. Kindleberger, *A Financial History of Western Europe* (London: George Allen & Unwin, 1984), 459. See also Salin, "The Choice of Currency in a Single European Market," *Cato Journal* 10, no. 2 (Fall 1990).

28. Andrew Fisher, "Germans Defend Treaty," *Financial Times*, June 16, 1992.

29. An exception is his constitutional proposal for Pinochet's Chile; see Nancy MacLean, *Democracy in Chains: The Deep History of the Radical Right's Stealth Plan for America* (New York: Viking, 2017), Chapter 10.

30. James Buchanan, *Une Constitution pour l'Europe? Etats-Unis 1787-Europe 1990* (Paris: Euro 92, 1990); Buchanan, "Möglichkeiten für eine europäische Verfassung: Eine amerikanische Sicht," *Ordo* 42 (1991): 127–37; Buchanan, "Europe's Constitutional Opportunity," in *Europe's Constitutional Future* (London: Institute of Economic Affairs, 1990); Buchanan, "An American Perspective on Europe's Constitutional Opportunity," *Cato Journal* 10, no. 3 (Winter 1991), 619–29.

31. Buchanan, "American Perspective," 623.

32. Ibid., 624.

33. Ibid., 628.

34. Ibid., 629.

35. Buchanan, *Socialism Is Dead, but Leviathan Lives On* (St. Leonards, Australia: The Centre for Independent Studies, 1990).

36. Buchanan, "An American Perspective," 625.

37. See Slobodian, *Globalists*, chapter 3; Or Rosenboim, *The Emergence of Globalism: Visions of World Order in Britain and the United States, 1939-1950* (Princeton, N.J.: Princeton University Press, 2017), Chapter 5.

38. Buchanan, "Response," in *Public Finance and Public Choice: Two Contrasting Visions of the State*, ed. James M. Buchanan and Richard A. Musgrave (Cambridge, Mass.: MIT Press, 1999), 180.

39. Victoria Curzon-Price, "Three Models of European Integration," in *Whose Europe? Competing Visions for 1992*, ed. Ralf Dahrendorf (London: Institute of Economic Affairs, 1989), 37.

40. Ibid., 38.

41. Antonio Martino, "A Monetary Constitution for Europe?," *Cato Journal* 10, no. 2 (Fall 1990): 519.

42. Plehwe and Bernhard Walpen, "Buena Vista Neoliberal? Eine klassentheoretische und organisationszentrierte Einführung in die transnationale Welt neoliberaler Ideen," in *Ideologien in der Weltpolitik*, ed. Klaus-Gerd Giessen (Wiesbaden: Springer, 2004), 78.

43. Ibid., 79.

44. Peter Bernholz, Gunnar Beck, Charles Beat Blankart, Francisco Cabrillo, Elena Leontjeva, Angelo Petroni, Pascal Salin, Friedrich Schneider, Jiri

Schwarz, Peter Stein, Roland Vaubel, and Frank Vibert, "European Constitutional Group Open Letter to the President of the European Council," *Open Europe Berlin*, December 1, 2015.

45. Brian Hindley and Martin Howe, *Better Off Out? The Benefits or Costs of EU Membership* (London: Institute of Economic Affairs, 1996), 99.

46. Chris R. Tame, *A Euro-Sceptical Directory*, Occasional Paper no. 29 (London: Bruges Group, 1997).

47. Jonathan Collett, "Euro-Scepticism: Past, Present and Future," *Bruges Group*, April 13, 1999.

48. Paul Belien, "The Brussels Capitalist Ball 2006," *Brussels Journal*, February 25, 2006.

49. Belien, "The Fatal Conceit of Europe," in *Visions of Europe: Summing Up the Political Choices*, ed. Stephen Hill (London: Duckworth, 1993). See Hayek, *The Collected Works of F. A. Hayek*, vol. 1, *The Fatal Conceit: The Errors of Socialism*, (Chicago: University of Chicago Press, 1988).

50. Belien, "Brussels Capitalist Ball 2006."

51. "Presentation: CNE Staff," http://www.cne.be, November 1, 1996; accessed through archive.org.

52. See, e.g., Belien and Kevin Vigilante, *The Health Care Dilemma* (Brussels: Centre for the New Europe, 1996); William Looney, *Drug Budgets: The Hidden Costs of Control; Impact of European Drug Payment Reform on Access, Quality and Innovation* (Brussels: Centre for the New Europe, 1995); Jeremy Rabkin, *Euro-Globalism? How Environmental Accords Promote EU Priorities into "Global Governance"—and Global Hazards* (Brussels: Centre for the New Europe, 1999).

53. Belien, "What Can Europe's Health Care Systems Tell Us about the Market's Role?," in *Healthy Incentives: Canadian Health Reform in an International Context*, ed. Cynthia Ramsay, Michael Walker, and William McArthur (Vancouver, B.C.: Fraser Institute, 1996).

54. Centre for the New Europe, *Introducing CNE* (Brussels: Centre for the New Europe, 1994), 6.

55. Ibid., 10.

56. Ibid., 28.

57. Belien, "Brussels Capitalist Ball 2006." On neoliberalism and social conservatism as mutually interdependent, see Melinda Cooper, *Family Values: Between Neoliberalism and the New Social Conservatism* (New York: Zone Books, 2017).

58. Digby Anderson, ed., *This Will Hurt: The Restoration of Virtue and Civic Order* (London: Social Affairs Unit, 1995).

59. Belien, *Abortus: Het grote taboe* (Zellik: Roularta, 1992).

60. Belien, *A History of the EC/EU by a Federalist Eurosceptic* (Brussels: Centre for the New Europe, 1994).

61. Secessie: Kwartaalblad voor de studie van Separatisme en Directe Democratie http://web.archive.org/web/20010722042051/http://secessie.nu. On Brimelow, see George Hawley, *Making Sense of the Alt-Right* (New York: Columbia University Press, 2017), 39.

62. Belien, "Anti-Immigration Party Banned in Belgium," *VDare*, November 9, 2004. https://vdare.com/articles/anti-immigration-party-banned-in -belgium.

63. "Geef ons wapens!," *Brussels Journal*, April 21, 2006.

64. Fred Singer, *The Scientific Case against the Global Climate Treaty* (Brussels: Centre for the New Europe, 2000), http://web.archive.org/web/ 20010418225100/http://www.cne-network.org:80/cne/index.htm, April 18, 2001.

65. See, e.g., Hardy Bouillon, "Libertarianismus—mit oder ohne Naturrecht?," *Eigentümlich Frei*, no. 6 (1999): 195–99.

66. André F. Lichtschlag, "Für die libertär-konservative Sezession," *Sezession*, October 2003.

67. On the paleo alliance from a participant, see Paul Gottfried, *The Conservative Movement*, rev. ed. (New York: Twayne, 1993), 144–59.

68. On Rothbard's split with Charles Koch and the Cato Institute, see Daniel Bessner, "Murray Rothbard, Political Strategy, and the Making of Modern Libertarianism," *Intellectual History Review* 24, no. 4 (2014). See also Hawley, *Making Sense of the Alt-Right*, 34.

69. Murray N. Rothbard, "A Strategy for the Right (January 1992)," in *The Irrepressible Rothbard*, ed. Llewellyn H. Rockwell (Burlingame, Calif.: Center for Libertarian Studies, 2000), 11.

70. Hans-Hermann Hoppe, "The Case for Free Trade and Restricted Immigration," *Journal of Libertarian Studies* 13, no. 2 (1998): 221–33; Hoppe, "Small Is Beautiful and Efficient: The Case for Secession," *Telos* 107 (Spring 1996): 95–101.

71. Hoppe, *Democracy: The God That Failed* (New Brunswick, N.J.: Transaction, 2001).

72. Bouillon, "A Note on Intellectual Property and Externalities," in *Property, Freedom & Society: Essays in Honor of Hans-Hermann Hoppe*, ed. Jörg Guido Hülsmann and Stephan Kinsella (Auburn, Ala.: Ludwig von Mises Institute, 2009), 149.

73. *Centre for the New Europe*, http://web.archive.org/web/20010418225100/ http://www.cne-network.org:80/cne/index.htm, April 18, 2001.

74. David Schah, "Mobilmachung der Libertären in Gummersbach," *Eigentümlich Frei*, August 2005, 36.

75. Ibid.

76. Bouillon, "Schlagermusik gegen Freiheitsabsenz," *Eigentümlich Frei*, October 2001, 18.

77. Lichtschlag, "Der 'CNE Capitalist Ball 2003,'" *Eigentümlich Frei*, April 2003.

78. See, e.g., Gerard Radnitzky, "Towards a Europe of Free Societies: Evolutionary Competition or Constructivistic Design," *Ordo* 42 (1991); "Die EU als Wegbereiter des globalen Steuerkartells," *Eigentümlich Frei*, April 2003; "'Demokratie' Eine Begriffsanalyse," *Eigentümlich Frei*, 3rd Quarter, 1998.

79. Detmar Doering, "'Sozialdarwinismus' die unterschwellige Perfidie eines Schlagwortes," *Eigentümlich Frei*, no. 6, 2nd Quarter, 1999; *Friedlicher Austritt: Braucht die Europäische Union ein Sezessionsrecht?* (Brussels: Centre for the New Europe, 2002).

80. Singer, *Scientific Case against the Global Climate Treaty*; Bouillon, "Which Ideas Matter? . . . Rather Than an Introduction," in *Do Ideas Matter?: Essays in Honour of Gerard Radnitzky*, ed. Bouillon (Brussels: Centre for the New Europe, 2001), 13.

81. The party changed its name (and acronym) to Alliance of Conservatives and Reformers in Europe (ACRE) in 2016.

82. LKR was originally known as Alliance for Progress and Renewal (Allianz für Fortschritt und Aufbruch, ALFA).

83. Roland Vaubel, "Banking Union: A Breach of Faith," *That Sinking Feeling*, Autumn 2015, 48–51; Joachim Starbatty, "Has Germany Benefitted from the Euro?," *That Sinking Feeling*, Autumn 2015.

84. Ryan Bourne, "Hayek Would Have Been a Brexiteer," *IEA Blog*, March 18, 2016.

85. Václav Klaus, "Mont Pelerin Society Speech in Korea," 2017.

86. Muthucumaraswamy Sornarajah, "Mutations of Neo-Liberalism in International Investment Law," *Trade, Law and Development* 3, no. 1 (2011): 203–32.

87. Dani Rodrik, "Populism and the Economics of Globalization," *Journal of International Business Policy* (2018).

Anti-Austerity on the Far Right

Melinda Cooper

If we have learned one thing from the global financial crisis, it is that the challenge to fiscal austerity is just as likely to come from the far right as the far left. Progressive theorists who hoped that the implosion of the financial system would naturally translate into a renewal of social democratic and socialist forces were left dumbfounded when the Front National in France and the Lega in Italy stepped into the breach and proclaimed themselves the only parties capable of engineering a genuine political alternative. Across Eastern and Western Europe, far-right parties from Golden Dawn and the Front National to Jobbik and CasaPound have seized on the event of sovereign debt crisis to position themselves as the only credible architects of a new post(neo) liberal political order, often borrowing from the work of left-wing and heterodox economists to work out the details of their economic agendas. We need only look at the programs of these parties—and beyond that to the far right mediasphere—to see that they and their constituencies are often surprisingly well-versed in heterodox theories of banking and money creation and just as willing as many on the left to entertain unconventional solutions to the threat of deflation.

In non-Eurozone Central and Eastern Europe, where the former communist left has more often than not discredited itself through years of acquiescence to market reforms, the authoritarian center right now finds itself jostling with the far right in its efforts to denounce the imperialist and perverting influence of neoliberal capitalism. In Hungary, the far-right Jobbik arose seemingly out of nowhere to assert itself as a major political force in the parliamentary elections of 2010, when it focused its campaign rhetoric on the decades of austerity engineered by parties of the center-left and right. Its leaders denounce the "neo-liberal pseudo-democracy—that under the guise of free competition divides society between a thin, very rich part, and a thick, very poor part" and apportion equal parts blame to the European Union, the IMF, gender deviants, the Roma, and their universal symbolic equivalent, the international Jew.[1] Its electoral program of 2010 begins with the observation that "global capitalism based on the free movement of multinational capital has failed" and calls for a bold new economic agenda involving the expansion and renationalization of welfare funds, an end to tax and investment subsidies to multinational corporations, and the subordination of central bank policy to national interests.[2]

Forced to contend with the rising political clout of the far right, Viktor Orbán's nationalist Fidesz has blatantly coopted elements of Jobbik's economic program: since his election in 2010, Orbán has unilaterally canceled a quarter of foreign-exchange debt held by households, imposed a crisis tax on foreign-owned banks, nationalized over \$14 billion in private pension assets, and made a mockery of central bank independence.[3] In stark contrast to his rivals in the Hungarian Socialist Party, Orbán has not hesitated to flout IMF rules in order to reduce the public deficit and debt, a victory through appropriation that has ultimately and unexpectedly won him the support of international bond markets.

In Bulgaria and Romania also, the far right has emerged as the most vocal champion of expansionary fiscal policy against the depredations of both international capitalism and the political left. As former communist parties defer to the dictates of international lenders, the Bulgarian Ataka and Greater Romania Party have consistently opposed the bondage of foreign debt and demanded an end to the straitjacket of central bank independence.[4] Their political imaginary points to the machinations of the IMF, the European Union, and the United States—behind which they discern the international of Jewish money-lenders—as the agents of both economic and cultural decline.[5]

But it is within the Eurozone itself (comprising those countries who have adopted the Euro and have adhered to the constitutional rules of the European Monetary Union) that the far right has been forced to exercise greatest creativity in its attempts to evade the imperatives of fiscal austerity and balanced budgets. In France, the Front National has often vacillated on the question of public debt, but when its current leader, Marine Le Pen, took office in 2012 she abandoned the neoliberal economic politics of her father, Jean-Marie Le Pen, in favor of an expansionary economic nationalism more reminiscent of National Socialism.[6] In her two most recent presidential campaigns, Marine Le Pen announced that, if elected, the Front National would exit the Eurozone (pending the results of a referendum) and restore the franc as the national currency for day-to-day transactions.[7] Further than this, Le Pen proposed to revoke the Pompidou-Giscard law of 1973 that allegedly put an end to the Banque de France's ability to "print money" through the purchase of treasury debt.[8] The Front National would accomplish its twin aims of increasing public spending and cutting taxes by returning to the regime of central-bank-financed fiscal deficits that prevailed in France up until the early 1970s—and that now represents an almost unimaginable affront to the orthodoxy of central bank independence.

In Italy, the far-right Lega's in-house economist and former sales manager at Deutsche Bank, Claudio Borghi Aquilini, also calls on his party to restore the lira and instruct the central bank to monetize treasury debt. "If a state has debt expressed in its own money and has monetary sovereignty it can never fail to honor the debt because it will always be able to 'print' the money it needs to pay it back."[9] The Lega has also toyed with the idea of introducing "fiscal money," a government-issued IOU that would allow the state to elude the vise of austerity without flouting the European Union's legal monopoly on issuing money. Interestingly, the concept of "fiscal money" was first proposed by a group of left-wing economists who have marketed the idea to groups from right across the political spectrum, from the far-right Lega to the politically nebulous but sometimes progressive Five Star Movement.[10] These economists are very conscious of the historical antecedents to their proposal. They point out that Hitler's central banker, Hjalmar Schacht, was the first to successfully create a parallel regime of fiscal money in circumstances very similar to those faced by the peripheral economies of the Eurozone and argue that we would do well to revisit such radical solutions today.[11]

We need not look far to find the reasons for this renewed interest in unconventional economic policy. In the wake of the crisis, central banks have themselves moved far into uncharted waters, adopting expansive balance sheet strategies that would have been unthinkable in the recent past and grappling with problems (such as near-zero interest rates and insufficient inflation) that were simply not countenanced in more tranquil times.[12] In the meantime, however, states have struggled to exert their full fiscal powers to stimulate the economy because of the continued hold of neoliberal financial orthodoxies over public spending decisions. One unintended consequence of the mantra of central bank independence is that monetary authorities have been far more active and far more politically engaged in their response to crisis than elected governments have. In a context where fiscal activism on the part of states remains tightly constrained, purportedly independent central banks have been forced to capitalize on their executive power to compensate for the inaction of states (much to the chagrin of central bankers such as Bernanke).[13]

The irony has not been lost on political insiders, who lament the fact that government action remains so paralyzed by the dogma of balanced budgets at a time when debt is almost cost free (thanks to near-zero interest rates) and central banks are performing acrobatics to stimulate inflation. Little wonder then that even mainstream economists are contemplating the most unorthodox solutions to the current impasse. These range from those who, like Lawrence Summers, call for a much more exuberant use of public debt to fund grand infrastructure projects[14] to those who recall that even Milton Friedman recommended the use of central bank money creation (so-called helicopter money) in a context where deflation, not inflation, was the primary threat[15] and those who, like Adair Turner of the Bank of England, recommend a more democratic use of central bank money creation to fund fiscal deficits and public spending. As Turner explains, so-called "monetary finance"—that is, the process by which the central bank creates money for the state ex nihilo by purchasing treasury bonds—was declared off limits toward the end of the 1970s, when it was tainted with the sin of accommodating rising wage demands and generating runaway inflation.[16] But the widespread recourse to quantitative easing in the wake of the financial crisis—a practice of money creation in the service of private financial institutions—has led many to call this taboo into question. If the central bank is capable of "printing money" to keep the private banking sector afloat, Turner asks, why could we not put the same technique to work in the service of public welfare?

The situation is even more fraught for countries belonging to the EMU, where the constraints on public spending and money creation are not merely conventional but constitutional, hence almost impossible to contest without a root-and-branch reform of the Eurozone itself. As has long been recognized by both heterodox (post-Keynesian) and mainstream (New Keynesian) economists, the monetary and fiscal constitution laid down in the Maastricht Treaty and supplemented by numerous treaties and pacts since then is beset with design flaws that are destined to subvert any prospects of an enduring political union.[17] While most other central banks are merely constrained by the convention of limited money creation, the European Central Bank is constitutionally prohibited from monetizing the debt of member states, but can offer no alternative source of stimulus, since it has no fiscal institution (comparable to the U.S. Treasury, for example) that might make up for the crippled spending power of individual states.[18] As such, its actions in the face of recessionary events such as the sovereign debt crisis of 2010 (and beyond) appear calculated to sabotage any hope of recovery: the ECB has consistently forced deficit countries to slash public spending, privatize assets, and implement regressive taxes, interventions that are bound to increase debt-to-GDP ratios and postpone debt repayment into the distant future. In the absence of all flexibility on the part of the EMU itself, any country or political party that wishes to evade its crippling budget restrictions has to be very creative in its efforts to imagine an alternative—or else contemplate the danger of complete exit. Under these circumstances, even mainstream economists such as Joseph Stiglitz appear to recognize that the creation of fiscal money or a parallel currency—by any standards, well outside the rulebook of mainstream macroeconomics—might now represent the only livable alternative for the peripheral countries of the Eurozone.[19]

I take it as given that the various methods for financing the state—from public borrowing to monetary finance—have no a priori political persuasion and may lend themselves to widely divergent politics of public spending.[20] In other words, unconventional methods of public financing such as monetary finance or fiscal money have no exclusive affinity with either communism or fascism, although they are certainly at odds with the (neo)liberal premises of sound finance and permanent austerity.

What then is the difference between an anti-austerity politics of the far left and the far right? And how is the left to respond to far-right movements that are just as willing to propose a radical alternative to neoliberal austerity? More to the point, what *should* be the difference between an anti-austerity politics of the far left and the far right? The distinction matters at a time when some on the left prefer to blur the boundaries by insisting, for instance, that support for the nationalist far right represents a form of worker consciousness gone awry, a consciousness that is therefore potentially rectifiable; that "we elites" must attend to the grievances of the white working class, even when they veer to the right; or simply that the national *Volk* need to be secured against the rootlessness of financial capital and migrants alike.[21] It matters at a time when left-wing economists are calling for a coalition of anti-Euro parties of the far left and right (Jacques Sapir in France) or have openly thrown in their lot with the far right (the post-Keynesian Alberto Bagnai in Italy). The temptation on the left has always been to dismiss the anti-capitalism of the far right as a form of elite dupery hiding an actual coalition with global finance (recall the so-called Dimitrov doctrine, according to which "fascism is the power of finance capital itself," the *"open, terrorist dictatorship of the most reactionary, most chauvinistic, and most imperialist elements of finance capital"*).[22]

This article seeks instead to address the economic politics of the far right as a real—not diversionary or fictitious—alternative to fiscal austerity but one whose distinct governing logic remains to be elucidated. I begin by delving into the long history of unconventional economic experiments on the far right to illuminate both the specific circumstances under which the far right has developed a critique of economic liberalism and the specific form of this critique with respect to its competitors on the left. Pointing to the disquieting parallels between the German experience of the Great Depression and the sovereign debt crisis currently afflicting the peripheral countries of the Eurozone, I consider the anti-liberal economic philosophy informing early National Socialism and its practical translation in the heterodox economic practice of the German central bank under the Third Reich. It was the Third Reich's willingness to embrace a heterodox alternative to austerity, I suggest, that explains its overwhelming popular success during its first years of rule. I then turn back to the present to assess the dangers of a national social (as opposed to national neoliberal) front on the contemporary European far right, looking in particular at recent events in France, Italy, and Germany. The national social or anti-neoliberal component of the far right is far from representing the entire spectrum of neofascist tendencies in Europe today. Indeed, until recently, the national neoliberal component of the far right appeared much more powerful. Both tendencies are extremely dangerous. But the national social configuration of the far right presents a particular threat to the left, especially at a moment when the left is struggling to enact a decisive political alternative to the austerity mandate embedded in the European Monetary Union.

The intransigence of European authorities in the face of the sovereign debt crisis—their overwhelming obsession with protecting the value of the

common currency, at whatever cost to its member states and their people—
has definitively vanquished the mythology of apolitical money. But it remains
unclear whether the far left or far right will emerge triumphant from this
revelation. Across much of Europe, the national social far right is calling
for an end to austerity and a return to fiscal expansion, by whatever means
necessary. In so doing, it finds itself working on the same terrain as centrist
practitioners such as Adair Turner at the Bank of England, social democratic
money activists such as Positive Money, and far-left advocates of fiscal money
or a so-called Plan B, all of whom are struggling to define a new politics of
money creation and a new imaginary of public finance. For the anti-capitalist
and antifascist left, the stakes could not be higher. The defeat of the far-
left economic alternative in Greece and the subsequent failure of the social
democratic left to push through with even a modest reform of the Eurozone
has left the door wide open for the far right. The victory of neoliberal parties
in France and the Netherlands has bought time, but has resolved neither the
economic stagnation of the Eurozone nor the threat of the far right. How we
understand and intervene in this conjuncture is of vital importance if we are
to avoid the worst, not least because we have been here before.

The Gold Standard and Austerity

More than a decade out from the financial crisis of 2007, it is hard not to
be struck by the parallels between the German deflation of the late Weimar
Republic and the depression-like conditions that continue to engulf the peripheral economies of the Eurozone.[23] In both instances, a seemingly local-
ized liquidity crisis triggered in the United States turned into a banking or
currency crisis in Europe before generating a full-blown sovereign debt crisis
among Europe's deficit economies. In twenty-first-century Greece as in Weimar Germany, a peripheral economy that had been held afloat by borrowed
funds in a fixed exchange rate was suddenly starved of funds and unable to
devalue its currency the moment these flows reversed direction. Both then
and now, the countries that were in a position of structural deficit vis-à-vis
gold or the Euro were most severely hit by the crisis.

As many economists have recognized, there are deep structural affinities
between the international gold standard regime and the economic constitutionalism of today's Eurozone.[24] Both impose fixed exchange rates, either by
pegging national currencies to gold, as in the interwar years of the early twentieth century, or abolishing national currencies altogether, as in the Euro-

pean Monetary Union of today. This makes it difficult, if not impossible, for countries to devalue their currency in response to crisis, forcing them instead to deflate wages and prices, cut social spending, and raise taxes in an effort to regain competitiveness and restore access to credit. Both regimes offer fiscal austerity as the only response to sovereign debt crisis and, when credit becomes scarce, tend to push deficit economies into deflationary spirals that can only aggravate public debt burdens and intensify political fractures.

The rules imposed by the international gold standard were unforgiving at the best of times. Money creation by the central bank was ruled out because it was deemed likely to undermine confidence in the currency. Short of building up an export surplus, a country on the gold standard could only borrow to fulfill its spending needs, an option that required studious deference to the orthodoxies of fiscal restraint and low inflation. But when a country was faced with a large balance-of-payments deficit and ongoing foreign debts, as was the case of Germany at the end of the Weimar Republic, the gold standard became catastrophic.[25] Unable to depreciate its currency while remaining on gold, a country in deficit could only hope to restore competitiveness by deflating domestic prices, of which wages formed the largest part.[26] Yet this strategy all too often proved self-defeating, plunging economies into deflationary spirals long before they could restore their credibility in the eyes of foreign investors.

Such was the path pursued by Chancellor Heinrich Brüning in the dying days of the Weimar Republic, when the heavily indebted Germany was plunged into crisis by a sudden outflow of gold reserves to the United States. By the time Brüning was appointed chancellor in March 1930, one-quarter of the German workforce was unemployed. But as conditions worsened and government deficits automatically swelled to meet the welfare needs of unemployed workers, Brüning maintained a single-minded focus on balancing the budget—the one response, he thought, that would reassure creditors and allow the country to replenish its gold reserves.[27] Accordingly, Brüning set about cutting public service wages, raising taxes, and steadily dismantling the social insurance system that had been built up under the Weimar Republic.[28] When he met with resistance from a divided parliament, Brüning simply resorted to a succession of emergency decrees to push through these measures. Workers who would have been covered by unemployment insurance in the past were pushed back into poor law systems of discretionary public assistance, strict time limits were placed on benefits, and whole classes of workers (mostly women) were excluded from benefits altogether.[29] As recession turned into deflation, Brüning—dubbed the hunger chancellor by the

German Communists—blamed spendthrift municipal governments for the parlous state of the German economy. His successor, the Catholic ultraconservative Franz von Papen, went further and blamed the Weimar welfare state for propagating class struggle and weakening the moral fiber of the nation.[30] Brüning's austerity drive was greatly helped by his conviction—shared by many on his own center-right Catholic party Zentrum but also by those much further to the right—that the Weimar welfare state had served to finance an alarming descent into moral degeneracy.[31] His merciless attack on welfare could therefore be justified in both economic liberal and moral conservative terms as an attempt to reinvigorate the (re)productive health of the nation.

Although behind the scenes, Brüning did more than most to stave off Hitler's arrival in power, his relentless campaign of fiscal austerity, pursued in the name of market freedom, paved the way for National Socialism. Well before Hitler, it was the economic liberal and social conservative Chancellor Brüning who invoked presidential emergency powers to dismantle the Weimar welfare state. And it was Brüning, not the National Socialists, who first called upon the ultraconservative jurist Carl Schmitt to justify the use of these extreme measures.[32] In so doing, the chancellor unwittingly revealed the autocratic underside of economic liberalism: when pushed to the extreme, the gold standard could not be maintained without the abrogation of constitutional safeguards and democratic process; an allegedly automatic, self-regulating system of market exchange required the brute executive force of the state to maintain its coherence. The lesson was all the more ironic in that Brüning had effectively abandoned the gold standard in the summer of 1931 when he opted to impose price controls to stem a run on the Reichsmark.[33] The gold standard subsequently only survived as an administrative fiction, and yet Brüning did not let up on its orthodoxies, convinced that the imposition of austerity would ultimately restore the currency's creditworthiness in the eyes of foreign lenders. By the time Brüning resigned from office, the deficit had been reduced to less than 1 percent of GDP, but economic and political consensus had collapsed as hunger strikers took to the streets and the Communists and Nazis engaged in open battle.[34]

Anti-Austerity in the Third Reich

The situation played perfectly into the hands of the National Socialists, who, since the Versailles Treaty, had developed an uncompromising critique of the imperialist powers of international capitalism. Hitler, it is often forgotten, came to National Socialism through a chance encounter with Gottfried Feder, a polemicist and self-taught economist who traveled Germany during the interwar years lecturing on the dangers of international financial capital and the Jewish bankers who allegedly controlled it. Feder saw himself as a nationalist and a socialist. He opposed communism on account of its internationalism and indifference to the biological unity of race. His socialism was selective. More strictly anti-liberal than anti-capitalist, he drew a sharp dividing line between productive capital (which was national, industrial, and rooted in agriculture) and unproductive capital (which was cosmopolitan, interest-bearing, or financial) and envisaged an economic future in which the former would thrive without the constant depredations of the latter.[35] Feder is widely thought to have composed the party's twenty-five-point program, in 1920, which called for unilateral debt default on the part of the German state, the death penalty for "usurers," and the exclusion of Jews from German political life.[36] Hitler, who had attended Feder's lectures in the interwar years, later explained the importance of these ideas to his own political vision:

> For the first time in my life I heard a discussion which dealt with the principles of stock-exchange capital and capital which was used for loan activities. . . . The absolute separation of stock-exchange capital from the economic life of the nation would make it possible to oppose the process of internationalization in German business without at the same time attacking capital as such, for to do this would jeopardize the foundations of our national independence. I clearly saw what was developing in Germany and I realized then that the stiffest fight we would have to wage would not be against the enemy nations but against international capital.[37]

When Germany returned to the gold standard under the Dawes Plan of 1924, the National Socialists incorporated this fact into their phantasmagoria of financial conspiracy, identifying the Jews as both reckless purveyors and hoarders of gold, puppet masters of the world economy who could corrupt a nation by flooding it with credit and withdraw it on a whim. At the height of the Depression, Gottfried Feder argued that the "anchoring of a currency in gold . . . leads only to the most dangerous shortage of the means of payment, and serves at bottom exclusively the interest of the gold-holder, or high finance."[38] The gold standard regime was held responsible for both the luxurious, unsustainable consumption of the Weimar credit boom—now denounced as a period of frivolous unproductive pleasures that had diverted profits to the Jewish financiers—and the terrible austerity that had followed.

"Jewish thought" had "placed gold at the center" and had "forced the peoples of the Western world to be the payers of interest and tribute to finance capital."[39] It was the Jews as marketers of consumer credit who had financed the sexual decadence of the Weimar boom years, encouraging perversion among the young and liberating women from their proper roles as mothers and housewives.[40] It was the Jews, more than Brüning the hunger chancellor, who subsequently withdrew these funds and reduced the German people to a state of near starvation.

At a time when the German Social Democrats were preaching deference to tight money and the German communists rejected any merely reformist attempt to rethink the organization of state finances, Feder and the National Socialists were openly calling on the German state to abandon gold and reclaim its power to create money.[41] Under the National Socialists, money and credit would no longer be constrained by an external anchor, forcing Germany into a state of near constant austerity, but instead could grow as fast as the productivity of the German worker.[42]

Looking back on the first five years of Nazi rule in the early 1940s, Hitler congratulated the regime for achieving Feder's vision and instituting an expansionary economy anchored solely in the labor power of German workers: "I . . . take care not to buy dead gold with the productive power of German workmen. I purchase the necessities of life with the productive power of German workmen. The results of our economic policy speak for us, not for the gold standard people."[43] Hitler envisaged the economics of National Socialism as an anti-capitalism divested of class conflict. Although radically opposed to the austerity mandate of the gold standard, he nevertheless sought to foreclose the possibility of class warfare by interpolating a unified nation of producers—embracing both workers and industrialists in the one form of address. "For we, the poor have abolished unemployment because we no longer pay homage to this madness, because we regard our entire economic existence as a production problem and no longer as a capitalistic problem. . . . We explained to the nation that it was madness to wage internal economic wars between the various classes, in which they all perish together."[44] These reflections were of a piece with Feder's vision of a national socialist economics.

Yet it was not Feder who would carry out the Nazi's economic policies. Instead, when Hitler came to power in January of 1933, he immediately appointed a new Reichsbank president, the experienced central banker Hjalmar Schacht, who had held the position several years before. The reappointment represented something of a conversion experience. Schacht, who had been a staunch defender of the gold standard under the Weimar Republic, now embarked on an extraordinary experiment in monetary and fiscal expansion that broke all the rules of the liberal financial regime and put the central bank entirely at the service of Hitler's political objectives: rearmament, reconstruction through a large public works program, and full employment. Under the gold standard, deficit spending had been tightly circumscribed and monetary finance (the process whereby the central bank lends to the treasury at zero interest, colloquially referred to as "printing money") was strictly prohibited. Turning his back on these rules, Schacht implemented an ingenious off-balance-sheet system that he thought could finance Hitler's ambitious public works and rearmament schemes without stimulating inflation or tipping off the Allied powers, who thought all German wealth should be dedicated to reparations.[45] Germany's largest industrial conglomerates were instructed to set up a dummy private company called the Society for Metallurgical Research (Metallurgische Forschungsgesellschaft), which would then create money by issuing IOUs, called MEFO bills. Described as "an ante litteram case of unconventional money-financed fiscal expansion" by contemporary advocates of fiscal money, these bills were used to pay state contractors and suppliers engaged in the regime's new public works program, effectively creating money and credit without recourse to lenders.[46]

Although Schacht ascribed himself sole credit for this coup in his testimony at the Nuremberg trial and later memoirs, the economic historian Avrahim Barkai observes that a similar initiative was put forward by Gregor Strasser in May of 1932, and publicized in the official Immediate Economic Program of the party.[47] It appears that the specifics of the plan had been devised a few years earlier by a Jewish statistician employed by the German Trade Union Federation. The plan was narrowly voted in by the trade unions, but tellingly, the Social Democrat and former finance minister Rudolf Hilferding managed to persuade Social Democrats in the Reichstag to oppose it on the grounds that it was "non-Marxist" and would undermine the necessarily international basis of the struggle against capitalism.[48] It is one of the terrible ironies of history that among the many warring factions that dominated German political life at this time, only the National Socialist far right was willing to challenge the structural constraints of the gold standard, making it the one party that could offer a credible alternative to austerity.[49]

The creation of money through MEFO bills helped fund the highways [*Autobahnen*] and a multitude of other civic projects in the first years of Hitler's rule. These work-creation projects, together with efforts to push women out of work and forcibly enroll the male unemployed in work teams, led to a rapid amelioration of job prospects for working-aged men. Unemployment levels fell by one-third during Schacht's first year in office; by 1936 close to full employment of male German citizens had been achieved. As state purchases revived demand in the private sector of the economy and incomes rose, the German Depression came to an end.

These early successes seemed to confirm the wisdom of National Socialist strategy vis-à-vis labor. During the Depression, the National Socialists had targeted their anti-austerity message to Germany's surplus population of long-term unemployed, hoping to exploit the collapse of organized labor to win over the traditional constituencies of the Communist Party.[50] In power, they pursued an authoritarian full-employment policy that criminalized strikes, outlawed trade unions, and reintroduced the forty-hour working week but also (under the administration of a new Labor Board) put an end to the freefall in workers' wages and, at least during the first five years of Nazi rule, pushed wages steadily upward.[51] Women were cajoled or forced back into the home by the use of marriage loans or outright banishment from positions they had "stolen" from working men.[52]

By contrast, those who remained without legitimate work in spite of the Nazi's welfare-to-work programs were treated ruthlessly. By seemingly refusing the benefits of full (if forced) employment, both the willfully unemployed and illegally employed confirmed their position as irredeemable surplus and were treated as such.[53] The homeless, the vagrant, the itinerant, beggars, criminals, and prostitutes were persecuted or interned because they seemed to embody the horror of un(re)productive, unemployed, or perhaps perversely (re)productive labor at a time when all labor needed to be harnessed to the ends of national (re)production. In some cases, this indicated an unproductivity of the will—the so-called asocials who simply refused to work or who chose a life of homelessness and vagrancy despite the most strenuous efforts to rehabilitate them. In other instances, inaptitude for productive labor seemed to represent an entrenched biological trait that could only be eradicated by the use of sterilization or extermination—such was the case of the itinerant and "dark" Sinti and Roma, the mentally ill, and the disabled.[54]

Homosexuals, for their part, were considered a direct threat to the reproductive future of the nation, and were condemned to re-education, voluntary castration, and, if this was refused, extermination in the concentration camps.[55] The Nazis understood homosexuality as a failure of the reproductive will (lesbians were less strenuously persecuted because the "will to procreate" was assumed to be male; women were simply recipients of this will and so remained reproductive despite their sexual preferences).[56] Women, however, could threaten this male procreative will by choosing abortion. It was not for nothing that when the Third Reich intensified its persecution of gay men and lesbians after 1936, it did so under the aegis of The Reich Office for the Combating of Homosexuality and Abortion: homosexuality was classified alongside abortion as a withdrawal of reproductive labor from the nation.

The Jews occupied a special position within the Nazis' pantheon of threats to national reproduction: if others were persecuted by virtue of their identification with unproductive *labor*, the Jews were singled out as the personification of unproductive *capital*. Their suspected absence of allegiance to the nation-state, the very precariousness of their claims to citizenship, seemed to demonstrate an elective affinity with the rootlessness and nation-destroying qualities of financial capital flows.[57] Their position as professional rentiers and bankers was held up as proof that they—not the unemployed Germans of the late Weimar Republic—were the true parasites, the agents of unproductive, sterile capital feeding off the vital energies of the nation.[58] Consequently, the treatment that was reserved for them resembled a macabre attempt to turn the German experience of austerity against its alleged causal agents: the extreme destitution, the near starvation that had been visited upon the entire working class (which, of course, included Jews) would now be reserved for the Jews in particular.[59] The alleged agents of the international gold standard regime would be forcibly dispossessed of their gold and forced to work themselves to the bone, as Germans had been during the deflationary years of the late Weimar Republic.

The task of expelling and dispossessing these surplus populations was essential to the success of the Nazis' economic program: short of implementing a wholesale program of redistribution, the regime could hardly have ensured "full employment" and rising wages unless it tightly circumscribed the population of legitimately productive workers. It is not the case then that the Nazis offered a "merely ideological" solution to debt crisis in lieu of an authentically economic solution, but rather that their economic solution took the form of a rigorous xenophobia, where "xenos" refers to the panoply of surplus figures—racial, gendered, and sexual—to be excluded from the biological nation. The innovation of Nazi economics was to have defied the dictates of liberal capitalism while defending the profits of large industrial capital and offering only minimal disturbance to the existing distribution of wealth among German citizens. This it did by using unconventional finance—prohibited under the liberal gold standard regime—to stimulate public investment and carefully restrict the class of persons qualified to benefit from it.

Here we can suggest a minimal definition of fascism as a heterodox economic formation, distinct from the equally heterodox methods of Keynesianism or socialism. The anti-austerity politics of the far right is defined by the attempt to overcome the threat of deflation without substantially threatening the existing distribution of wealth and income. The National Socialists were willing and (thanks to the seizure of executive power) spectacularly able to undertake the most unconventional experiments in monetary and fiscal policy, in complete defiance of the liberal gold standard. But their antipathy to economic liberalism never extended to the question of economic inequality per se. Insofar as they discerned economic inequalities of wealth and income, it was refracted through the lens of ethnic, biological, or cultural conflict and rendered as an innate distinction between the (re)productive citizen and the un(re)productive or illegitimately (re)productive non-citizen. The true German was (re)productive by nature and by right; the Jews, the Sinti, the Roma, the Communists, and homosexuals were biological threats to the legitimate (re)production of the nation. Once this translation work had been accomplished, it was possible to imagine that capitalism's crises tendencies (made manifest in recurrent surpluses of unemployed or underemployed workers) could be permanently and definitively resolved through the exclusion of figures defined as *surplus by nature*.

Anti-Austerity on the New European Far Right

How serious is the threat of a national social "anti-capitalist" far right in Europe today? At the very least, it can be said that the enduring failure of European elites to offer any credible reform of the EMU at the federal level has tended to favor those elements on the far right that offer a national welfarist alternative to austerity. The sheer duration of the sovereign debt crisis, with its legacy of Depression-like conditions across Greece, Italy, Spain, and Portugal, has created fertile ground for resurgent national social tendencies within the European far right. The shift is most evident beyond the boundaries of the parliamentary far right in direct action and social movement groups such as CasaPound Italia or in the youth wings of the established far-right parties. But it has also become increasingly evident on the parliamentary far right itself where national social factions have been rapidly gaining ground since the sovereign debt crisis of 2010. Yet the resurgent national social far right exists in close competition with a national neoliberal far right that until recently was dominant throughout most of Europe. A case in point, the French Front National, has gone through several metamorphoses since its creation in 1972, evolving from national neoliberalism under Jean-Marie le Pen to national welfarism under Marine le Pen, only, it appears, to have moved back toward a national neoliberal position after the defeat of the 2017 presidential elections.

The tension between these two positions has deep roots in the post-war French far right. The so-called Nouvelle Droite or New Right (in fact, the new far right) emerged in the 1960s out of the ashes of defeat. Forced into refuge after the ignominy of French collaboration under the Vichy regime and the triumph of the anticolonial movement in Algeria, the remnants of the French far right regrouped as an essentially cultural and intellectual movement under the shadow of the new left of 1968. Under the intellectual leadership of Alain de Benoist, one of its founding groups, le GRECE, or Groupement de recherche et d'études pour la civilisation européenne, gradually shed the markers of mid-century biological racism to instead develop a celebration of essential cultural differences closely molded on the anti-racist thinking of postwar cultural anthropology. Conceding defeat on the question of imperialism, de Benoist now aligned himself with the cause of Third World nationalists (and later fundamentalists) seeking to defend their culture against the homogenizing influence of a nebulous Western/American cultural imperialism. It was de Benoist who coined the term "right wing Gramscism" to describe what he saw as the most suitable strategy for the far right in these years of retreat—one of long-term cultural infiltration rather than parliamentary compromise.[60] This led to some interesting political contortions: the French were addressed as "natives" whose unique cultural traditions were equally threatened by the empire of global capitalism and the forced integration of North African Muslim migrants in France.[61] It also led to some unexpected political collaborations: a brief National-Bolshevist dalliance with former members of the French Communist Party in the 1990s and ongoing exchanges with intellectuals on the academic left (first in the pages of *Éléments* magazine, then *Krisis*).[62]

Not all members of the Nouvelle Droite subscribed to de Benoist's strategy of passive or cultural revolution. In 1974, several members of the Nouvelle Droite established a think tank called the Club de l'Horloge, with the express aim of infiltrating the mainstream parliamentary right.[63] Its cadres had close links to France's premier institutional hothouse for high-ranking civil servants and politicians, the *Ecole Nationale d'Administration*, or ENA, and were intent on pursuing careers in the mainstream center-right parties.[64] Intellectually, they remained much more closely wedded to the ideas of the old, mid-century Vichyist far right—biological racism, Catholic integralism, and nationalism—and were not prepared to follow de Benoist in cultivating a mimetic relationship to the left. Indeed, the Club de l'Horloge was firmly committed to the neoliberal ideas that were rapidly gaining ground in Britain and the United States and just as promptly being imported back into France by the so-called nouveaux économistes. In its first collective publication, the Club de l'Horloge called for a synthesis between the most traditionalist of French nationalisms, replete with predictions of imminent demographic decline, and the most radical neoliberal prescriptions against the bloated French welfare state.[65]

This was bound to create tensions with GRECE, which aligned itself firmly with the romantic anticapitalist tradition of the European far right and was one of the earliest sources of intellectual opposition to neoliberalism in France. The position was well entrenched in France, where, according to the historian Zeev Sternhell, European fascism finds its true intellectual sources. Sternhell observes that during the late nineteenth century, under the Third Republic, France first saw the coming together of xenophobic and traditionalist nationalism with a form of socialism that presented itself as either anti-Marxist or post-Marxist.[66] This particular strain of "nationalist socialism" sought to resolve the felt contradictions of modern capitalist existence without fueling the antagonism between workers and wealth-holders. As the anarcho-syndicalist writer Georges Sorel would make clear, anticapitalist revolution was possible, even preferable, without class conflict: the ultimate end of revolutionary struggle, in his view, was to unite workers and capitalists in a monumental revolt against the spiritual decadence of modern life, to revive the lost values of faith and tradition through an act of orgiastic violence, not the humdrum business of equalizing the conditions of existence.[67] It was these figures, along with the anticapitalist nationalists of the 1920s German Conservative Revolution, that formed the intellectual background to de Benoist's late twentieth-century reinvention of fascism.

As time progressed, relations between the two offspring of the Nouvelle Droite became increasingly strained. Simmering tensions came to the fore in 1990 when GRECE dedicated an entire issue of its magazine, *Éléments*, to attacking the national-neoliberal politics of the Club de l'Horloge. The issue included a long critique of Hayek by de Benoist. In the preface to this article, de Benoist took direct aim at the Club de l'Horloge, which had spent its last annual autumn school investigating the possibility of an alliance between neo-liberalism and conservatism. Here de Benoist accused the Horlogers of "polit-ical opportunism" and denounced neoliberalism itself as utterly incompatible with the conservative revolution.[68] Hayek's anti-egalitarianism was welcome (this much de Benoist shared with his peers of the Club de l'Horloge), but Hayek's neoliberalism had pushed individualism so far that it dispensed with any idea of social justice, thereby disabling the conservative welfarism that de Benoist saw as an integral component of fascist revolution.[69] The article spoke in two registers that would have been perfectly legible to de Benoist's peers: while the body of the text unfolded a meticulous philosophical critique of Hayek, the footnotes to the article extended this critique to the neoliberal economists of the Club de l'Horloge. The following year, Henry de Lesquen, one of the founders of the Club de l'Horloge and a close intimate of Jean-Marie le Pen, published a "right of response" in which he accused de Benoist of willful misrepresentation and, worse, of playing into the hands of the left.[70] De Benoist doubled down, pointing to what he saw as the insuper-able contradictions between neoliberalism and traditionalism: "Monsieur de Lesquen wishes to unite liberalism and nationhood, even though free-trade self-evidently implies a blindness to borders. He contends that liberalism can go together with tradition, even though all traditions are *collective* and liberal society was born out of the complete destruction of traditions. . . . In short, he adheres to the national-liberal right that has always served the interests of the bourgeois business class first and foremost."[71]

For the time being, however, it was the national-neoliberal proclivities of the Club de l'Horloge that prevailed in the Front National. Finding little traction on the mainstream right, senior members of the Club de l'Horloge began to defect to Jean-Marie le Pen's Front National from 1985 onward, where they were duly rewarded with senior strategic positions.[72] Here they imbued Front National propaganda with the idea of "national preference" while excoriating the cultural liberalism of cosmopolitan elites. By the 1990s, the traditionalist neoliberals of the Club de l'Horloge were one of the ma-jor ideological influences within the Front National, second only to their friends the Catholic integralists. In the meantime, the national social vision of GRECE remained popular among the ranks of the young Frontists in the Front National de la Jeunesse and the far-right militants of the GUD (Groupe union défense) at the elite law school of Assas. It was among these circles rather than the neoliberal Club de l'Horloge that Jean-Marie le Pen's daughter, Marine, underwent her political apprenticeship.[73]

It was this alternative heritage of the far right—anti-American, anti-neoliberal and welfarist—that returned to the political stage when Marine le Pen succeeded her father as president of the Front National in 2011. In truth, the Front National of Jean-Marie le Pen had been making small concessions in this direction since the French general strike of 1995 and in response to the party's growing success among working-class voters. However, it was only when Marine le Pen took power that the Front's social and economic program turned abruptly to the "left," thanks in no small part to the influence of her strategic campaign director Florian Philippot, a former supporter of the left-wing sovereigntist and Euroskeptic Jean-Pierre Chevènement.[74] The moment was propitious: the sovereign debt crisis that engulfed the European Monetary Union in the winter of 2009 was followed by an intensification of fiscal austerity measures across the union, as political leaders from the left and right pursued the now default strategy of devaluing wages and slashing public spending to ensure the credibility of their public debt. In the absence of a serious alternative from the left—at least prior to the rise of Jean-Luc Mélenchon—Marine le Pen was able to exploit the sheer frustration of voters to present the Front National as the only viable response to austerity.

Published in 2012, Marine le Pen's political biography *cum* campaign manifesto, *Pour que vive la France*, presents a remarkable document of the wedge strategy she was pursuing at this time. The book begins with a denunciation of the fatalism with which French elites on both the left and right had acquiesced to the dictates of the European Monetary Union and addresses an impassioned plea to those who might once have voted for the Communist left. For generations born in the 1970s, she observes with some justification, the experience of fiscal consolidation is far from new; the fiscal austerity measures imposed by European leaders after the sovereign debt crisis are merely an acute version of the disinflationary policies adopted by both the mainstream right and the French Socialists after Mitterand's infamous "turn to austerity" in 1982. "For decades we've been told that unemployment is inevitable, that endless crisis is our fate. At the same time, we have it drilled into us that the ultraliberal remedies administered to the patient are the only ones capable of curing him—yet the long-awaited cure is endlessly deferred. '*There is no alternative,*' is what Margaret Thatcher said, thus giving rise to the TINA acronym. TINA, there is no alternative, rhapsodize our leaders and intellectuals today."[75] There is no need to invoke conspiracy theories to explain the collusion of political leaders on the left and right, she continues—such collusion simply reflects the real convergence of interests among the 1 percent. "It's not as if obscure plots are being hatched in international forums such as the Mont Pèlerin Society, the Bilderberg group or Davos. These are simply '*melting pots*' for politicians from the left and right, for bankers from the left and right, and CEOs from the left and the right"[76]

Yet despite her conviction that neoliberalism is "beyond left and right," le Pen reserves her harshest words for the left, which she accuses of having abandoned the French working class after the fall of the Soviet Union. "Why did the left, the traditional defender of the working class, the poor, the excluded, resolute opponent of the excesses of financial capitalism, rally so wholeheartedly behind the project of liberal globalization?"[77] Le Pen traces the roots of this betrayal to the fatal turning point of May 1968, when the left abandoned its commitment to the founding institutions of nation, church, and family and instead embraced the cause of cultural liberalism—inseparable, according to her, from the larger project of economic neoliberalism. "The calculated death of the left . . . derives from a combination of the ideas of May 1968 and the great comeback, at the very same time, of economic liberalism. . . . The left called for man's liberation from all the shackles—national, religious and familial—that weighed him down. . . . Recall liberalism's claim to free humankind from everything that prevents him from being a rational consumer in a free market."[78] Failing to discern the symbiotic relationship between economic and cultural neoliberalism, the left offered a rigorous (and useful) critique of financial globalization but was unwilling to acknowledge its necessary link to cultural deracination.[79] It is because the far right recognizes the malaise of cultural rootlessness—and more than this, identifies its actual embodiment in the form of the migrant or the gender deviant—that it is able to go one step further than the left.

Accordingly, Marine le Pen's 2012 economic program borrows assiduously from the progressive and far left when it comes to developing a critique of the Eurozone but supplements this with what she sees as its logical and necessary counterpart, a program of unabashed racial purification. In a chapter of her book dedicated to the sovereign debt crisis and the failure of neoliberalism, le Pen unfolds a rigorous critique of the constitutional design flaws of the EMU, drawing on the work of such respected left-wing and left-liberal figures as Philippe Askenazy, Emmanuel Todd, and Jean-Luc Mélenchon.[80] And in her public speeches, le Pen lavishes praise on the work of the progressive but orthodox New Keynesian economist Joseph Stiglitz, whose forensic critique of the Euro as a currency without fiscal authority lends mainstream economic support to the views of post-Keynesian, Marxist, and other heterodox economists (Stiglitz, in the meantime, has been at pains to distance himself from the political positions le Pen has drawn from his economic analysis).[81] But it is the work of Jacques Sapir, a heterodox economist and one-time supporter of the far left Front de Gauche, who seems to have most directly influenced the Front National's strategy vis-à-vis the Euro. Sapir's far-left critique of the Euro, along with his strategic analysis of heterodox alternatives, was one of the primary sources of inspiration for the Front National's economic program of 2012, which outlined a plan for bypassing Eurozone rules and restoring the full monetary and fiscal powers of the French state.[82] Both le Pen and Florian Philippot are reputed to be close readers of the work of Jacques Sapir.[83] The admiration appears to be mutual. In a 2015 interview, Sapir suggested that the Eurozone's austerity mandate could only be successfully challenged by a popular front uniting the far left and far right. "Eventually," he added, "the question of our relationship with the Front National . . . will come up. We need to understand very clearly that this is no longer a time for sectarianism."[84] When these remarks were met with outrage from the left, Sapir insisted that the new Front National of Marine le Pen and Florian Philippot had completely abandoned the xenophobia of Jean-Marie le Pen.[85]

In truth, xenophobia is a critical element of the Front National's socioeconomic agenda which champions fiscal expansion only insofar as it feeds into its nativist and natalist vision of the welfare state. In her 2017 presidential campaign, le Pen vows to abolish the recently passed "labor law" (la loi du travail or la loi El Khomri) that has weakened worker protections in France, to withdraw France from the European directive allowing employers to contract workers from countries with weaker labor protections, to increase minimum social benefits for old age, to maintain a thirty-five-hour week, to decrease taxes for those in the lowest tax brackets, and to lower the official retirement age to sixty.[86] True to the national socialist dictum that the contradictions of capitalism can be resolved without recourse to class struggle, le Pen proposes to achieve this program without involving the unions (who would be immediately dissolved in favor of a corporatist labor board) and without in any way questioning the distribution of wealth within the nation (except perhaps between large and medium-to-small enterprises). Rather, she hopes to overcome the insecurity of the French worker through the selective reining in of *foreign* capital (a more vigorous pursuit of tax fraud on the part of multinationals, a tax of 3 percent on all imports, a law obliging the French public sector to favor French suppliers and contractors and a limit on foreign investment in French corporations) and, a fortiori, the marginalization of non-French citizens from the fruits of economic expansion (an immediate exit from the Schengen agreement with its provisions for free movement within the European Union, abolition of le droit du sol, the exclusion of non-French citizens from welfare protections, and the promotion of a "true pronatalism" reserving family allowances for French citizens).[87]

Le Pen's resounding defeat in the second round of the 2017 elections, where she had hoped to recuperate voters from the far-left Jean-Luc Mélenchon, brought her national social strategy to an end. In the wake of this defeat, the Front National (now rebaptized as the Rassemblement National and divested of its strategic advisor, Florian Philippot) has changed tack once again and appears to be returning to the national neoliberal position of Jean-Marie le Pen.[88] But if the threat of a national social far right is for the moment extinguished in France, it has flared up in a slightly different guise in Italy, where an unexpected alliance between the far-right Lega and the populist Five Star Movement was formed in early 2017. Having declared its intention to flout Eurozone rules on deficit spending, the coalition promises to forge ahead with plans to implement a universal citizen's wage and restore the full pension rights that were eroded under Italy's fiscal consolidation program.[89] If successful, this would represent the first serious injection of public money into the Italian economy after a decade of crippling austerity and the first serious challenge to the EMU after Syriza's failed attempt to force concessions from the Troika in the summer of 2015.

Beyond this, the Lega has proposed an extensive program of public spending including the provision of free nurseries, the doubling of the disability pension, and a more generous system of family allowances and tax concessions for large families. Coauthored by the Lega's current minister of families and disability, Lorenzo Fontana, and the Catholic economist Ettore Gotti Tedeschi, the Lega's welfare program is shaped by an obsession with demographic decline, as evidenced by falling birth rates among white Italian women and a growing migrant population from West Africa and Syria.[90] Accordingly, Fontana and Tedeschi are at pains to point out that the Lega's expanded welfare benefits should be reserved for heterosexual couples and Italian citizens with at least twenty years of residence—to be funded by taxes on foreign capital and migration.

The Lega has undergone a profound transformation under the leadership of Matteo Salvini, who in the 1990s was already attempting to forge an improbable electoral alliance between Lega Nord secessionism and communism.[91] When Salvini ousted the Lega's founder and former leader, Umberto Bossi, in 2013, the party was still parading under the name of the Lega Nord and saw itself as a regionalist movement protecting the interests of productive, tax-paying Northerners against corrupt political elites in Rome and lazy Southerners.[92] The economic program of the Lega Nord under Umberto Bossi can be described as a kind of regionalist neoliberalism—dedicated to protecting the interests of small business and private-sector workers against the overbearing state, which it accused of tax extortion on behalf of the South.[93] The Lega Nord called for less regulation, more privatization, and a generalized tax revolt against the Italian state. It vociferated against Italy's large public debt, which it saw as a symptom of the exorbitant public spending on the South and called for the creation of a separate "Padanian" republic in the North.

However, the changing political climate generated by Italy's debt crisis, which brought crushing poverty and unemployment to large swathes of the North as well as the South, together with the unexpected success of the politically amorphous but Euroskeptic Five Star Movement, convinced Salvini that a change of tack was needed. The public debt crisis that unfolded in Italy in the summer of 2011—when yields on Italian government bonds reached above 7 percent—sent shudders through the European Monetary Union as its leaders contemplated the prospect of default on the part of the Eurozone's third-largest economy. In an effort to prevent contagion, the ECB convinced the Italian president to appoint an unelected technocrat, Mario Monti, as prime minister with the express mandate of consolidating Italy's finances.[94] What followed was an extraordinary austerity drive that saw continuing cuts to public spending, massive tax hikes, and the inclusion of a balanced budget amendment in the Italian constitution. By some accounts, the deflationary effects on the Italian economy have been more profound than during the Great Depression.[95] At a time when all Italians were feeling the brunt of directives from Brussels, it no longer made sense to pursue secession from Rome. If anything, Italy as a whole needed to secede from the Eurozone. Accordingly, Salvini performed a radical makeover of the Lega Nord, transforming it from a separatist faction committed to the interests of small business owners into a nationalist movement, the Lega, closely aligned with the xenophobic welfarism of Marine le Pen's Front National. The new Lega has made no secret of its desire to foster close relations with the militant extraparliamentary far right.[96]

Before this transition point, the Lega Nord cultivated an ambivalent attitude toward the European Union. Lega Nord deputies were unanimous in contesting the nomination of the technocrat Mario Monti (the other votes of no confidence came from the far right, Alessandra Mussolini, and two deputies from the far left).[97] But while the Lega Nord's then leader railed against Monti's exactions in public, behind the scenes it was made clear that the party would rubber-stamp everything he did.[98]

Under Salvini, all tergiversation on the subject of the Eurozone has disappeared. In power, Salvini has made no secret of his resolve to contest the budgetary mandates of the Eurozone, whether this means negotiating a larger deficit or resorting to a Plan B and the creation of a parallel currency. Behind him, he has recruited an impressive lineup of economists and finance market practitioners. These include the former Deutsche Bank sales manager and investment banker Claudio Borghi Aquilini, with his professional expertise in financial markets; Paolo Savona, a renowned mainstream economist who studied under Franco Modigliani at MIT and who has occupied leading roles in Italian public administration and industry; and, most alarmingly, Alberto Bagnai, a respected post-Keynesian economist and self-identified man of the left, who now describes himself as a "socialist, populist and nationalist."[99] Each of these advisors has written extensively on the structural failings of the Eurozone and the possibilities of exit. Like Hjalmar Schacht under the Third Reich, they lend professional and institutional credibility to the economic agenda of the Lega, without necessarily subscribing to its nativist politics.

In some respects, however, the Lega's economic program remains ambivalent and retains at least some traces of its earlier pro-business inclinations: the decision, for example, to replace Mario Monti's regressive tax reforms with an equally regressive flat tax has been openly contested by the post-Keynesian Alberto Bagnai.[100] Much less ambivalent on the issue of economic reform are the frankly fascistic movements that reside to the right of the Lega and that provide much of its extraparliamentary support base. A case in point here is CasaPound Italia, a far right social movement *cum* party that is directly inspired by the social tradition of Italian fascism and the anti-Semitic, anti-usurious "economics" of the American poet and supporter of Mussolini Ezra Pound.[101] CasaPound's political program of 2018 calls for immediate exit from the Eurozone, a return to monetary sovereignty, the removal of Mario Monti's "balanced budget" amendment to the constitution ("in order to plan for growth, development and widespread prosperity, the state can and must operate in deficit"), an end to precarity, a revamped pronatalist welfare state—and the mass expulsion of undocumented migrants.[102] Thus far, CasaPound's electoral incursions have been minimal. However, it has had considerable success in infiltrating the social arena at a level that is not often accessible to mainstream parliamentary parties. Drawing inspiration from the "social centers" of the autonomist left, CasaPound has developed a strategy of samizdat welfarism that seeks to pursue fascist revolution from the ground up (its social ventures extend from squats, public housing, health care clinics, and soup kitchens for impoverished Italians). Its student organization is active in over forty cities, and its members reportedly "control" dozens of bars, restaurants, bookstores, and sports clubs. It would be easy to dismiss CasaPound on the basis of its poor electoral results. But its extensive presence on the ground is extremely valuable to a party such as the Lega, which must maintain the veneer of parliamentary respectability while delegating the work of vigilantism to others.

If there is one country in the Eurozone that seemed least likely to produce a national-social far right, it is Germany. The reasons are obvious: Germany as a creditor and export economy has gained the most from the introduction of the Euro, and its elites have played no small role in enforcing the Eurozone's austerity regime on debtor economies in the south. Accordingly, Germany's far right has until very recently been dominated by a form of neoliberal nationalism preaching a paradoxical mix of free-market economics and isolationism. The Alternative für Deutschland was founded in 2013 by Bernd Lucke, an ordoliberal economist based at the University of Hamburg. During the first two years of its existence, the party was overseen by a board of like-minded economists who developed a uniquely German, nationalist-neoliberal critique of the Euro. These economists saw European federalism as imposing unfair tax burdens on the Germans to fund the bailouts of other member states and called for Germany to abandon the Eurozone in the interests of national sovereignty.[103] During this period, the AfD's default response to widespread precarity within Germany was to deflect the focus onto the European Union, the peripheral economies of Southern Europe, and migrants. In terms of its domestic politics, the AfD was firmly committed to a neoliberal politics of low taxes, restricted deficit spending, continued labor market flexibilization, and privatization. As suggested by Dieter Plehwe and Quinn Slobodian, this alliance of nationalist isolationism and free-market economics was true to the original spirit of German ordoliberalism, despite the widespread conviction among critical scholars that the economic constitutionalism of the EMU was the brainchild of ordoliberals.[104]

However, even the AfD has seen significant change in recent years. When Lucke was ousted from the party in July of 2015, the balance of power shifted unexpectedly in favor of state chairmen in the former east (Björn Höcke, leader of the Thuringia-AfD, and Alexander Gauland of the Brandenburg-AfD) who wanted the party to abandon its neoliberal line to instead pursue the votes of low-wage workers, the unemployed, and the precarious.[105] At the same time, figures such as Höcke have made no secret of their sympathy for the overtly fascist, extraparliamentary far right. In early 2017, Höcke urged Germans to abandon the cult of guilt around the Nazi past, an incident that almost had him excluded from the party, but that in the long run has only strengthened his position.[106]

There is now a clear factional split within the party, as state leaders in the former east attempt to wrest power from national neoliberal cadres. A clear sign of the shifting balance of powers, the national social wing of the AfD won over a third of the delegate positions at the party's annual congress of 2017.[107] More important is the fact that AfD candidates close to Höcke are now polling at around 22 percent among unionized workers in the former east of Germany.[108] It appears that Höcke is banking on success among this new constituency to transform the AfD from within and simultaneously to undermine the support base of the left and Social Democrats.

In the meantime, a Gramscian culture war is being conducted on the ground, on the model of Alain de Benoist's "metapolitics." At the 18th Winter School of the Institut für Staatspolitik, a far-right think tank with close links to the French New Right and the Höcke wing of the AfD, delegates reflected on the history of right-wing anti-capitalism from the Conservative Revolution to Alain de Benoist.[109] Benedikt Kaiser, a regular contributor to the magazine *Sezession*, published by the Institut für Staatspolitik, is one of the chief exponents of Alain de Benoist's far-right anti-capitalism in Germany, and it appears that Höcke, too, is heavily influenced by the French New Right.[110]

A lucid expression of Höcke's ideological strategy vis-à-vis the left can be found in a speech he delivered in late 2017. Here he laments the death of the "old, authentic left"—nationalist, socialist, and patriotic—now entirely absorbed within a "globalist left" that has become "the socialist appendage to global finance capital."[111] True to the fascist tradition, he identifies the migrant as the materialization of capitalism's abstract equivalence and denounces the left for failing to erect any border against its relentless logic—its "liquefaction" of all foundations. Here, he insists, lies the fundamental contradiction of the left that on the one hand "praise[s] the welfare state and at the same time destroy[s] its foundations and prerequisites; on the one hand, uphold[s] solidarity and at the same time destroy[s] the growth of solidarity-building communities."[112] The primary social conflict, in other words, does not reside between classes but between the inside and outside of the nation-state, between citizen and stranger. Leveraging what he sees as the failure of the left to recognize this essential truth, Höcke vows to "defend the social achievements of 150 years of the workers movement against the destructive forces of predatory capitalism!"[113]

How successful Höcke will be in transforming the AfD from within remains to be seen. In any event, the fact that the national social faction within the AfD has made such rapid headway in Germany, the one country that appeared immune to this temptation in the immediate aftermath of the sovereign debt crisis, is surely significant. After four decades of "competitive disinflation" throughout the European Union and almost an entire decade of crippling austerity across its periphery, it is the national social far right that is most attuned to growing popular discontent with neoliberal elites. In this respect at least, Marine le Pen's decision to revert to the national neoliberal line of her father appears strategically misguided—and serendipitous for the left. Here perhaps lies a small window of opportunity for the left to reinvigorate the experiment first launched, then prematurely aborted by Syriza. If the left were able to exploit this reprieve to advance a comprehensive—macroeconomic and constitutional—alternative to the Eurozone, it might still have some chance of stemming the rising tide of the far right.

Notes

1. Quoted in Mihai Varga, "Hungary's 'Anti-Capitalist' Far-Right: Jobbik and the Hungarian Guard," *Nationalities Papers* 42, no. 5 (2014): 798.

2. Quoted in Varga, "Hungary's 'Anti-Capitalist' Far-Right," 798.

3. Juliet Johnson and Andrew Barnes, "Financial Nationalism and Its International Enablers: The Hungarian Experience," *Review of International Political Economy* 22, no. 3 (2015): 535–69, and Andrea L. P. Pirro, "Hardly Ever Relevant? An Appraisal of Nativist Economics through the Hungarian Case," *Acta Politica* 52, no. 3 (2017): 339–60.

4. Pirro, "Hardly Ever Relevant?," 345.

5. Kristen Ghodsee, "Left Wing, Right Wing, Everything: Xenophobia, Neo-Totalitarianism, and Populist Politics in Bulgaria," *Problems of Post-Communism* 55, no. 3 (2008): 26–39.

6. On this shift, see Gilles Ivaldi, "Towards the Median Economic Crisis Voter? The New Leftist Economic Agenda of the Front National in France," *French Politics* 13, no 4 (2015): 346–69. The Front National was renamed the Rassemblement National after Marine le Pen's defeat in the presidential elec-

tions of 2017. However, I will be using the term "Front National" throughout this chapter, as I am primarily referring to events prior to 2017.

7. Rémi Bazillier et al., *Petit manuel économique anti-FN* (Paris: Le Cavalier Bleu, 2017), 49–69.

8. Alexis Le Castel, *Marine le Pen n'est pas celle que vous croyez* (Paris: Editions Lulu, 2013), 27. This pamphlet summarizes Marine le Pen's electoral program of 2012, which is no longer available online. In fact, as detailed by Benjamin Lemoine, the 1973 law was widely considered redundant by those working for the treasury and Banque de France. The treasury had not been able to directly sell its debt to the central bank for a very long time. It was, however, able to borrow at low or no interest from the central bank. This possibility was subsequently suppressed by the Maastricht Treaty of 1992, which therefore represents the most important intervention; see Lemoine, *L'ordre de la dette: Enquête sur les infortunes de l'état et la prospérité du marché* (Paris: La découverte, 2016), 33–44.

9. Claudio Borghi Aquilini, *Basta Euro: Come uscire dall'incubo* (Milan: Lega Nord, 2014), 13–14.

10. Biagio Bossone, Marco Cattaneo, Enrico Grazzini, and Stefano Sylos Labini, eds., *Per una moneta fiscale gratuita: Come uscire dall'austerità senza spaccare l'Euro* (Rome: MicroMega, 2015), and Monica Rubino, "I 'prof' della moneta fiscale: 'Uno strumento trasversale utile al futuro governo del paese,'" *La Repubblica*, March 28, 2017, http://www.repubblica.it/politica/2017/03/28/news/i_prof_della_moneta_fiscale_uno_strumento_trasversale_utile_al_futuro_governo_del_paese_-161623442/.

11. Bossone and Labini, "Macroeconomics in Germany: The Forgotten Lesson of Hjalmar Schacht," VOX: CEPR's Policy Portal, July 1, 2016, http://voxeu.org/article/macroeconomics-germany-forgotten-lesson-hjalmar-schacht.

12. Andrew Bowman et al., "Central Bank-Led Capitalism?" *Seattle University Law Review* 36, no. 2 (2013): 455–87.

13. Matthew O'Brien, "Bernanke's Secret Message to Congress: More Stimulus, Please," *Atlantic*, December 28, 2012.

14. J. Bradford Delong and Lawrence Summers, "Fiscal Policy in a Depressed Economy," *Brookings Papers on Economic Activity*, March 20, 2012.

15. Milton Friedman, "A Monetary and Fiscal Framework for Economic Stability," *American Economic Review* 38, no. 3 (1948): 245–64; Ben Bernanke, "Deflation: Making Sure 'It' Doesn't Happen Here; Remarks by Governor Ben S. Bernanke before the National Economists Club, Washington, D.C," Federal Reserve Board, November 21, 2002.

16. Adair Turner, *Between Debt and the Devil: Money, Credit, and Fixing Global Finance* (Princeton, N.J.: Princeton University Press, 2015).

17. See, for instance, Bill Lucarelli, "German Neomercantilism and the European Sovereign Debt Crisis," *Journal of Post Keynesian Economics* 34, no. 2 (December 2011): 205–24, and Joseph E. Stiglitz, *The Euro and Its Threat to the Future of Europe* (London: Penguin, 2016).

18. Lucarelli, "German Neomercantilism," 210–17.

19. Stiglitz, "How to Exit the Eurozone," *Politico*, June 26, 2018.

20. In this respect, I follow the observation of Abba P. Lerner, who proposed to understand the different uses of finance solely from a "functional" point of view. In Lerner's words, "Functional Finance is not especially related to democracy or to private enterprise. It is applicable to a communist society just as well as to a fascist society or a democratic society. It is applicable to a society in which money is used as an important element in the economic mechanism. It consists of the simple principle of giving up our preconceptions of what is proper or sound or traditional, of what 'is done' and instead considering the *functions* performed in the economy by government taxing and spending and borrowing and lending"; Lerner, "Functional Finance and the Federal Debt," *Social Research* 10, no. 1 (1943): 50–51.

21. See, for example, Wolfgang Streeck, "The Return of the Repressed," *New Left Review* 104 (2017): 5–18.

22. The Dimitrov doctrine refers to the work of the Bulgarian Communist leader Georgi Dimitrov; Dimitrov, *The Fascist Offensive and the Tasks of the Communist International in the Struggle of the Working Class against Fascism, Main Report Delivered at the Seventh World Congress of the Communist International 1935* (New York: Prism Key, 2012), 11.

23. Harold James, "Weimar Europe?" *Project Syndicate*, February 24, 2012, and Paul Krugman, "Weimar on the Aegean," *New York Times*, February 16, 2015.

24. Barry Eichengreen and Peter Temin, "Fetters of Gold and Paper," *Oxford Review of Economic Policy* 26, no. 3 (2010): 370–84, and Stiglitz, *The Euro and Its Threat to the Future of Europe*.

25. Peter Temin, *Lessons from the Great Depression* (Cambridge, Mass.: MIT Press, 1999).

26. Eichengreen and Temin, "Fetters of Gold and Paper," 183; Paul McCulley and Zoltan Pozsar, "Does Central Bank Independence Frustrate the Optimal Fiscal-Monetary Policy Mix in a Liquidity Trap?," Paper Presented at the Inaugural Meeting of the Global Interdependence Center's Society of Fellows, Banque de France, March 26, 2012, 13.

27. Liaquat Ahamed, *Lords of Finance: The Bankers Who Broke the World* (London: Penguin, 2009), 399–402; McCulley and Pozsar, "Does Central Bank Independence Frustrate the Optimal Fiscal-Monetary Policy Mix?," 19–20.

28. Young-Sun Hong, *Welfare, Modernity, and the Weimar State* (Princeton, N.J.: Princeton University Press, 1998), 205–9.

29. David F. Crew, *Germans on Welfare: From Weimar to Hitler* (Oxford: Oxford University Press, 1998), 152–65.

30. Hong, *Welfare, Modernity, and the Weimar State*, 208.

31. Laurie Marhoefer, *Sex and the Weimar Republic* (Toronto: University of Toronto Press, 2015), 184–85.

32. Joseph J. Bendersky, *Carl Schmitt: Theorist for the Reich* (Princeton, N.J.: Princeton University Press, 2014), 123.

33. Eichengreen and Temin, "The Gold Standard and the Great Depression," *Contemporary European History* 9, no. 2 (2000): 203.

34. Ibid., 202; Ahamed, *Lords of Finance*, 400.

35. Gottfried Feder, *The German State on a National and Socialist Foundation* (1923; repr. London: Black House, 2015).

36. Feder, *The Programme of the NSDAP: The National Socialist German Workers' Party and Its General Conceptions* (1932; repr. London: Black House, 2016).

37. Adolf Hitler, *Mein Kampf*, trans. James Murphy (London: Hurst and Blackett, 1939), 168 and 171.

38. Feder, *Kampf gegen die Hochfinanz* (Munich: Franz Eher, 1933), 348. For an illuminating discussion of this passage, see Mark Loeffler, "Populists and Parasites: On Producerist Reason," in *Transformations of Populism in Europe and the Americas: History and Recent Tendencies*, ed. John Abromeit, York Norman, Gary Marotta, and Bridget Maria Chesterton (London: Bloomsbury, 2015), 272. I have borrowed Loeffler's translation of Feder here.

39. Feder, *Kampf gegen die Hochfinanz*, 348.

40. Shelley Baranowski, *Strength through Joy: Consumerism and Mass Tourism in the Third Reich* (Cambridge: Cambridge University Press, 2007), 31–32.

41. Feder, *Kampf gegen die Hochfinanz*, 343–48.

42. Feder, *German State on a National and Socialist Foundation*, 110.

43. Adolf Hitler, "Speech by Chancellor Hitler to the Nazi Party in Munich (February 1941)," Munich, Germany, February 24, 1941.

44. Ibid.

45. Avraham Barkai, *Nazi Economics: Ideology, Theory, and Policy* (Munich: Berg, 1990), 165–67; Ton Notermans, *Money, Markets, and the State: Social Democratic Economic Policies Since 1918* (Cambridge: Cambridge University Press, 2000), 146; Adam Tooze, *The Wages of Destruction: The Making and Breaking of the Nazi Economy* (London: Penguin, 2007), 37–66; Pierpaolo Barbieri, *Hitler's Shadow Empire: Nazi Economics and the Spanish Civil War* (Cambridge, Mass.: Harvard University Press, 2015), 114–15; Bossone and Labini, "Macroeconomics in Germany."

46. Bossone and Labini, "Macroeconomics in Germany," 3.

47. Barkai, *Nazi Economics*, 40–47.

48. Ibid., 51–53.

49. There were inklings of a reflationary turn under Chancellor von Papen, who, in the summer of 1932, engaged in a covert program of money creation involving the issuing of business tax coupons that were rediscountable at the Reichsbank. However, unlike Hitler, von Papen did not give up on the policy of wage suppression; see Notermans, *Money, Markets, and the State*, 145.

50. Crew, *Germans on Welfare*, 202.

51. Notermans, *Money, Markets, and the State*, 137–38.

52. Birgit Wulff, "The Third Reich and the Unemployed: National Socialist Work-Creation Schemes in Hamburg 1933–4," in *The German Unemployed: Experiences and Consequences of Mass Unemployment from the Weimar Republic to*

the Third Reich, ed. Richard J. Evans and Dick Geary (London: Croom Helm, 1987), 290–92.

53. Michael Stolleis, *Origins of the German Welfare State: Social Policy in Germany to 1945*, trans. Thomas Dunlap (Berlin: Springer, 2013), 137–39.

54. Richard Weikart, *Hitler's Ethic: The Nazi Pursuit of Evolutionary Progress* (London: Palgrave Macmillan, 2009), 118–19.

55. Günter Grau, "Persecution, 'Re-education' or 'Eradication' of Male Homosexuals between 1933 and 1945: Consequences of the Eugenic Concept of Assured Reproduction," in *Hidden Holocaust? Gay and Lesbian Persecution in Germany 1933–45*, ed. Günter Grau, trans. Patrick Camiller (London: Cassel, 1995), 1–7.

56. Claudia Schoppmann, "The Position of Lesbian Women in the Nazi Period," in Grau, *Hidden Holocaust?*, 10.

57. Moishe Postone, "Anti-Semitism and National Socialism: Notes on the German Reaction to 'Holocaust,'" *New German Critique* 19, no. 1 (1980): 97–115.

58. Jeffrey Herf, *Reactionary Modernism: Technology, Culture and Politics in Weimar and the Third Reich* (Cambridge: Cambridge University Press, 1984), 55–60, 190–91.

59. This interpretation of German anti-Semitism has been made by others. See, for example, Bernd Widdig, *Culture and Inflation in Weimar Germany* (Berkeley: University of California Press, 2001), 228–32, who applies it to the experience of the German hyperinflation of 1922–23. I believe that the argument makes more sense when applied to the German deflation of the late Weimar years.

60. Alain de Benoist, *Vu de droite: Anthologie critique des idées contemporaines* (1977; repr. Paris: Labyrinthe, 2001), 456–60.

61. Benoist, *Europe, tiers monde, même combat* (Paris: Robert Laffont, 1986).

62. Tamir Bar-On, *Where Have All the Fascists Gone?* (Aldershot, UK: Ashgate 2007), 49–50.

63. Tom McCulloch, "The Nouvelle Droite in the 1980s and 1990s: Ideology and Entryism, the Relationship with the Front National," *French Politics* 4 (2006): 163.

64. François Denord, "La conversion au néo-libéralisme: Droite et libéralisme économique dans les années 1980," *Mouvements* 35 (2004/2005): 17–23.

65. Club de l'Horloge, *Les racines du futur: Demain la France* (Paris: Masson, 1977).

66. Zeev Sternhell, *Neither Right nor Left: Fascist Ideology in France*, trans. David Maisel (Princeton, N.J.: Princeton University Press, 1995).

67. Georges Sorel, *Réflexions sur la violence* (Paris: Marcel Rivière et Cie, 1908), and Sternhell, Mario Sznajder, and Maia Ashéri, "Georges Sorel and the Antimaterialist Revision of Marxism," in *The Birth of Fascist Ideology: From Cultural Rebellion to Political Revolution* (Princeton, N.J.: Princeton University Press, 1994), 36–91.

68. Benoist, "Hayek: La loi de la jungle," *Éléments* 68 (Summer 1990): 5–14. The essay was reprinted in English as "Hayek: A Critique," *Telos* 110 (1998): 71–104.

69. Benoist, "Hayek: La loi de la jungle," 14.

70. Henry de Lesquen, "Droit de réponse," *Éléments* 71 (Autumn 1991): 28.

71. Benoist, "Droit de réponse," *Éléments* 71 (Autumn 1991): 29.

72. Pierre-André Taguieff, "Origines et métamorphoses de la nouvelle droite," *Vingtième siècle: Revue d'histoire* 40 (October–December 1993): 3–4 and 17; McCulloch, "Nouvelle Droite in the 1980s and 1990s," 158–78.

73. Michel Eltchaninoff, *Inside the Mind of Marine le Pen* (London: Hurst, 2018), 108.

74. Ivaldi, "Towards the Median Economic Crisis Voter?," 346–69.

75. Marine le Pen, *Pour que vive la France* (Paris: Jacques Grancher, 2012), 9.

76. Ibid., 98.

77. Ibid., 147.

78. Ibid., 147–48.

79. Here Marine le Pen references the work of French intellectual Jean-Claude Michéa, an avant-garde reactionary whose denunciations of cultural and sexual freedom as symptoms of late capitalism have endeared him to the anti-neoliberal far right; ibid., 147.

80. Ibid., 21–102.

81. Stiglitz, *The Euro and Its Threat to the Future of Europe*; Marie Charrel, "Stiglitz s'agace d'être récupéré par Marine Le Pen," *Le Monde*, April 20, 2017.

82. Dominique Albertini, "Le programme économique de le Pen par ceux qui l'ont 'inspiré,'" *Slate*, April 15, 2011. After Sapir expressed his reservations concerning some of the details of this program, it was duly revised to conform more closely to his suggestions. A selection of Sapir's media articles on the Eurozone appears in book form in Jacques Sapir, *Faut-il sortir de l'euro?* (Paris: Seuil, 2012).

83. Emmanuel Galiero, "Un économiste proche de Jacques Sapir rejoint Marine Le Pen," *Le Figaro*, May 2014.

84. The original version of the interview was published in FigaroVox. The longer version, which contains the offending quotes, is published online in Sapir, "Réflexions sur la Grèce et l'Europe: Interview with Alexandre Delvecchio," August 21, 2015.

85. Albertini, "Jacques Sapir: 'On ne peut plus nier que le FN ait changé,'" *Libération*, August 2015, 3.

86. Marine Présidente, *Engagements présidentiels 2017*, accessed May 1, 2017, https://www.marine2017.fr/programme/.

87. Ibid.

88. Alexandre Sulzer, "Sans Florian Philippot, Marine Le Pen libérée ou Marine Le Pen en danger?" *L'Express*, October 22, 2017.

89. Nicola Lillo, "Deficit Widens: Citizens' Income, Tax Cuts and Pension Reform," *La Stampa*, September 29, 2018.

90. Lorenzo Fontana and Ettore Gotti Tedeschi, *La culla vuota della civiltà: All'origine della crisi*, with preface by Matteo Salvini (Verona: Gondolin, 2018).

91. Luigi Mastrodonato, "L'eterna transizione politica di Matteo Salvini," *Vision*, February 5, 2018.

92. Marco Brunazzo and Mark Gilbert, "Insurgents against Brussels: Euroscepticism and the Right-Wing Populist Turn of the Lega Nord since 2013," *Journal of Modern Italian Studies* 22, no. 5 (2017): 624–41.

93. For a fuller analysis of the economic politics of the Lega Nord, see Andrej Zaslove, *The Reinvention of the European Radical Right: Populism, Regionalism and the Italian Lega Nord* (Montreal: McGill-Queen's University Press, 2011), 132–54.

94. Giuseppe Fonte, "Italy PM Unveils Sweeping Austerity Package," *Reuters*, December 4, 2011.

95. Sergio Rame, "Crisi, è peggio del '29: Crollo degli investimenti," *Il Giornale*, April 13, 2013.

96. Federico Marconi, "La Lega alla festa neofascista: C'è anche il 'braccio destro' di Salvini," *L'Espresso*, June 28, 2018.

97. "Fiducia alla camera, nasce il governo Monti. Berlusconi: 'Non staccherò la spina,'" *Il Fatto Quotidiano*, November 18, 2011.

98. Brunazzo and Gilbert, "Insurgents against Brussels," 634.

99. Edoardo Petti, "Chi è Alberto Bagnai, l'economista anti euro di sinistra corteggiato dalla destra," *Formiche*, December 5, 2013, https://formiche.net/blog/2013/12/grillo-bagnai-euro-alemanno/. The following works by Savona and Bagnai have been especially important in influencing political debate on the Euro in Italy: Paolo Savona, *Come un incubo e come un sogno* (Catanzaro: Rubbettino, 2018), and Alberto Bagnai, *Il tramonto dell'Euro: Come e perché la fine della moneta unica salverebbe democrazia e benessere in Europe* (2012; Milan: Mondadori: 2018).

100. Lillo, "Economisti o casinisti? Gli ideologi della lega, Bagnai e Siri, litigano sulla flat tax," *Dagospia*, June 5, 2018.

101. Matteo Albanese, Georgia Bulli, Pietro Castelli Gattinara, and Caterina Froio, *Fascisti di un altro millennio? Crisi e partecipazione in CasaPound Italia* (Rome: Bonanno Editore, 2014).

102. CasaPound Italia, *Una nazione: Programma politico 2018* (Rome: CasaPound Italia, 2018), https://www.docdroid.net/Bg8qGdw/programma-casapound-2018.pdf. The quote on deficit spending can be found on page 3.

103. Simon Franzmann, "A Right-Wing Populist Party Founded by Economists: The Strange Case of Germany's AfD," *LSE Blogs*, March 11, 2017.

104. See Quinn Slobodian and Dieter Plehwe, "Neoliberals against Europe," in this volume.

105. Severin Weiland, "Strategie der Rechtspopulisten: Wie die AfD bei SPD und Linken fischt," *Spiegel*, July 2018.

106. Matthias Kamann, "Was Höcke mit der 'Denkmal der Schande'-Rede bezweckt," *Welt*, January 18, 2017.

107. Volkhard Mosler, "Die AfD auf dem Weg zur faschistischen Partei," *Marx 21*, December 8, 2017.

108. Weiland, "Strategie der Rechtspopulisten."

109. The brochure for the event, "Wirtschaft: Hegung und Entgren-zung," *Institut fur Staatspolitik*, can be found here: https://staatspolitik.com/wp -content/uploads/2017/12/18.-WiAk_IfS.pdf.

110. On Benedikt Kaiser and the connection to Alain de Benoist's New Right, see Richard Gebhardt, "Eine neue 'Querfront'?" *Der Rechte Rand*, November 2017, https://www.der-rechte-rand.de/archive/2824/neue-querfront/. On Höcke and the French New Right, see Michael Kraske, "Der Code der Neuen Rechten," *Übermedien*, December 2016.

111. Björn Höcke, "Widerstand gegen den Raubtierkapitalismus," *Compact* 1 (2018): 47.

112. Ibid., 47.

113. Ibid., 48.

Disposing of the Discredited:
A European Project

Michel Feher

Elected at the turn of the 1980s on the promise to make the "free world" vibrant again, Margaret Thatcher and Ronald Reagan claimed a mandate to impose market discipline on everyone. The "Iron Lady" and her friend the "Great Communicator" faulted their predecessors for responding to the restive 1960s by inordinately raising the minimum wage and social benefits—thereby causing inflation to soar. They also blamed the CEOs of large corporations for balancing the wishes of shareholders with the demands of labor unions and consumer advocates—thereby causing profits to wane. Finally, they lamented that the propensity of politicians and employers to placate "special interest" groups enticed wage earners to rely more on wealth redistribution and collective bargaining than on their own hard work and initiative.

The architects of the "conservative revolution" argued that harnessing the power of the state to help markets do their job was not only good for business. More importantly, it helped encourage the entire population to think and behave like self-reliant entrepreneurs. In their view, awakening the entrepreneurial spirit of every citizen required the creation of an environment where private companies, public administrations, and individual consumers in need

of resources would have to compete for private funding. To that end, they ini-
tiated a process purported to lift the constraints that had hitherto limited the
transnational circulation of capital, kept the various branches of the financial
industry separate, and checked the creativity of financial engineering.

Deregulation certainly enabled financial institutions to act as the arbiters
of valuable endeavors. However, the order of priorities that resulted from the
ascendency of finance turned out to be quite different from what its political
facilitators had envisioned. For *financial* markets, as John Maynard Keynes
warned, do not operate like other markets. More than coordinating transactions, their specific function is pooling predictions: the signals they produce
are not *prices* representing the outcome of negotiations between buyers and
sellers but *ratings* expressing the speculations of investors on the value of a
project. Moreover, Keynes added, what investors speculate upon is not the
eventual yield of an endeavor—be it the long-term profitability of an enterprise or the social impact of a public program—but its chances to draw the
attention of their peers in the immediate future.

Corporations were the first type of economic agents to internalize the
guessing game of their potential backers. For almost four decades, CEOs have
been less intent on maximizing commercial profits (conceived as the difference between sales revenues and production costs) than on bolstering their
company's financial credit (measured by the market value of its stock). Unre-
alized capital gain, rather than operating cash flow, is the metric of success—
which explains why firms use so much of their resources to "buy back" their
own shares.

But the primacy of ratings is not confined to the private sector. From the
1980s on, governments keen on improving the attractiveness of companies
based in their own territories catered to investors' preferences for business-
friendly tax codes and flexible labor markets. As the subsequent loss of fiscal revenues forced them to borrow the funds they could no longer collect,
elected officials have become increasingly dependent on the value of their
sovereign debt in the bond market. Maintaining the trust of bondholders is
arguably the main concern of policy makers—over and above the rate of economic growth or the welfare of their fellow citizens.

In time, the sway of shareholders' and bondholders' valuations has extended to households and individuals. While vying for investors' attention,
employers no longer provide lifelong careers and political leaders no longer
secure a robust safety net. It is now up to job applicants to make themselves
valuable by advertising their highly prized skills, by brandishing their appeal-

ing social networks, or, failing that, by presenting their unlimited availability and flexibility as valuable assets.

Furthermore, once faced with precarious jobs and receding social benefits, large swaths of the wage-earning population have been forced to borrow, whether to access housing, to study, or simply to survive. Yet anyone hoping to obtain a loan must offer guarantees. In the absence of sizeable possessions, aspiring borrowers rely on the estimated worth of what they want to acquire and on the reputation for reliability they earned by repaying previous loans. Here again, being deemed *creditworthy* is what enables people to navigate our brave new world.

Altogether, the conduct fashioned by investors' speculations scarcely fit the entrepreneurial type that the conservative revolution was supposed to mold. Pro-market reforms purported to create a world where capital owners, wage earners, and even the unemployed would envision their lives as a profit-seeking business, calculating the cost and benefit of every decision. However, what financialized capitalism has actually bred are credit-seeking portfolio managers primarily concerned with the appraisal of their assets in the form of both material and human capital.

Arguably, advocates of the "Third Way" were the first elected leaders to address their constituents in terms of this growing preoccupation with creditworthiness. Bill Clinton, Tony Blair, and Gerhard Schröder were hardly inclined to revive the promises of economic security or gradual upward mobility that had sustained the postwar social compact. But they did not merely echo the conservative revolution's pledge to free hard-working taxpayers from a burdensome fiscal state and parasitical special interest groups. In their view, if public officials were to curb their fellow citizens' dependency on guaranteed employment and benefits, they needed to help them become more appreciable—so as to attract recruiters, find sponsors, and reassure lenders.

On the one hand, Third Way governments sought to address the growing dearth of stable jobs by improving job seekers' employability with education and welfare reforms. Their purpose was to equip the young with more bankable skills and to entice the unemployed to keep up with a labor market that needed flexibility and availability. On the other hand, to make up for increasingly ungenerous social programs, the new center-left facilitated the access of middle- and working-class households to commercial credit—both by providing conditional government guarantees on their debt and by authorizing private lenders to take more risks. For its architects, these reforms were supposed to foster a new social compact that would provide the citizenry with autonomy and care while maintaining the trust of bondholders. An employable and solvent population, so the argument went, would be as attractive to investors as a business-friendly tax code and flexible labor market.

By the turn of the twenty-first century, however, the financially responsible welfare state envisioned by Third Way governments was delivering more precariousness than appreciation for its constituents (with exception of the already well endowed). Public officials were thus compelled to base the appeasement of the middle and working classes on increasingly loose conditions for accessing commercial credit.

The 2008 collapse of the subprime mortgage market certainly drove a wrench into the economic model of previous decades. Yet the quick refurbishing of the banking system, under the stewardship of the Federal Reserve, hardly foreshadowed a return to the Keynesian fiscal policies and embedded markets of the postwar era.[1] Instead, the decision to manage the bailout's impact on public finances with fresh austerity measures, made at a G7 meeting in the winter of 2010, effectively perpetuated a regime of capital accumulation predicated on asset appreciation. Boosting the estimated worth of their fellow citizens has thus remained a core commitment of elected officials—albeit one with a novel inflection.

In the early 2010s, European authorities proved especially inclined to make their territory attractive by ridding it of those residents least attuned to investors' expectations. At the time, the Berlin-led EU was responding to the speculative attacks on the sovereign debt of its more fragile member states with harsh consolidation measures, thereby inciting their governments to cover up the socially disastrous effects of austerity. Moreover, the violent backlash following the so-called Arab Springs of 2011 provided fresh fuel for the politicization of xenophobia, thereby raising institutional inhospitality to unprecedented heights.

Reducing the visibility and (when possible) the presence of unattractive individuals has involved a variety of measures. They have alternatively been designed to render disability programs less accessible, clear the unemployment registers, deny residency or asylum to most applicants, and, in some cases, pressure poorly rated nationals to emigrate. While still meant to improve the per-capita valuation of human capital in the population, these pruning techniques seek to decrease the denominator of the ratio rather than increase its numerator.

Disposing of the discredited has become a multidimensional European project rich in public-private partnerships. The project has involved letting migrants drown in the Mediterranean Sea, making life unbearable for allegedly undesirable populations such as the Roma, pushing an increasing number of insufficiently malleable employees to suicide, erasing from official registers any trace of a large proportion of the unemployed, and pushing more and more young nationals to migrate from countries like Greece, Portugal, and Ireland. This chapter examines the dynamic process of discarding the discredited, focusing on the time period through the winter of 2015. Tumultuous as they have been, the major events of the past years—from a near Grexit, to an actual Brexit, to the increasing power of nationalist political parties—unfortunately both confirm and accentuate trends that began prior to 2015. In the afterword of this chapter, I take stock of their overlapping logics.

Actually Existing Neoliberalism

"Actually existing socialism," as those who experienced the Cold War will recall, was the name given to the regime of the Soviet Union and its partners in the Warsaw Pact. The most likely individuals to resort to this phrase were then embarrassed left-wingers (who used it to convey that this was not all socialism could or should be) and sneering right-wingers (who used it as another way of saying "we told you so"). Yet despite the difference in tone and intent, both groups agreed there was a huge gap between what socialists had promised and what states calling themselves socialist had delivered.

My contention here is that there is a similarly dramatic discrepancy between the neoliberal program itself—by which I mean the measures Friedrich Hayek, Milton Friedman, and their respective followers devised when elected officials were not yet listening to them—and what its implementation actually effected when sympathetic politicians took the reins of the world's most developed countries. From 1947 onward, the "neoliberal" scholars of the Freiburg and Chicago schools of economics gathered around Hayek at the Mont Pèlerin Society. They shared the conviction that the Free World, with Keynesian economists at its helm, would descend into socialism. They did not imagine the bang of a revolution, however, but rather the whimper of countercyclical fiscal policies. The neoliberals complained that, as governments tinkered with the price mechanism, both employers and employees would forgo competition by staking their prosperity on the state's ability to prevent market failures and ensure full employment.

To prevent liberal societies from sliding down the road to totalitarian serfdom, these neoliberal economists devised a three-pronged program. Their purpose was to create an environment in which:

1. Corporate managers would be enticed to regain their eagerness to compete—instead of seeking state support and advantages for their company's stakeholders;

2. Governmental agencies would be retooled to shield fragile market mechanisms from the sway of "special interests"—instead of protecting the latter from the alleged rough market conditions;

3. And the salaried classes would be actively encouraged to adopt the entrepreneurial ethos of their employers—instead of letting them assume that their welfare clashed with the interests of the business class.[2]

Neoliberal reformers realized that time-honored liberal principles, such as the right to vote and to form an association, were responsible for the illiberal evolution of Western societies—namely, the stifling encroachment on the economy of welfare programs and militant labor unions. Yet since they were reluctant to call for sacrificing democratic institutions in order to preserve "free choice" (with the exception of "peripheral" countries like Chile), they argued that the redemption of liberalism depended on the conversion of all economic agents to the outlook of profit-seeking entrepreneurs—from corporations and public institutions to workers and even the unemployed.

The protracted stagflation of the 1970s provided conditions for the neoliberal agenda's rise to prominence. With the monetarist shock instigated by Paul Volcker's Fed and the trademark fiscal policies of Thatcher and Reagan, Hayek and Friedman's influence loomed large. The implementation of the Mont Pèlerin Society's three-pronged program, however, would produce a very different world than what its architects had portrayed.

The authors of *The Road to Serfdom* and *Capitalism and Freedom* identified as an "old Whig" and a "laissez faire" advocate, respectively.[3] Though they presented their project as a restoration of the original spirit of liberalism, the chasm between "planned" and "actually existing" neoliberalism stems from the different meanings of "competition" in the old-fashioned liberals and their self-appointed redeemers. For classical and neoclassical economists, and even for the German ordoliberals, competition primarily refers to producers competing for consumers and to businesses vying for clients. Hence, staving off the formation of oligopolistic markets (or worse, of monopolies) is one of the main tasks assigned to a liberal government.

For Hayek, the Chicago School economists and their brainchild "Law and Economics" movement, however, monopolistic situations are benign— because necessarily temporary—as long as the state does not get involved in creating or sustaining them.[4] What is problematic and needs mending, in the eyes of Friedman and his disciples, is corporate managers' propensity to put their own standing among the stakeholders above the interests of the shareholders of the firm. Therefore, what competitiveness really involves is a mechanism that will keep managers on their toes, which is to say, exclusively focused on creating value for the owners of the company that employs them.[5] Hence the institution of a "market for corporate control," whereby current but also potential shareholders (that is, investors at large) will be enabled to choose and replace CEOs, as well as other top managers, according to their ability to raise the shareholder value of the corporation.[6] In short, what "Law and Economics" scholars call competition no longer pertains to producers endeavoring to snatch consumers from their rivals, but instead, to managers competing for investors.

Once predicated on this latter definition, the implementation of the neo-liberal agenda was bound to stray from the restoration of market discipline heralded by its champions. First, as managers were made to internalize the new rules of "good governance"—both through the menace of hostile lever-age buyouts and the lure of bonuses and stock options—they learned that their primary job was no longer about optimizing the commercial *profit* of their corporation over time—about tending to the difference between the accumulated income generated by the sales of commodities and the aggre-gate costs incurred to produce them—but about increasing the *credit* of the corporation's stock in the eyes of impatient investors—about tending to the difference between the projected results of the company and the doubts that financial markets might harbor about its ability to deliver them.

Second, in order to create an environment that would keep managers on their toes—to wit, focused on the creation of shareholder value—public au-thorities were required to lift all forms of obstacles to the flow of financial capital. Indeed, if investors were to impress upon business executives that raising the market value of the corporation's shares was the only way for them to keep their jobs, they needed to be free: free to move across national borders so as to reward good governance on a global scale; free to mount whatever takeover scam imaginable so as to raid underperforming firms; free to ignore the boundaries separating the different types of financial institutions so as to leave no savings behind with regard to the fulfillment of their mission; free to invent novel financial instruments so as to protect the volume of available liquidities from the vagaries of the business cycle. While justified in the name of "competition"—of the will to render corporations more competitive—

these manifold deregulations were clearly at odds with what classical liberalism envisioned as the prime responsibility of a liberal government—namely, establishing a strong antitrust legislation.

Third, as national governments heeded the call of "Law and Economics" scholars, thereby assuming that their own calling was now to make the territory under their jurisdiction attractive to investors, they quickly learned that liquidity handlers had simple and stable tastes: what lured them almost unfailingly included low labor costs (that is, a flexible labor market) and a business-friendly tax code (especially with respect to capital gain) as well strong and pervasive intellectual property rights (to make sure no potentially money-making idea would remain unpatented). While eager to placate investors, elected officials could not help but realize that meeting their demands translated into precarious labor conditions for most wage earners, drastic budgetary cuts affecting social programs and public services, and the privatization of hitherto common resources.

In spite of the ideological climate that the proponents of the "conservative revolution" had managed to create—whereby "special interests" and welfare provisions were respectively accused of short-changing and dispiriting "main street" folks—political leaders were still worried that their new priorities could cost them their reelection or even cause social unrest. Thus, instead of simply sacrificing the welfare of their constituents to the wishes of the investing community, they sought to make up for the loss of tax revenues that were resulting from their fiscal and labor policies by borrowing the money they needed from the very investors they meant to attract.

Though happy to be of service, the purveyors of credit were careful to attach strict conditions to their loans, making them incumbent on commitments to welfare reform, leaner public institutions, improved flexibility in the labor market, and fresh tax cuts. Since the depositaries of popular sovereignty no longer were in a position to refuse or even argue with their backers—having allowed financial capital to choose its havens freely—their approach to government underwent the same transformation as that which had affected corporate management. Indeed, just as managers had reneged on the Fordist ideal of sustainable profitability to embrace a mode of governance exclusively geared toward the pursuit of shareholder value, elected representatives not only renounced their Keynesian preoccupations with full employment and sustained growth, but also elected what the German sociologist Wolfgang Streeck aptly calls the "bondholder value" of their national debt as the main compass of their policies.[7]

Fourth, as the twin pursuit of shareholder and bondholder values translated into new modes of corporate and public management, the incidence of what business manuals refer to as "best practices" began permeating people's behavior as well. Having CEOs obsess about the shareholder value of their stock and political leaders focus on the bondholder value of their national debt, respectively, caused jobs to become either scarcer or more precarious and social benefits to shrink or, at least, get attached to a number of strings. Consequently, large sections of the population found it increasingly hazardous to stake their material welfare on the stability of their employment, the regular progression of their wages, and the added protection of a publicly funded safety net.

Governments quickly realized that they could not make the territory under their jurisdiction attractive to investors and, at the same time, enable the majority of their constituents to reap sufficient income from the sale of their labor power. Moreover, the conditions under which bondholders agreed to purchase and hold their treasury bills made it quite clear that incurring more debt to compensate for the loss of tax revenues did not spare public institutions from subjecting their programs to drastic budgetary cuts. Torn, once again, between the demands of their financial backers and the looming discontent of their electorate, public officials decided to do for private citizens what they had done for themselves—namely, substitute borrowed for earned money. In other words, what people could no longer purchase thanks to the income of their labor, they would still be able to buy, albeit on credit.[8]

Understandably, financial institutions were eager to oblige: for once properly securitized, proliferating loans would dramatically increase the volume of circulating liquidity, thereby widening and, at the same time, tightening the hold of investors on the rest of society. Yet, despite their confidence in the prowess of financial engineering, lenders still needed the recipients of their largesse to be able to offer valuable assets as collateral. Thus, for those who did not have much to show as guarantee, access to credit was dependent on the estimated worth of what they wished to acquire—be it the very house for which they requested a mortgage or the projected value of the university degree for which they sought a student loan—as well as on their past reputation as borrowers—an asset that, in many countries, is rated by the famed FICO credit score.[9] Altogether, what primarily enabled the classes formerly known as salaried to remain solvent consumers was not the income they made as employees but the various types of capital that qualified them as creditworthy.[10]

Of course, stagnant wages and precarious jobs did not simply change working people into idle borrowers. However, an increasingly large proportion of them ceased to receive a regular salary and became contingent workers instead—as is already the case for a third of the working population in the United States. Hailed by the surviving architects of the neoliberal program as a decisive step toward the generalization of the entrepreneurial ethos, the gradual substitution of this new status of "free agent" for the wage earner of yore turned out to fashion a very different type of character. Indeed, rather than businesspeople selling the commodities they produce, contingent workers are induced to see themselves as the managers of their assets—whether their occupation involves performing tasks predicated on their skills or renting out the capital goods they own. Some cash in on their talents—be it by designing computer programs for outsourcing companies or mounting Ikea furniture for clumsy households—others survive thanks to their availability and flexibility—as in the case of the German mini-jobs and the British zero-hour jobs—still others endeavor to lease the space, time, and durable goods at their disposal—a room in their flat, a drive in their car, an extra camera or vacuum cleaner sitting in their closet.[11]

Insofar as independent contractors and casual laborers make a living by multiplying temporary commercial contracts—instead of being offered labor contracts accompanied by pension and health care plans—the success of their operations very much depends on their capacities to advertise what they have to offer and attest to their proficiency and trustworthiness. In short, the reputation they manage to build—regarding the efficiency of their performances, the quality of their amenities, or their willingness to be ruthlessly exploited—is their crucial asset. The credit they manage to muster thus proves equally essential to their abilities to work and to consume. For the so-called free agent, self-branding becomes the way to live, and in some cases the only way to survive: a way that involves techniques analogous to the "best practices" of corporate managers seeking to raise the shareholder value of their firm and of public officials preoccupied with the bondholder value of their treasury bills.

To the extent that my schematic description of it is correct, life under *financialized* capitalism is a far cry from what the neoliberal luminaries had envisioned—or at least from the "free society" they championed and eventually managed to sell. Hayek and Friedman had likened the implementation of their program to the advent of a world where the mindset and behavior of corporations, governments, and individuals—including wage earners and even the unemployed—would be modeled on the reasoning and pursuits of the profit-seeking entrepreneur. Yet, what we got instead—albeit through the implementation of the neoliberal program—is a world where the mindset and behavior of corporations, governments, and individuals—at least the growing number of "free agents" among them—are modeled on the reasoning and pursuits of a credit-seeking asset manager. Between "actually existing" and planned neoliberalism, the gap is thus arguably as wide as the distance from socialist ideals to Soviet reality.

Quoting Adam Ferguson, Friedrich Hayek liked to claim that human societies are "the result of human action, but not the execution of any human design."[12] Accordingly, neoliberal society, if this is what we should call ours, can be said to result from neoliberal actions, while not reflecting the professed intentions of neoliberal scholars. Yet, Hayek is not the only one whose favorite proclamations have been subjected to an ironic spin. In his 1937 magnum opus, John Maynard Keynes, Hayek's archrival, not only advocated the "euthanasia of the rentier" but also announced it as the logical outcome of an impending process that would see the state take "an ever-greater responsibility for directly organising investment."[13] In the world of actually existing neoliberalism, however, far from having been administered a painless death, rentiers rule. Better still, the rule they have managed to impose is largely about inducing everyone to emulate them—by virtue of staking their livelihood on the capital value of the assets they happen to have.

Whether exercised by public or private institutions, the mode of government distinctive of actually existing neoliberalism endeavors to fashion individuals who are mindful enough of their creditworthiness to invest in the goods, services, and conduct that they believe likely to increase it—or at least to prevent the depreciation of what they either possess or project. However, enticing people to seek the appreciation of their portfolio requires offering them a number of guarantees and protections. In that respect, neoliberal governing agencies are no longer in a position to assure wage earners that the income of their labor will gradually increase—or that welfare programs will provide for the ill, the old, and the unemployed. On the other hand, what they must do their best to sustain is the capital value of the assets off of which credit-seeking subjects are purported to live. In other words, for a neoliberal social compact to emerge, those who have savings, real estate property, or appreciable skills need to be assured that public authorities will tend to the markets where financial, physical, and human capitals are valued, whereas those who merely have their flexibility and availability to offer must at least be given the opportunity to advertise their willingness to be overexploited.

Moreover, in situations of credit crunch—such as that which developed countries have been experiencing after the financial crisis of 2008—public authorities take it upon themselves to let their constituents rely on race, ethnicity, autochthony, religion, or gender as assets of last resort. "I don't have much but at least I am white," or "at least I am from here," are statements that, while hardly new, take on a singular credit-seeking dimension under actually existing neoliberalism. The latter's way of dealing with systemic discriminations is thus ambivalent. For on the one hand, its promoters claim that the markets where creditworthiness is evaluated should be open to everyone regardless of color, nationality, sex, faith, gender, or sexual orientation. But on the other hand, they understand that people will try to turn whatever they have at their disposal into a relatively valuable asset—including the fact that they are not of foreign descent or that they are not members of a disadvantaged or allegedly suspicious minority.

Consequently, while actually existing neoliberal governments make it their calling to support the creation and attend to the sustaining of capital markets, the social compact that they produce by means of protecting an ever-expanding range of assets is not one that provides universal coverage. Quite to the contrary, the advent of a political regime devoted to the fashioning of credit-seeking portfolio managers is bound to generate an ever-growing number of discredited individuals whose very existence ends up being burdensome. Indeed, when reassuring bondholders and creating value for the shareholders are the respective priorities of public officials and corporate managers, people who lack valuable assets can neither be cared for nor simply left to fend for themselves. On the one hand, boosting their creditworthiness requires an expansive fiscal policy that investors are likely to find unappealing. Yet, on the other hand, allowing their sorry lot to appear in plain view will prove just as damaging to the attractiveness of the territory in which they reside. Therefore, no matter how unsavory, disposing of the discredited— either by rendering them invisible or by making them actually disappear— figures among the missions that actually existing neoliberal institutions are expected to accomplish.

European Biopolitics

The European Union, especially since the financial crisis of 2008, offers a good illustration of how the discredited are both produced and disposed of under actually existing neoliberalism. To a large extent, both the EU itself and the nation-states comprising it are similar to the other parts of the developed world that have adopted a mode of government predicated on the quest for credit. Thus, like any territory subjected to the tastes of choosy and mobile investors, Europe is ruled by governing agencies who address the population they govern as a collection of asset-bearing individuals and who consider that raising the ratio of capital value per capita should be their chief objective. To reach such a goal, two paths can be followed, either alternatively or in combination. The first one involves equipping current nationals and residents with appreciable skills as well as bringing in either skilled or especially flexible foreigners. The second one concentrates on relieving the land from those who are regarded uncreditworthy— or, to quote Achille Mbembe's *Critique of Black Reason*, from those who are deemed "un-exploitable."[14]

Since the mid-1990s, "investment in human capital" has become the central feature of what could be called actually existing neoliberalism *with a human face*. In the preceding decade, the structural reforms advocated by the architects of the "conservative revolution" had been exclusively couched in the rhetoric of the neoliberal planners—to wit, the twin promise of turning everyone into a self-reliant profit-seeking entrepreneur and of administering nothing but tough love to anyone who resisted. But with the advent of "Third Way" governments—namely, those of Tony Blair in the UK, Bill Clinton in the U.S., and Gerhard Schröder in Germany—a new type of discourse emerged. Eager to "help people help themselves" or to give back "the will to win" to the "workless class," Clinton and Blair shed Reagan and Thatcher's talk of freedom and discipline and replaced it with the language of "recovery." The role of government, they claimed, was to cure its self-depreciating constituents of their addiction to the social benefits and full employment policies of yore by giving them the tools and desire to make themselves appreciable. Constituents should likewise learn to welcome appreciable foreigners who work hard for little pay and protection. In the 2000s, the numerous reports of the OECD expounding the merits of large investments in education, empathetic workfare, and relatively open borders became the template of actually existing neoliberalism with a human face. Along with policy recommendations, these reports also like to cite the poster children of their approach: Finland with respect to education, Denmark's "flexsecurity" with respect to welfare reform, and Canada with respect to immigration.

Though hardly advertised as such, the second path to enhanced attractiveness—the "disposing of the discredited" approach—was never entirely forgone. For instance, while celebrating immigration for the talented and the flexible, Tony Blair never failed to contrast them with the allegedly "fake" asylum seekers whose only motive was to take advantage of Britain's generosity. In the first years of his presidency, Nicolas Sarkozy resorted to the same binary between what he called "chosen" immigration and the "burden" he associated with the beneficiaries of family reunification laws. Thus, for him as for the former British prime minister, getting rid of burdensome migrants, or at least denying them entry, was at least as important as attracting the migrants of choice. Yet, in the wake of the financial crisis, the techniques of government purporting to dispose of the discredited ceased to represent the dark underside of population management. Instead, they became the predominant way of sustaining the ratio of valuable assets per capita, most notably within the confines of the European Union.

That Europe embraced such a pruning approach to the pursuit of credit, both more vigorously and more systematically than other parts of the developed world, can be attributed to two major factors:

First, while both the EU and the U.S. responded to the crisis by refurbishing the financial system without reforming it substantially, the Obama administration at least complemented the rescue of Wall Street with a fiscal stimulus—however insufficient in the eyes of Keynesian economists—while the Fed endeavored to stimulate the economy by means of engaging in quantitative easing (that is, purchasing bonds so as to raise their price while lowering their interest rate). In Europe, however, the German authorities used their dominant position to persuade their partners that lax fiscal policies were not the way to go. Meanwhile the European Central Bank—also a German creation—remained faithful to what is supposed to be its sole calling: namely, ensuring price stability regardless of the circumstances, even at the cost of inducing deflation. Consequently, once the losses incurred by financial institutions were duly socialized—thereby causing the national debts of the more fragile member states to soar dramatically—the ensuing austerity measures proved especially drastic, particularly because they were neither preceded nor accompanied by countercyclical measures.

As countries like Greece, Spain, Italy, and Ireland faced financial collapse, the ECB was forced to circumvent its own bylaws—which forbid it to finance states directly—albeit not without attaching stringent conditions to its loans: the governments of indebted countries could borrow what they needed to round out their budgets, but only if they committed to crushing spending cuts. Official proclamations notwithstanding, debt reduction was hardly the purpose of austerity programs—and, indeed, in most cases, just the opposite happened. The real raison d'être of these programs is to assure creditors that their loans will be serviced ahead of any other consideration—and thus to ensure that a sizable portion of the wealth produced by indebted nations will be permanently used to keep an unreformed financial system afloat. In short, the creditworthiness of a country is ultimately incumbent on its willingness to sustain the credit of those who hold its bonds—with the consequence of multiplying the number of the discredited among its own population.

Second, in the fall of 2008, the anxiety generated by the looming Great Recession caused European leaders to promise their constituents protection from the wreckage that irresponsible speculators had wrought. However, as these same leaders used the political credit that their promises had given them to restore the hegemony of the very institutions they had accused of irresponsibility, the protection on offer no longer looked like a new New Deal. Unable to shield their population from the exigencies of investors, they offered instead to protect them against the impending flood of non-European migrants—primarily, though not exclusively, from Africa—as well as from the creeping identity trouble created by the presence of culturally alien minorities on their soil. The menace of a huge inflow of migrants was totally imaginary at first—if only because emigration from developing countries tends to be closely linked to the state of labor supply in developed countries, which means that a high rate of unemployment is usually much more dissuasive than tightened border control. Yet, the violent aftermath of the so-called Arab Springs gave it a modicum of credibility by virtue of swelling the numbers of asylum seekers desperately trying to cross the Mediterranean Sea. Thus, for European authorities, curbing immigration—and blaming the budgetary deficits on the cost of resident foreigners—became a privileged way of showing care and protectiveness to a population subjected to the pain and worries caused by their own austerity programs.

Altogether, a persistent preference for deflationary measures and the increasing appeal of fanning xenophobic sentiments explain why Europe has chosen to maintain its credit by purging its territory of ostensibly uncreditworthy people—or, at least, by keeping them from affecting its reputation in the eyes of investors. Whether deployed at the level of the European Community, assumed by member-states, or fine-tuned as public-private partnerships, the techniques of government involved in such an endeavor can be divided into four main categories: manipulation of statistics, relentless harassment, population swapping, and malign neglect.

OBFUSCATION

The first way of reducing the negative impact that a discredited population produces on the attractiveness of a territory is to remove it from the statistics revealing its sorry state. In the EU, as in many other places, the unemployed are the main targets of such obfuscation. Of course, one may wonder why financial markets would be turned off by high unemployment: couldn't they perceive it as a sign that both public officials and corporate managers are doing all they can to reduce labor costs? Thus, provided that, thanks to welfare reforms, the times of lasting "generous benefits" are over, what is wrong with unemployment? The answer is that investors are torn between two opposite anxieties. On the one hand, they fear that, out of weakness toward their constituents and their stakeholders, elected politicians and corporate managers will fail, respectively, to sustain the bondholder value of their debt and the shareholder value of their company. But on the other hand, investors are also worried about the recessive effects of their own exigencies—since a downturn in the economic activity is bound to reduce the opportunities for lucrative investments. Therefore, it is incumbent on governing agencies to appease creditors and stockholders by concealing the troubling consequences of their demands.

Practically, three major techniques are used to reduce the official number of unemployed people:

First, employment seekers can be given another status, thus removing them from the statistics. In Sweden, the Netherlands, and Britain, for instance, long-term unemployment was customarily converted into invalidity, whereas in France, early retirement was the substitution of choice—until the governments of these countries realized that the pensions they needed to pay to those they declared invalid or retired clashed with the budgetary cuts they were expected to make. Still, status manipulation remains operative, albeit at a subtler level. Hence for Pôle emploi, the French employment office, any employment seeker who has recently worked for a short period of time or who is currently holding an unpaid internship immediately ceases to be included among the unemployed.

Second, insofar as the International Labor Office defines unemployment as the condition of a person who does not have a job but is actively looking for one, the civil servants in charge of receiving and guiding job-seekers have been tasked with showing that the people who come to their office are often insufficiently motivated in their search to keep the right of calling themselves unemployed. The criteria that can be invoked to expose a damning lack of motivation include missing an appointment with one's employment officer (regardless of the circumstances) and refusing a job offer—even when the pay, location, and job description do not fit the profile of the person to whom it is offered.

Third, when employment seekers cannot be forcibly removed from the unemployment registers—whether by putting them in another category or by depriving them of the status and benefits that the unemployed are entitled to claim—the most expedient way to proceed is to persuade them to remove themselves. In other words, inducing discouragement—or better still self-depreciation—is another mission, and perhaps the most important one, that employment offices expect their staff to fulfill. To that end, the officers in charge of managing the unemployed are incited to send the people under their care to job interviews that they have no chance of passing successfully, thereby imparting to them that they are unfit for the job market.

HARASSMENT

The unemployed are not the only group of discredited whose self-depreciation is deliberately pursued. To induce suicidal depression through systematic ha-rassment also figures among the well-honed techniques that the students of new public management have applied to the beneficiaries of social programs subjected to severe cuts and that the practitioners of good corporate gover-nance have tested on the employees they mean to get rid of. The following two stories, one involving the British government, the other a major French company, illustrate quite eloquently the rationale for harassing expendable people to death.

The tragic hero of the first story is, or rather was, Brian McArdle, a night watchman from Glasgow.[15] On December 26, 2011, Brian, who was fifty-seven years old, had a stroke that left him blind in one eye, paralyzed on his left side, and aphasiac. In the wake of his stroke, he filed for an invalidity pension, which he got, but not for long. In the winter of 2012, David Cameron had already realized that, while beneficial for unemployment statistics, turning ageing and long-term employment seekers into invalids proved too costly for public finances. Thus, he decided that, having lost their positive effect on the credit-worthiness of the country, invalidity pensions should not be granted too eas-ily. To justify his decision, the British prime minister resorted to an argument dear to the architects of planned neoliberalism—namely, that many pension recipients were not really invalid—thereby shortchanging those who really were and abusing the generosity of public authorities. Although the Brit-ish Department of Labor and Pensions contested Cameron's allegations—showing that abusive claims amounted to two million pounds at most, about

1 percent of the available funds—the conservative PM remained undeterred. In order to identify fake claimants, the government hired a private company, Atos Healthcare, with the assignment of testing potential pension beneficiaries and delivering "Work Capacity Assessments" based on those tests. Atos Healthcare's bill amounted to 400 million pounds—two hundred times more than the abuses the company was meant to check. (But then again, a nation's bondholder value is less about actual cost reduction than about showing creditors that you care about their concerns.) Though already a beneficiary of an invalidity pension, Brian McArdle was among the people summoned for testing. A couple of weeks after being evaluated by Atos Healthcare, he received a notice from the Labor and Pension Department declaring him fit to work and thus deprived of all benefits. The next day, he died from another stroke. Far from being the only victim of Cameron's war on pension abuse, Brian McArdle is merely one out of 1,300 people who passed away soon after being tested by Atos Healthcare; strokes and suicides were among the most frequent causes of death.[16]

The main character of the second story is Didier Lombard, the former CEO of France Telecom—a company currently known as Orange. Privatized in 1997, France Telecom became the corporation carrying the largest debt in the world by 2002—about 68 billion Euros. The cause of this abysmal deficit was not the high-salaries-cum-generous-benefits customarily attributed to French firms—especially when the state owns part of its capital—but the fact that, taking advantage of the deregulation of the telecom sector in Europe, France Telecom had bought into the capital of a large number of private telephone providers throughout the continent. As the stock value of these companies plummeted when the dot-com bubble burst, their French shareholder found itself in dire straits. To address the issue, France Telecom appointed a team of so-called cost killers whose mission was to restore the company's finances and credit. Although labor costs had played no part in the firm's debacle, they were soon singled out as the main target of the cost killers. Upon taking office, in 2006, Didier Lombard did not merely pursue the efforts of his predecessor, Thierry Breton. Eager to bring the cost-killing concept to a whole new level, he devised the so-called plan NEXT, ostensibly purported to endow France Telecom with a lean and flexible management style, but actually aimed at ridding the corporation of 22,000 employees—17 percent of its personnel. However, since firing people is costly—especially at France Telecom where some of the staff still enjoyed a civil servant status—Lombard's goal was to persuade them to quit. To that end, he ordered his human resources staff to set up a system of relentless harassment, whereby employees were constantly asked to change location, alter their priorities, and modify their schedule, with the explicit purpose of making them collapse psychologically and physically—indeed, the bonuses offered to the harassers were indexed on the number of so-called voluntary departures they managed to induce. While most of the people targeted by Lombard's human resources team were still alive when they left France Telecom "voluntarily," during the best three years of "plan Next"—2008, 2009, and 2010—fifty-eight of them committed suicide and another thirty-three tried but failed. These suicides, which Lombard likened to a "fad" (*mode*) during a 2009 press conference, were hardly an unintended consequence of France Telecom's cost killing spree. In a memo dating from late 2006, the new CEO vowed that, under his tenure, 22,000 employees would be made to leave— "whether through the door or through the window," he added.[17] And indeed, defenestration turned out to be one of the preferred modes of suicide in the Didier Lombard days at France Telecom.

Of course, the art of bringing supposedly abusive welfare recipients and allegedly superfluous staff to suicidal depression is hardly unknown outside of Europe. However, it is important to recall that, prior to the neoliberal era, European citizens were especially prone to identify social benefits with vested rights and to assume that laid-off workers should be compensated. Thus, I would argue that their lasting attachment to the welfare state of yore is what makes harassment especially appealing to European governments and corporations. The former find it politically riskier to suppress a social program altogether than to tell its recipients that they don't deserve the benefits to which they claim, while the latter find it more expedient to make their employees feel unworthy of their jobs than either pay the required firing compensation or wait for drastic reforms of the labor laws.

How far can governing agencies afford to go in order to lock people in their discredited condition? In some European countries such as Hungary, Rumania, and Bulgaria, as well as France and Italy, the treatment inflicted on the Roma offers a frightening answer to this question. As the French sociologist Éric Fassin recently noticed,[18] the kind of harassment to which the Roma are subjected does not quite fit in with Michel Foucault's famous opposition between the sovereign's license to kill and the right to let some people die, which the author of *The Will to Knowledge* associates with biopolitical power. For, on the one hand, even the openly Romaphobic regime of Viktor Orban, the Hungarian prime minister, refrains from orchestrating the pogroms organized by the fascist militants of its sometimes partner Jobbik. But on the other hand, it would be highly inadequate to claim that the Roma are merely neglected.

For instance, in the French context, which is Fassin's focus, public authorities actively endeavor to render the life of the Roma population unbearable. Called nomadic because they are so frequently expelled from the insalubrious quarters in which they attempt to settle, portrayed as dirty because garbage trucks and sanitation services carefully avoid the zones where they live, the 18,000 Roma dwelling on French soil are also castigated for not sending their children to school—regardless of the fact that they are never allowed to stay long enough in the same place to register them. They are also accused of being culturally disposed to beg instead of looking for a job—regardless of the fact that they are denied access to legal working permits. In sum, far from turning a blind eye to the Roma's lot, French elected officials—such as ex-socialist Prime Minister Manuel Valls—interpret their condition as the expression of a radically alien culture. Although their European citizenship protects them against effective deportation—or, rather, *because* they cannot be expelled once and for all—Romanian and Bulgarian Roma are made to understand that going back to their country of origin is their "calling."

Constructed—and made to identify—as the absolutely discredited people, the Roma are the ultimate testing ground for harassing techniques. Yet, paradoxically, their treatment at the hands of some European governments can also be perceived as the last cruel remnant of actually existing neoliberalism with a human face. Indeed, to the extent that their lack of valuable assets is allegedly unredeemable—since it is supposed to be a cultural trait—their very presence is both a blemish with respect to the attractiveness of the country hosting them and a mode of reaccreditation for the relatively discredited minorities who live in their vicinity. For the latter, complaining about the nuisances attributed to the Roma helps them feel closer to the creditworthy majority—whose members are expected to share their sentiment—and thus part of a neoliberal social compact predicated on comparative appreciation. To put it bluntly, Romaphobia can be an asset, especially for those who don't have much in their portfolio.

REPLACEMENT

Remarkably at odds with the OECD's virtuous recommendations—regarding the necessity of investing in human capital—the third major technique purported to boost the credit of a country consists in fostering the emigration of its educated youth. Whereas in Greece and Spain, the drought of job opportunities persuaded many people to try their luck elsewhere, for both the Irish and Portuguese governments, encouraging their own population to leave became a deliberate and explicit policy.

In Ireland, a country with a population of 4.6 million people, more than 500,000 nationals left between 2008 and 2014—a 289 percent increase compared to the previous six years. At the moment of peak emigration in the summer of 2013, 16,000 Irish citizens were emigrating every week. While 87 percent of these half-million emigrants were less than forty-four years old when they left,[19] 67 percent had at least a college degree. Before 2008, Ireland figured among the OECD countries with the most people under thirty—about 16 percent. Soon enough, the number was down to 12 percent, and continued falling. Considering that the rate of unemployment among the people under twenty-five was 28.6 percent, the fact that the Irish youth migrated en masse is not surprising. According to a survey commissioned by the National Youth Council of Ireland, one of every two Irish young people seriously contemplated emigration as the only way to survive.

Far from passive, Irish public authorities did not just acknowledge the situation; they actively supported the trend through indirect stimulation and direct encouragements. On the one hand, to make sure that young people thinking about emigration would get their act together and actually do it, the government drastically reduced welfare benefits for people under twenty-five—from 144 to 100 Euros per week. Moreover, thanks to the so-called Jobbridge internships, whereby most of the young people who work are only paid fifty Euros more per week than if they were unemployed, the ministry of labor made sure that living below the poverty line was not the privilege of the jobless youth. On the other hand, public institutions offered explicit encouragements to putative emigrants: in 2013, the Irish employment office sent more than 6,000 letters to young employment seekers about job offers in Australia, Canada, the U.S., and the UK. Hence the accusation of deliberately forcing young people to emigrate leveled at the government by a member of the Sinn Fein opposition.

Now, to be fair, the Irish authorities did not push everybody out. While they seem to have decided that, by staying at home, their young and educated citizens would most probably face a depreciation of their human capital— thereby bringing down the capital value, and thus the attractiveness, of the entire country, with them—Dublin proved most welcoming to tax-averse multinationals like Apple, Google, and Facebook. In a country known for its frequent rainfalls that recently gave its residents a new water tax, companies enjoy the lowest tax rate in Europe—12.5 percent, austerity notwithstanding, compared to an average rate of 27 percent for the rest of the EU. Better still, until 2020, Apple and its peers will benefit from the so-called "double Irish" scam, which entitles corporations to divide their fiscal duty between Ireland (where the rate is very low) and tax shelters such as the Virgin Islands (where there is no rate at all). Exemplary of actually existing neoliberal reasoning, the efforts deployed by the Irish government to lure big multinational corporations are the exact counterpart of its determination to persuade young and educated Irish people that they should leave. Now of course, trading human capital for glowing brands makes little business sense—since the companies for which these brands stand produce nothing on Irish soil. Yet, from the perspective of creditworthiness, the swap is a clear win-win operation— since the assets of the emigrating youth are unlikely to be appreciated in the short run.

While Dublin's authorities were still cautious about asking their young constituents to migrate—nudging is as far as they go—Portuguese officials had no qualms about being explicit. "If you are unemployed, you have to leave your comfort zone and go beyond borders," the sports minister told his young compatriots in 2011.[20] Adopting a more positive tone, one of his colleagues added that emigration would endow the Portuguese youth with a much-needed "cosmopolitan outlook." The prime minister himself, Pedro Coelho, soon joined his voice to the chorus, calling upon jobless teachers to exercise their profession in Brazil or Angola—otherwise, he probably meant, those countries would have been colonized in vain.

Like in Ireland, large numbers of young college-educated Portuguese citizens have left their country. In 2012, the year after encouraging emigration officially became a public policy, about 10,000 people were leaving a country of 5.6 million every month, half of them under thirty and highly skilled. Portugal has been subjected to the same austerity program as Ireland—in both cases, courtesy of the infamous Troika (the European Commission, the European Central Bank, and the International Monetary Fund). The two countries shared the same high rates of unemployment, especially among young people. Where Portugal differs from Ireland, however, is in the nature of the swap. Rather than substituting prestigious corporate brands for home-grown human capital, Pedro Coelho's team endeavored to replace educated but prospect-less Portuguese youth with foreign but affluent retirees. In January 2013, Lisbon's authorities created the status of "non-habitual fiscal resident." The beneficiaries of this status are exonerated of all income tax for ten years—a Portuguese version of the "double Irish"—provided they buy real-estate property and reside in Portugal for at least 183 days every year. As with the Irish swap, it would seem that, in the long run, trading young and skilled locals for wealthy but retired foreigners is not such a profitable deal. But then again, actually existing neoliberalism is about raising the credit of a country *now*—about boosting its per capita capital-value *immediately*—and not about ensuring sustained profitability.

NEGLECT

Finally, a fourth way of attending to the creditworthiness of the European population is to curb the inflow of people who are not presumed to be very bankable. To this end, both European institutions and member states have been especially careful to keep African migrants and asylum seekers from reaching the shores of southern Europe too easily. Two kinds of statistical evidence attest to the intensity of their efforts. First, between 1994 and 2014, a minimum of 25,000 people died while trying to cross the Mediterranean—some from drowning, others because their boats were simply left to drift for weeks. And this despite the heavy patrolling and permanent scrutiny to which European authorities subject the sea.[21] Second, with respect to refugees, it is noteworthy that, until the 1990s, 85 percent of the people who sought asylum in Europe got it; more recently, however, the rejection rate is around 85 percent.[22]

The number of casualties has dramatically soared in recent years. Before the infamous "summer of migration" in 2015,[23] 3,419 people died in the Mediterranean in 2014 alone. However, what European governments call their efforts to "regulate" immigration date back to the 1990s, which is precisely when they were busy deregulating financial markets. Throughout the period preceding the crash of 2008, the proponents of neoliberalism with a human face were already engaged in dissuasive tactics—such as blocking access to the most convenient points of entry so as to increase the distance and the danger of migrants' journeys—but without disavowing their alleged attachment to bring the talented and hardworking to Europe. Thus, one preferred way of keeping their noses clean, so to speak, involved outsourcing the dirty work of "regulated" immigration to the so-called transit countries of North Africa—especially Libya and Morocco. Indeed, the latter received ample funding, either from individual states like Italy and Spain or from the

European Commission, both to upgrade their navy and police forces and to build detention camps for aspirant migrants from sub-Saharan Africa. Though such camps were not held to very high human rights standards—as surviving detainees reported—sometimes the Europe-funded police of the transit countries found it more expedient to dispose of the migrants in more radical ways. For instance, in October 2005, members of Doctors Without Borders found a group of around five hundred men, women, and children who, after being expelled from the Spanish enclaves of Ceuta and Melilla, had been brought by the Moroccan police to the desert neighboring the Algerian border and simply abandoned there without food or water.[24]

Prior to 2008, outsourcing the roughest aspects of their immigration policy enabled European authorities to maintain their ostensibly balanced approach, according to which immigration was a good thing, for migrants and for the countries hosting them, as long as it was properly regulated. However, once the recession hit, the language of regulation quickly gave way to that of restriction: Europe, according to its political leaders, could no longer afford to be so generous. Until the winter of 2011, the change of rhetoric was not very consequential, as the economic downturn in the North considerably reduced the flow of emigrants coming from the South. Yet, when the bloody aftermath of most Arab Springs turned parts of North Africa and the Middle East into war zones, substantial cohorts of asylum seekers attempted to cross the Mediterranean to European shores—200,000 in 2014.

Determined to take in as few refugees as possible, European governments were nonetheless a little reluctant to openly assume their inhospitality—especially once they decided to intervene militarily in Libya, in the name of humanitarianism. Thus, from early 2011 to fall 2013, their attitude toward people fleeing wars in Libya and later in Syria was essentially one of malign neglect. Exemplary in this respect is the case of the so-called left-to-die boat carrying seventy-two people who escaped from Tripoli, in March 2011[25]—at a time when French and British ships were besieging the Libyan capital. As the survivors later recounted, the boat ran out of fuel and drifted for two weeks before landing back on the Libyan coast. By then, sixty-three passengers had perished, and two more died in the following days. During that period, the migrants successively saw a military aircraft and a military helicopter fly over them—the latter came back a second time to drop a few bottles of water and packets of biscuits on their boat—and a French military ship that provided no assistance at all—though its crew took some pictures of them before departing.

This neglectful approach to the swelling number of asylum seekers lasted until October 2013, when a boat carrying Eritrean and Somali refugees sank near the Italian island of Lampedusa: 366 people drowned. The magnitude of the tragedy produced enough of a shock, in Italy at least, to persuade Enrico Letta, who was then head of the Italian government, that letting asylum seekers die at such a high rate was no longer an option—if only because Italy's reputation was at stake. He thus launched the operation Mare Nostrum, whereby the Italian navy, police, and army were mobilized, not only to patrol the Mediterranean but also, and primarily, to rescue the boats carrying African and Middle Eastern refugees. While human rights and humanitarian organizations largely recognized the merits of Mare Nostrum—in less than one year, about 160,000 migrants were rescued—Italy's European partners refused to contribute to the operation. Their alleged motive was that the humanitarian nature of the operation actually encouraged asylum seekers and other migrants to try their luck, thereby increasing the chance of more shipwrecks, but also the overall inflow of asset-less foreigners. Faced with Europe's' enduring neglectfulness—as well as domestic complaints about the operation's cost—Matteo Rienzi, Letta's successor, ended operation Mare Nostrum in November 2014. What replaced it was a fully European operation called Triton. Whereas the Italian endeavor was primarily about rescuing people and operated on a budget of about nine million Euros per month, Triton costs about one-third of that sum—divided among twenty-one members of the EU—and focuses primarily on what European institutions call "border management." In other words, its main purpose is to patrol European territorial waters, intercept migrant boats, detain their passengers, send them back to the southern side of the Mediterranean, and, by that token, hopefully dissuade future candidates. The results of the new European operation have been stark. On February 11, 2015, an estimated 300 people died attempting to reach the island of Lampedusa from Libya. Europe's policies of malign neglect are back in place.

Obfuscating unemployment numbers, harassing to death superfluous employees and burdensome welfare recipients, swapping underpaid college-educated youths for glossy brands or rich retirees, and, last but not least, turning a blind eye to drowning asylum seekers: such are the core components of actually existing neoliberal endeavors. Disposing of the discredited is an effort to boost Europe's standing in the eyes of potential investors. Using the same logic, Wolfgang Schäuble, the former German finance minister and arguably the most influential European leader during his tenure, floated the idea of extending the weeding-out process to the entire country of Greece—though his heart's desire, the "Grexit" experiment, was ultimately not to be.

Once again, the EU is certainly not the only actually existing neoliberal power that resorts to such techniques of government. The Economic Policy Institute shows that the decreasing rate of unemployment in the U.S. is largely due to what the researchers call "the missing workers," meaning the 2.8 million Americans between the ages of eighteen and sixty-two—half of them between twenty-five and fifty-four—who stopped looking for a job and were thus removed from the official statistics.[26] As for the treatment of migrants and asylum seekers, Australia's policies, under its conservative government, makes the EU look like it actually does put a human face on its immigration controls. But what is distinctive about Europe's pursuit of creditworthiness is the fact that, like Japan, a rapidly ageing population is its main demographic feature. Indeed, most of the EU members states have a low and regularly declining birthrate, while the life expectancy of their senior population continues to increase. It is under these conditions that the European political agenda wages a passive-aggressive war on immigration, pushes the young and skilled to emigrate, and invites foreign retirees to take their place. Contrary to what disenchanted Europhiles often claim, this shows that there is such a thing as a "European project." And what this project involves is turning the EU into a gated community for aging yet affluent white Europeans—a project that often goes by the name "Fortress Europe."[27]

Some may object that, no matter how hard they try, European authorities will of course never succeed in disposing of all the people who are presumed to lower their territory's credit. Still, what truly matters is that they actually have a project (even if it has a utopian dimension) and that they pursue it to the best of their abilities. Finally, yet another objection could be raised, though this time about the sustainability of such a project. For if Portugal's previous plot is the template of things to come, what Europe is facing, short of discovering fresh reserves of rich retirees, is a new twist in Keynes's prediction—namely, that the rentiers whose demise he announced have decided to take protracted euthanasia into their own hands. But then again, we should remember that long-term considerations are foreign to credit-seeking asset managers. This is not only because, as Keynes also wrote, in the long run we are all dead. For while they are hardly preoccupied about how their gambling impacts other people's present, speculators are equally unfazed by the prospect of a catastrophic after-tomorrow. No matter how gloomy the distant future promises to be, they are confident that, as long as financial markets are protected, the near future, which is the only time they care about, will always come first.

At first glance, one would probably be hard-pressed to find a silver lining in what I have presented. Yet, I believe that there is one. Admittedly, the pursuit of creditworthiness so far has been informed by what investors are expected to find attractive. But it does not need to be so. What makes actually existing neoliberalism so objectionable, I contend, is not that it substitutes credit for profit—as if there were so much to regret—but rather what it considers to be valuable assets. The problem is not credit *per se*, but who gets it, and for what. In other words, instead of lamenting the hegemony of predatory speculators, opposing actually existing neoliberal agencies should be about challenging them on their own turf. Against the self-depreciating effects of left melancholy, "another speculation is possible" could be a valuable rallying cry.

Afterword

In January 2015, Alexis Tsipras, the leader of the left-wing party Syriza, won the legislative elections in Greece and received a mandate to reject the debt consolidation program imposed on the country by the so-called Troika. What his platform questioned was the very notion that a democratically elected government was required to submit the needs of its constituents to the demands of its creditors. However, after a dramatic six-month standoff and despite a referendum confirming the Greek electorate's defiance, Athens was eventually blackmailed into subservience. Though reelected in the wake of his capitulation, Alexis Tsipras became little more than a local enforcer of the EU's agenda.

Merely a few weeks after the Greek government's surrender, the European consensus faced a second major challenge. But this time the threat did not come from a subaltern member-state; it came from the European Union's own headquarters. In the closing days of August, Chancellor Angela Merkel declared that welcoming asylum seekers onto European soil—and especially refugees from war-torn Syria—was both morally mandatory and economically feasible. European leaders were understandably taken aback by this sudden plea for hospitality. For until Merkel's unexpected turnaround, a main area of agreement among EU officials had been to represent immigration as a problem in need of tougher border control and increasingly dissuasive legislation.

Acting as the towering champion of fiscal discipline, German finance minister Schäuble had proved remarkably successful at persuading his European partners that Syriza's proposals had to be met with unwavering intransigence. Even elected representatives of nations almost as debt-ridden and impoverished as Greece—Ireland, Spain, Italy, Portugal—refrained from questioning Berlin. Regardless of whether crushing budgetary cuts required them to reduce their deficits, Germany said that debtors cannot not be choosers. Berlin's notoriously irresistible influence did not extend so far, however, when Angela Merkel spoke of "fundamental European values."

By the fall, the chancellor found herself increasingly isolated. Domestically, prominent members of her Christian Democratic party—and even of her own cabinet—openly expressed discontent with her appeal to *Wilkommenskultur*, "a culture of hospitality." Internationally, opposition did not merely come from overtly xenophobic regimes in Central and Eastern Europe. Following the ISIS attacks in Paris, the vast majority of European public officials claimed that the terrorist menace called for a more restrictive asylum policy. Thus, after Merkel looked in vain for a compromise that might save her from reneging on her initial commitments without further alienating her partners, she eventually gave her voice to the European choir. Inhospitality, she reckoned, was as nonnegotiable as austerity. Nonnegotiable, that is, even despite an ageing population and a deflation-ridden economy that could eventually render Europe unattractive to investors.

In the short run, quelling the "Athens Spring" and frustrating Merkel's "German Dream" preserved Europe's approach to financial attractiveness. Yet it hardly improved the standing of EU leadership among European citizens. For measures purported to valorize the most appreciated portfolios and to discount the allegedly unappreciable ones do not address the lot of those credit seekers who neither benefit from market deregulations and regressive tax reforms nor range among the disposable segments of the population. Given the disappointing record of the Third Way governments' employability programs and the disastrous outcome of debt securitization schemes designed to create what George W. Bush labeled an "ownership society," appeasing the anxieties of the middle class was going to require fresh modes of asset appreciation.

Whether conservative, liberal, or nominally social-democratic, European governments did not wait for the outcome of the Brexit referendum or the Donald Trump election to co-opt the concerns—and even the recommendations—articulated by the far right. Mainstreaming phobias kindled by populist firebrands has accompanied the financial turn of European capitalism with varying degrees of intensity. And in doing so, it has served two purposes. First, blaming unemployment, stagnating wages, and bankrupt public services on migration and on the cultural elites who deny its costs and dangers proved an expedient way to divert popular discontent with the social impact of debt consolidation policies. Second, the ensuing rise of extreme right parties proved useful during electoral campaigns, since it persuaded left-leaning voters to treat mainstream parties as a lesser evil.

However, the political use of nationalist rancor has recently extended beyond the purposes of an outlet or a foil. Encouraged by the surprising events of 2016—and notwithstanding their dismay with British secessionism and American protectionism—most European leaders are now reconciled with the idea of investing in a new category of assets. Through discursive as well as practical incentives, underappreciated yet undisposable nationals are enticed to experience their status as natives, the color of their skin, the gender norms they uphold, and the cultural traditions they identify with as so many valuable assets in their portfolio. Hence the growing number of EU member-states— Italy, Austria, Finland, Denmark, Hungary, Poland, Slovakia, Bulgaria— whose governments have either included or enjoyed the support of openly xenophobic parties.

In Europe and across the developed world, asset appreciation has become the main engine of growth at both microeconomic and macroeconomic levels. But because the pursuit of capital gains hardly causes wealth to "trickle down," public officials who stake the prosperity of their country on its financial attractiveness are engaging in a different kind of wager. They are increasingly inclined to dispose of the poorly rated segments of their population and to valorize the features that enable citizens to distinguish themselves from the discredited. Far from being a challenge to the hegemony of global finance, the resurgence of European nationalisms—in the name of ethnic, cultural, or religious integrity—is integral to its speculative logic.

Notes

1. See Adam Tooze, *Crashed: How a Decade of Financial Crises Changed the World* (New York: Penguin Random House, 2018).
2. On the fashioning of the neoliberal agenda, see among many other accounts, Philip Mirowski and Dieter Plehwe, eds., *The Road from Mont Pèlerin:*

The Making of the Neoliberal Thought Collective (Cambridge, Mass.: Harvard University Press, 2009); Daniel Stedman Jones, *Masters of the Universe: Hayek, Friedman, and the Birth of Neoliberal Politics* (Princeton, N.J.: Princeton University Press, 2012); Angus Burgin, *The Great Persuasion: Reinventing Free Markets since the Depression* (Cambridge, Mass.: Harvard University Press, 2012); and Christopher Payne, *The Consumer, Credit and Neoliberalism: Governing the Modern Economy* (New York: Routledge, 2012).

3. Friedrich A. Hayek, "Why I Am Not a Conservative," in *The Constitution of Liberty* (Chicago: University of Chicago Press, 1960), 406–7.

4. On the Chicago School's approach to competition—developed in the 1950s by the Chicago Antitrust Project whose directors were Milton Friedman, Aaron Director, and Edward Levi—see Rob van Horn, "Reinventing Monopoly and the Role of Corporations: The Roots of Chicago law and Economics," in *The Road from Mont Pelerin*, 204–36.

5. The principles and agenda of the Law and Economics movement can be traced to Michael C. Jensen and William H. Meckling, "Theory of the Firm: Managerial Behavior, Agency Cost and Ownership Structure," *Journal of Financial Economics* 3 (1976).

6. See Henry Manne, "Mergers and the Market for Corporate Control," *Journal of Political Economy* 73 (1965). The impact of Law and Economics on corporate governance—and on the dissolution of the corporation—is brilliantly described in Gerald Davis, *Managed by the Markets: How Finance Reshaped America* (Oxford: Oxford University Press, 2011), 59–101.

7. Wolfgang Streeck, *Buying Time: The Delayed Crisis of Democratic Capitalism* (London: Verso, 2014), 80.

8. See Streeck, "The Crises of Democratic Capitalism," *New Left Review* 71 (September–October 2011): 7–9.

9. See Martha Poon, "From New Deal Institutions to Capital Markets: Commercial Consumer Risk Scores and the Making of Subprime Mortgage Finance," *Accounting, Organizations and Society*, special issue, *Tracking the Numbers: Across Acounting and Finance, Organizations, Markets and Cultures, Models and Realities* (2008).

10. Marion Fourcade and Kieran Healy, "Classifications Situations: Life-Chances in the Neoliberal Era," *Accounting, Organizations and Society* 38 (2013): 539–72, and Davis, *Managed by the Markets*, 191–234.

11. See David Weill, *The Fissured Workplace: Why Work Became So Bad for So Many and What Can Be Done to Improve It* (Cambridge, Mass.: Harvard University Press, 2014).

12. Adam Ferguson, *An Essay on The History of Civil Society* (Cambridge: Cambridge University Press, 1996), 119, and Hayek, *New Studies in Philosophy, Economics and the History of Ideas* (London: Routledge and Kegan Paul, 1978), 264.

13. John Maynard Keynes, Chapter 12, "The State of Long-term Expectation," in *The General Theory of Employment, Interest and Money* (1935; repr. London: Palgrave Macmillan, 2007).

14. Achille Mbembe, *Critique de la raison nègre* (Paris: La Découverte, 2013).

15. This story was told by David Stuckler and Sanjay Basu, in *The Body Economic: Why Austerity Kills* (New York: Basic Books, 2013).

16. "Atos Comes under Attacks in Emotional Commons Debate," *Guardian*, January 17, 2013.

17. "Suicides à France Telecom: Un document accablant," *Le Parisien*, May 7, 2013.

18. Éric Fassin, Carine Fouteau, Serge Guichard, and Aurélie Windels, *Roms et riverains: Une politique municipale de la race* (Paris: La Fabrique, 2014).

19. Irial Glynn, Tomás Kelly, and Piaras MacÉinri, *Irish Emigration in an Age of Austerity* (Cork: Irish Research Council, University College Cork, 2013).

20. "Como Passos e outros governantes apelaram à emigração," *DN Política*, January 17, 2013.

21. For the number of migrants who died on their way to Europe, the two main sources are a report from the International Organization for Migration (IOM), *Fatal Journeys: Tracking Lives Lost During Migration*, 2014, and data collected by the Migrant Files (European consortium of journalists).

22. Anthropologist Michel Agier, in *Rapport d'Audit de la Politique d'immigration de Nicolas Sarkozy: À de mauvaises questions, apporter de pires réponses*, Cette France-là, 2011, http://www.cettefrancela.net/IMG/pdf/CetteFrance La-rapport_audit.pdf.

23. Sonja Buckel, "Welcome Management: Making Sense of the 'Summer of Migration,'" *Near Futures Online* 1, "Europe at a Crossroads," March 2016, http://nearfuturesonline.org/welcome-management-making-sense-of-the -summer-of-migration/.

24. *Le livre noir de Ceuta et Melilla*, Migreurop, 2006, http://www.migreurop .org/article981.html?lang=fr.

25. Forensic Oceanography—*Report on the "Left-To-Die Boat,"* Charles Heller, Lorenzo Pezzani, and SITU Studio, part of the European Research Council project "Forensic Architecture," Centre for Research Architecture, Goldsmiths, University of London, https://forensic-architecture.org/investigation/the-left -to-die-boat. See also Charles Heller and Lorenzo Pezzani, "Ebbing and Flowing: The EU's Shifting Practices of (Non-)Assistance and Bordering in a Time of Crisis," *Near Futures Online* 1, "Europe at a Crossroads," March 2016, http:// nearfuturesonline.org/ebbing-and-flowing-the-eus-shifting-practices-of-non -assistance-and-bordering-in-a-time-of-crisis/.

26. "Missing Workers: The Missing Part of the Unemployment Story," Economic Policy Institute, https://www.epi.org/publication/missing-workers/.

27. Fassin and Windels, "The German Dream: Neoliberalism and Fortress Europe," *Near Futures Online* 1, "Europe at a Crossroads," March 2016.

Neoliberalism, Rationality, and the Savage Slot

Julia Elyachar

In the early decades of the twentieth century, liberalism was in crisis, and its utilitarian roots were compromised.[1] The bloody savagery of WWI threw the Western world into debates about the meanings of "rationality" and "irrationality" and about how to distinguish the "civilized" from the "savage" after the boundaries between them had been repeatedly challenged on multiple fronts. The debates drew in intellectuals and polemicists from the German-speaking world, whom we now read separately in anthropology, economics (of a particular kind), sociology, political science, and law.[2] Putting this broader context into view can help us better comprehend some of neoliberalism's mutations during this centenary year of the Versailles Peace Treaty of 1919. In this chapter, I trace the outlines of this grand debate about rationality vs. irrationality and the civilized vs. the savage out of two empires dismantled at the close of WWI: the Austro-Hungarian Empire and the Ottoman Empire.

My immediate focus is on a concept from this period in which debates about rationality and irrationality in economy overlapped: "tacit knowledge." The concept played a minor but crucial role in debates among exiled Austro-Hungarians during the interwar period, which were formative for neoliberalism, before drifting into management and organizational theory during the 1990s. This intellectual history is important in and of itself.[3] But my concern here is otherwise. By reading together key texts in foundational moments of anthropology and of what we now call "neoliberalism," I show how an obsession with the "primitive" and the "irrational" was shared across emergent fields of economics and anthropology and should be read as part of one discursive terrain shaping political discourse 100 years later.

To foreshadow my argument, I will show how reactionary liberal theorists who gave birth to neoliberalism confronted the "irrational" at the heart of the civilized world, blaming it not on the Great War but on delusional and traitorous efforts of socialists to undermine the free market and its constitutive form of rationality. In this moment, and in the fateful decades to come, socialists moved into the "savage slot" of the civilized world, to draw on the influential phrase of Michel-Rolph Trouillot.[4] While early neoliberals uncovered the irrational in socialist efforts to institute economic planning, early anthropologists located the "rational" in ritual exchange practices of primitive man. Decades later, when the Soviet Union collapsed and the utopian vision of a "global free market" reigned triumphant, tacit knowledge migrated into the management laboratories of corporate America roaming the globe in search of new terrain for profit. At the centenary of the Versailles Peace Treaty in 2019, accusations that socialists, indigenous activists, and climate rebels are willfully undermining Western Civilization increasingly resound from militarized fortresses of neoliberal market fundamentalism.

A "Nation at Risk" and Tacit Knowledge in the Corporate Body

In 1983 the United States Department of Education published a report called "A Nation at Risk" to call attention to a growing "knowledge gap" between the United States and the Soviet Union. That report prompted the CEO of the Xerox Corporation, David Kearns, to establish the Xerox Palo Alto Research Center (PARC) to help "rethink learning" and to "look at the wide variety of ways people learn successfully in daily life." Jean Lave's seminal concept of "communities of practice," formulated during her ethnographic research with tailors in Liberia, gave PARC an analytic frame to reconsider the "knowledge problem" framed during the calculation debate and early neoliberal conflicts with victories of collectivism and socialist planning. Lave's student Étienne Wenger took the concept of communities of practice into the corporate world, where such communities could be vessels for the cultivation of tacit knowledge and the free source of profits it promised.[5] A vast literature in management and organizational theory on tacit knowledge focused on how organizations could learn how to learn and profit from this tacit knowledge. By learning how to find and format tacit knowledge, corporations could better compete in a neoliberalizing global market economy.[6]

The Soviet Union collapsed in 1991, and fear in the United States that it was losing the knowledge wars receded. But research on tacit knowledge flourished. By the late 1990s, academic and corporate ethnographers had studied practices of photocopy repair technicians, bakers, and weavers, to name just some examples of the kinds of tacit knowledge analyzed by social scientists in the management and organizational literature.[7] By the 2000s, tacit knowledge had become a strategic resource of the nimble learning corporation. In a cover story of *Business Week* called "Eureka, We Failed! How Smart Companies Learn from their Failures," readers learned the extent to which learning—learning how to learn, and learning how to benefit from learning within companies and among customers—was the key for survival in a globalized economy where breakthrough innovation was imperative for survival. In a world where product cycles were shorter than ever, the *Business Week* article went on, organizations had to be "well-honed" and "built for efficiency and speed to do what feels unnatural: Explore. Experiment. Foul up, sometimes. Then repeat." As the managing director of the consulting firm Innosight put it, "Figuring out how to master this process of failing fast and failing cheap and fumbling toward success is probably the most important thing companies have to get good at."[8] This kind of fumbling toward success, drawing on all pockets of neglected tacit knowledge in the corporation, lay at the core of success in a global neoliberal political economy. But to unravel the forgotten warp and weave of neoliberalism and the irrational in our world today, we need to go further back.

The Socialist Calculation Debate and the Question of Rationality

The notion of tacit knowledge is usually attributed to Michael Polanyi and his book *The Tacit Dimension*.[9] M. Polanyi has mainly been read as a philosopher of science and would seem to have little to do with Austrian economist and neoliberal polemicist Friedrich von Hayek. In fact, the two were interlocutors and part of the same community of Austro-Hungarian exiles in the interwar period.[10] The link between them, and the problem of irrationality that tacit knowledge aimed to solve, goes back years, just after the Versailles Peace

Treaty and the Bolshevik Revolution when economists took up the problem of how to measure value in a world without price.

The "socialist calculation debate" of the 1920s and '30s arose after the establishment of the Soviet Union turned theoretical debates about value and price in the critique of political economy into urgent real-time problems. Could an economy be run without the price mechanisms of a "free market"? If so, how? Socialists argued that it could. Reorganizing society on the basis of a planned economy could give a rational basis for organizing society's affairs. Here it is important to note a crucial difference in how the two sides of this debate used the word "rational."[11] From the theoretical approach of a Marxist political economy, "rational" here implies a world where the distorting veil of price and commodity fetishism has been stripped away together with the ownership rights of individual capitalists. From this perspective, prices were an epiphenomenon distorting real value. Nascent neoliberals would draw on a quite different perspective on "rationality" to launch their attack.

The debate began when Ludwig von Mises, secretary of the Vienna Chamber of Commerce since 1909 and organizer of one of the most prominent seminars of the period (which involved his student Friedrich von Hayek) attacked Lenin, singling out a problem where the Bolsheviks were at their weakest. In the third section of his essay "Economic Calculation in the Socialist Republic," Mises quotes and immediately attacks Lenin's statement from 1918 that "the immediate and most pressing task of Russian communism was 'the organization of bookkeeping and control of those concerns, in which the capitalists have already been expropriated, and of all other economic concerns.'"[12] Mises also took on the argument of Otto Neurath, a leading Vienna intellectual—and during the short-lived Bavarian Soviet Republic its head of planning in Munich—that "lessons of the war economy" could be drawn on for a centrally planned "natural economy" without money or prices.[13] In Mises's view, both Lenin and Neurath were tragically wrong. With the attempt to calculate in a socialist commonwealth, "an entirely new problem is here involved which it is impossible to solve with the conceptual instruments of 'bourgeois culture' or with lessons from the so-called 'natural economy'"[14]

Mises scoffed at Lenin for wanting to "re-introduce into Soviet business 'bourgeois' bookkeeping carried on a monetary basis" and transform banks "into the nodal point of social bookkeeping under socialism." Socialism could not solve its problems by importing techniques of accounting via money price from a capitalist to a socialist setting.[15] In a passage that sounds remarkably like Marx on the capitalist in the first volume of *Capital*, Mises wrote, "It is not a knowledge of bookkeeping, or business organization, or of the style of commercial correspondence, or even a dispensation from a commercial high-school, which makes the merchant, but his characteristic position in the pro-duction process, which allows of the identification of the firm's and his own interests."[16] Mises's polemics against Lenin were extended in his critique of Neurath, who was equally deluded. Socialists, Mises proclaimed had not even begun to think seriously about the issues involved with socialist economics.

Mises framed his question as follows: Could an economy be organized in rational fashion without a free market and the price system? His answer was a definitive no. The word "rational" is key here—likewise, its different meaning for Mises vs. for Lenin or Neurath. According to Mises, a price sys-tem based on private ownership of the means of production was about more than increasing production or profits. It was a vast calculating device through which something that Paul Samuelson would in the next decade call "revealed preferences" of embodied subjective value could be accessed and expressed.[17] The price system was a translation device; it rendered the inexplicable ex-plicable and the incommensurable commensurable in the universal language of money price. The price system "effectively computes the solution to an enormous number of mathematical conditions."[18] From Mises's perspective, planning could never achieve a Pareto-optimum equilibrium condition of ef-ficient resource allocation.[19]

Socialist Irrationality and the Willful Primitive

It would be a mistake to read this clash as involving only different approaches to economics or political economy or as a difference in political philosophy. Rationality itself was at stake. And rationality was the distinguishing hallmark that liberalism claimed for itself and Western civilization. Mises made his ar-gument against the socialists with recourse to words like "delusion" and "in-sanity." Socialists were "deluded" about the possibility of rational economic planning. This delusion further abetted the tendency among intellectuals and members of political elites in the U.S. and Europe to fall into the "confused embrace of collectivist and socialist fantasies" that put the "precious legacy of European liberalism" even more at risk.

With any attempt to impose even piecemeal measures of central planning, techniques of planning would spread like cancer and "inevitably lead to a completely centrally planned economy, which would in turn be devoid of any 'rational economic system.'"[20] On the one hand, Mises reduced both economy and rationality to the problem and techniques of economic calculation. Rationality as the hallmark of Western civilization became economic rationality as he understood it. Then, he hypostasized economic action as human action as such. (In the process, he anticipated key aspects of the "formalist" position in economic anthropology some thirty years later.) Without what Mises called "economic calculation" there could be neither economy nor rationality. In a socialist state wherein the pursuit of economic calculation was, by his definition, impossible, there could be no economy and no rationality. In trivial and secondary matters rational conduct might still be possible, but in general it would be impossible to speak of rational production anymore. There would be no means of determining what was "economically rational." It was even questionable if there could be any such thing as rational conduct at all under socialism—even among "civilized" Europeans.

Mises took pervasive debates about rationality and irrationality that the Great War had moved out of the province of the "primitive" into the heartland of Europe and pinpointed responsibility for irrationality among civilized Europeans on socialists and collectivists. Socialists willfully cultivated the conditions of irrationality that early anthropologists and travelers had said characterized "primitives." Rationality here can be read through Talcott Parson's translations of Max Weber, in terms of "instrumental rationality" *cum* weighing of alternative means to reach given ends (and what formalist anthropologists would soon call "economization"). How could rationality continue in the European heartland when socialists divorced it from the very grounds of its generation?[21]

Theories and Politics of Value

In the eyes of civilized Europeans before the Great War, rationality versus irrationality overlay the dividing line between the civilized and the primitive. In the interwar period, a broad range of writers trying to save and renew "liberalism" portrayed "collectivism" as an attack on "Western" or "European" civilization, or on "civilization" as a whole.[22] This is an overlooked but central aspect of the calculation debate. It was in this context that Mises accused the socialists of willful irrationality. Changes in economic theory also shaped terms of clash in the calculation debate. An emergent "subjective theory of value" that focused on changes at the margin moved economic theory away from an "objective theory of value" in political economy of the English-speaking tradition, with its focus on a lump amount of a certain good (or use value). The "marginalist turn" is usually identified as the significant break with political economy. But the associated rise of a subjective theory of value—which originated with the thought of sociologist Georg Simmel as much as with anyone read today as an economist—stems from a time when in the German language economics and sociology were not yet distinct and separate fields.[23]

Along with notions of rationality, theories of value were changing. Value is a central category in the history of political economy, and a simple storyline of the history of economic thought goes something like this: for mercantilists, gold is the source of value; for the physiocrats, land was the source of value; in classical political economy of the nineteenth century, labor is the source of value, and it remained so (with revisions) in Marx. All of these theories shared the assumption of an objective source of value. For Mises and the rest of the Austrian School, value existed in the relation between two people and a desired object or between two objects and one individual. Value was a triadic relation. Without prices there would be no way to render value comprehensible and commensurate and to rationally organize economic life. By way of contrast, in the Marxist tradition, labor-power was the source of value, and labor-time was the yardstick for its measurement. Real value had been veiled by price under capitalist relations of production. Under socialism, value as congealed socially necessary labor time—not money price—could be accounted for directly. But knotty theoretical dilemmas of the "transformation problem" of value to price in production cycles were difficult to work out. That said, for decades the consensus was that the socialists had won this debate. The modes of economic planning they developed were long successful and their contributions to macroeconomic theory many.[24] That success and those contributions were rendered invisible in the years of neoliberalism's hegemony and need to be remembered in these years of its mutating ideological demise.

From Primitive Irrationality to The Sensory Order

In the first round of the calculation debate in the aftermath of WWI, the question of rationality and irrationality was directly stated. The issue was not yet formulated as a "knowledge problem" in which tacit and irrational preconceptual impulses could find rational expression only on the free market. The solution to civilizational irrationality courted by socialists would only emerge in the 1930s, in the work of Mises's student, Friedrich von Hayek. The concept of "tacit knowledge," usually credited to Michael Polanyi, was decisive in this transition.[25]

Michael Polanyi was a chemist and polymath who became an anticommunist after visiting the Soviet Union to investigate Soviet claims to a proletarian science. Polanyi studied chemistry, served in the Austro-Hungarian Army during the Great War as a medical officer, and became a professor of chemistry in Berlin. He left Germany for a position in chemistry in Manchester when the Nazi Party came to power in 1933 and shifted to the social sciences in 1948. After a visit to the Soviet Union in 1936, he spoke publicly and often against the idea of state involvement in the conduct of science. In scientific inquiry, matters must be left to evolve as a "spontaneous order." The phrase "spontaneous order" was in turn associated with tacit knowledge. This linked pair became key to a second phase of the neoliberal attack on socialism after WWII. Whether the concepts should be credited to Polanyi or to Hayek is a matter of debate.[26]

Polanyi spent the rest of his life arguing that tacit knowledge proved the necessity of "freedom" in scientific and economic life. Even in his own field of chemistry, the "most exact of sciences," Polanyi argued, something "inexact" was essential to scientific discovery.[27] This inexact source of knowledge lay inside the discrete individual. It was a semi-spiritual and yet physiological essence that shaped even the most explicit of pursuits—scientific inquiry. Tacit knowledge was present in all kinds of thought of which we are but "subsidiarily aware," as Polanyi put it, lying behind the "focal content of our thinking."[28] This kind of knowledge could not be made explicit or available to individuals, let alone collectivist economic planners.

Hayek was born into a family of intellectuals and landowners. He claimed relation to Ludwig Wittgenstein as a second cousin and, after the latter's success, noted Wittgenstein's influence on his early work.[29] Hayek studied brain anatomy as a young man and was part of research projects critical of empiricists and logical positivists. Already in the 1920s, before he began to study economics, Hayek began his first research project, which would be published as a book called *The Sensory Order* only in 1952.[30] In the language of early twenty-first-century neuropsychology, Hayek showed that much of perception is "pre-conceptual" and not readily accessible to conscious thought.[31] While sympathetic to socialism in his youth, as the student of Mises his intellectual agenda was shaped by anticommunism and anti-collectivism as much as his earlier interest in neuropsychology.

Michael Polanyi and Hayek were part of the same intellectual world. Through whatever process, they came to share key metaphors in their quite different areas of work. Polanyi used metaphors of the free market to discuss science; Hayek used the concept of tacit knowledge to give new foundations to antisocialist polemics. Polanyi argued that there should be no central control, planning, or "any form of association that determined the actions of its members" in science or, by extension, in economy. A businessman needed to rely on "freely available information to adjust the prices of his goods," thus helping in this indirect way to steer the course of production. This was just like how "the scientist used the results published by other scientists in determining the course of his own research; and knowledge accumulated as a result." The scientist needed to be like "an independent businessman in liberal society."[32]

For both Mises and Hayek, planning was objectively impossible. Formal economic models and statistics gathered by the state could not take into account unsystematized forms of knowledge that are experienced as part of the body itself, rather than being formed in the brain through the study of books. This is what Hayek used the concept of tacit knowledge to convey. In a free market system, with wide distribution of ownership of the means of production, price was an existential matter. For the market is a mechanism for transmission of irrational impulses and tacit knowledge across communicative channels that are an essential infrastructure of economic life.[33] Without this price mechanism no one can "know" the economy—certainly not one person, party, or state organization. The price system alone provides that communicative infrastructure essential for the economic provision for human needs. Any movement attempting to strip away the price system, meanwhile, was seen as launching an existential attack on human order, civilization, and rationality.

The Politics of Irrationality

The British Empire and its allies had been victorious in WWI. But ideological underpinnings of the British Empire and its "civilizing mission" had come unhinged. Assumptions of the superior rationality of Western "civilized" man were central to British liberal imperialism. That mission had been challenged in different realms of empire; at home, capitalism had been challenged in waves of socialist and communist revolt. Liberal imperialism and utilitarian classical political economy implied that natives under British imperial rule could be weaned away from their irrational impulsive nature by alterations in social arrangements (unlike earlier biological theories of racism). Even the most backward subject of empire had the potential to develop and act rationally. The British Empire had exactly this "civilizing mission."

Liberal free market rationalities were under attack on all sides after the Great War. Communists, socialists, fascists, and progressive liberals all wanted to overcome the atomizing and corrosive impact of the unrestrained free market by developing new techniques of planning and calculation.[34] Mises took them all on. These debates were enmeshed in broader political problems that today we think of as separate. The National Socialists rejected liberal political order because it led to the domination of partial economic interests over things of existential importance for the nation as a whole. A faction of the Nazi movement (including a translator of Adam Smith's *The Wealth of Nations*) was opposed to the domination of Anglo-American financial power and "capitalist imperialism" internationally.[35] The German Empire had less of a colonial presence than the other victorious British and French; territories it formally possessed were confiscated and handed over to the Mandate System after the Great War. Post–WWI colonial efforts were sporadic and troubled; continued efforts to colonize inside Europe were both tragic and far beyond the scope of my discussion here. For European powers without many colonized peoples seen as "primitives" abroad, socialists at home took over the "savage slot" that so obsessed European thinkers in the British and French empires.[36]

With victory of the Bolshevik Revolution and communist victories in Central Europe, irrationality—and reckless abandonment of civilization—seemed to be sweeping into the heartland of Europe. For reactionary liberals like Mises, socialists were just that: voluntary "primitives." Socialists and collectivists stripped themselves of the price system—at best, through delusion, and at worst, to devastate the Western world. In the process they destroyed the possibility of a functioning economy and fatally undermined rationality itself. Denuded of rationality, what would remain to distinguish civilized European men from the primitive other of the Western civilized self? This was not a new fear. The figure of the "primitive man" is prominent in most early economics textbooks: it was the essential figure against which *homo œconomicus* was built. Mises brought this lurking background of the primitive to the center of debate about rationality and civilization via economy in the aftermath of the Great War.

Rationality and Irrationality: Austro-Hungarians among the "Primitives"

While Mises accused socialists of unleashing irrationality in civilized Europe, anthropologist Bronisław Malinowski was asking similar questions about rationality among "the primitives." Malinowski's *Argonauts of the Western Pacific* (1922) is long credited, if now controversially, with giving birth to the anthropological method of ethnography and to economic anthropology. Just like Mises and Hayek, Malinowski was born a subject of the late Austro-Hungarian Empire. Like Hayek, Malinowski would end his life a British subject and employed for much of his career at the London School of Economics (LSE). Like the early Hayek as well, Malinowski was immersed in reflection on the nature of rationality and economic life.

Malinowski's first studies had been in mathematics and physical sciences; his Ph.D. dissertation in philosophy was called "On the Principle of the Economy of Thought."[37] After reading Frazier's *The Golden Bough*, he was famously inspired to study anthropology and went to London to study with Charles Seligman, first professor of ethnology, and Edvard Westermarck, professor of sociology at the London School of Economics. Another well-known (and critiqued) origin story of anthropology: Malinowski had wanted to go to Australia to conduct research on aboriginals (then considered to be the best living exemplar of "primitive man") and only ended up staying in the Trobriand Islands as an Austro-Hungarian enemy and alien of the British Empire due to the outbreak of WWI.

When Malinowski embarked on his fieldwork, he expected to find something quite distinct from the maximizing rational English economic man. He hoped to find a nonmaximizing nonutilitarian man. To his surprise, after he set up his tent in the center of the Trobriand villages, he found activity that he recognized as economic and yet, as stated by Frazier in a preface to Malinowski's 1922 *Argonauts*, "not based on a simple calculation of utility." Something beyond utility prevailed: exchange could also satisfy "emotional and aesthetic needs of a high order."[38] Here, too, we see the pervasive interest at the time in rationality and high-order values. Malinowski transferred into British social anthropology the kind of German-language debates about rationality, which I discussed earlier, in the work of Mises and his followers (as well as in Max Weber and others).[39]

The centerpiece of Malinowski's book on the Trobriand Islands is the chapter "The Secret of the Kula." The kula would become a hallmark of thinking about the workings of a nonmarket society, building on Mauss's seminal notion of the gift as the counterpart to the "invisible hand" in the market. The kula consisted of two forms of exchange: "ritual exchange" of arm-shells and necklaces in which high-status men alone participated and ordinary trade and bartering like street markets that circle a main colonial square in many cities of the world. Both aspects of the kula were rational in their own way: they both served a function, albeit in relation to different aspects of man's needs and ultimate values—be they biological, aesthetic, or emotional. Primitive man was revealed to be enmeshed in a parallel kind of "spontaneous order" that gave underlying rationality to his actions, even if there was no price system to reveal that which lay inside:

> What appears to us an extensive, complicated, and yet well-ordered institution is the outcome of ever so many doings and pursuits, carried on by savages, who have no laws or aims or charters definitely laid down. They have no knowledge of the total outline of any of their social structure. . . . Not even the most intelligent native has any clear idea of the Kula as a big, organized social construction, still less of its sociological function and implications.[40]

Malinowski used the word "economic" repeatedly in his analysis of kula. That "economic" had nothing to do with markets, let alone a free market with dispersed ownership of the means of production (such as preoccupied Mises and the Austrian school of economics). Nor was there any production in play. But kula was economic in Malinowski's terms: it served a function in an overall system. Kula mediated systems of power and prestige in the region; it shaped systems of barter and trade in everyday useful objects that were clearly "economic"; and it revealed a form of value, with these odd, apparently useless trinkets mediating passions and interests of these "primitive peoples." The vast chain of kula exchanges across the Trobriand Islands created a huge trading network something like long-distance interisland trade. Primitives were rational even while driven by a powerful desire to possess, and then give away, seemingly worthless kula shells.

Malinowski's analysis of kula would become the iconic example of reciprocity and gift—even as it was, in his view, an "economic institution." Learning about this economic institution was of utmost importance to him: there is "no other aspect of primitive life where our knowledge is scantier and our understanding more superficial than in Economics."[41] Malinowski may have hoped to find in the Trobriands among the "primitives" an "ideal type" of man that was the opposite of utilitarian *homo œconomicus* of liberal British imperialism that had rested from the start on contrast with a fictitious "primitive man." In the end, Malinowski's "primitive" man was rational and could no longer serve as a counterpart for the disappearing rationality of Western civilized man after the Great War.

Concluding Thoughts

Questions about rationality and irrationality, and the primitive versus the civilized were shared between neoliberals and anthropologists of economy in this historic moment. Anthropology has long recognized that the "savage" colonial subject was coeval with the civilized colonizing West. But we have barely remembered how much these theories are coeval as well.[42] They are part of a broad reckoning with the disasters of WWI, the end of empires, and the transposition of debates about rationality into "economy" in the foundational moves of economics away from political economy. Like the discipline of anthropology itself, neoliberalism was constituted in an encounter with mass violence, collapse of empire, and the struggle against socialism, seen as a new locus of the irrational primitive other.

Malinowski and Mises need to be read together; just like the worlds they studied, they are coeval. Theories thought to be about the primitive were in part a projection of self onto subjected other. And theories invented in the study of "primitive economies" have turned out to be at least as useful for twenty-first-century business models as utilitarian liberal theory or neoclassical economic theory in its undergraduate level formulas with rational individual actors weighing options in a world of perfect information. Tacit knowledge took off in the business world in the 1990s; with the rise of social networks and brand building in a digital world, the gift and kula became intuitive ways of pursuing profit.

Hayek, I have said, naturalized the "willful irrationality" that his teacher Mises had said was cultivated by the socialist European. Both the economics we know as "Austrian" and the ideology we call "neoliberal" naturalized Mises's obsession with the willful irrationality of the socialists. If Hayek naturalized irrationality in the civilized, then what happened to his fellow Austro-Hungarian's discovery of the rationality of the so-called primitive? I cannot pursue this part of the story in the same detail here, but in short: Malinowski's student Evans-Pritchard made a parallel move to that of Hayek and his naturalization of irrationality: Evans-Pritchard naturalized the "rationality" of "the primitive." Here, I refer to Evans-Pritchard's famous discussion of rationality and irrationality in the case of Azande witchcraft. Based on his discussions with his "informants," Evans-Pritchard proposed that "we" take seriously the Azande theory that something called a "witchcraft substance" could be located in the body.[43] The presence of witchcraft substance in the physical body of the witch (in the context of a pervasive social belief in witchcraft), Evans-Pritchard argued, did not prevent the Azande from having a perfectly rational and logical understanding of causality in other aspects of life. Like any rational civilized Westerner, the Azande had the capacity to distinguish between proximate and ultimate cause in a chain of events, even if ultimate cause was culturally specific.[44] The "primitive" was rational. Only his ultimate causes, or secondary values, were different than those of *homo œconomicus*. Witchcraft substance, the anthropological equivalent of tacit knowledge, was located inside the body.

By the turn of the millennium, in anthropology and other modes of critical inquiry, "neoliberalism" had become a curse word—a "floating signifier" for something we were all against but could not quite define.[45] In such a context, I have argued, locating and analyzing transformations and transmutations of some mythical, pure, original neoliberalism is insufficient. Something else is needed. In this chapter, I thus returned to the broader discursive field out of which two matched pairs of thinkers—neoliberals and anthropologists hailing from the same (former) region of the world—pursued and transposed questions of rationality and irrationality into the sphere of economy. I noted that socialists were committed to rationality and objective value as a basis for collective life. This was methodologically opposed to the theory of subjective value and fetishization of the individual in the neoliberal critique of discredited liberal thought. I then pulled this thread of tacit knowledge out from the tangled mess that neoliberalism has wrought, beginning with the first stages of the Central European debate. The concept of tacit knowledge, I showed, was central to Mises and Hayek's argument about why only the price system could extract unconscious irrational impulses into actionable information and why, according to the neoliberals, socialism was but a pernicious delusion and utopian dream. By now, of course, we know that the free market they espoused against socialism was at least as utopian. Reading Mises together with Malinowski, and Hayek with Evans-Pritchard, as part of a shared world, makes all of this much easier to see.

Along with others after the Great War, Mises perceived the multiple ways in which the irrational played itself out in the action of civilized Western man. He chipped away at the possibilities for an objective theory of value. But his religion of one—the individual agent, brought together with others only through the market and price—overwrote all. This individual agent was an illusion, and yet critiques of early neoliberal thinkers have overlooked the implications. Other solutions might be sought with inspiration from the distributed agency of the Egyptian popular masses in times of revolt, or in the collective agency of Brazilian masses demanding elections, or in the distributed neural networks of the brain.[46] From these perspectives, the entire basis of the neoliberal critique of socialist planning dissolves. The notion that a discrete individual could be the basis of anything—including that individual businessman enshrined by Michael Polanyi and Hayek as the model for scientific inquiry and economic action alike—appears as much an artifact of ensorcelled colonialism as do colonial displays of indigenous sacred objects in a museum. But legacies of socialism's appeals to "rationality" need to be overcome as well.

To exorcise hauntings of the world we inherited from the last crisis of liberalism, now 100 years after the signing of the Treaty of Versailles, we cannot simply accept the terms in which these problems of neoliberalism and rationality have been framed. Even tracking a simple concept such as "tacit knowledge" that weaves through the great debates and their consequential solutions of the long twentieth century helps us see how this is so. Charges of treason launched by Mises against socialists who willfully upended the fundamental values of Western civilization were no random flourish of rhetorical excess. As socialism gains renewed appeal among young people coming of age in the devastation that neoliberal fundamentalism has wrought, we can expect to hear accusations of irrationality and treason once again.

Notes

1. My reading of the crisis of liberalism is influenced by Tomaž Mastnak, *Liberalizem, fašizem, neoliberalizem* (Ljubljana: Založba, 2015).

2. In Germany, economists were doctors *rerum politicarum* (not *economicarum*) and worked together with jurists.

3. I present some of this history in Julia Elyachar, "Before (and after) Neoliberalism: Tacit Knowledge, Secrets of the Trade, and the Public Sector in Egypt," *Cultural Anthropology* 27, no. 1 (2012): 76–96.

4. I borrow this concept from Trouillot; see Michel-Rolph Trouillot, "Anthropology and the Savage Slot: The Poetics and Politics of Otherness,"

republished in Trouillot, *Global Transformations: Anthropology and the Modern World* (New York: Palgrave Macmillan, 2004).

5. For discussions of this history, see Jean Lave, *Apprenticeship in Critical Ethnographic Practice*, Lewis Henry Morgan Lecture Series (Chicago: University of Chicago Press, 2011); John Seely Brown and Paul Duguid, "Organizational Learning and Communities of Practice: Toward a Unified View of Working, Learning, and Innovation," *Organizational Science* 2, no. 1, Special Issue, *Organizational Learning: Papers in Honor of (and by) James G. March* (1991): 40–57.

6. Research then moved into the problems of how to help organizations benefit from this revealed knowledge. Chris Argyris's influential concepts of double-loop learning and learning resistance addressed problems that arose when the knowledge garnered from the study of workers was formatted into knowledge from which managers were supposed to benefit; see Argyris, Robert Putnam, and Diana McLain Smith, *Action Science* (San Francisco: Jossey-Bass, 1985).

7. See, for example, Haridimos Tsoukas and Nikolaos Mylonopoulos, "What Does It Mean to View Organizations as Knowledge Systems?," in *Organizations as Knowledge Systems: Knowledge, Learning and Dynamic Capabilities*, ed. Haridimos Tsoukas and Nikolaos Mylonopoulos (New York: Palgrave Macmillan, 2004); Marleen Huysman, "Communities of Practice: Facilitating Social Learning While Frustrating Organizational Learning," in Tsoukas and Mylonopoulos, *Organizations as Knowledge Systems*; and Ikujiro Nonaka and Hirotaka Takeuchi, *The Knowledge-Creating Company* (New York: Oxford University Press, 1995).

8. Both quotes are from the article "Eureka, We Failed! How Smart Companies Learn from their Failures," by Morton Skogly, in *Businessweek*, July 10, 2006, 44. As noted to me by William Callison, this supports Jamie Peck's 2010 analysis of neoliberalism as perpetually "failing forward"; see Peck, *Constructions of Neoliberal Reason* (Oxford: Oxford University Press, 2010).

9. Michael Polanyi, *The Tacit Dimension* (Garden City, N.Y.: Doubleday, 1966).

10. See Richard Hull, "The Great Lie: Markets, Freedom and Knowledge," in *Neoliberal Hegemony: A Global Critique*, ed. Dieter Plehwe, Bernhard Walpen, and Gisela Neunhoffer (New York: Routledge, 2006), 141–55; and Philip Mirowski, "Economics, Science, and Knowledge: Polanyi vs. Hayek." *Tradition and Discovery* 25, no. 1 (1998): 29–42. Even those who reject the notion that Polanyi had an influence on Hayek point out that theories considered "Hayekian" or "Austrian" might better be thought of as "Austro-Hungarian"; see John P. Bladel, "Against Polanyi-Centrism: Hayek and the Re-Emergence of the 'Spontaneous Order,'" *Quarterly Journal of Austrian Economics* 8, no. 4 (2005): 15.

11. For one discussion, see William Callison, "Politics of the Rational: The Austrian School, Max Weber, and the Socialist Calculation Debate," in "Political Deficits: The Dawn of Neoliberal Rationality and the Eclipse of Critical Theory" (Ph.D. diss., University of California, Berkeley, 2019).

12. Ludwig von Mises, "Economic Calculation in the Socialist Commonwealth," in Collectivist Economic Planning: Critical Studies on the Possibilities

of Socialism, ed. F.A. Hayek (1935; repr. London: Routledge and Kegan Paul 1963), 125. The passage he cites from Lenin is from Vladimir Lenin, "On the Immediate Tasks of the Soviet Government," April 30, 1918. Mises cited the German translation, "Die Nächsten Aufgaben der Sowjetmacht" (Berlin: Verlag der Kommunistischen Bibliothek, 1918).

13. See Otto Neurath, "Wesen und Weg der Sozialisierung," in *Wissenschaftliche Weltauffassung, Sozialismus und Logischer Empirismus*, ed. Rainer Hegselmann (1919; repr. Frankfurt am Main: Suhrkamp, 1979), 242–61; Neurath, *Economic Writings: Selections 1904–1945*, with an introduction by Thomas E. Uebel (Dordrecht: Kluwer, 2004); Gunther Chaloupek, "Otto Neurath's Concepts of Socialization and Economic Calculation and His Socialist Critics," in *Otto Neurath's Economics in Context*, ed. Elisabeth Nemeth, Stefan W. Schmitz, and Thomas E. Uebel, Vienna Circle Institute Yearbook 13 (2007): 61–76; Hull, "Great Lie," 146.

14. Mises, "Economic Calculation in the Socialist Commonwealth," in *Collectivist Economic Planning*, ed. F. A. Hayek (1920; repr. London: Routledge and Kegan Paul, 1935), 125–26.

15. Ibid., 121.

16. Ibid.

17. Paul Samuelson, "A Note on the Pure Theory of Consumer's Behavior," *Economia*, n.s., no. 5 (1938): 61–71.

18. Ibid.

19. Duncan Foley, *Adam's Fallacy: A Guide to Economic Theology* (Cambridge, Mass.: Harvard University Press, 2006). As Foley notes, outside of the socialist world, theories of market socialism contributed to the rise of mathematical general equilibrium theory in the 1930s and 1940s.

20. Mises, "Economic Calculation," 121.

21. Foley, *Adam's Fallacy*, 18.

22. See Mises, *Liberalism: The Classical Tradition* (Indianapolis: Liberty Fund, 2005); Hayek, *The Road to Serfdom*, with Foreword by John Chamberlain (Chicago: University of Chicago Press, 1944); Walter Lippmann, *An Inquiry into the Principles of the Good Society* (Boston: Little, Brown, 1937).

23. For this line of argument, see Jörg Guido Hülsmann, "Introduction to the Third Edition: From Value Theory to Praxeology," in *Epistemological Problems of Economics*, trans. George Reisman, 3rd ed. (Auburn, Ala.: Ludwig von Mises Institute, 2003).

24. Foley, *Adam's Fallacy*.

25. Michael Polanyi was the brother of Karl Polanyi, author of *The Great Transformation*. For a brilliant analysis of their intellectual world, see Hull, "Great Lie."

26. "Spontaneous order" is usually associated with Hayek, but the consensus has shifted to his having borrowed the concept from Polanyi, even if publications of The Mises Institute still claim it for Hayek. For the view that it was Michael Polanyi's concept, see Struan Jacobs, "Spontaneous Order: Michael

Polanyi and Friedrich Hayek," *Review of International Social and Political Philosophy* 3, no. 4 (2000). Claiming the concept for Hayek is Bladel, "Against Polanyi-Centrism," 15–30. Istvan Hont, on the other hand, traces the concept of spontaneous order back to Adam Smith; see Hont, *Jealousy of Trade: International Competition and the Nation-State in Historical Perspective* (Cambridge, Mass.: Harvard University Press, 2005).

27. See, for example, Jerry H. Gill, *The Tacit Mode: Michael Polanyi's Postmodern Philosophy* (Albany: State University of New York Press, 2000); Michael Polanyi, *Personal Knowledge: Toward a Post-Critical Philosophy* (Chicago: University of Chicago Press, 1974); and Michael Polanyi, *Tacit Dimension* (1966).

28. Polanyi, *Tacit Dimension*, x–xi.

29. Alan O. Ebenstein, *Friedrich Hayek: A Biography* (Chicago: University of Chicago Press, 2003), 305.

30. Hayek, *The Sensory Order: An Inquiry into the Foundations of Theoretical Psychology*, with an introduction by Heinrich Klüver (Chicago: University of Chicago Press, 1952).

31. See, for example, the writings of José Luis Bermúdez, on how "phenomenological insights into bodily awareness and its role in agency can be developed and illuminated by research into somatic proprioception and motor control"; Bermúdez, *The Bodily Self: Selected Essays* (Cambridge, Mass.: MIT Press, 2018), 15.

32. John R. Baker, "Michael Polanyi's Contributions to the Cause of Freedom in Science," *Minerva* 16, no. 3 (1978): 382–96.

33. Julia Elyachar, "Phatic Labor, Infrastructure, and the Question of Empowerment in Cairo," *American Ethnologist* 37, no. 3 (2010): 452–64; Elyachar, *Semiotic Infrastructure: Phatic Labor, Collective Goods, and Theory from the Semi-Civilized* (forthcoming, 2019); Kockelman, "Enemies, Parasites, and Noise: How to Take Up Residence in a System Without Becoming a Term in It," *Linguistic Anthropology* (November 2010).

34. Mastnak, *Liberalizem, fašizem, neoliberalizem.*

35. Ibid.

36. See Trouillot, "Anthropology and the Savage Slot." We could also analyze the ongoing string of substitutions of these ratios of equivalence to note the importance of the "Slavic slot" in German National Socialism. Thanks to Paul Kockelman for pointing this out to me.

37. On Malinowski's studies and early writing, see Andrzej K. Paluch, "The Polish Background to Malinowski's Work," *Man*, n.s., 16, no. 2 (June 1981), 276–85.

38. Bronisław Malinowski, *Argonauts of the Western Pacific* (London: Routledge, 1922/1984), 83.

39. See Callison, "Politics of the Rational."

40. Malinowski, *Argonauts.*

41. Ibid., 84.

42. An exception, if with a different analysis, is Chris Hann and Keith Hart, *Economic Anthropology* (Cambridge and Malden, Mass.: Polity Press, 2011).

43. E. E. Evans-Pritchard, *Witchcraft, Oracles, and Magic among the Azande* (1937; repr. Oxford: Clarendon Paperbacks, 1958), 1.

44. See the classic book by Stanley Tambiah, *Magic, Science and Religion and the Scope of Rationality* (Cambridge: Cambridge University Press, 1990).

45. See especially the concept of Claude Levi-Strauss, "Introduction à l'oeuvre de Marcel Mauss," in *Sociologie et anthropologie*, by Marcel Mauss (Paris: Presses Universitaires de France, 1950); English translation *Introduction to the Work of Marcel Mauss*, trans. Felicity Baker (London: Routledge and Kegan Paul, 1987), 62–63. I also have in mind Catherine Malabou's revisiting of Levi-Strauss's concept in her lecture "The Floating Signifier Revisited," Gauss Seminars in Criticism, Princeton University, February 2018.

46. On distributed agency in times of revolt, see Elyachar, "Upending Infrastructure: Rethinking Agency after the January 25th Revolution in Egypt," in *Distributed Agency*, ed. Paul Kockelman and Nick Enfield (New York: Oxford University Press, 2016); and the opening paragraphs of Miguel Nicolelis, *Beyond Boundaries: The New Neuroscience of Connecting Brains with Machines—and How it Will Change Our Lives* (New York: St. Martins, 2011).

SEVEN

Sexing Homo Œconomicus:
Finding Masculinity at Work

Leslie Salzinger

At the fulcrum of neoliberalism stands a choosing subject: homo œconomicus.[1] Despite his central role in the system, he is a present absence, a "correlate of governmentality" who "rationally" (thus predictably) responds to threats and incentives.[2] The neoliberal self is intentionally skeletal, thinned to a productive receptivity that presumes no interfering identity, affect, body, or intimate context. That elegant figure is misleading however. In presuming that it is possible to divorce the subject from his animating content and context, neoliberal theorists ignore the patriarchal relations and gendered performances that make him tick. In the following pages we will track him in situ—from his Foucauldian portrait to his home in the market to media accounts of his bestial alter ego. Scrutinizing these sites reveals a fuller character, a normative man buttressed by the prerogatives of patriarchal power, incited by the pleasures of masculine performance and vulnerable to aspersions of its escape from control. Thus viewing him in context(s) reveals masculinity's pivotal role and varied manifestations at crucial moments in the functioning of the neoliberal economy.

Of course, as multiple historical accounts suggest,[3] capitalism has long been dependent on discourses and enactments of masculinity. There is nothing unique about masculinity's consequential role in neoliberalism. However, across contexts, difference works differently. It is all too easy to confuse masculinity's reiterated presence in capitalism with either analytic necessity or identity across time.[4] The substance and role of masculinity in capitalism are not fixed, and delineating how these unfold in practice is an essential element in understanding the functioning of actually existing neoliberalism.[5] Thus my goal in exploring the distinct ways that the gendered nature of homo œconomicus matters in neoliberalism is precisely to underline the historical specificity of this relationship and to argue for a more fully fleshed understanding of how neoliberalism actually operates in space and time.[6]

In carrying out this project, we will move through three arenas: Foucault's text on homo œconomicus; an ethnographic account of a trading desk set at a hub of the global money supply; and the scientific investigation and public discussion of the disruptive role of testosterone in financial markets during the 2008 crisis. Each account illuminates a distinctive way in which neoliberal capitalism's operations are premised upon masculinity's persistent and persistently naturalized presence. In the first case, the purportedly ungendered figure of homo œconomicus obscures the social context that enables his economic functioning and hence keeps the question of reproductive labor from coming into view. In the second case, masculine challenges and displays both undergird and fuel the operations of foreign exchange markets. And in the third, anxieties over "irrational exuberance" are projected onto the male body, sidelining discussions of institutional and regulatory failures. Together, these accounts illustrate some of the many ways that the unacknowledged gendering of the paradigmatic figure of neoliberal reason obscures the social context of the economy itself. Neoliberalism—notoriously encapsulated in Thatcher's dictum "there is no society"—is premised on a fundamental refusal to recognize social structure. Within the actual market, masculinity's unmarked form proves to be an ideal partner for that truly antisocial project.

View 1: Homo Œconomicus in the Text

Foucault's 1979 lectures on neoliberalism come early in his object's emergence. His writing traces the contours of the theory that both describes and prescribes the era as it emerges. Defining American neoliberalism as the "unlimited generalization of the form of the market,"[7] he dedicates these lectures to surveying the enactment and consequences of market logics for

noneconomic spheres and thus, characteristically, to interrogating the formations of the subjects such logics address. Principal among the neoliberal
claims he analyzes is their construal of the economy as made up of multiple
holders of capital, each of whom is an "entrepreneur of himself" who invests
in his own "human capital" and reaps its rewards. These analyses have the
virtue of "adopt[ing] the point of view of the worker" and making the study
of his "internal rationality" the central task of economic analysis.[8] Hence he
introduces his protagonist: *homo œconomicus*, neoliberalism's economic man.
Homo œconomicus is the calculating self who, in working to augment his
human capital, responds rationally to incentives. In so doing, he "accept[s]
reality" and becomes susceptible to the neoliberal governance that shapes the
options to which he responds.

The shift from an analysis of processes and relations to an analysis of the
rationality of an agentic subject raises some questions Foucault does not address. Primary among these is the question of gender. What are we to make
of the grammatical masculinity of homo œconomicus? Are we in the realm
of the neuter, the androgynous, the truly unmarked? Or is he more like the
"generic he"[9]—a normalizing masculine standard slipped into conventional
speech in the guise of grammatical convenience? Perhaps, rather than being
truly neuter, he is a man in disguise.

In a sense, of course, he is neither: homo œconomicus is not a human
being, he is "the surface of contact between the individual and the power
exercised on him."[10] Yet that contact requires an infrastructure to work, and
in this sense, the figure of homo œconomicus *is* socially masculine. Reading
the lectures alert to the social organization that enables him, we stumble over
"his family" listed amid his "private property,"[11] a wife negotiating over love-
making and feeding chickens, and a "mother" busy "forming" human capital.
After all, the rational, self-interested self who responds to "incentives," the
obsessed developer and custodian of his own human capital, the "entrepreneur of himself," requires a certain context. The state of single-minded focus
and permanent availability required to be an "enterprise for [one]self" implies another kind of self nearby, shouldering the labor involved in caring for
children, aging parents, and other forms of "inevitable dependency."[12] The
issue is not just that those who enact traditional femininity are excluded, but
more fundamentally, that the subject invoked here only makes sense if one
presumes an underlying support structure, constituted by a distinctive subject
whose attention is as resolutely focused elsewhere. As in many such contexts,
the unencumbered focus of some is premised upon its inverse in others.

This situation is elucidated elegantly by Melinda Cooper in her discussion of the incongruous alliance of neoliberal and neoconservative theorists in the arena of actually existing politics.[13] The apparent disjuncture between the purportedly amoral individualism of neoliberal ideology and the deeply moral critiques of new conservatives, she argues, is an illusion. In fact, welfare-state retrenchment, even if done in the name of individual autonomy, always requires someone to pick up the pieces—the old, the young, and the sick—in the end. And here the patriarchal family suddenly reemerges like a rabbit from a hat, to respond to the accidents of birth and death that ultimately define what it means to be human, no matter what political or economic system we live in.

Homo œconomicus's peculiar autonomy requires not only an underlying social scaffolding, but an affective one as well. Economic man is embedded in "civil society," Foucault tells us, but that embedding does not appear to entangle him emotionally. To the contrary, the more resolutely selfish he is, the more effectively the "invisible hand" can coordinate his self-interested actions with those of others, producing more for all. Brought to life in the "abstract" worker,"[14] his moral obligation is to single-mindedly develop his own human capital in the interest of a family whose actual care he can, and indeed must, ignore. In this formulation, love, caring, and personal obligations can only act as crude impediments. Nonetheless, someone must provide an affective container for this constrained subject, whose feelings are ruled out of court by definition. Homo œconomicus can only exist if others pick up the emotional slack, and so we return to a familiar gendered terrain.

This social situation, ironically, is made most vivid in Foucault's description of neoliberals' analysis of mothering, which he provides to demonstrate the impact of market logics outside the context of markets themselves.[15] And indeed at first it appears that the mother herself—the paradigmatic nonmarket actor—can be folded into the same narrative as a rational investor in the welfare of her children; we are all homo œconomicus now. But it turns out the mother is homo œconomicus with a twist. Unlike the normal economic man, whose investment redounds to his own human capital, her investments augment the human capital of her child, her own repayment not pragmatic, but in "psychical income"—the only figure whose rational investments do not improve her own "ability stream."[16] Luckily for the species, the mother's human capital, unlike that of the normal masculine homo œconomicus, is at one with her child's, thus allowing neoliberal theorists to subsume her within their framework, while still noting her ineluctable difference. Thus even as the argument attempts to contain reproductive labor and care work within its confines, they overflow its bounds. It is only through the mother's distinctively feminine commitment to a being outside herself that the family form presumed throughout the narrative can function.[17]

Homo œconomicus is certainly not biologically male, not even exactly a man, but his form of subjectivity and habitual social practices are viable only within the framework of the patriarchal family. That is, the productive fiction of economic man is enabled and constituted by heteronormativity as a structure as well as by the masculinity that it assumes, requires, and supports. Homo œconomicus's purportedly autonomous masculinity is a vital element in a system that obscures human needs and desires and thereby makes invisible the material, social, and affective labor that goes into responding to them. It is precisely the manly man, secretly lurking in the purportedly ungendered rational decisionmaker, who makes it possible for the latter to function and thus for the system that depends on him to operate. As such, this necessarily unmarked gendering is a vital element in the ideological functioning of neoliberalism overall.

View 2: The Man in the Market

Homo œconomicus is a theoretical fiction, but it is a fiction with teeth. If Foucault's analysis of homo œconomicus is one window onto its functioning, another portal is empirical. The economists describing neoliberalism were making it as they described it, and the markets they helped establish depend on traders who understand themselves and their decisions through the trope of homo œconomicus—rational, autonomous, and self-interested.[18] In markets on the ground, the idea of economic man is less descriptive than prescriptive, a model traders strive to approximate. In the flesh, however, economic man's manliness is no longer obscured. To the contrary, traders perform that self in explicitly masculine terms.

I am an ethnographer, and between 2001 and 2006, I spent six periods observing coupled "emerging markets" foreign-exchange trading desks in New York and Mexico City, both in a major transnational bank I call Globank. Global foreign-exchange markets are the largest, most liquid, and least regulated markets on the planet. What's more, the early 2000s was a defining period in Mexico's move from a "developing nation," theoretically accountable to its citizens, to an "emerging market," accountable instead to investor and global market—a neoliberalizing shift accomplished in part on this market terrain. In this context, Globank dominated global foreign exchange, with an especially powerful presence in Latin American markets. That makes these linked desks ideal sites in which to investigate homo œconomicus at work. During my time at the bank, I watched mostly Latin American young men trade Latin American currencies for dollars, in constant interaction with colleagues both crammed into the same desk and across national borders on open phone lines, and through screens with colleagues and competitors around the globe.[19]

Trading in a contemporary financial market requires a calculating self, fully immersed in the economic task at hand. It requires the capacity to make instantaneous decisions and not look back, to be located in a discrete present, diverted by neither hopes nor regrets. Foreign-exchange traders dealing in the currencies of their countries of origin—whether they are physically located at "home" or outside—cannot be distracted by nostalgia, dreams, or allegiances. Instead, such traders must hone the capacity for intense compartmentalization between public and private welfare, between patriotism and workday obligation, between citizenship and market role.

Speculating against one's homeland in turbulent moments, especially in emerging markets where the position held might tip the balance against a currency already close to the edge, is a psychologically complex task. But experiencing that conflict is a luxury allowed by neither a nearby boss nor a demanding market. "You can't be emotional," the Argentine trader shrugged stoically as the currency tumbled in one of his country's many crises. The bank helps this process by bringing traders up from their native countries and paying them in dollars for several years at a time, pragmatically forestalling any overidentification with the currency of home. Set in front of computers, their countries of origin made numbers on the screen, traders are hailed as rational decisionmakers, socially disembedded and accountable only to the bottom line, and they respond as such. Here is homo œconomicus incarnate.

However, it turns out even economic man traffics in meanings, and over time spent watching, these come into view. Globank traders were (and are) among the peso/dollar market's most powerful and dependable "market makers." That is, they commit, as representatives of the bank, to exchange pesos for dollars at a "fair" price to other market participants. At request, they will provide a "spread," in which they commit to a price in pesos at which they would be willing to buy dollars and a price at which they'd be willing to sell. The spread is kept narrow by market convention, the bid and offer yoked.

This forecloses the option to simply buy low and sell high, so the art of making money while making markets is intuiting whether the "aggressor" wants to buy or sell and then shading the prices so that whichever way the trade goes, it strengthens their own "position" overall. But profit or not, the most fundamental commitment, the trader point of "honor," is to give prices and to abide by the commitment made in so offering. It is only insofar as they and others engage in these rituals that the price-clearing market of neoclassical theory can come to life in practice.

Foreign-exchange markets are the world's least regulated financial markets. Although banks are institutionally bound by national legal systems, there is no supervising body empowered to regulate and sanction trading behavior in transnational space, thus there is no one who can legally force a trader to go through with a trade once accepted, even if the response turns out not to be profitable. This essential function is played instead by a set of informal expectations and sanctions, held by traders themselves, articulated through a masculinized rhetoric of "honor" and enforced both through an always already internalized idea of what a "professional" trader does, as well as by the external pressures of gossip and reputation. Thus a New York trader tells me:

> The most important thing you have is your credibility inside and outside the bank. . . . If you lose your credibility you're worth nothing. . . . Your word is everything. Like your honor. . . . If you renege on a deal, that guy will take care of making sure the whole market knows, the trade went against you and you pulled out.

Here, we find masculinized concepts of honor repeatedly cited by traders as fundamental guides, undergirding the very structure of the market itself.

This often implicit, earnestly held concept of masculine selfhood is located within a more theatrical version as well. On both desks I observed, traders explicitly performed masculinity at every opportunity, often with a wink at their own performance, but persistently nonetheless. They opened the day with punches and slaps, threw things at each other when things got slow, slammed phones down so hard they broke, played frequent, sometimes cruel, practical jokes on each other, sent and received dirty jokes on line. These performances were most striking in the process of trading itself, where traders routinely addressed each other *as* men, and masculinity became a kind of trading fuel. "Do it! Be a man!" a trader pushed his colleague, as he consulted on whether he should take a riskier position. "Oh, so now he's turned into a lady!" mocked another, hearing from his broker that someone didn't want to do a deal. "I thought you had balls," a third typed back to a counterparty and friend in re-sponse to an overly cautious price. The senior trader described "training" an intern as, "I'm on him, on him. Can you take the pressure?" Winning and los-ing were described in vividly gendered and sexualized terms, in which sexual position was often all one needed to know to estimate profit or loss: I fucked him; he fucked me; he doesn't have balls; he's a fag; he's a whore; I've got him tied down! Whatever they did, they did through a caricatured masculinized rhetoric, performing homo œconomicus as made-for-primetime tough guy.

The traders I observed were almost all men, of course, but the rare woman among them if anything further emphasized the powerful link between trad-ing and the masculine self. Among the thirteen traders in New York and the approximately twenty in Mexico City, there were two women traders. In New York, the only woman on the desk traded smaller currencies and so did not "carry risk," her presence thereby strengthening the ironclad link between masculinity and risk-taking. Her colleague in Mexico City, on the other hand, was known as the "ice queen," a formidable presence whose power in the mar-ket was rivaled only by the obsessive enactment of gendered difference, both on her part and on the part of her colleagues, outside it. In her presence dur-ing trading lulls, her colleagues' manly self-presentation shifted momentarily from tough guy to gentlemanly, even protective, courtly gestures re-marking her fundamental distinction. This dissonance finally came to a head at the end of my first period of fieldwork, when she resigned, fearing that it was the pressures of her job that were keeping her from being able to get pregnant with her second child.

One turbulent day on Globank's Mexico desk, I saw this in-market, mascu-line performance, and its economic consequences, with particular vividness. The desk forwards trader, after upholding the peso against the rest of the market for several weeks, realized he was too outnumbered and needed to cut his position to keep from being swamped by the rest of the market. At that point he could have started quietly unloading his position. But he instead, he started yelling, "If it's gonna blow, it'll be *me* who blows it!" "They want to stick it to me, I'm going to be the biggest bastard in the market!" He began yelling on the phone in English to his broker in New Jersey. "Damage! Dam-age! Damage! They want assholes, they've got assholes! Push it up! They want to fucking blow it, here goes!" A friend at another bank he'd been work-ing with called, furious, but he wouldn't take the man's calls. "Tell him not to put himself in front of me, tell him to get out of the way." His friend and boss, sitting beside him, laughed uproariously throughout, anxiety and admiration mingled in his comments: "It's going to hurt a bit next month." "What a mess we made!" Several hours later the market had moved a full percentage point, and traders around the city and across North America were licking their wounds. Notes started appearing his screen. "You're the king. . . ." "You're the greatest!" "I'd like to thank you for today. Hope you can give me a job." A local broker called. "The whole world's saying you're the king. . . . You made the market shake. . . . You're really something. . . . I take my hat off. . . . Even in New York they're saying it."[20]

In the market, the "professional" honor and calculating rationality of economic man are claimed without hesitation. Traders talk about responding to reality, about complex forms of autonomy and choice, about building their personal positions (in all senses), about efficiently responding to the conditions they are dealt. But they do so embedded within an explicitly masculine rhetoric, performed at high volume, and this rhetoric in turn is fundamental to the way the market works as a social space. As the New York–based spot trader recounted in talking about a female boss he'd had during his first job, "But really she was a man. She'd stand and shout across the room, 'You know why I don't wear a skirt? I've got balls!'" He laughs in understanding.

Unlike homo œconomicus in theory, here in an actual financial market, no one thinks economic man is gender neutral. To the contrary, his masculinity is self-evident, even as it is knowingly enacted. Both performed and performative: masculine market discourses address traders as men and in so doing regulate and fuel the neoliberal market itself.

View 3: The Body as Fall Guy

Homo œconomicus's masculine persona undergirds the logic of his functioning in theory, and his cartoonish performance greases the wheels of unregulated neoliberal markets in practice. But perhaps the clearest illustration of the figure's masculinity can be found in a set of expressions of anxiety around the male *body*, emergent during a period in which the market's "irrational exuberance" and subsequent crisis threw its purportedly machine-like workings into question. Homo œconomicus and his market analogs brim with confident self-assurance, but as markets bust and prognosticators lose their edge, we find a spate of market narratives in which masculine figures are replaced by male bodies—hormonal containers, alternately fueled and buffeted by chemicals that operate beneath their consciousness and yet that determine their most consequential moves. In this mediated arena, we can finally limn the consequences of a masculine term unable to give an account of its own etiology. As we shift the angle from which we view the neoliberal economy, masculinity's role comes most clearly into focus where it is most denied, where the role of the social itself is obscured by the presence of a male biology assumed to be prior by definition, to be always already in place.

The last few decades have seen a surge of research into the biological bases of human behavior, and the results have been breathlessly covered in the media. Much of this research and discussion has focused on gender, often with reference to testosterone and frequently located in the newer branches of neuroscience. "Neuroeconomics" is one such field, coupling a growing social obsession with the mechanics of the economy with biological explanations that locate its foundations beyond conscious human intervention. John Coates is a prominent figure in this field,[21] a retired trader educated in the academic humanities whose collaborations with colleagues in the neurosciences on the role of testosterone in trading behavior received outsize attention when their publication coincided with the 2008 financial crash.[22]

On April 13, 2008, a day before the publication of Coates's first article, the *New York Times* published a reassessment of Milton Friedman's legacy and of the mechanistic model that had heretofore guided the management of the U.S. economy under his influence:

> The downward spiral of the economy is challenging a notion that has underpinned American economic policy for a quarter-century—the idea that prosperity springs from markets left free of government interference.[23]

On April 14, with fortuitous timing, Coates published the first of several collaborative studies, all arguing for "a hypothesis he had developed while working on Wall Street—that endogenous steroids were shifting risk-preferences systematically across the market cycle, exaggerating the peaks and troughs."[24] "Endogenous Steroids and Financial Risk Taking on a London Trading Floor" looked at seventeen male traders over eight days, correlating testosterone and cortisol levels (established through saliva samples taken at the beginning and end of each trading day) with individual profit levels and indicators of "uncertainty" (market volatility). The authors argued that men with higher testosterone levels made higher profits, but that this was not an unmitigated boon. In the paper they cautioned:

> Cortisol is likely . . . to rise in a market crash and, by increasing risk aversion, to exaggerate the market's downward movement. Testosterone . . . is likely to rise

in a bubble and, by increasing risk taking, to exaggerate the market's upward movement. These steroid feedback loops may help explain why people caught up in bubbles and crashes often find it difficult to make rational choices.[25]

In a brief description of the work published in *Nature* online, the two authors disagreed on the implications of the study.[26] Coates argued that hormonal levels and swings led to profits and losses, while his neuroscientist collaborator argued more cautiously that they had established correlation between hormones and profits, not causation.

In Coates's second study, "Second-to-Fourth Digit Ratio Predicts Success Among High-Frequency Financial Traders," published nine months later, he and a second set of coauthors moved to investigate another aspect of the role of testosterone in trading. The study took as axiomatic the (contested)[27] claim that the ratio between the length of the second and fourth finger (termed 2D4D) was a "marker" for levels of prenatal androgen exposure and thus for adult men's sensitivity to the testosterone circulating in their systems. Given that premise, the authors looked at the relationship between finger-length ratios and monthly profits and losses over a twenty-month period among forty-four high-frequency traders in interest rate securities. They found that lower 2D4D ratios predicted higher profits during that time.[28] In a 2010 article summarizing the two studies, Coates argued that "economic agents are more hormonal than is assumed by theories of rational expectation," leading to exaggerated "appetites for risk" in the presence of testosterone and equally disproportionate caution in the presence of cortisol.[29, 30]

The epistemological logics, and hence the empirical claims, of this literature have been devastatingly critiqued by an impressive group of natural and social scientists.[31] They argue that these kinds of studies tend to read social expectations into biological data and to confound correlation with causation and thus to take biological primacy for granted. My interest is less in the "science" itself, however, than in what these studies can tell us about the gendering of the market subject. For this I turn to the media and blogosphere, where, in the context of the financial crisis, the possible pathology of the once acclaimed risk-takers who populated financial markets emerged as an issue and the studies became widespread objects of fascination.

In 2008 and 2009 there was a spate of coverage, at least fifty articles in major papers (including the *Economist*, the *Wall Street Journal*, the *New York Times*, *Businessweek*, and *Time*), coverage on all the large TV networks in the U.S. and the UK, and hundreds of reports in less major outlets on television and radio. The blogosphere, unsurprisingly, was awash in commentary, and in 2010, after the dust from the crisis had begun to settle, a Google search identified 632 discrete pages discussing the studies on line. Although Coates's own articles were written entirely straight, many of these articles were less so—by turns ironic and pedantic, funny and alarming, overflowing with irresistible sexual puns ("yes, size matters" was a frequent setup for these accounts). Yet these articles were ultimately not joking. To the contrary, in acknowledging that they were sophisticated enough to understand how silly it sounded, they managed to communicate that these "scientific" claims were no laughing matter.

These newspaper articles and commentaries made a series of claims about both traders and the markets they participated in. First, there were biological claims about traders themselves. A *Washington Post* article from April opened with the statement that traders are "slaves to their hormones" and continued by quoting Coates saying, "this is the biological substrate for winning and losing."[32] Elsewhere Coates was quoted discussing traders' possible "addiction"[33] to testosterone and the possibility that "chronic cortisol exposure [may] end up in a mental state known as 'learned helplessness.'"[34] Both Coates and the language of the articles themselves implied a perfect isomorphism between individual and collectivity, moving seamlessly between putative individual effects and market consequences. For instance, following this discussion of learned helplessness, Coates commented, "If this [learned helplessness] happens, central banks may lower interest rates only to find traders still refuse to buy risky assets. At times like these economics has to consider the physiology of investors, not just their rationality."[35] Another scientist interviewed commented, "[The study] might give an explanation for irrational exuberance and why a crisis changes into a recession or a depression."[36] A *Guardian* article was more straightforward yet: "For every boom it creates, testosterone is most likely behind every bust too." It followed with a quote from Coates, "I think this molecule is partly responsible for financial instability."[37]

The second, smaller flurry of reporting started in mid-September, as Coates took the opportunity provided by the developing crisis to write a commentary of his own.[38] In it he added a new argument, unfounded in his empirical work, that hormone swings are "contagious" and that this may also be operating on trading floors. "Either through smell, vision or hearing, one animal's surge in testosterone or cortisol can be spread throughout a herd and trigger aggression or panic."[39] It was in this second wave of coverage that Coates's suggestion that banks hire more women and older men in order to promote stability was taken up by other commentators, in line with the focus on solutions pervading public discourse on the economy in general after 2008.[40]

Thus, as markets faltered and as the mechanisms of neoliberal governance themselves seemed increasingly incapable of guaranteeing growth or even stability, the male body emerged with increasing prominence in public discourse. Side by side with concerns around regulation and corruption, the man in the market now looked less Jekyll and more Hyde, less man and more beast. In discussions of the market, the social masculinity that animated homo œconomicus was increasingly replaced by a male body understood to operate outside the purview of biopolitical mechanisms. Homo œconomicus, the socially masculine body, can be addressed by the market, but testosterone lies beyond the reach of market coordination, a bodily disruption of the social market form.

This panicked read of masculinity as unsettling maleness led, ironically, to a new assessment of women's comparative "hormonal stability" in the many editorial discussions of this work. Whereas once it was men whose minds ruled their bodies with implacable control, Coates argued, it is in fact women who "may be less hormonally reactive."[41] Given that, he concluded in still another op-ed, perhaps "a risk reduction strategy for banks might entail diversifying the endocrine profiles on their trading floors."[42] Coates was not alone in looking to the "opposite sex" for solutions. The arguments were picked up and became the subject of a panel at Davos in early 2009 that asked, "Would the world be in this financial mess if it had been Lehman Sisters?"[43] In the *Economist*, a columnist was sufficiently concerned by what he called "the new feminism" to counsel women making these arguments that "it would be a grave mistake to abandon old-fashioned meritocracy just at the time when it is turning to women's advantage."[44] In the *New York Times* the issue was picked up by none other than Nick Kristoff, who discussed the Coates research and asked rhetorically, "Could it be that the problem on Wall Street wasn't subprime mortgages, but elevated testosterone?"[45] His response to proposals to make the Lehman Brothers the "Lehman Sisters" accepted the terms of debate and placed a characteristically liberal spin on the question. It was not female dominance but "diversity" that would protect market function.[46] The depth of the links between neoliberal markets, homo œconomicus, and masculinity was revealed with particular clarity in these suggestions as the market crisis sent commentators not to new regulations or even to new trading behaviors, but instead to subjects distinguished precisely by their sex. In this moment of panic, the recriminations against homo œconomicus's failures targeted not a congenital human irrationality, but a specifically male version. Maleness emerged as a problem during the crisis, because homo œconomicus was a man all along.

Sexing the Subject

Sexing homo œconomicus reveals gender: masculinity at work in the neoliberal economy. The rational, unencumbered, neoliberal subject is contingent upon the gendered familial and affective structure that enables him to attend to economic decisions without reference to the messy business of caring and caretaking lurking behind them. This self as market "correlate" is produced and enabled by masculinity and by the feminine shadow attached at its heel. Outside the Foucauldian text, men as men make up financial markets, performing masculinity as a routine part of the job. In this theater, masculinity is productive, acting as grease for trading relations and fuel for the risk-taking that is the substance of market work. That fuel can be combustible, however, and in the absence of external regulation, masculinity contributes to the repetitive normalization of risk-taking even as it spirals out of control. Public response to this situation has been to attend neither to regulation nor to masculinity, however; instead, made salient by the biological sciences' move to the center of power and knowledge, the male body has emerged as culprit, a center of anxious public discussion and recrimination. It is precisely because homo œconomicus is masculine that it can be undone by maleness, its underlying ideological double, the animal body lurking in the unmarked male subject. These discussions are symptoms of crisis, a way of making sense within neoliberalism of a form of coordination that is no longer "productive" even in its own terms. Just as masculinity as a social form undergirds the functioning market and the logics that spawn it, so the male body becomes a way to articulate the limits of economic governance.

Under neoliberalism, market logics have gotten loose, swarmed from their home in the economy to frame our every action, reconstituting the operations of intimacy, punishment, and governance more broadly. This process feels inexorable, catalyzed by developments in financial capitalism and a creeping logic of calculation that pervades everyday practices and common sense. However, rereading these developments through a gendered lens suggests that they and the agents they evoke are saturated in other forms of meaning;

they do not act alone or in a vacuum. Despite the seductive elegance of parsimonious explanation, social life works otherwise.

Conceptualizing capitalism as if it barrels along in isolation, flattening everything in its path, is neither accurate nor politically productive. Theorists are increasingly documenting capitalism's deep historical imbrication with gender and race, both in the moments of its emergence[47] and in its relentless reproduction.[48] This is no less true of neoliberalism than it was of previous eras. Neoliberalism is most fundamentally distinguished from earlier periods by its organization around the indexical claim that all human agency is motivated by asocial self-interest. Such an assertion could only emerge in a social universe that was always already structured around women's multidimensional reproductive labor: some are free to perform their calculating selves only because others can be relied upon to attend to feelings, community and the needs of dependents. Without this care infrastructure, homo œconomicus and the neoliberal world he makes and inhabits would be unthinkable. Similarly, although the association of risk and masculinity is of comparatively recent vintage,[49] and one might imagine rhetorics of risk that did not operate with reference to gender, that is not the case now.[50] As we have seen, the actually existing links between neoliberalism, risk, and speculation, whether for good or for ill, run through a gendered terrain. There has never been a version of neoliberalism that operated in gender-neutral terms.

If masculinity inhabits the agent at the heart of neoliberalism, then resisting its calculating logics requires forms of resistance that respond to that deep imbrication. In recent years, we find pundits arguing that the crisis of neoliberal finance can be solved by changing the sex of its personnel.[51] We find lean-in "feminists"[52] arguing that women, too, can incarnate the rational man as long as they can find "other" women to pick up the care-work slack.[53] But the failure of these interventions to make a dent either in the situation of most women or in neoliberalism's depredations overall suggests that we need to challenge homo œconomicus on his home turf. We can no longer survive the gendered and raced assumption that it is possible for some to be pure agents of calculation, because they can implicitly rely on "others" in their home back offices to do the loving and community building upon which the rest of life depends. Rather than suggesting the "Lehman Sisters" can save us, we need to ask how we might undo the binaries that dole out distinct aspects of human responsibility and experience by gender. This alone is surely not enough to undo neoliberal logics, but it is an indispensable first step. It is only by challenging the system's gendered infrastructure more broadly that we can begin to destabilize its imperialist, calculating common sense.

Notes

1. Many thanks to audiences at UC Santa Cruz and UC Berkeley for thoughtful comments in presentations of earlier iterations of this work. And a special thanks to Margaret Phillips for her help in gathering the data for View 3. This essay is dedicated to the memory of my father, Kurt Salzinger, indefatigable writer, 1929–2018.

2. Michel Foucault, *The Birth of Biopolitics: Lectures at the College de France 1978-1979* (London: Palgrave MacMillan, 2008), 215–16.

3. See Leonore Davidoff and Catherine Hall, *Family Fortunes: Men and Women of the English Middle Class, 1780–1850* (Chicago: University of Chicago Press, 1987); Marieke de Goede, *Virtue, Fortune, and Faith: A Genealogy of Finance* (Minneapolis: University of Minnesota Press, 2005); and Heidi Hartmann, "Capitalism, Patriarchy, and Job Segregation by Sex," *Signs: Journal of Women in Culture and Society* 1, no. 3 (Spring 1976): 137–69.

4. See Denise Riley, *"Am I That Name?": Feminism and the Category of "Women" in History* (Minneapolis: University of Minnesota Press, 1988), for a fuller discussion of the danger in confounding gender's repetitive nature with inevitability and permanence.

5. For analogous arguments that, however capitalism might have operated in theory, in practice it has always functioned within the context of preexisting gendered and raced meanings and practices, see (respectively) Silvia Federici, *Caliban and the Witch* (2004; repr. New York: Autonomedia, 2014) and Cedric Robinson, *Black Marxism: The Making of the Black Radical Tradition* (1983; repr. Chapel Hill: University of North Carolina Press, 2000).

6. For a resonant discussion of the emergence of "varieties of capitalism" in theorizing the persistent but shifting relationship of race and capitalism over time, see Nikhil Singh, "On Race, Violence, and So-Called Primitive Accumulation," *Social Text* 34, no. 3 (2016): 39.

7. Foucault, *Birth of Biopolitics*, 243.

8. Ibid., 223.

9. Catherine MacKinnon, "Difference and Dominance," in *Feminism Unmodified* (Cambridge, Mass.: Harvard University Press, 1987), 32–45.

10. Foucault, *Birth of Biopolitics*, 252.

11. Ibid., 241.

12. Martha Fineman, "Cracking the Foundational Myths: Independence, Autonomy and Self-Sufficiency," *American Journal of Gender, Social Policy, and the Law* 8 (2000).

13. Melinda Cooper, *Family Values: Between Neoliberalism and the New Social Conservatism* (Cambridge, Mass.: MIT Press, 2017).

14. Joan Acker, "Hierarchies, Jobs, Bodies: A Theory of Gendered Organizations," *Gender and Society* 4, no. 2 (1990): 151.

15. Foucault, *Birth of Biopolitics*, 244.

16. Ibid., 244.

17. For an elegant version of this argument, see Wendy Brown, *Undoing the Demos: Neoliberalism's Stealth Revolution* (New York: Zone Books, 2015).

18. Sara Babb, *Managing Mexico: Economists from Nationalism to Neoliberalism* (Princeton, N.J.: Princeton University Press, 2001).

19. My project was directed at the Mexican market, hence my location in New York City and Mexico City. However, the Mexican peso was traded in Globank, New York, on a desk that focused on all the Latin American currencies and traded other "emerging market" currencies as well. This structure was a vital part of how the bank operated in Mexico and more generally, so while in New York I observed and interacted with traders of all the currencies traded on the desk.

20. On the transnational power dynamics and structuring of these markets, see Leslie Salzinger, "Beneath the Model: From 'Developing Nation' to 'Emerging Market,' Deal by Deal." Institute for Work and Employment Research Seminar, MIT, April 26, 2011.

21. John Coates received his Ph.D. in the humanities at Cambridge, publishing a book on Wittgenstein in 1996 before beginning his work as a trader at Goldman Sachs and Deutsche Bank. Today he is jointly affiliated with the Department of Physiology, Development and Neuroscience and the Judge Business School at the University of Cambridge and, since 2008, has coauthored a series of papers that seek to identify a "biological substrate to economic action."

22. John Coates and Joe Herbert, "Endogenous Steroids and Financial Risk Taking on a London Trading Floor," Proceedings of the National Academy of Sciences 105, no. 15 (April 22, 2008).

23. Peter Goodman, "A Fresh Look at the Apostle of Free Markets," *New York Times*, April 13, 2008.

24. John Coates, "John Coates," University of Cambridge Judge Business School, http://www.jbs.cam.ac.uk/research/associates/coatesj.html.

25. Coates and Herbert, "Endogenous Steroids and Financial Risk Taking on a London Trading Floor."

26. Geoff Brumfiel, "The Testosterone of Trading," *Nature*, April 14, 2008.

27. See Rebecca M. Jordan-Young's *Brain Storm* (Cambridge, Mass.: Harvard University Press, 2010) for a thorough and devastating takedown of this claim.

28. John Coates, Mark Gurnell, and Aldo Rustichini, "Second-to-Fourth Digit Ratio Predicts Success among High-Frequency Financial Traders," *Proceedings of the National Academy of Sciences* 106 (January 13, 2009).

29. John Coates, Mark Gurnell, and Zoltan Sarnyai, "From Molecule to Market: Steroid Hormones and Financial Risk-Taking," *Philosophical Transactions of the Royal Society B* 365 (2010).

30. A third study, reanalyzing the data and published in 2010, argued that testosterone levels predicted risk-taking but not the profits made per unit of risk, thus further disaggregating the trading self and pathologizing testosterone as a root of risk taking on its own. All this work was summarized and popularized in a book by John Coates, directed at the lay reader, entitled *The Hour Between Dog*

and Wolf: How Risk Taking Transforms Us, Body and Mind (New York: Penguin, 2012).

31. See Anne Fausto-Sterling, "The Bare Bones of Sex: Part 1—Sex and Gender," *Signs* 30, no. 2 (2005); Katrina Karkazis, "The Masculine Mystique of T," *New York Review of Books*, June 28, 2018, https://www.nybooks.com/daily/2018/06/28/the-masculine-mystique-of-t/; Jordan-Young, *Brain Storm*; and Robert Sapolsky, "The Trouble with Testosterone," in *The Trouble with Testosterone and Other Essays on the Human Predicament* (New York: Touchstone, 1997).

32. Rob Stein, "Hormones Tied to Traders' Deal-Making, Study Finds," *Washington Post*, April 21, 2008.

33. Mark Henderson, "Rush of Hormones May Be Behind Credit Crunch," *Times (London)*, April 15, 2008.

34. Andrew Levy, "How Testosterone Can Make a Trader Much Slicker in the City," *Daily Mail*, April 15, 2008; Staff "Hormones; Testosterone Levels Predict City Traders' Profitability," *Drug Week*, May 2, 2008.

35. Staff, "Hormones; Testosterone Levels Predict City Traders' Profitability."

36. Stein, "Hormones Tied to Traders' Deal-Making, Study Finds."

37. James Randerson, "Scientists Find Secret Ingredient for Making (and Losing) Lots of Money—Testosterone," *Guardian*, April 15, 2008.

38. The 2009 study got somewhat less coverage because, although the mechanism actually being tested was new, its political message was not—already old news. Nonetheless, it did make it into the *Washington Post*, where one of the study's authors was quoted saying flatly, "'Testosterone is the hormone of irrational exuberance.' . . . 'The bubble preceding the current crash may have been due to euphoria related to high levels of testosterone, or high sensitivity to it.'"

39. John Coates, "Hormones May Be Hurting Stock Markets," *Daily Telegraph*, September 19, 2008.

40. Associated Press, "Male Sex Hormone May Affect Stock Trades," *New York Times*, April 15, 2008.

41. The ironies here are glaring, as for centuries Western thinkers have argued that women's general hormonal instability and (consequent) hysteria are precisely what makes them unsuitable for a host of important social functions.

42. Associated Press, "Male Sex Hormone May Affect Stock Trades."

43. Katrin Bennhold, "Where Would We Be If Women Ran Wall Street?" *New York Times*, February 1, 2009.

44. Schumpeter, "Womenomics," *Economist* (London), January 2, 2010.

45. Nicholas Kristof, "Mistresses of the Universe." *New York Times*, February 7, 2009.

46. As I ("Re-Marking Men: Masculinity as a Terrain of the Neoliberal Economy," *Critical Historical Studies* 3, no. 1 [2016]) and others ("Empowered Women, Failed Patriarchs: Neoliberalism and Global Gender Anxieties," by Smitha Radhakrishnan and Cinzia Solari, *Sociology Compass* 9, no. 9 [2015]) have argued elsewhere, masculinity has been increasingly stigmatized in the lower reaches of many parts of the global economy. However, it is a measure of the

depth of the 2008 crisis and the long-standing masculinization of the financial sector that, even as men continue to dominate political and economic institutions globally, we see that stigma touch these men at the top.

47. See Robinson, *Black Marxism*, and Federici, *Caliban and the Witch*.

48. See Saidiya Hartman, "The Belly of the World: A Note on Black Women's Labors," *Souls* 18, no. 1 (2016), and Cooper, *Family Values*.

49. De Goede, *Virtue, Fortune, and Faith*.

50. Miranda Joseph, *Debt to Society: Accounting for Life under Capitalism* (Minneapolis: University of Minnesota Press, 2014).

51. Bennhold, "Where Would We Be If Women Ran Wall Street?"

52. Sheryl Sandberg, *Women, Work, and the Will to Lead* (New York: Knopf, 2013).

53. For key analyses of the racial and transnational structuring of care work, see Evelyn Nakano Glenn, *Forced to Care: Coercion and Caregiving in America* (Cambridge, Mass.: Harvard University Press, 2010), and Arlie Hochschild, "Global Care Chains and Emotional Surplus Value," in *Global Capitalism*, ed. Will Hutton and Anthony Giddens (New York: New Press, 2000), 130–46.

Feminist Theory Redux:
Neoliberalism's Public-Private Divide

Megan Moodie and Lisa Rofel

Whether invoked by boosters or critics, the concept of privatization is pervasive in discussions of neoliberalism. This essay seeks to develop a more nuanced approach to privatization—both its conceptualization and its practice—than is currently available. We make two interrelated arguments: first, feminist theories have developed elaborate deconstructions of the public/private division that can help us in understanding the operations of neoliberal capitalism. Feminist theorists have long argued that "public" and "private" are ideologically defined and vary historically and cross-culturally, that this division is empirically unfounded, and that their usage obscures their role in the maintenance of gender hierarchies. Yet, with a few notable exceptions,[1] feminist insights about the public/private divide have been consistently ignored in analyses of neoliberalism and, more generally, capitalism. We employ feminist critique to analyze the multiple meanings and practices of privatization, including the often-blurred relationships among them.

Second, and relatedly, theories of neoliberalism have underestimated the legacies of socialism and the Cold War. Whether from the left or the right, theorists of neoliberalism tend to take for granted that the Cold War is over and treat socialism as a completed, surpassed historical project. We contend that this understanding of "postsocialism"—as a historical phase that has overcome socialism—is insufficient. Our respective research in China (Rofel) and India (Moodie), coupled with a deep engagement with feminist theory, has brought to light how prevailing narratives of neoliberalism depend on a particular imagination of a public/private divide that does not apply in post-socialist locations. Further, many actually existing formerly socialist countries, for different reasons, feel compelled to bring aspects of the socialist past into their postsocialist present, particularly as they pertain to possibilities for more livable futures.

We begin by laying out our two-part argument: we show that a feminist approach to the public/private divide not only provides a more rigorous framework for the study of contemporary capitalism, but specifically brings to light a problematic set of assumptions about the "end" of socialism. Then, using ethnographic insights we have garnered from China and India, we demonstrate how this approach might work, focusing on two aspects of neoliberalization in these locations: labor regimes and what we call "profitization." Finally, we offer a set of thoughts about how the feminist theory redux of the public/private might enhance fights for social justice: this approach centers subaltern dreams that are often not articulated in legible ways by scholars of neoliberalism precisely because they straddle a public/private imaginary.

Theories of Neoliberalism and Feminist Theory Redux

There is no question that neoliberal policies and practices have sought to bring about a new relationship between private economic interests and the state (theoretically the guarantor of the public good), one in which the public sector as well as previously nonproductive areas of social life have become financialized and profoundly oriented toward profit-seeking.[2] However, some scholars emphasize that neoliberalism is not merely about the market or a set of economic principles but more capaciously is a mode of reason—that is, a governmental rationality that reconfigures all aspects of human endeavors according to a model of the market.[3] All of these writings emphasize that neoliberalism is plural and dynamic in terms of both political philosophy and political practice and transnational in its historically evolving formations.[4] And yet, while there is obviously wide variation in foci on different aspects of neoliberalism, as well as the recognition that neoliberalism is inventive and has evolved and changed over time, we nonetheless contend that a vision of the public/private divide derived from North American and non(post)socialist European social arrangements and imaginaries underlies the description of privatization under neoliberalism in contemporary scholarship.

Despite its deep problematization by feminist and allied scholars since the 1970s, an oppositional model of social life in which there is a separation between "public" and "private" realms of behavior and experience—realms that often map onto male and female genders—has proven remarkably tenacious. In contemporary discussions of neoliberalism the idea that its proponents are first and foremost committed to something called "privatization" has become "common sense."[5] For example, in David Harvey's well-known account of the rise of neoliberal thinking and policy across the globe, privatization is the first sign and symptom of a movement away from temporally prior ownership patterns and welfare commitments that we might call "public." This process, for Harvey, is fairly simple to diagnose, as it consists of "the transfer of assets from the public and popular realms to the private and class-privileged domains," a process he also refers to as "accumulation by dispossession."[6] The political stakes in Harvey's analysis are high, and it is certainly the case that in many instances and sites such a transfer of public wealth into private hands has indeed taken place, with disastrous effects for all of us, but especially for those who are most vulnerable when states retreat from welfare commitments.

We want to suggest nonetheless that many discussions of privatization, like Harvey's, presume what they ought to explain: namely, the dynamic arenas in which social life unfolds. Our analysis of the public/private rearrangements in postsocialist countries such as China and India draws on the long-standing critique of the distinction between the private and the public developed by feminist scholars and activists.

If feminist scholarship in the 1970s was characterized by a search for the origins of a universal male dominance that was located in the division between a (valued) public, political, male sphere and a (devalued) private, domestic, female sphere,[7] subsequent decades saw this explanatory framework questioned, unpacked, and historicized.

While feminists in the 1970s initially drew on the domestic/public distinction to explain gender inequality,[8] a consensus emerged that this dichotomy was analytically unproductive, empirically unfounded,[9] and based on the universalizing and biologically essentialist notion that the mother-child bond forms the core of domestic relations.[10] They further argued that domestic relationships were often so inextricably intermeshed with political alliances that to separate the domestic from the political was to misconstrue them.[11] Black feminist scholars further highlighted how the "private" was never an attainable sphere for black women and families in the U.S.[12] The metaphor of "separate spheres" always involved exclusions, as it was based largely on white, middle-class women's experiences in the United States[13] as well as on the centrality of colonialism to ideas about emancipation of women from the domestic/public division.[14]

Thus, as feminist theorists and activists demonstrated, getting caught up in drawing strict boundaries between the public and the private is less an exercise in analytical rigor than a displacement of attention from how both public and private structures of power are reinforced and reproduced. Such boundary drawing especially neglects how the state uses its public resources to support corporate profit. Feminists were not contesting that understanding the public/private model was essential for both political activism and scholarly analysis. They were, however, questioning who might *benefit* from the maintenance of the separate sphere model, given that it does not map onto much of activity and feeling of daily life. *The public/private model is not itself politically neutral,* and it is this insight that seems to have gotten lost in the recent literature on neoliberalism.

Recent years have seen the emergence of studies of public-private partnerships rather than what we might call "simple privatization."[15] Yet whenever the private/public division is discussed in relation to capitalism, the existence of these two spheres is rarely interrogated. One result has been the entrenchment of a model of social life that may obscure all kinds of political-economic relations, particularly in postsocialist locations.

Cold War Lens

We contend that the understanding of postsocialism as a historical phase that is completed is insufficient on several grounds that attention to neoliberal processes in China and India make clear. First, as Rofel's discussion of China shows, China's transition to a market-based economy has not meant the dismantling of the entire preceding socialist ideology; it thus casts a shadow over most familiar developmentalist globalization narratives. In the case of India, too, recent political coalitions, including the Communist Party of India–Marxist (CPIM) and labor unions, have blocked the resource capture—and resultant unemployment—that would have come from the selling off of private assets and enterprises. Two states, Kerala and West Bengal, have longstanding communist governments. And even the current regime, with its dual focus on foreign and nonresident Indian investment and employment/development, is in some sense an extreme Hindu-nationalist, mutated form of an ongoing commitment to redistributive politics, social welfare, and "depressed classes."

Second, as Neda Atanasoski argues, postsocialism can more productively be thought of "as a conceptual frame denoting the displacement as well as the ongoing significance of socialism," one in which there is not a clean break from the past. Rather, all contemporary political economic imaginaries, including neoliberalism and criticisms thereof, contain "inheritances of previous fantasies about the global good."[16] But this is rarely the approach taken in studies of neoliberal ideology or policy. An otherwise extremely cogent analysis of recent theorizations of neoliberalism, "Postneoliberalism and Its Malcontents," provides a telling example.[17] These authors take up and critique Gusenbauer's contention that "the fall of Wall St. is to neoliberalism what the fall of the Berlin Wall was to communism" on the grounds that neoliberalism was never a singular, historically detached process, but rather something *dynamic*.[18] Therefore, it could not simply collapse in total failure. Peck et al.[19] then propose the term "neoliberal*ization*" to talk about the open-ended and polymorphic nature of this process. But in retaining the distinction between these two events and stressing their stark difference from one another, the authors implicitly leave unchecked their assumption that communism was singular and coherent and that the Berlin Wall moment signaled the same thing to a vast array of different nation-states, and groups within nation-states, who were pursuing socialist policies and strategies of some kind.

If we look at the recent political economy of China and India as signaling exactly the same kind of open-ended and processual nature for what is glossed as "communism" or "socialism" as we want to insist on for neoliberalization, we can better account for the entanglements of the three worlds in twentieth-century history and thereby provide an important corrective to the Eurocentrism of the neoliberalism story. In India, for example, while today there is a great deal of focus on connections to the United States via the tech industry and the U.S. Indian diaspora, the celebration of this friendship belies the decades during which money, but more importantly, technical know-how, came to India from Moscow and East Europe, which provided a symbolic center for development efforts.[20] Nirmal Kumar Chandra argues persuasively not only that it was Soviet and East European expertise that encouraged industrialization in India after independence, but that this was a direct outcome of the Marshall Plan, which pushed the USSR to expand its own development efforts abroad. This is an especially interesting point because, as Chandra discusses, many commentators look at the Marshall Plan through the lens of the neoliberal present and refer to it as "the first structural adjustment program."[21] But in its implementation of the Marshall Plan, the U.S. was decidedly unconcerned with how Western European nations restructured their economies—or not—along free-market ideological lines. France and Britain nationalized large industries, India was taking direct monetary and technical assistance from the USSR and its satellites (particularly in the oil and steel industries), and countries like Japan seemed to combine both Soviet-style planning and free-market capitalism. Indeed, the U.S.'s own economy was engaged in one of the biggest social welfare projects in its history: the G.I. Bill.

Similarly, China, which had initially received a great deal of technological, political, and economic support from the USSR, turned itself into a source of aid to Third World countries after the split with the Soviet Union and in competition with them. China's past aid to countries in Africa and Southeast Asia, as well as Latin America and the Caribbean, especially Cuba, remains an important ideological resource in the current era as China turns once again to these countries, but now in search of natural resources for their own development. Within China, there is an ongoing debate about whether and to what extent to privatize land. This, too, speaks loudly of the aftereffects of socialism and the Cold War, as free access to land was a mainstay of how China claimed distinction from the capitalist West.

We are concerned with this correction not just at the level of theoretical clarification, but also, and perhaps more importantly, because the social imaginaries of many of the workers with whom we have engaged in our combined last several decades of ethnographic research in China and India retain important ideas about what Atanasoski calls "the global good" from more explicitly socialist eras. It may be precisely because these ideas straddle a public-private divide that they do not usually capture the imagination of neoliberalism's commentators.

In the following two sections, we demonstrate the importance of a feminist approach to the public/private for analyses of neoliberalism, particularly how it brings to light many of the ongoing aftereffects of the Cold War that are elided in stories that treat 1989 as the hinge between two distinct historical epochs. We look at two arenas in which political-economic arrangements have been strongly affected by neoliberal ideas and practices—labor regimes and profitization—and in each of these show how ethnographic attention to when, how, and by whom public/private distinctions are drawn illuminates that the creation and mobilization of the categories are part of what is at stake in—rather than the social pregiven for—neoliberalization. Feminist theory alerts us to the many ways in which the operative model of privatization presumes what it ought to explain: namely, meaningful categories of social life such as, but not limited to, "public" and "private," and through which social relations are enacted and contested in contemporary capitalism.

Labor Regimes

CHINA (ROFEL)

By the end of the twentieth century, China had become known as the sweatshop of the world. With the full collusion of and encouragement by the Chinese state, the multinational corporate displacement of production to China had produced, in addition to commodity chains, the relentless labor conditions in Chinese factories, including work precarity. These were a decided transformation in labor conditions from the socialist era, which began with the turn to a full-market economy in the 1980s (we discuss labor arrangements under the socialist state in the next section).[22] The state has abandoned workers—or at least allowed factory owners a great deal of leeway in how they treat workers—a radical rearrangement of workers' social and economic lives that was initially motivated by a desire to attract foreign direct investment. The rearrangement of private/public relations—or the relationship of capital and the state—is central to the changing nature of subaltern exploitation.

Since the beginning of the turn to a market economy, factories in China have hired predominantly migrant workers from the countryside. Factory managers and owners take advantage of the fact that China has a discriminatory legal system that maintains an urban/rural residence system (*hukou*) that does not allow migrants from the countryside to obtain permanent legal urban residence. Thus, they are denied benefits urban residents take for granted, including, most importantly, housing and public education for their children. Migrant workers must leave their children behind in the countryside. Urban residents, in turn, tend to treat rural migrant workers as the source of pollution and criminality. Factory owners rely on the classic uneven development structure in which migrant workers must depend on the countryside for their reproductive needs.

The replacement of the urban working class with rural migrant labor both enabled and was hastened by the "privatization" of China's factories that began in the 1990s and then proceeded more rapidly after 2001, when China joined the World Trade Organization (WTO). This process has occurred in a context in which the Chinese state simultaneously retains and discards aspects of the socialist past. Previously, all factories were subsumed under various state bureaus—central, provincial, and municipal. But in the past fifteen years, these state bureaus—now calling themselves corporations—have forced these factories to "privatize." They did so by "selling" the factories to one or a group of the factories' managers. In this process, the state corporation chose who should be the owners. These managers' ownership was enabled by loans from one of the state banks in China that, if the factory went bankrupt, in effect did not have to be repaid.[23] Thus state-owned banks basically handed over state-owned resources to party officials. In addition, factory office employees (though not workers on the production lines) were essentially forced to buy shares in the newly privatized entity.

Clearly, in China one finds individuals who have amassed wealth through "accumulation by dispossession." But this story is complicated by the fact that often these individuals are working within *state-run* corporations that have continued to maintain "public" ownership of resources. By contrast, those who are given the "advantage" of turning former state-owned resources, especially factories, into their individual private property are in vulnerable industries with heavy welfare burdens. This is clearly to the advantage of the state, which aims to slough off the welfare obligations and difficulties of making a profit in labor-intensive industries.

The factories under the aegis of state corporations have thus been "privatized" in the sense that the newly minted owners are now fully responsible for their profits as well as losses, in addition to workers' welfare, without any support from the state corporation they used to rely on. They are then allowed—or forced—to find their own way toward profitizing. As one state corporation official said to me about this process in Zhejiang province: "It used to be that everyone ate out of one big pot (*chi daguo fan*), but now the government doesn't have that much money to give out to support everyone."

The resulting privatization has led to insecure working conditions and backbreaking work schedules that make the former three-shift system appear benign. In textile factories for export—especially export of fashion clothing—the problem is less constant overwork or even horrible factory conditions than the risk and insecurity workers face due to the uncertain and ever-changing schedules associated with garment supply chains. Workers get paid by piecework; when there is work, they have to work continuously, with no days off. Sometimes they even sleep by their machines as they work overtime in twenty-four-hour cycles to finish an order for export. When there is no work, they get sent home with no pay. Workers do not have a regular work week or regular days off. There is no guaranteed wage in factories for export that are privately owned. Workers in this sector are essentially being taught to be entrepreneurial about their factory labor—to accept this risk and uncertainty as part of the very conditions of their labor; thus, workers try to move around to different factories in the hope of finding marginally better working conditions. They are quite aware of the structural inequalities that shape their daily work experiences.

In this sense, some parts of state-owned corporations that oversee manufacturing have fully privatized, if by "fully privatized" we mean that the state no longer is involved in any way in the mitigation of losses and no longer takes any responsibility whatsoever for workers' wages and benefits. Most of this type of privatization has occurred at the bottom of the hierarchy of production—that is, the factories themselves. Commodity chains then resignify the meaning of "privatization." Commodity chains are the structural heart of multinational corporate displacement of production processes to China and other countries of the global South. Conversely, they are the major means through which China conducts exports and accumulates foreign currency reserves.

While some individual factories manage to create their own subcontracting arrangements with foreign corporations—mostly those from Taiwan and Hong Kong—the vast majority of factories actually subcontract through state-owned import-export corporations. This is because most multinational corporations find it extremely difficult to link directly with production factories. The Chinese state made this direct link structurally impossible prior to its joining the WTO. But even without the formal structural barriers, most multinational corporations do not have the means to assess which factories are appropriate for their needs. They generally turn to the state-owned corporations to act as their mediating link. Factories' very survival therefore depends on their ability to obtain contracts from the state-owned corporations under whose aegis they used to exist under socialism. Commodity chain production must be brought more clearly into focus in order to understand how the state is more fully implicated in workers' working conditions. The multinational structuration of production through commodity chains thus binds "privatized" factories to the state in conditions that blur private/public even as ideologically—and legally—the factories are defined as "private." Given the Chinese state's intimate involvement in this structuration, it would be misleading to argue that labor questions in China have been fully privatized. Once again, this recalls the insights of feminists, reminding us that questions of privatization require detailed analysis of the particular social and political powers reshaping the public-private divide.

INDIA (MOODIE)

In India, labor is even less easily parsed as public or private than in China, especially in low-wage, manual-labor positions. This blurriness is not simply because some previously public sectors have not been privatized, but because for many workers the experience of toiling as a day laborer for a private entity and working as a low-level employee for the state are nearly identical. In both cases, groups including those who have had guaranteed government employment via India's vast "reservation" system—quotas of jobs held aside for members of "formerly" oppressed groups known as the Scheduled Castes (Dalits/so-called Untouchables) and Scheduled Tribes (adivasis/indigenous groups)—find themselves at the mercy of caste-based middlemen and an opaque contract system that provides few of the possibilities for upward mobility previously held out by government employment. If we take a worker's-eye view of what in India has been called "liberalization," public and private labor regimes are nearly identical.

Using "liberalization" as the preferred term to describe the opening of Indian markets to foreign investment and, more importantly, to the import of items like washing machines and VCRs that increasingly define a new middle-class beginning in the early 1990s, speaks precisely to the break with an earlier, socialist era often depicted as the "license-permit raj."[24] This was not a new era of retooling global economic relations, but one of opening up to consumer goods and an individualized "liberal" (that is, nonsocialist) model of democracy as much as market forces. It was also therefore an implicit shift away from the more Gandhian notion of *swaraj* (anticolonial self-rule and national production) that held rhetorical, if not actual, sway for many who had been involved in the independence movement and came into power in the second half of the twentieth century.

One of the most interesting places to see the remolding of the public and private spheres is in the realm of public utilities. This is in part because different utilities have had quite different neoliberalization trajectories: electricity has shifted almost entirely to private production and distribution, while water and sewage have proved more resistant to privatization and comprise a kaleidoscopic patchwork. This inconsistency among various essential utilities itself is evidence that there is a great deal more to privatization than simple resource capture through the selling-off of public assets. A number of recent studies have described the privatization of electricity production and provision in major metropolitan areas such as Delhi and Mumbai.[25] While there are regional differences related to everything from state budgets to party politics, the general finding of these studies is that the transition to private electricity access and decentralization has not been met without protest, and extralegal access continues such that most residents of large cities encounter electricity through both public and private channels.[26]

In the case of water and sewage, the picture is different such that, as Nikhil Anand puts it, "water networks in India . . . have consistently troubled privatization."[27] In the smaller city where I have conducted research, Jaipur, the capital of the state of Rajasthan, the privatization of electricity has actually served as a cautionary tale for those worried about the future of water. My ethnographic study of an urban Scheduled Tribe group, the Dhanka, who have worked in the city's Public Health and Engineering (PHED) Department, the body that manages the city's waterworks, including its sewer system, is instructive.[28] Because of their status as a protected group, Dhanka men were able to obtain government jobs in the PHED for the last several generations, which led to notable upward mobility for many families in the community. Alongside these official postings, however, many men also engaged in contracted temporary labor—known as *thekedari*, meaning "of the contract [*theka*]" or "hired by a contractor [*thekedar*]"—for private businessowners hired by individual households to fix pipes, dig wells, and, sometimes, set up illegal connections to the city system. Such *thekedari* posts had, of course, low pay, no job security, and lasted only as long as any given project.

Since I began conducting research with the Dhanka in 2002, employment in the PHED has come to resemble the *thekedari* system. In both government and private postings, most of the hiring is done on a short-term, contractual basis; both also reportedly, and unofficially of course, require the payment of large bribes that are often out of reach for poor Dhanka families. One important difference between public and private forms of employment remains, however: there are still strict laws determining the duration of contract work for the state. These laws were put into place to protect workers from just the sort of exploitation the *thekedar* system depends on. What this means in practice, though, is that both employers and employees find creative ways to get around regularizing government employment, which would add benefits, security, and other guarantees for the worker. One method is for a government department to hire a worker on a temporary basis, allow him to serve out his contract, and once that has ended, rehire him under a new, false name with forged documents. In 2012, a Dalit/Scheduled Caste employee of PHED told me he had been working on temporary contracts for fifteen years, a claim vehemently denied by PHED officials who insist they do not use contract labor at all. Whether this is willful subterfuge or a creative interpretation of the current bureaucratic regime in the state is hard to determine.

What concerns laborers a great deal, besides the fact that there are fewer and fewer government posts with less and less protection, is the way that caste—called *jati* or *samaj* locally—may work differently and to the great disadvantage of groups like the Dhanka who at present enjoy legal protections for their job quotas. Every worker I encountered insisted that each *jati* has its own *thekedars* who will only hire from within their own community. If one's *jati* does not have a contractor in a particular sector, or if that contractor loses its ties to larger private or public hiring entities, one cannot find work at all. There is no loyalty to workers, they say, except via the ties of one's *samaj*. Therefore, *thekedars* are rarely criticized as exploiters; rather, they are praised for their perseverance and loyalty.[29]

In a way, caste itself and its ongoing role in labor regimes in India, particularly from the colonial period onward, can be seen as a set of social practices that muddle public-private distinctions with regard to the kind of work one does and how work is obtained. We should not be surprised, then, that caste is often at the heart of the (re)negotiations that accompany the broader political-economic changes characterized as liberalization. Caste is still often understood as endogamous adherence to an occupational group ranked by its proximity to defiling substances.[30] The current *thekedari* system shows us that, perhaps rather than reproducing caste for its own sake and to reinforce hierarchical status, in the so-called neoliberal era, endogamy and loyalty to the *samaj* are strategic choices within a labor regime built around loyalties that are always both "private" (that is, should not matter in a meritocratic system and maintained through marriage practices) and "public" (that is, codified in the legal protections necessary for oppressed groups to find and maintain employment).

To reiterate, then, at the bottom rungs of employment hierarchies in India—and leaving aside the informal economies of, for instance, urban garbage scavengers—individuals have to go through quite similar processes: find a middleman who is a member of one's caste to make a connection, pay a bribe and secure a temporary position, work without health and retirement benefits for the duration of a contract, and then try to get hired back under different terms—or a different name.

It is important to note that this collapsing of the difference between public and private employment has not gone uncontested. The rise of the *thekedari* system was the primary complaint of most of the men I encountered between the ages of eighteen and fifty during my field research. One interlocutor was considering filing a complaint against his boss, who had repeatedly promised him a permanent position—to which he was by law entitled after years of working on a contract basis—but grappling with the very real possibility that that would also mean he would be out of a job for a very long time to come. In response to the era of *thekedari*, Dhanka men's assertions of their Scheduled Tribe status have grown stronger and more urgent, leading some to pursue lawsuits when denied the certification of their tribal identity. When the Dhankas' status as a tribal group was questioned by a rival community in the state with whom they compete for reserved seats, community elders fought a protracted legal battle to assert their constitutional right to special protection under the law, including the right to a quota of government postings.[31] Thus, the current labor regime has had the unintended side effect of mobilizing not only workers'-rights-based protest, but caste-based conflict as well.

The case of the Dhanka in Jaipur also reminds us that all workers, even those in low-paying and devalued jobs, are also consumers. When privatization occurred in the electricity industry in Rajasthan, the effect was not only, or even perhaps in the main, to limit employment opportunities. It also reportedly raised electricity bills by several orders of magnitude. Once again, an overly strong private-public distinction might highlight Dhanka struggles as workers but neglect the domestic-facing impacts of changes in utilities. Both matter a great deal as men and women wake up each day and worry about their children's futures.

Toward a Feminist Rethinking of Neoliberal Privatization

The arguments presented in this section about changing labor regimes in China and India reveal the extent to which "privatization" must be studied ethnographically. While in many accounts of neoliberalism privatization is an implicit shorthand for Harvey's "accumulation by dispossession," we have argued that from a worker's-eye view the division of "public" and "private" is not so clear-cut, even as the blurring between the two can be ideologically obscured by invocations of privatization that might even be enacted in the law. To reiterate, the retreat of the welfare state is as important a feature of privatization as simple resource capture (which has, of course, occurred in both locations). Whether in the form of direct subsidies for housing and daily living expenses (more visible in China) or affirmative action guarantees in public sector jobs (India) or worker support in the form of health care and pensions (both China and India), we find that in an earlier, avowedly socialist era, in both cases the state demonstrated forms of accountability to workers' well-being. We do not want to romanticize conditions under twentieth-century socialism, but neither can we ignore the fact that, first, the erosion of welfare provisions through neoliberalization has made the welfare commitments of socialism perhaps more obvious in the breach, and, second, that these provisions retain a great deal of power in workers' imagination of the good life today (a point to which we return later).

It is not a coincidence that our view of the blurred division of the public and private, informed by feminist theory, highlights issues such as welfare that touch more closely on those activities and relations often referred to as "reproductive." Feminists have long made use of this category, derived from Marx but especially from Friedrich Engels's *Origins of the Family, Private Property, and the State*, to point to how the conditions of reproduction are tied to modes of production (and vice versa), and that changes in one "sphere" create changes in the other.[32] Indeed, it takes a great deal of cultural work to make productive and reproductive worlds appear separate, and it is precisely this breakdown that workers are addressing when they critique current labor regimes.

It is also telling that, whatever their blurred ownership structure, business enterprises in both China and India make use of pre-extant forms of social difference to produce profit. In China, this difference is urban versus rural residence and the fact that the enticements of the city could bring in new, lower-paid workers. Ironically, this is a difference that was hardened under socialism. In India, as shown by Moodie, caste is reoperationalized. Our findings are thus very much in accord with other feminist analyses of globalized commodity chains that stress not how such connections create sameness and homogenization, but in fact how they rely on and reinforce social inequalities of race, gender, class, religion, and so on.[33] While studies of neoliberalism have stressed the emergence of new subjectivities, these feminist analyses show us that older ideas about social order and the good life—including those derived from the socialist era that has been supposedly supplanted—are often entwined with newer ideas about the self-maximizing rational actor, the paragon of neoliberalism.

Based on our earlier ethnographic discussion, in the next section we suggest that rather than continuing to use the term "privatization" to describe a multitude of practices and contexts that may be very dissimilar, our analyses of capitalism might be better served by attention to the goals of a particular rearrangement of the public-private. We propose "profitization" as a more apt descriptor for the changes we note in China and India and continue to mark the many ways in which the afterlife of the Cold War informs and shapes these changes.

Profitization

CHINA (ROFEL)

As we argued in the introduction, the practices enacted under the rubric of privatization are not as singular or as universal as is often assumed. Scholars have raised an important ethnographic question with regard to China: is a particular corporate entity privately or state-owned?[34] The major concern of these scholars is to assess whether a "true" market economy can exist in China. Thus, they tend to measure the extent to which a company is able to operate apart from the state. I found that for many state-owned corporations, an intentional obfuscation is enacted to present themselves as private or at least partially private. Why would a state-owned corporation bother to dress itself up as a private one? The answer, in brief, is that the pursuit of state-inflected privatization involves two goals: first, to attract foreign investors and second, to distance state corporations themselves from the socialist past. Privatization is a performance, if you will, of enactment of these two intertwined goals.

Prior to China's entry into the WTO, foreign investors were required to work with a state entity. But since 2001, these investors have been allowed to seek out private, or nonstate, companies that have evolved out of the market economy rather than from a state bureau. State corporations have thus found themselves potentially in competition in certain sectors with companies that might appear to be independent of the state. There is a widespread view in China that the ability of government officials to maintain power enables them to have a monopoly on profit-seeking activities. They are further accused of using this monopoly to benefit their families over employees in state corporations, even to the extent of siphoning profits out of the corporation rather than making it profitable: in a word, what is considered in China to be "corruption." This corruption is said to derive from the socialist past and its inequalities based in political networks.

Government officials in charge of state corporations have gone to great lengths to distance themselves from that view. Performing a move away from the socialist past is an important means of casting the inequalities emerging in the present as holdovers from that past, rather than as produced by the capitalist activities that state officials engage in and encourage in others. Yet state officials, as part of the socialist obligations of that lingering past, also feel the need to display some response to these inequalities, especially in light of the many demonstrations that occur in China about working conditions, land reallocation, and social welfare. One might point out that these demonstrations also speak to the lingering of the socialist past, a past that avowed support for a decent life for all. Thus, state officials, somewhat paradoxically, cast their profit-seeking activities from within the state as a diffuse sense of seeking the welfare of the nation. State officials' revisionist history criticizes the socialist era not through the discourse of corruption but through a developmentalist logic: that the socialist era held China back from proper development. Distancing oneself from the socialist past enables those working within state entities to craft this revisionist history while simultaneously continuing with the legacies of certain socialist institutional practices. These include the power to determine the parameters of multinational corporate activity in China. The ongoing anticolonial, nationalist structure of feeling among those working within as well as outside of government corporations subtends a determination not to allow the United States to weaken China.

That which state corporations call privatization can be seen in the establishment of companies with all the legal trappings of a private entity. This privatization process is especially prevalent among industries that are export-oriented. Even with the emergence of a substantial middle class and the rise of domestic consumption, China depends on exports to create wealth. Thus, the matter of control of exports is central to the complexity of the privatization process within state corporations.

One important means to enact a version of privatization is to create joint ventures or linked commodity chain production relations with foreign investors that appear to be separated from these state corporations. Based on ethnographic research conducted from 2002 to 2013 of a state-owned import-export corporation in the Zhejiang silk industry that I had previously studied in the 1980s and 1990s,[35] I found that these "private" entities were not as independent from the state as they are made to appear.[36]

By the mid-2000s, this state-owned corporation had several joint ventures with companies from Italy, Germany, and France. This corporation's "true" nature—that is, whether it had fully privatized or was still part of the state—was difficult at first to discern even as it was clearly seeking to create profit. I slowly came to realize that this import-export corporation was not so much a hybrid entity as a blurred entity that is profit-seeking, partially privatized, and still part of the state. This blurred status is distinct from those who describe hybrid public-private entities, which are a combination of an already existing private company with a state agency.

Several characteristics eventually revealed the blurred character of the corporation. The most important was the formation of a company, Splendid China [a pseudonym], out of the state corporation that was described to me as a new company that was privatizing the import-export aspect of the state corporation. Splendid China was formed to manage joint ventures with foreign investors. This company took the appearance of a private company and was described to me that way. But through several years of conversation with its head manager, whom I will call Manager Li, as well as discussion with others in the state corporation, it became clear it was more like a general holding company for the state corporation.

One practice that would conventionally indicate privatization was a process of selling stock. Employees were encouraged, cajoled, and pressured to buy stock in Spendid China. About 44 percent of Splendid China's stock was owned by employees.[37] This stock-buying campaign did not turn employees into the owners. Like U.S. corporations, the fact that stockholders buy securities in a corporation does not mean that the corporation itself—or one of its holding companies—is no longer the major owner.

Splendid China was also required by government regulation to find a few other companies to buy their stock so that this process—whether privatization or profitization—did not look like stark originary accumulation; that is, it should not look as if the government handed over public resources to the top managers to make a profit for themselves. Three other companies bought a total of 5 percent of the stock in Splendid China. It is more than likely that these companies represent the state corporation, as many state-owned corporations have pursued this strategy of creating multiple holding companies.

Thus, the silk corporation is most likely still the majority shareholder of Splendid China. Selling stock, then, can have multiple implications: it can indicate a "privatization" process, it can make the company "public" in the sense of appearing on the stock market, and it can mean "public" in the sense of still belonging under the aegis of a state-owned corporation. In Splendid China's case, it was not listed on the stock market; shares in the company were internally distributed.[38]

In addition to stock ownership, other practices indicated that a clean line between private and public was difficult to draw and that a more ambiguous state of affairs existed. One was the development of "branch companies." Splendid China has eight branch companies that engage in foreign trade and form joint ventures. Manager Li also called them *bumen*. *Bumen* is one of the key terms that links Splendid China with the government. *Bumen* means department, or section, of a larger entity. It is a term that has been in use since the 1950s to describe offices within a state bureau. Branch companies, or *bumen*, under the aegis of Splendid China can engage in a wide variety of profit-seeking activities, including joint ventures, domestic production, and buying and selling of raw materials and fabric for the domestic market and for export. Yet that does not make them independent entities. None of the independent companies in China have anything they would call "branch companies" that are responsible for their own profits. The larger nonstate private companies have established "franchises."

Splendid China also has what they call "children companies" (*zi gongsi*). These were acknowledged to be dependent agents. Splendid China owns 70 percent of these companies, and the employee who runs one of these children companies owns 30 percent. Splendid China organizes the customers for these children companies, and the financial arrangements and the management structure are unified with Splendid China. If Splendid China were a fully "independent" or "private" company, it is unlikely they would encourage their employees to take potential profit away from them. However, given the greater likelihood that Splendid China is still under the aegis of the state silk corporation, the fact that employees generate more profit on their own initiative can only be seen as a benefit for Splendid China/the state corporation/the state.

The term "children companies" is not simply a metaphor. Given the difficulty of finding good jobs in China and the culturally accepted norm to help one's children and other kin members, it is not surprising that a good number of these companies are managed by the actual children of government officials. While I do not have the space to discuss the issue further here, suffice it to say that the status of "family firms" is ambiguous in China, given these entangled relations labeled "corrupt."

In sum, my research led me to conclude that Splendid China is a profitizing trading company within the Zhejiang silk corporation. It creates its own profit-seeking activities and is responsible for its losses. On the other hand, it generates profits that are partially used by the state silk corporation.[39] This corporation and many others in China represent the kind of blurred entity that is profit-seeking, partially privatized, and still part of the state. Analytically, this ambiguity reveals the historically contingent and continuously changing nature of the private-public distinction as well as profit-seeking activities within capitalism, not only in China but elsewhere.

INDIA (MOODIE)

India's turn to liberalization and its relationship to global regimes and rhetorics of neoliberalism runs along what are perhaps more familiar lines for those in the West. In 1991, the Indian state—a socialist democracy, it is important to remember—found itself in a serious debt repayment crisis. As a result, and with consultation from the World Bank and neoliberal economists, the Congress Party–led government began divesting itself of shares of public-sector enterprises (PSEs) and allowing foreign investors to bid for them in addition to the general public, financial institutions, and workers. The only public-sector company from which the government fully divested was the automobile company Maruti Udyog, which was sold to Suzuki.[40] In fact, many economic commentators have noted that privatization per se—the selling off of PSEs, which in India remain numerous—has been the least consistently implemented policy of post-1991 reforms. Whether economists celebrate[41] or bemoan[42] this fact, as Sunila Kale puts it, "privatization and the scaling back of the public sector have proven to be the least successful [reforms] and most susceptible to political derailing."[43] Much of the pushback against privatization has come from labor unions and India's various communist parties.

Aside from recommending financial and trade restructuring, global powers like the World Bank had to contend with the reality that in 1990, the Bank itself was estimating that about 45 percent of the country still lived under the (very low) poverty line. High-level economic changes would only go so far toward helping the vast majority of the nation's poor, rural residents.

Another set of recommendations pertained to the decentralization of welfare functions and their transfer from the state to nongovernmental organizations [NGOs]. In the 1990s, NGOs sprang up on nearly every street corner in India with support from international donors such as the World Bank, UNICEF, and Planned Parenthood and, sometimes, from the state itself, creating the bizarre acronym GONGO. NGOs were seen as an efficient, nimble, and less corrupt alternative to the great behemoth of Indian bureaucracy and the widespread corruption of government officials.[44]

The NGO-ization[45] of the so-called developing world since the 1990s has called into question neat public-private divisions insofar as so much of its institutional and discursive attention has been trained on poor households and, in particular, poor women. Looking at gender and development as part of neoliberalization also highlights, however, that rather than "privatization," which may be a tempting characterization of the turn to NGOs, we may do well to specify which kind of privatization. For instance, in my work on microfinance—perhaps the most "successful" gender and development paradigm of all time given its current status as common sense among policy planners—"financialization" perhaps better describes changes in the approach to women and development than simple privatization.

Microfinance has always been about blurring the public-private divide. From the famous quip by Muhamed Yunus, Grameen Bank (GB) founder and World Bank darling, that "credit given to a woman brings about change faster than when given to a man"[46] to the oft-stated goal of GB and other microfinance institutions (hereafter MFIs) to both allow women to undertake their income-generating work within the home and traverse into the public sphere if they so desire, the very point seems to be to reinforce the deep imbrication of public and domestic. The "enterprises" undertaken by women in MFIs are almost universally domestic or reproductive in nature, from basket making to raising chickens for eggs, and, planners like Yunus promise, their proceeds will immediately and almost universally go the welfare of their children.[47]

Few, if any, MFI projects have ever been "private" to begin with. As Milford Bateman has shown, in the vast majority of cases around the world—including in Bangladesh, home of Yunus and the famous Grameen Bank—already resource-starved governments have supplied the start-up capital and bureaucratic infrastructure to get MFIs off the ground.[48] The Bangladeshi government, for instance, gave Yunus an initial loan to get GB up and running and has been a major shareholder throughout its many iterations. The risks of any given loan default are certainly borne entirely by individual women (and are thus "private"),[49] but the resource base of microfinance has been public in the sense that it is shared by taxpayers and implemented by extant state bureaucracies.

An example from my fieldwork in Rajasthan is instructive. The Women's Development Programme (WDP) was a women's empowerment initiative formed as a joint venture between the government of Rajasthan, the Institute of Development Studies, Jaipur, and a (now-defunct) NGO monitoring organization called the Information and Development Resource Agency (IDARA). Founded in 1984, in the waning days of the UN Decade on Women, with six years of funding from UNICEF, the WDP became emblematic in India and across the world of the idea of bottom-up development for women. Eschewing traditional agendas for women's empowerment in India, which often centered on reproduction and population control, the WDP encouraged local women to join together in groups, forge their own agendas on everything from domestic violence to agricultural work injuries to grazing rights, and learn how to bring their concerns to the relevant bodies, whether these be local elected representatives, *panchayats*, or the court system.[50]

By all accounts, for the first few years of its operation the WDP did provide an avenue for some important forms of radical change. WDP employees, known as *sathins* (which can be translated as something like "female friend" or "female accomplice"), became outspoken advocates for their fellow women. In fact, it may be that the WDP was too effective: several *sathins* were attacked in the line of duty, the most brutal and infamous case being the gang-rape of Bhanwari Devi, a *sathin* in a village not far outside the state capital of Jaipur, who was working to stop a child marriage. She was assaulted by males from the caste group planning the weddings; all accused were eventually acquitted.

The Bhanwari Devi case coincided with the national take-off of neoliberal ideas about development and the call for the retreat of the welfare state. Over the following decade, the WDP was substantially defunded. By the time I was conducting fieldwork and living in the home of one of the women who was trained early on as a *sathin*, the grassroots activities that had made the WDP effective—role-playing, stage plays, group songs that spoke from and to the lives of rural women—had been almost entirely replaced by the lending and borrowing of money.[51] WDP had taken up microcredit, and though some of the *sathins* were able to use this transition to their benefit, including my hostess, many women in Rajasthan were simply in a tangle of snowballing debt with little sense of who or what was behind the loan money that suddenly seemed to be flooding rural areas, earmarked for women.[52]

To describe the history of microfinance, then, as simply a process of privatization is to miss some key points. First, the initial outlays for MFI-building projects, at least in India and other well-known cases from South Asia, often came from the state. Some, like the Grameen Bank, were entirely "public." Second, even in their view of the perfect entrepreneurial female subject, MFIs relied on women's ongoing role as the caretaker of children and elders to lend credence to their assertion that through such small-scale interventions large-scale changes could be made.

What has been depoliticized, or rendered into "anti-politics," a term that may also be preferable to "privatized,"[53] is the implementation of social welfare measures. It is not and was not the case that there is no money for development. It is simply that elected officials are no longer accountable for the vexing social life of development efforts—the daily dramas of lending and building and losing and dealing with the inevitable catastrophes that often accompany life in poor homes and regions—as they might have been if such welfare efforts were undertaken by government departments. Instead, social messiness and human deprivation are now the purview of international planners and NGO workers who have little, if any, accountability to the people they serve.

In this section, we have pointed to the always already imbricated nature of public-private relations vis-à-vis the state. In the case of China, it is often impossible to parse a clear divide between public and private when state-owned corporations profitize through legalistic strategies of privatization. Similarly, in the case of India, the changes in the public sector, especially the NGOization of welfare, do not remove the state from people's lives—especially poor people's lives—so much as rearrange and outsource welfare programs. Risk is shifted away from the state, which can still opportunistically claim to be dedicated to goals like women's empowerment as and when it becomes politically salient within and beyond national politics.

One key aspect worth emphasizing is that we cannot tell a straightforward story of the private sector taking over the state. The processes we describe here do not simply begin from the private sector anxious to take over public resources. Even the World Bank's efforts to privatize the Indian state come up against the overwhelming evidence of the need to address poverty. Thus, what is striking in this section's discussion is that the transformations move in the opposite direction. That is, the initiatives originate largely from *within* the state. Moreover, these initiatives remind us of the afterlives of the Cold War, as the governments of both China and India feel the need to continue to address questions of social welfare, even if in attenuated and depoliticized forms.

This section also reminds us of the feminist point that, as Wendy Brown so cogently put it some time ago, we still find the man in the state.[54] It is not merely that the domestic realm gets pulled into public financial arrangements, but that we can never understand the domestic realm without taking into account how the state—or, rather, political power and authority—shape domestic labor and relations from their inception. In the case of India, microfinance arrangements press women both to engage in "domestic" enterprises and to financialize their debt so that they are ever more closely tied to the state, now through a debt relationship. In the case of China, the entanglement of family relations and profitizing practices has been a key aspect of discourses on corruption, even as the pressures to find decent work lead people to rely on their families.

Conclusion

Given the explosion of studies dedicated to understanding, unpacking, historicizing, and critiquing neoliberalism, it is striking that one of its key terms, "privatization," has been largely treated as a transparent process that unfolds in similar ways across the globe as "accumulation by dispossession."[55] Our feminist training alerts us to a term like this, with its invocation of a private sphere of political economic activity. Long histories of the creation, management, and continual renegotiation of social imaginaries of separate spheres called "the private" and "the public" have been documented by feminists since the 1970s. Their lesson is clear. Rather than taking neoliberalism at its word about what labor relations, economic processes, or visions of the future it engenders through so-called privatization, we must learn to ask, "What is being made public or private? By whom? Through which social processes?" And, importantly, "In whose interests?" We contend that privatization needs to be opened up for closer inspection, its messiness exposed, not just for the sake of empirical fidelity (though that is also important at times), but to encourage new thinking in the search for social justice. As we stated in our introduction, if the problem were really just that public resources have been sold off for profit, we could simply fight for renationalization, for instance.

Unfortunately, the situation is more blurred and more dire. In this article, we have proposed that using a processual postsocialist lens that does not presume the end of the Cold War but instead points to moments and contexts in which its afterlife becomes salient—such as in workers' articulations of their dreams for the future—is essential to the project of understanding contemporary capitalism. In both cases we describe, China and India, the socialist "past" is not fully supplanted by capitalist political economic arrangements—both have communist parties that are alive and well. Furthermore, long-standing debates about configurations of private investment and profit versus public need and shared responsibility take place in languages (not to mention geopolitical connections) birthed during the Cold War.

We also point to the way feminist theorizations of the public-private relationship—and, ultimately, their blurriness except in moments of ideological production—can help us take a broader view of the political economic processes that are killing off species, heating the planet, making us sick, and increasing inequality around the world. We have shown that rather than presume what we need to explain—namely, that neoliberalism is characterized by the process of privatization (to the extent that they are sometimes synonymous)—an ethnographic approach can help us distill more specific descriptions of exploitative capitalist relations. For instance, we proposed that the term "profitization" has more descriptive power for the situations we described in China and India. Again, this is not just theoretical parsimony, but rather suggests exactly where political pressure might be applied in the service of justice.

We are ultimately arguing that it is important to keep our eyes on the prize. Our goal as social scientists and observers of political economy is not simply to describe neoliberalism in greater detail—though we think the specificity provided by ethnography is an important first step. Rather, it is to locate the sites, sources, and relations of capitalist exploitation and take them apart—one by complicated one, if necessary.

But we fear that using privatization as a shorthand for complex political economic processes can also, in effect, take neoliberalism at its word. If private companies have taken "our" resources, we simply need to fight to get them back. Deep ethnographic study of the social relations that constitute and are constituted by processes now referred to as privatization, however, shows that the picture is much messier and, we might add, more challenging than even our best accounts have yet conveyed.

Notes

1. Matthew Carlin and Silvia Federici, "The Exploitation of Women, Social Reproduction, and the Struggle against Global Capital," *Theory & Event* 17,

no. 3 (2014), http://muse.jhu.edu/article/553382; Kathi Weeks, *The Problem with Work: Feminism, Marxism, Antiwork Politics, and Postwork Imaginaries* (Durham, N.C.: Duke University Press, 2011).

2. William Davies, "Neoliberalism: A Bibliographic Review," *Theory, Culture & Society* 31, no. 7/8 (2014): 309–17; Davies, *The Limits of Neoliberalism* (London: Sage, 2014); Nik Heynen et al., eds., *Neoliberal Environments: False Promises and Unnatural Consequences* (New York: Routledge, 2007); Stephen H. Linder, "Coming to Terms with the Public-Private Partnership: A Grammar of Multiple Meanings," *American Behavioral Scientist* 43, no. 1 (1999): 35–51; James McCarthy, "Privatizing Conditions of Production: Trade Agreements as Neoliberal Environmental Governance," *Geoforum* 35, no. 3 (2004): 327–41; Lisa Rofel, *Desiring China: Experiments in Neoliberalism, Sexuality, and Public Culture* (Durham, N.C.: Duke University Press, 2007).

3. Wendy Brown, *Undoing the Demos: Neoliberalism's Stealth Revolution* (New York: Zone Books, 2015); Aihwa Ong, *Neoliberalism as Exception: Mutations in Citizenship and Sovereignty* (Durham, N.C.: Duke University Press, 2006); Nikolas Rose, *Powers of Freedom: Reframing Political Thought* (Cambridge: Cambridge University Press, 1999). In this version of neoliberalism as a modality of governance, economic framings replace political ones such that all values are subsumed under economic efficiencies and capital enhancements. This includes rendering human beings as human capital whose constant aim is to entrepreneurialize their individual value. Certain scholars thus conclude that neoliberalism is most importantly an ethical as well as political vision and not merely an economic one, because it fosters an ethos of competitiveness in all aspects of individual and social life.

4. Plehwe, "Introduction," in *Road from Mont Pèlerin*; Timothy Mitchell, "How Neoliberalism Makes Its World: The Urban Property Rights Project in Peru," in *Road from Mont Pèlerin*, 392–416; Rofel, "Capitalism and the Private/Public Division," *Theorizing the Contemporary*, Cultural Anthropology website, March 30, 2015, https://culanth.org/fieldsights/653-capitalism-and-the-private-public-division; Rofel and Sylvia J. Yanagisako, *Fabricating Transnational Capitalism: A Collaborative Ethnography of Italian-Chinese Global Fashion* (Durham, N.C.: Duke University Press, 2019).

5. See Antonio Gramsci, *Selection from the Prison Notebooks*, trans. Quintin Hoare and Geoffrey Nowell-Smith (New York: International Publishers, 1972).

6. David Harvey, *A Brief History of Neoliberalism* (New York: Oxford University Press, 2007), 161–62.

7. Michelle Zimbalist Rosaldo and Louise Lamphere, eds., *Woman, Culture, and Society* (Stanford, Calif.: Stanford University Press, 1974).

8. Rosaldo, "Woman, Culture and Society: A Theoretical Overview," in Rosaldo and Lamphere, *Woman, Culture, and Society*, 17–42.

9. Jane Fishburne Collier and Sylvia Junko Yanagisako, eds., *Gender and Kinship: Essays Toward a Unified Analysis* (Stanford, Calif.: Stanford University Press, 1987); Rayna Rapp, "Family and Class in Contemporary America: Notes toward

an Understanding of Ideology," *Science & Society* 42, no. 3 (1978): 278–300; Rapp, "Anthropology," *Signs: Journal of Women in Culture and Society* 4, no. 3 (1979): 497–513; Rosaldo, "The Use and Abuse of Anthropology: Reflections on Feminism and Cross-Cultural Understanding," *Signs: Journal of Women in Culture and Society* 5, no. 3 (1980): 389–417; Yanagisako, "Family and Household: The Analysis of Domestic Groups," *Annual Review of Anthropology* 8, no. 1 (1979): 161–205; Yanagisako and Carol Delaney, eds., *Naturalizing Power: Essays in Feminist Cultural Analysis* (New York: Routledge, 1995).

10. Yanagisako, "Family and Household."

11. Marilyn Strathern, *The Gender of the Gift: Problems with Women and Problems with Society in Melanesia* (Berkeley: University of California Press, 1990).

12. Patricia Hill Collins, *Black Feminist Thought: Knowledge, Consciousness, and the Politics of Empowerment* (New York: Routledge, 1990); Kimberle Crenshaw, "Demarginalizing the Intersection of Race and Sex: A Black Feminist Critique of Antidiscrimination Doctrine, Feminist Theory and Antiracist Politics," *University of Chicago Legal Forum*, 1989, 139–68; Patricia J. Williams, *Alchemy of Race and Rights* (Cambridge, Mass.: Harvard University Press, 1991).

13. Linda K. Kerber, "Separate Spheres, Female Worlds, Woman's Place: The Rhetoric of Women's History," *Journal of American History* 75, no. 1 (1988): 9–39.

14. Antoinette Burton, *At the Heart of the Empire: Indians and the Colonial Encounter in Late-Victorian Britain* (Berkeley: University of California Press, 1998).

15. The focus of these topics has varied considerably. For urban development and infrastructure, see Vincanne Adams, *Markets of Sorrow, Labors of Faith: New Orleans in the Wake of Katrina* (Durham, N.C.: Duke University Press, 2013); Linder, "Coming to Terms with the Public-Private Partnership"; Matti Siemiatycki, "Public-Private Partnership Networks: Exploring Business-Government Relationships in United Kingdom Transportation Projects," *Economic Geography* 87, no. 3 (2011): 309–34; Gavin Shatkin, "The City and the Bottom Line: Urban Megaprojects and the Privatization of Planning in Southeast Asia," *Environment and Planning A* 40, no. 2 (2008): 383–401; for "resources" such as water, transportation, and energy, see Karen Bakker, *Privatizing Water: Governance Failure and the World's Urban Water Crisis* (Ithaca, N.Y.: Cornell University Press, 2010); Laura Bear, *Navigating Austerity: Currents of Debt along a South Asian River* (Stanford, Calif.: Stanford University Press, 2015); Pedro Pirez, "Buenos Aires: Fragmentation and Privatization of the Metropolitan City," *Environment and Urbanization* 14, no. 1 (2002): 145–58; for medical care, see Sara McLafferty, "The Geographical Restructuring of Urban Hospitals: Spatial Dimensions of Corporate Strategy," *Social Science & Medicine* 23, no. 10 (1986): 1079–86; Sandy Smith-Nonini, "Health 'Anti-Reform' in El Salvador: Community Health NGOs and the State in the Neoliberal Era," *PoLAR: Political and Legal Anthropology Review* 21, no. 1 (1998): 99–113; for social welfare, see Jesook Song, *South Koreans in the Debt Crisis: The Creation of a Neoliberal Welfare Society* (Durham, N.C.: Duke University Press, 2009); for plant self-cloning, see Matt Hodges, "The Politics of Emergence: Public–Private Partnerships and the Con-

flictive Timescapes of Apomixis Technology Development," *BioSocieties* 7, no. 1 (2012): 23–49; for NGOs, see Sangeeta Kamat, "The Privatization of Public Interest: Theorizing NGO Discourse in a Neoliberal Era," *Review of International Political Economy* 11, no. 1 (2004): 155–76; for information technologies, see Renee Kuriyan and Isha Ray, "Outsourcing the State? Public–Private Partnerships and Information Technologies in India," *World Development* 37, no. 10 (2009): 1663–73; Becky Mansfield, ed., *Privatization: Property and the Remaking of Nature-Society Relations* (Oxford: Blackwell, 2008).

16. Neda Atanasoski, *Humanitarian Violence: The U.S. Deployment of Diversity* (Minneapolis: University of Minnesota Press, 2013), 23.

17. Jamie Peck, Nik Theodore, and Neil Brenner, "Postneoliberalism and Its Malcontents," *Antipode* 41, no. S1 (2010): 94–116.

18. Alfred Gusenbauer, "La Strada on Wall Street," *Project Syndicate*, October 6, 2008, https://www.project-syndicate.org/commentary/la-strada-on-wall-street, quoted in Peck, Theodore, and Brenner, "Postneoliberalism and Its Malcontents," 99.

19. Peck, "Postneoliberalism and Its Malcontents."

20. Sushil Khanna, "The Transformation of India's Public Sector: Political Economy of Growth and Change," *Economic & Political Weekly* 50, no. 5 (2015): 47–60.

21. Nirmal Kumar Chandra, "Relevance of Soviet Economic Model for Non-Socialist Countries," *Economic and Political Weekly* 39, no. 22 (2004): 2287.

22. Ralph Litzinger, "The Labor Question in China: Apple and Beyond," *South Atlantic Quarterly* 112, no. 1 (2013): 172–78; Ngai Pun, *Made in China: Women Factory Workers in a Global Workplace* (Durham, N.C.: Duke University Press, 2005); Pun and Jenny Chan, "The Spatial Politics of Labor in China: Life, Labor, and a New Generation of Migrant Workers," *South Atlantic Quarterly* 112, no. 1 (2013): 179–90.

23. Kellee S. Tsai, *Back-Alley Banking: Private Entrepreneurs in China* (Ithaca, N.Y.: Cornell University Press, 2002); Tsai, *Capitalism without Democracy: The Private Sector in Contemporary China* (Ithaca, N.Y.: Cornell University Press, 2007).

24. Leela Fernandes, *India's New Middle Class: Democratic Politics in an Era of Economic Reform* (Minneapolis: University of Minnesota Press, 2006).

25. See, for example, Sunila Kale, "Current Reforms: The Politics of Policy Change in India's Electricity Sector," *Pacific Affairs* 77, no. 3 (2004): 467–91.

26. Leo Coleman, *A Moral Technology: Electrification as Political Ritual in New Delhi* (Ithaca, N.Y.: Cornell University Press, 2017).

27. Nikhil Anand, *Hydraulic City: Water and the Infrastructures of Citizenship in Mumbai* (Durham, N.C.: Duke University Press, 2017), 18; see also Lisa Björkman, *Pipe Politics, Contested Waters: Embedded Infrastructures of Millennial Mumbai* (Durham, N.C.: Duke University Press, 2015).

28. For more detail, see Megan Moodie, *We Were Adivasis: Aspiration in an Indian Scheduled Tribe* (Chicago: University of Chicago Press, 2015).

29. Ibid., 168–69.

30. This is the classic view outlined in Louis Dumont, *Homo Hierarchicus: An Essay on the Caste System*, trans. Mark Sainsbury (Chicago: University of Chicago Press, 1970).

31. See Moodie, "Microfinance and the Gender of Risk: The Case of Kiva. Org," *Signs: Journal of Women in Culture and Society* 38, no. 2 (2013): 279–302; Moodie, *We Were Adivasis*, 177–80.

32. Eleanor Burke Leacock, "Introduction," in *The Origin of the Family, Private Property, and the State, in the Light of the Researches of Lewis H. Morgan*, by Friedrich Engels (New York: International Publishers, 1972), 7–66; Moodie, "Feminist Theory and Reproduction: An Important Legacy for the Political Anthropology of the U.S.," in *Handbook of Political Anthropology*, ed. Harald Wydra and Bjørn Thomassen (Cheltenham, UK: Edward Elgar, 2018); Weeks, *Problem with Work*; Yanagisako and Delaney, *Naturalizing Power*.

33. See Bear et al., "Generating Capitalism," *Theorizing the Contemporary*, Cultural Anthropology website, March 30, 2015, https://culanth.org/fieldsights/650-generating-capitalism; Rofel and Yanagisako, *Fabricating Transnational Capitalism*; Anna Lowenhaupt Tsing, *The Mushroom at the End of the World: On the Possibility of Life in Capitalist Ruins* (Princeton, N.J.: Princeton University Press, 2015).

34. See, for example, Yasheng Huang, *Capitalism with Chinese Characteristics: Entrepreneurship and the State* (Cambridge: Cambridge University Press, 2008). I distinguish my argument here from the idea that the Chinese state is disingenuous, that it "pretends" to privatize but does not really do so. Or, more to the point, I distinguish my argument from those who argue that because the Chinese state has not followed a particular capitalist path toward privatization, it therefore has not truly instituted capitalism. Such a view universalizes the ideology of Adam Smith about the particular path one must follow in order to foster profit-seeking activity.

35. Rofel, *Other Modernities* (Berkeley: University of California Press, 1999).

36. This research was part of a collaborative ethnography with Sylvia Yanagisako; see Rofel and Yanagisako, *Fabricating Transnational Capitalism*.

37. Needless to say, migrant workers in Splendid China's factories were not given the option to buy stock. Only office employees—the technicians, designers, and marketing personnel—were part of this arrangement.

38. The majority of companies that have gone "public" and are listed on the Shanghai stock market as selling stock are state-owned firms. Thus, they are both "public" and "state-owned." Hence, stock can be held in Splendid China by individuals and various independent entities, but it can also be held by the Zhejiang silk corporation through the Zhejiang Silk Group--that is, by the state.

39. This might have been especially true after the 2003 tax reform, which put greater pressure on local governments to produce their own profits.

40. Khanna, "Transformation of India's Public Sector," 51.

41. Ibid.

42. Kale, "The Political Economy of India's Second-Generation Reforms," *Journal of Strategic Studies* 25, no. 4 (2002): 207–25.

43. Ibid., 207.

44. Akhil Gupta, *Postcolonial Developments: Agriculture in the Making of Modern India* (Durham, N.C.: Duke University Press, 1998); Gupta, *Red Tape: Bureaucracy, Structural Violence, and Poverty in India* (Durham, N.C.: Duke University Press, 2012).

45. Victoria Bernal and Inderpal Grewal, "The NGO Form: Feminist Struggles, States, and Neoliberalism," in *Theorizing NGOs: States, Feminisms, and Neoliberalism*, ed. Victoria Bernal and Inderpal Grewal (Durham, N.C.: Duke University Press, 2014), 1–18.

46. Muhammad Yunus, *Banker to the Poor: Micro-Lending and the Battle against World Poverty* (New York: Public Affairs, 1999), 72.

47. Ibid.; see also Lamia Karim, *Microfinance and Its Discontents: Women in Debt in Bangladesh* (Minneapolis: University of Minnesota Press, 2011); Moodie, "Microfinance and the Gender of Risk."

48. Milford Bateman, *Why Doesn't Microfinance Work?: The Destructive Rise of Local Neoliberalism* (London: Zed, 2010).

49. See Moodie, "Microfinance and the Gender of Risk."

50. See Sumi Madhok, *Rethinking Agency: Developmentalism, Gender and Rights* (London: Routledge, 2013).

51. C. P. Sujaya, Lakshmi Murthy Kumud Sharma, and Uma Chakravarti, *The Independent Review of the Women's Development Program, Rajasthan* (Jaipur: Government of Rajasthan, 2002).

52. Moodie, "Enter Microcredit: A New Culture of Women's Empowerment in Rajasthan?," *American Ethnologist* 35, no. 3 (2008): 454–65.

53. James Ferguson, *The Anti-Politics Machine: Development, Depoliticization, and Bureaucratic Power in Lesotho* (Minneapolis: University of Minnesota Press, 1994).

54. Brown, "Finding the Man in the State," *Feminist Studies* 18, no. 1 (1992): 7–34.

55. Harvey, *Brief History of Neoliberalism*.

"Innovation" Discourse and the Neoliberal University:
Top Ten Reasons to Abolish Disruptive Innovation

Christopher Newfield

If I had to nominate a biopolitical discourse for eminent domain over the contemporary university, it would be the discourse of *innovation*—disruptive innovation in particular. Universities are of interest to the top brass in politics and business largely to the extent that they produce disruptive technologies and innovation-ready human capital. University laboratories are expected to be world-class centers of innovation, and a discipline that is not serving innovation or subjecting itself to innovation becomes an object of disregard. The discourse of innovation now has almost unlimited managerial authority. Innovation binds the various practices of higher education to an economy where competitive success is assumed to depend on superior powers of disruptive innovation. A university that continuously innovates on itself is thought to be the one most likely to offer innovation to the economy. One widely noted feature of neoliberal societies is the translation of formerly independent political, social, or cultural aims into economic ones.[1] Innovation is a discourse that lashes the university firmly to the economy and its imperatives of pecuniary gain (revenues, salaries, assets). It is also a form of what Randy Martin called neoliberalism's "crisis-oriented sociality," which involves everyone in a "risk economy" that, conveniently, requires continuous managerial involvement.[2] While liberal arts colleges and regional four-year universities may focus on personal development or job training, innovation is a mandatory feature of research universities. Innovation is thus a classical kind of biopower—it is positive, generative, and constitutive rather than simply repressive, while functioning as an effective governmentality that disfavors or excludes a range of educational values and goals. Michel Foucault developed the notion of bio-power in large part through his studies of the history of sexuality.[3] For its nonstudents at least, innovation is the university's sexuality.

These first two paragraphs that you have just read form a recognizable mode of opening a chapter in a book of critical theory about an epic so-cial formation like neoliberalism. I introduced three conceptual categories (innovation, neoliberalism, the university), linked them through categorical generalities, and implied that they are always mutually reinforcing. What is likely to follow such a beginning is a learned discussion of some of the specific modes, claims, evidence, and discursive moves through which a discourse of innovation subjugates diverse institutional practices—the university's—to neoliberal capitalism.

In fact, this *does* describe a portion of what is to come. But the relations between neoliberal governance, innovation, and the university are much less stable and determinate than my first two paragraphs suggest. I don't treat the apparent durability and power of neoliberalism as a given, but as a mystery. It doesn't work very well if "work" is defined as achieving official goals. After thirty years of pumping universities full of innovation and staffing them with its fans, a standard metric of innovation—university patenting revenues—has shown little growth.[4] The university's research contribution to the econ-omy has grown at no better pace than the rate of GDP growth and remains very small.[5] Nor has neoliberalism inspired the corporate world to increase its rates of investment in new plants and processes or to increase the rate of productivity growth to anything like its 1950s or 1990s levels. When the economist David Kotz reviewed the post-2008 period in the United States, he called his piece, "End of the Neoliberal Era? Crisis and Restructuring in American Capitalism."[6] I share his doubts about the internal coherence of the economic system—and about the governmentality that it has so effectively persuaded many people is a kind of natural law.

The mystery, then, is the following: Why does the *failure* of neoliberalism produce more neoliberalism?[7] A large part of the answer is that neoliberalism's legitimacy rests on its reputation for innovation, which is as hard for society to oppose ideologically as, say, the divine right of kings was for an earlier period. Various publics would have an easier time rejecting innovation were it not for a second factor: the designated experts are almost all in favor. The main groupings of professionals and managers define innovation as right and necessary, efficient and inevitable, which makes it harder for regular folks to object. They must object in the teeth of official knowledge from law, business, economics, finance, and all technology fields. These fields contain skeptics and critics of multiple aspects of neoliberalism, of course, but they are minority dissidents, and their views rarely appear in nonexpert media. (A Thomas Piketty is the exception that proves the rule.) Whatever the mixed motives of individuals, the "professional-managerial class" (really "classes") has justified, streamlined, and curated a key aspect of neoliberalism—disruptive innovation—rather than opposing or overcoming it. I'll focus on the innovation theory of Clayton Christensen to explore the difficulty academic professionals, including left-wing humanities academics, have in developing an alternative.

I'll also address a second question: where might this alternative come from? That is, what forces might break the neoliberal deadlock? This question has particular urgency given the failure of the 2008 financial crisis and its long aftermath to prompt non-neoliberal models of Western economies. I'll suggest that there are large systemic forces that neoliberalism and disruptive innovation no longer master—and that academic professionals are going to need to enter the fray. Neoliberalism can function as a "political rationality" or as "governmentality," or as "biopower," to use just three Foucauldian terms for a systematicity that perpetuates itself *because of the political demobilization of professionals*.

Now more than ever we need to answer the question "Can the cognitariat speak?"[8]

Defining Disruptive Innovation

Although innovation seems like a nebulous term, its popular business meaning is narrow. It always refers to putting a novel idea to a use that creates monetary value. Its complementary term is *invention*, which is honored as the result of acts of creativity that bring a novelty forth into the world. As business writer David Burkus puts it, "Creativity, the ability to generate novel and useful ideas, is the seed of innovation but unless it's applied and scaled it's still just an idea."[9] Innovation is a further step. It's "a solution that adds value from a customer's perspective," writes Nick Skillicorn. Most simply, innovation is the copula or bridge in the movement expressed by the name of the organization that posted these definitions: "Idea to Value." Innovation translates thought, or intellectual capital, into pecuniary returns, which become financial capital. Innovation describes the process of capitalizing on an idea—on the capacity for creativity itself—and being rewarded with monetary gain.

The standard contrast between creativity and innovation also makes innovation post-educational. Creativity depends on the individual's education in a discipline's array of knowledges and practices. One of the most influential models of creativity, Mihaly Csikszentmihalyi's "flow," grounds the celebrated breakthrough moment of creative insight in a long prehistory of "preparation" and "incubation."[10] This includes the nearly two decades of learning that precedes the university, and then university learning for those who attend. Innovation takes educational formation for granted: it is priced into the person a lab or firm hires to innovate. In public discourse, high-value economies are traced to entities like "pools of talent" whose educational ingredients have long since disappeared into the mix.[11] The tech industry's indifference to the plight of nonelite colleges and universities stems in part from taking education for granted as innovation's archaic resource.

It's almost a matter of definition, then, that an innovative university is measured by its *pecuniary* effects. Universities do have other valued intellectual and social outcomes, but innovation relegates these to secondary status. An innovative university must show its payoff in the form of commercialized technology, general economic impact, the economic mobility of its graduates, or human capital formation measured by salary increments. The contrapositive is also true: a university that does not show measurable pecuniary benefits is not innovative. More on this later. My point here is that this nebulous-seeming term, "innovation," is in practice rather strict.

While U.S. colleges might have seemed close to pure forms of intellectual cultivation, research universities have always been shaped by pecuniary aims.[12] These coexisted with humanistic, social, spiritual, and other goals, sometimes loosely modeled on Weber's notion of the vocation as a profoundly nonpecuniary ambition.[13] The business university rose to the top of the academic heap in the late nineteenth century and has remained there, containing and diluting various forms of radical humanism and social movements without eliminating them.[14] The long détente between forces of fairly similar strength has been eroded by a second feature of innovation, beyond its monetary fixation, which is disruption.[15]

By the 1990s, innovation allowed society to have new products and economic progress allegedly by disrupting everything. The theory of disruptive innovation came to be used to justify an endless procession of company downsizings and closings over the past thirty years.[16] By the late 2010s, corporate America, health care, manufacturing, and the contemporary university have all tied their reputations to their delivery of innovation. The theory of disruptive innovation has justified continuous turmoil, unilateral decision-making, and steady managerial interference with how people do their jobs.

The dean of this innovation theory is Clayton Christensen, whose books *The Innovator's Dilemma* (1997) and *The Innovator's Solution* (2003) did more than any other works to change the collective corporate understanding of technical innovation from "steady, incremental improvement" arising from basic research to a market function.[17] Adding insult to injury, the value of innovation was decided not only by customers, but by the most backward customers, the ones who were way behind the adoption curve and wanted a *worse* product (that they could afford), not a better one.

Christensen nailed this feature in the less famous sequel book, *The Innovator's Solution*. He noted that technological sophistication did not protect famous companies like Xerox from clearly inferior products. The problem, he wrote, was commodification. You could spend a decade designing and building the fastest, most reliable copier or the best magnetic disk technology and get a couple of years' profits out of it before imitators stole most of your market. They would do this not by innovating a better disk drive, but a somewhat worse one that was a lot cheaper. What Christensen saw more clearly than nearly anyone else in the corporate world was the ease with which the most difficult technology could be commodified, which cut or killed its profit margins through imitation, and the general abundance of knowledge that typified the age of digital communications.

Christensen argued that "making highly differentiable products with strong cost advantages" is indeed a "license to print money, and lots of it," which only occurs when a firm is offering a distinctive and yet "not-good-enough" product protected by proprietary architectures.[18] An example from the past was Xerox Corporation, so dominant that its name became synonymous with the act of photocopying. Competition pressures the company into continuous innovation to get an always-better product that will make their customers happier and grow their market share. But what happens instead is that the company "overshoots the functionality and reliability that customers in lower tiers of the market can utilize." Imitators swoop in and *disrupt* the market from below, which slowly guts the big, high-quality incumbents and the sector overall. The result is a commercial double bind:

> A company that finds itself in a more-than-good-enough circumstance simply can't win: Either disruption will steal its markets, or commoditization will steal its profits. Most incumbents eventually end up the victim of both, because, although the pace of commoditization varies by industry, it is inevitable, and nimble new entrants rarely miss an opportunity to exploit a disruptive foothold.[19]

Companies must constantly strive to decommodify their own products. Apple does this with its iPhone via a steady stream of new models with supposedly unique new features. Christensen's key idea is that a firm stays on top not by innovating for higher quality per se, but by innovating for proprietary differentiation. Products must be different and be protected from imitation through intellectual property or trade secrecy or some other means. The iPhone's position depends not on superior quality—which is arguable at best—but on a brand ecosystem of software and product tie-ins that stabilize market share.

There are lots of ins and outs we don't need to ponder in order to grasp the theory's main points: innovation only happens through disruption; disruption is always driven by market price, not quality goals; market price means innovation is about achieving minimal or least-acceptable quality. When Christensen later coauthored *The Innovative University*, he said the same thing. Demand that comes from the bottom of the market, from weaker students who often didn't finish or even start college, is the source of disruption. Universities must address it by moving *down* the quality scale, toward standardized, modularized, simplified, less sophisticated, less advanced, even less intellectual education.[20] There is always a place for premium brands like Harvard and Williams, but the vast majority of colleges and universities, 95 to 97 percent, can thrive only by moving downmarket to the mass of customers. (It's possible to pursue this downmarketing with integrity, but only by setting disruption aside, as I'll argue later.)

Let's posit that Christensen is correct about his core idea—technology superiority does not guarantee business dominance. In an era of globalized manufacturing and relatively open information flows, technological breakthroughs create only temporary advantages. We might actually credit Christensen with a Marxian insight into the fundamental power of commodification: scientific progress and the rules of capitalism are two completely different things.[21] If you want to win at capitalism, don't try to win at science.

That means focusing not on innovation toward superior quality but instead on decommodification.

We have a handful of core features of innovation now: always pecuniary, market-ruled, and (mostly) tending toward lower quality (since disruption comes generally from the cheaper rather than the better).[22] In markets, volume rules: the masses speak, not professional elites who mark the leading edge.

Disruption Means Critique

And yet we should still ask, must dealing with disruption be so disruptive? The main claim of Jill Lepore's widely admired takedown of Christensen was that in fact successful companies *minimized* disruption or at least discontinuity in their own innovation process. She argued that Christensen was empirically wrong, since key tech sectors like disk drives are dominated by incremental innovators.[23]

Lepore understated the intelligence of Christensen's earlier work on the innovation process (from the mid-1990s to mid-2000s), written before he achieved guru status and came to stand for disruption as such. In *the Innovator's Solution*, the real goal was not disruption but decommodification; disruption was often a sign that you needed to start decommodification, not how you achieved the decommodification process. One of Christensen's most interesting insights took him on an intellectual orbit where he might briefly have intersected with Paul de Man's "blindness and insight"—managers routinely "assume that the *customer*'s world is structured in the same way that [their company] data are aggregated." In reality, the conceptual systems of the corporation and the world must be seen as distinct. Managers need to be self-reflective about this lethal aporia: "When managers define market segments along the lines for which data are available rather than the jobs that customers need to get done, it becomes impossible to predict whether a product idea will connect with an important customer job."[24] The problem is not that all innovation must disrupt the company, market, workforce, and community. The problem is epistemological capture within the managerial class.

When the "innovator's dilemma" is recast this way, the "innovator's solution" becomes something other than incessant disruption of everyone's processes through reorganizations, layoffs, and everything else. To the contrary, it means two things. First, the company (or university) should focus not on the characteristics of the product (and how smart and innovative it is), but on "the jobs that customers need to get done." This requires a kind of negative capability and populist interest in ordinary people outside the firm. It requires an interest not in their consumer desires but in their everyday *needs*. The question is not what kind of cool product they want to buy, but what they need help accomplishing in their lives.

Second, innovation strategy must not just be "deliberate," run by top-down procedures, but "emergent." Emergent strategy "bubbles up from within the organization, is the cumulative effect of day-to-day prioritization and investment decisions made by middle managers, engineers, salespeople, and financial staff. These tend to be tactical, day-to-day operating decisions made by people who are not in a visionary, futuristic, or strategic state of mind."[25]

To put these two features together, sustainable innovation requires that management keep a company, sector, workforce, community, and region relatively *undisrupted* so that its frontline employees can focus on the customer's job and how to help them do it. (Lepore was quite right about this.) The non-disruption helps support a distributed human intelligence system that uses quantitative data but embeds it in complex and collective "actor-networks" that combine people, activities, and things, including the company's products. Business becomes a kind of support for everyday society, offering new solutions that have a concrete positive impact on people's ordinary lives. Profit is first and foremost a source of sustained improvement in "doing the customer's job" rather than something to extract from them for the benefit of corporate owners.[26]

But in practice, these aspects of Christensen's innovation theory did not get taken up. This was mainly Christensen's doing. He did not at all emphasize the "empowerment" of frontline employees or bring forward the Douglas McGregor–Tom Peters line of "human relations" management theory that had long opposed Taylorism and autocratic managerialism.[27]

In other words, your employees' genuine love of excellence is not the solution: it's the problem. They will keep making better, higher-quality products (Theory Y is true!). Meanwhile, disruptive innovation will steal your market share with crappier products at lower prices. Your employees *do* want to focus on higher quality and smarter technology. But these are *always*, in the Christensen model, "sustaining innovations," which are *bad* for profits. So a firm needs to *lower* the quality of goods like photocopying or college teaching. Prof. Christensen often goaded managers with the inability of great firms with great products to develop worse stuff quickly enough to save themselves.

To move downmarket fast enough, they must *control* their excellence-oriented, highly effective, quality-focused workers and resubjugate them to the firm's value proposition.

This brings us to perhaps the most important feature of innovation as a contemporary neoliberal discourse. It functions not so much as an idiom of applied creativity as a *justification of managerial authority*. It became an ideology that explained why management had the right, indeed the obligation, to dispose through its own judgment of every "stakeholder" condition, such as job security, tax-funded public infrastructure, or carefully nurtured, high-quality product lines. Lepore wrote, "Disruptive innovation is competitive strategy for an age seized by terror." This is quite right, if we expand our notion of terror to include the Anglo-American managerial response to globalized price competition after the "great doubling" of the world's labor force at the bottom of the wage scale.[28] It justified a host of specific, corrosive social terrors, like being left behind by a change deemed irreversible, or being excluded from debate about alternatives to mass layoffs, or ignoring the costs of undermining entire regional economies through tax breaks to companies that offshore production.

One effect of disruptive innovation as neoliberal ideology has been the shocking complacency of the U.S. political class about the national devastation wrought by deindustrialization. We call a whole section of the country the "rust belt," and half-ruined cities like Newark and Detroit experience wide areas of social and economic decline amidst enormous wealth *because* business and political leaders were taught by consultants that capitalism must destroy in order to advance. Christensen's interpretations supported destruction by casting it as inevitable and right. He remains the leading heir to Joseph A. Schumpeter's theory of "creative destruction," in which social systems, cultural relations, political norms, and bureaucratic proceduralism are all the enemies of progress defined by the exceptional entrepreneur. Governments, publics, regulations, communities, traditions, habits, faculty senates, zoning boards, teachers' unions, homeowners' groups, professional organizations, and, last but not least, business corporations do *not* in this view create value but interfere with its creation.[29] Journalists might come along and chronicle the horrible human costs of the decline of the steel industry in, say, Youngstown, Ohio.[30] But by the time journalists know they should go there, decline has been baked into the regional cake.

Disruptive innovation was arguably head baker. Once it escaped the process of strategizing product development and became an ideology of market society, it taught politicians in Youngstown and elsewhere that industries like steel and their unionized employees had been judged by an impartial market to be outmoded. Consultants would routinely opine that the only logical response to falling profits was mass layoff and/or factory closure. In *The Disposable American* (2007), Louis Uchitelle had shown that layoffs were not wars of necessity but wars of choice, and yet to say that deindustrialization expressed a cultural entitlement rather than an economic law was to whistle in the wind.[31] Slowly but surely, Youngstown and every place like it no longer had economies that supported a stable middle class. In addition, like Beckett's Godot, the renewal to which this disruption was to lead never actually arrived.

Lepore's critique of disruptive innovation tapped into a pervasive, long-term anger about a ruin in America that the corporate and political classes deemed necessary. Innovation had shifted from the expression of "American ingenuity" to an engine of deindustrialization and post-middle-class inequality.

The Disrupted University

By 2000, innovation was university gospel. The term had acquired a number of default features. It was always pecuniary, market-ruled, and disruptive (implying replacement). Fourth, responses tend toward lower quality. This naturalizes lower quality and lowered expectations, especially for mass consumer products. This is not such a problem when a Canon office copier replaces a Xerox corporate machine; it is a major problem when public universities no longer even aspire to educational quality that is roughly equivalent to that offered by elite private universities.

The fifth feature of contemporary innovation discourse is the glorification of destruction as the necessary outcome of the entrepreneur's creativity. It has been the corporate version of the frontier's "regeneration through violence," the alleged rediscovery of America's primordial instincts to dominate with the vanishing of the adversary and its allies (e.g., local employees) as natural and right.[32]

The sixth has been the recasting of regular citizens—formal equals in political and social rights—as mostly backward customers. Mass democracy becomes a semi-undifferentiated body of late adopters who don't need good things because they aren't smart enough to use them. They can be sold inferior products. This supposedly doesn't violate democratic norms but rather fulfills them, because the mass customer *wants* worse (and cheaper) stuff. We are only starting to grasp the fundamentally anti-democratic nature of disruptive innovation theory, though we are moving in the right direction.

The seventh feature is the triumph of managers, particularly over the professionals. This ascent became easier when careful study of the customer (or society's) "jobs to be done" and of the current product line was less important than the appearance of innovativeness and the practice of disruption. In the flux of reengineering, mergers, stock buybacks, long marketing sieges, and the unending battlefield action of corporate repositioning, professional assessments of customers or products were less important.

Of course, management literature, including Christensen's, warns against this kind of churning. But the shift from professional to managerial authority has been a demonstrable trend.[33] Christensen became a pivotal figure in management history by using innovation to re-empower management. We can see him, in retrospect, as offering a comprehensive antidote to what American capitalists could only regard as the poison of neo-workplace democracy. Some 1980s business blockbusters were telling stockholders and executives to share power with a new, insufferably smart-ass "no-collar" generation of knowledge workers and that only this concession would turn the tables on the Japanese.[34] Many owners and executives must have felt that this price of recovery was too high. Christensen developed a theory that was less about maximizing innovation than it was about controlling it.

The shift of power away from professionals was intensified by the "shareholders revolt" inspired in part by another Harvard B-school professor, Michael Jensen: behind top executives were owners, who had resolved the old "principal-agent" problem in their favor.[35] Christensen's role was particularly important in "learning organizations" (the subtitle of a 1990 bestseller, by Peter M. Senge, that disruptive innovation also eclipsed).[36] Had the future belonged to the Peters—Senge as well as managerial theorist Peter Drucker—universities might by now have subjected financial management to the judgments of the *collegium*, a term used by Jim Sleeper. In a post-neoliberal university, administration would execute decisions made by faculty and staff collaborating with students in everyday operations and in strategy. But belatedly echoing the established shift from "learning" to "innovation," universities have gone in the opposite direction, with their managers unilaterally controlling the allocation of resources that determine the academic mission. They are also increasingly in charge of that core area of faculty expertise, the curriculum, and its delivery, in the name of learning innovation.

This is very much Christensen and his coauthor Henry Eyring's model in *The Innovative University*. The book recounts how top managers at BYU-Idaho pushed through unpopular changes like the elimination of sports teams and of summer teaching breaks on the basis of unilateral decision rights—in their case rooted in collaboration with the senior leadership of the Church of Latter-Day Saints. The revisions were directed by "heavyweight teams" and implemented by former Harvard Business School dean Kim Clark. BYU-Idaho has an interesting teaching model that deserves independent analysis: my point here is that it was imposed through top-down managerialism wearing innovation's clothing.

There's a further aspect of the Christensen antidote to knowledge-worker autonomy. In contrast to professional authority, which is grounded in expertise and expert communities, managerial authority flows from its ties to owners and is formally independent of embedded or subject-area expertise. Management obviously should be competent, but competence need not require either substantive expertise with the firm's products or meaningful contact with employees. The absence of contact with and substantive knowledge of core activities, in managerial culture, functions as an operational strength. In universities, faculty administrators are now likely to lose peer and governing-board support when they are seen as too close to the faculty. In the well-known story that Lepore retold, the head of the University of Virginia's Board of Visitors decided to fire the university president because she would not push online innovation with the speed recommended by a *Wall Street Journal* article.[37] The Christensen model does not favor university managers who understand what happens in the library, lab, and classroom and who bring students and faculty into the strategy process. For employees and customers are exactly the people who want to sustain and improve what they already have, which in disruptive capitalism is a loser's game.

The power of the Christensen script can be seen in the ways ed-tech advocates have been following it since 2012. In the first wave, Massive Open Online Courses cast universities as overbuilt incumbents, the kind of places that do indeed hire nonfaculty professionals at ten times the rate of full-time tenured faculty in order to chase high-end customers and avoid the less demanding and underserved masses.[38] Second, MOOCsters slammed instructional employees as *opposed* to innovation: articles or books by analysts like Mark C. Taylor, Ann Kirschner, and Richard A. DeMillo heaped scorn on what DeMillo called "faculty-centered" universities.[39] Third, during the 2012–13 boom, MOOC entrepreneurs bypassed faculty to connect directly with venture capitalists, politicians, business leaders, and senior university managers. One triumph of the campaign was the Udacity–San José State contract for three MOOC courses, which must have been the first time in history in which a university's outsourcing contract for one department's remedial curriculum was signed in the presence of a state governor.[40] 2014's MOOC

business plays continued the outreach to academic managers and the sidelining of teaching professionals.[41] MOOCs moved in so easily because they fit
with managerial ascendency over the professional authority of professors.[42]
This is a widespread *institutional* effect of disruptive innovation.

Imagining Political Economy after Innovation

Universities need to enter a different era, one in which they are allowed
to find sustainable financing and to support sustaining innovations on their
own terms. (Something analogous needs to happen for technologies that have
huge social value, like polymer solar cells, that can't attract enough private
capital to be made to work quickly enough to thrive.) Attacks on disruption-
as-such aren't yet making a difference in part because of an absence of broad
faculty support for restoring the status of professional knowledge after its
decades-long undermining, in large part through the ideology of disruptive
innovation.

To understand the difficulties we need to see the full list of innovation
challenges. In the current environment, innovation is to be:

1. pecuniary
2. market-ruled
3. disruptive (implying replacement or extinction)
4. (mostly) tending toward lower quality
5. socially destructive
6. overrunning the respectful study of ordinary, everyday (customer)
   needs
7. with managerial authority in charge of professional expertise
8. Embedded in science and especially technology, and not social and
   cultural knowledge less than 1 percent of national research and
   development funding for sociocultural research
9. Replacing public (political) analysis with data-based audit
10. Replacing interpretation with programming.

I have analyzed feature 8 at length on many occasions, and only note here that
it has produced a quasi-colonial situation in universities, in which science is
the "Lexus" and socioculture the "olive tree" of relative backwardness, allowing "metropolitan" officials to ignore the impoverished native informants of
vernacular culture once their presence has been granted, and not make them

the recipients of research investment.[43] Scholars have been rightly calling for decolonizing the Western university and its knowledges.[44] Raising almost nonexisting humanities and arts funding would be one concrete mechanism for moving in this direction. The theory of disruptive innovation makes that seem like a waste of money.

Ninth, disruptive innovation has supported a particular kind of managerial over professional knowledge—audit—that makes accounting systems the evaluative mechanism of managerial judgment.[45] The multiplication of metrics like college rankings is one major symptom of the general reduction of qualitative interpretation to indicators, as is the gifting of intellectual authority to them.[46] Most audit is private and part of confidential processes involving personnel, financial, or commercially sensitive information. This nonpublic dimension has been extended by another key aspect of the audit society—what the British sociologist William Davies describes as a movement from "facts" to "data," in which public statistics are eclipsed by the algorithmic analysis of very large data sets. Davies argues that the latter is "an entirely different type of knowledge" than statistics:

> There is no equivalent of an Office for National Statistics for commercially collected big data. We live in an age in which our feelings, identities and affiliations can be tracked and analysed with unprecedented speed and sensitivity—but there is nothing that anchors this new capacity in the public interest or public debate. . . . The anonymity and secrecy of the new analysts potentially make them far more politically powerful than any social scientist.[47]

Nor does data analytics have a fixed scale or use pre-existing settled categories:

> Analogue statistical techniques, such as surveys, require us to present our views and preferences in deliberate, objective, and coherent terms, often with a moment of reflection. By contrast, digital platforms only require us all to carry on emoting and demanding whatever and however we wish, and the algorithms will detect patterns in the mess that arises. No finite number of classifications or identifiers (such as "employed," "unemployed," "self-employed") needs to be selected in advance. Feelings do not need to be rendered conscious or verbal in order to be captured. Everything can be discerned from whatever words, images, and trails happen to be left lying around.[48]

Disruptive innovation prizes exactly the kind of quasi-conscious flow of desire and reaction that typifies digital life—even if it doesn't actually produce its equally prized marketable products. The shift from a centuries-old form of public calculation raises major epistemological and political questions for which we currently lack clear answers. Davies makes a persuasive claim that the rise of data analytics has made it easier for "populist" leaders to denigrate expertise: studies of climate change and reproductive health are now joining university-based sociocultural fields in the public doghouse. Making data-based audit publicly accessible and modifiable will be a long and painful struggle. But if it does not take place, the university and its nondigital knowledges will continue to decline.

Tenth and finally, disruptive innovation has sought since Joseph Schumpeter to replace workers with technology. Machines were thought always to be cheaper after an initial investment, and also more docile, more accurate, and more reliable. Frederick Taylor and others developed "scientific management" to replace the discretion of production workers with optimized procedures that would be micro-managed; Amazon's warehouse employee trackers are the direct descendent of these longstanding attempts to turn people into robots when they couldn't actually be replaced.[49] Constraining worker judgment reduced important kinds of efficiency at the same time as it raised others.[50] This kind of concern was no match for "cold war rationality" and the technology trends we've been discussing here.[51] In short, I'm claiming that we can see more clearly what we are up against if we rename "disruptive innovation" as "managerial innovation."

I'd like to conclude this chapter by claiming that we need to take two possibilities seriously: first, we are starting to see the economic *decline* of the algorithm as such (and its "innovation" housing); second, nothing much will change unless the "cognitariat" enters the fray as, so far, it has mostly refused to do.

We might ask ourselves: What if economic change isn't moving always toward more technology and management, but now is moving away from it? What if history does not side simply with technology, but with more complex forms of sociocultural-technological knowledge?

I'll posit, to get us thinking more about this, that the Schumpeter-Christensen model of innovation has been revived as a way of returning American business to a more familiar past—one of "manageable" technological change. In this context, Google is more like General Motors than it is like the organizations that will work in the next economy. Partly in response to an industrial model that was being extended digitally, Christensen reconsecrated a managerial class that opposes, as it did in the earlier twentieth century, the democratization of invention. It's quite likely that none of our current chal-

lenges can be faced when the best-educated people with the most access to resources come from a small and narrowly educated elite—not climate change,
not expanding refugee populations, not continuous warfare, not hardening
inequality.

The blindness of Schumpeter's model was its elitist notion of invention and
innovation alike. Christensen and today's advanced corporate world—Apple,
Amazon, Wall Street—function with the same concentrations of elite professionals set up in *contrast* to the forms of knowledge in the wider vernacular
culture. Christensen's model is at best indifferent to creative labor on a mass
scale and looks to entrepreneurs supported by venture capital. But what if
this indifference to labor—in addition to traditional exploitation, racism, and
injustice—is precisely what has been eroding Western capitalism?

By contrast, there is the economic (though not the political) success of
China. Americans often assume that China offers only a low-wage Western
developmental pathway, doing the same kind of production, dark satanic mills
style, at a much lower price. In reality, Chinese electronics manufacturing
is not the cheapest manufacturing but, in many cases, the *best* manufacturing in the world.[52] The same is true in the crucial area of renewable energy:
China rapidly took over the solar photovoltaic manufacturing sector after
2010 with a combination of trade and industrial policy, and the United States
will meet its defossilization goals by buying Chinese technology.[53] China's
success with scale, scope, and complexity is not a simple question of workforce exploitation, though there is lots of that, but of a rejection of the rules of
neoliberalism—indeed, of disruptive innovation—as they are ritualistically
applied in the West. The result is that Apple won't be able to manufacture
the iPhone 11, 15, or 20 back in the U.S. at any price. Even Silicon Valley
doesn't have the high-skilled labor, the sophisticated supply chain, the quality
transportation infrastructure, the capacity for public-good investment, or the
cultural interest in the intelligence of the *ensemble*. Capitalism needs more
intensive social factors of production than ever, and the U.S. simply doesn't
have them at a global level.

There's a deeper pattern here that to my mind has been best explained by
Giovanni Arrighi's version of world-systems theory. In *Adam Smith in Beijing*,
he argued that the "Western pathway" of capitalist development, which was
good at its chosen task for two hundred years, has reached a hard limit.[54] His
contrast was with East Asia, where there was a kind of market economics that
was more successful than the European kind until 1820 or so, when it became
less successful than the Western pathway. This "East Asia" pathway was *not*

technology-intensive and did *not*, to the same extent, replace human labor with machines. It was labor-*intensive*. Arrighi borrowed from Hayami Akira the term "Industrious Revolution" to label this East Asian path.

Arrighi worked for decades on capitalist accumulation cycles and on the *end* of "accumulation regimes" that in their time seemed like the end of history. He argued at length that the West has overestimated "large-scale production and the technical division of labor" and misread as our business or technological genius—whether we were Genoan, Dutch, Victorian, or Bush-era American—the effects of military superiority and resource extraction, slavery very much included. In reality, Arrighi insisted, there is *no innate superiority* to the Western path of capitalist development. The tide may have been running against the Western model since around 1950. Our period of financialization—from the Savings and Loan crisis of the 1980s through the housing bubble and the financial crisis of the current period—looks like the kind of "belle epoque" that, in Arrighi's historical studies, signals the decline of a regime of accumulation.

This is not to say that Japan or China has the answers to our economic, environmental, social, or cultural problems. The essential point is that East Asian modernization has been based not so much on the imitation of the Western Industrial Revolution as on the revival of features of the indigenous, skills-based Industrious Revolution.[55] The issue is not that it is Chinese or Asian capitalism, but that the next economic order, wherever it appears, represents the overcoming of the limiting features of the Western pathway—its colossal demand for energy, enabled by energy-dense fossil fuels, its dependence on military dominance, and its mass use of coerced wage labor, which, as we have seen, for the great majority of workers, it generally de-skills or replaces with technology.

It's fairly obvious that ecological survival now depends on the continuous reduction of energy used per unit output.[56] But just as profoundly, advanced innovation now depends on *labor-intensive* complex practices, on *up-skilling* mass labor rather than de-skilling it. All regions could potentially update the "industrious revolution" for our not-yet decarbonizing, climate-changing, permanent war-making times. Northern Europe has a start on this. I think Arrighi is correct that the future's sustainable economies and stable societies will be those that shift away from the technological *replacement* of labor toward *high*-skill labor served by technology. Remember Donna Haraway's cyborg manifesto.

So a humanities question for our times is: Will the United States manage to achieve this transition? And my answer is, no—absolutely not. Not, that is, unless the humanities—critical theory—can critique and help change macroeconomics with a new militancy about the formation of complex creative skills rooted in uncoerced interpretation.[57]

How would the humanities break—in both theory and practice—not only with the capitalist university but with Western capitalism in its current form? Of course, we think this is grandiose, and impossible, and ridiculous. And yet the situation has been shifting toward high-skill and new-skill labor for years, with one catch: sustainable high skills will be as interpretative as they are technical. The liberal-arts side of universities hasn't much thought about and planned enough for a generative role in changes already underway.

In *The Undercommons*, Stefano Harney and Fred Moten write that our practice must assert "a metapolitical surrealism that sees and sees through the evidence of mass incapacity."[58] This is exactly right, and oddly enough, especially right on the matter of innovation. The humanities offers a surrealism of concepts, found in a mainstream tradition, from Socrates through the Stoics on to Friedrich Schleiermacher, Ida B. Wells, Dewey, C. L. R. James, and Hannah Arendt that has always had a (carefully suppressed) *economic* destiny.

Table 9-1 depicts a few pieces of a long tradition in a reductive schema. Column 1 is a summary of our post-democratic period in which commoditized creative labor loses its value and value-added becomes an elite product. Column 2 is our current innovation culture, with its techno-supremacist tendencies. Column 3 references the strong humanities as a bland inclusive term for critical theory. Column 4 is the institutional body that houses these humanities.

My point about the humanities disciplines as schematized in column 3 is that they contradict the disruptive innovation of capitalism's "Western pathway" (column 2). They have been doing this at the same time they are providing founding elements of a sustainable postcapitalism. Humanities scholars are familiar with the items in the first and third rows. Our elitism means we will need to do more with pioneer authors over a long historical arc from Frederick Douglass to Jacques Rancière to develop the idea of *universal* intellectuality. That will be the core feature of a future world that can no longer live by the elite educations of its 1 percent but needs the help of pretty much everybody to solve its problems.

Egalitarianism, row 3, has been the pervasive implication of the humanities renaissance that global academia has induced over the last seventy years. In conjunction with social movements, it has helped produce new forms of criticism through feminism, gender studies, deconstruction, queer theory, social history, and much more. Faculty are not spontaneous egalitarians. But

TABLE 9-1. Humanities vs. Disruptive Capitalism

Challenge	S-Innovation	Strong Humanities	Public University
Post-democracy; plutocracy	Minoritarian democracy of tech talented tenth	Mass intellectuality: participation of 100%	Free/open access
"Global auction": high-skills can go with low-wages	Plutonomy with precarity	Industrious revolution based on diverse craft capabilities, cultural agency	Bildung: deep personal development
Naturalization of all kinds of inequality (race, class, nation)	Assimilate to innovation culture (Spencerian technogenesis)	Egalitarian non-assimilationist pluralisms of specific experience	Egalitarian inclusion and diversified curriculum

to improve the situation of both the humanities and the transition to a post-Western economic pathway, we will need to act systematically on the basis of the implications of our own research.

Regarding the second row, craft labor is an old-fashioned term; we don't talk much about craft skills even in writing programs. But we're moving toward this. Doris Sommer's concept of cultural agency is a huge help; so is Martha Nussbaum on "creative capabilities"; so is John Warner's idea of writing as the struggle to think; so is Gayatri Chakravorty Spivak's notion of reading as translation and translation as the "trace of the other."[59] So is Badiou's "third historical sequence of the communist hypothesis" (equality, the polymorphousness of human labor, politics without a coercive state).[60] Whatever terms we use, they won't change the fact that the acquisition of the ability to do something with thought and language changes the life we're told that we are born into.

My general claim assumes that Arrighi is correct in seeing a hard limit to the current Western regime of accumulation and in claiming an inevitable transition out of it. Whether the U.S. economy does well or badly in the transition is an open question. In addition, sustainable uses of technology and energy resources will require us to scale up *autonomous labor* via *mass access to self-governed interpretative practices*. Large-scale *self*-management will in this scenario gradually change both manufacturing and service organizations—and will move the economy away from the energy-intensive replacement of people with machines and programming that has been the hallmark of the

Western pathway for over two centuries. The current ideology of disruptive innovation impedes this kind of large-scale cultural expansion.

What is the university's role in this transition out of the current cycle of late finance capitalism? A pivotal one. Autonomous interpretation is both the key to the transition *and* a key outcome of university practice. The strengths of the Industrious Revolution are specifically the strengths of university knowledge production rooted in combinations of technical and qualitative disciplines.

This all sounds quite pecuniary. In fact, the university's public good goes far beyond helping the economy. The university's core role is to cultivate mass intelligence. I have a more limited point here: the interpretative disciplines fight the sense of inevitable defeat at the hands of economics and technology. I've used Arrighi to sketch in the most simplistic way the very real possibility of reframing contemporary Western capitalism as a system at its limit. U.S. and similar societies will be asking the university to serve not only as a place of refuge but as a place that imagines an economy after disruptive innovation and provides the hybrid knowledges that can bring that into being.

Notes

1. A particularly comprehensive and forceful account is Wendy Brown, *Undoing the Demos: Neoliberalism's Stealth Revolution* (New York: Zone Books, 2015). Another lucid overview is William Davies, *The Limits of Neoliberalism: Authority, Sovereignty and the Logic of Competition* (London: Sage, 2014).

2. Randy Martin, "From the Race War to the War on Terror," in *Beyond Biopolitics: Essays on the Governance of Life and Death*, ed. Patricia Ticineto Clough and Craig Willse (Durham, N.C.: Duke University Press, 2011), 261.

3. Michel Foucault, *The History of Sexuality*, vol. 1, *The Will to Knowledge*, trans. R. Hurley (1976; repr. New York: Vintage, 1998).

4. The University of California is a good bellwether; its growth was propelled by federally sponsored science and has uncritically tethered itself to tech transfer outcomes. For one snapshot, see UC Office of the President, "Technology Commercialization Report, 2017," https://www.ucop.edu/innovation-alliances-services/_files/ott/genresources/documents/IE_Rpt_FY2017_FINAL.p.

5. See, for example, Lori Pressman et al., "The Economic Contribution of University/Nonprofit Inventions in the United States: 1996–2015" (Washington, D.C.: Association of University Technology Managers, 2015), 15–16, https://www.autm.net/AUTMMain/media/Advocacy/Documents/June-2017-Update-of-I-O-Economic-Impact-Model.pdf.

6. David Kotz, "End of the Neoliberal Era? Crisis and Restructuring in American Capitalism," *New Left Review* 113 (September–October 2018): 29–55.

7. I am recasting Michael Power's dictum, "The failure of audit means more audit"; *The Audit Society* (Oxford: Oxford University Press, 1997).

8. Isabelle Bruno and Christopher Newfield, "Can the Cognitariat Speak?," *e-flux journal* no. 14 (March 2010), https://www.e-flux.com/journal/14/61316/can-the-cognitariat-speak/.

9. Multiple authors, "What Is Innovation? 15 Experts Share Their Innovation Definition," *Idea to Value*, https://www.ideatovalue.com/inno/nickskillicorn/2016/03/innovation-15-experts-share-innovation-definition/.

10. Mihaly Csikszentmihalyi, *Creativity: Flow and the Psychology of Discovery and Invention* (New York: HarperPerennial, 1996), 79–80.

11. Eduardo Porter, "The Hard Truths of Trying to 'Save' the Rural Economy," *New York Times*, December 14, 2018, https://www.nytimes.com/interactive/2018/12/14/opinion/rural-america-trump-decline.html.

12. Thorstein Veblen, *The Higher Learning in America* (1918; repr. Baltimore: Johns Hopkins University Press, 2015); see also Newfield, "Professorial Anger, Then and Now," *Chronicle of Higher Education*, October 25, 2015, http://chronicle.com/article/Professorial-Anger-Then-and/233856.

13. Wendy Brown, "The Vocation of the Public University," typescript, author's files: "For Weber, having a genuine vocation for something means being compelled by and dedicated to the activity's worldly value, combined with a willingness to navigate and withstand often miserable conditions or rewards for pursuing it. Being animated by a calling is precisely the opposite of an egoistic or self-benefiting pursuit. Further, Weber's account of political leadership and scholarly inquiry involved bringing into relief how beset and even imperiled both endeavors were in his time, and how small the possibilities were for recognition or success in either domain. This led him to formulate the calling for politics and scholarship as requiring a capacity to simultaneously reckon with and resist these conditions—facing them squarely without submitting to them. The sobriety, maturity and asceticism he established as comprising the ethic appropriate to each extends, then, even to their uptake; those seeking glory, glamour, wealth, certainty of success or simple gratification should look elsewhere."

14. Newfield, *Ivy and Industry: Business and the Making of the American University, 1880-1980* (Durham, N.C.: Duke University Press, 2003).

15. The following section draws from Newfield, "Christensen's Disruptive Innovation after the Lepore Critique: Remaking the University," *Remaking the University*, June 22, 2014, http://utotherescue.blogspot.com/2014/06/christensens-disruptive-innovation.html.

16. Bill Bamberger and Cathy N. Davidson, *Closing: The Life and Death of an American Factory* (New York: W. W. Norton, 1998).

17. Clayton M. Christensen, *The Innovator's Dilemma: When New Technologies Cause Great Firms to Fail* (1997; repr. Boston: Harvard Business Review Press, 2013); Christensen and Michael E. Raynor, *The Innovator's Solution: Creating and Sustaining Successful Growth* (Boston: Harvard Business Review Press, 2013).

18. Christensen and Raynor, *Innovator's Solution*, 151.

19. Ibid., 152.

20. Christensen and Henry J. Eyring, *The Innovative University: Changing the DNA of Higher Education from the Inside Out*, 1st ed. (San Francisco: Jossey-Bass, 2011).

21. Christensen is not a Marxist, of course. He has quite a different understanding of the valorization process, among many other things.

22. Christensen and Raynor do describe strategy processes for incumbent companies to scramble "up-market" (*Innovator's Solution*, chapters 8 and 9), but this process is somewhat marginal to the general innovation process and also shrouded in likely failure.

23. Jill Lepore, "The Innovation Machine: What the Gospel of Innovation Gets Wrong," *New Yorker*, June 23, 2014, https://www.newyorker.com/magazine/2014/06/23/the-disruption-machine.

24. Christensen and Raynor, *Innovator's Solution*.

25. Ibid., 215.

26. For a remarkable sketch of an economy in which business is not a way to make lots of money but about useful services, see Douglas Rushkoff, *Throwing Rocks at the Google Bus: How Growth Became the Enemy of Prosperity* (New York: Portfolio, 2016), chapter 5.

27. In the mid-1990s, the management book to beat was still *In Search of Excellence* (New York: Harper and Row, 1982), which Tom Peters coauthored with Robert H. Waterman. These two management consultants had done a particularly good job of facing up to the decline of American manufacturing, particularly in relation to Japan, which had been influentially analyzed in works as different as Chalmers Johnson, *MITI and the Japanese Miracle* (1982), Barry Bluestone and Bennett Harrison, *The Deindustrialization of America* (1984), Michael J. Piore and Charles F. Sabel, *The Second Industrial Divide* (1984), and Rosabeth Moss Kanter, *The Change Masters* (1985). By the time David Harvey's *The Condition of Postmodernity* (1991) came along to declare a fundamental change in capitalism's mode of production, prominent business writers had been trying to revive capitalism by exposing the deficiencies of top-down corporate management.

Most famously, Mr. Peters and Mr. Waterman indecorously criticized management's selfish cynicism about the capabilities of their employees. They argued that American executives adhered to an outmoded Theory X, "the assumption of the mediocrity of the masses." Executives wrongly believed, in the words of Theory X's codifier, the MIT industrial psychologist Douglas McGregor (*Human Side of Enterprise*, 1960), that the masses "need to be coerced, controlled, directed, and threatened with punishment to get them to put forward adequate effort" (Peters and Waterman's paraphrase). Theory Y, which Peters and Waterman upheld, like McGregor before them, "assumes. . . that the expenditure of physical and mental effort in work is as natural as in play or rest . . . and the capacity to exercise a relatively high degree of imagination, ingenuity, and creativity in the solution of organizational problems is widely, not narrowly, distributed in the population" (Peters and Waterman, *Excellence*, emphasis omitted, 95). (For a discussion of MOOC-based Theory X in higher education discussed earlier, see Christopher Newfield, "Quality Public Higher Ed: From Udacity to Theory Y," *Remaking the University*, June 6, 2012, http:// utotherescue.blogspot.com/2012/06/quality-public-higher-ed-from-udacity .html.) *In Search of Excellence* implied that American management was holding the American worker back. The way to compete with Japan, Germany, etc., was general employee empowerment. Peters called a later tome *Liberation Management* (1992), claiming that a kind of self-organized worker activity would grow the company's bottom line through the creative pursuit of higher quality. Oddly enough, this kind of "human relations" management theory surged during the Reagan years. One culmination was *Post-Capitalist Society* (1993), in which the godfather of management theorists, Peter Drucker, prophesied the replacement of the firm's managerial layers with the "intellectual capital" of knowledge workers, who would use their pension-based ownership of their companies to take capitalism away from passive capitalists and their managerial proxies. Christensen sidestepped this entire tradition. This probably helped him spread his influence among top corporate executives.

28. Richard Freeman, "The Great Doubling: The Challenge of the New Global Labor Market," Econometrics Laboratory, UC Berkeley (August 2006), https://eml.berkeley.edu/~webfac/eichengreen/e183_sp07/great_doub.pdf.

29. Joseph A. Schumpeter, *Capitalism, Socialism, and Democracy*, 3rd ed. (New York: Harper Perennial Modern Classics, 2008).

30. See the Tammy Thomas sections in George Packer, *The Unwinding: An Inner History of the New America* (New York: Farrar, Straus and Giroux, 2013).

31. Louis Uchitelle, *The Disposable American: Layoffs and Their Consequences*, 1st ed. (New York: Vintage, 2007).

32. Richard Slotkin, *Regeneration through Violence: The Mythology of the American Frontier, 1600–1860* (Middletown, Conn.: Wesleyan University Press, 1973).

33. As one revealing case study in a large literature on the institutional effects of financialization, see Christopher M. Muellerleile, "Financialization Takes Off at Boeing," *Journal of Economic Geography* 9, no. 5 (September 2009): 663–77.

34. Andrew Ross, *No-Collar: The Hidden Cost of The Humane Workplace* (New York: Basic Books, 2002).

35. For an early salvo, see Michael C. Jensen and William H. Meckling, "Theory of the Firm: Managerial Behavior, Agency Costs and Ownership Structure," *Journal of Financial Economics* 3, no. 4 (October 1976): 305–60. For history and critique, see Lynn Stout, *The Shareholder Value Myth: How Putting Shareholders First Harms Investors, Corporations, and the Public* (San Francisco: Berrett-Koehler, 2012).

36. Peter M. Senge, *The Fifth Discipline: The Art & Practice of The Learning Organization* (1990; repr. New York: Crown Business, 2006).

37. Newfield, "All Hell Breaks Loose at the Professional-Managerial Divide: University of Virginia Edition," *Remaking the University*, June 19, 2012, http:// utotherescue.blogspot.com/2012/06/all-hell-breaks-loose-at-professional.html.

38. Newfield, "Is This What President Napolitano Meant by Teaching for California?," April 26, 2014, http://utotherescue.blogspot.com/2014/04/is-this-what-president-napolitano-meant.html.

39. Mark C. Taylor, "Opinion: End the University as We Know It," *New York Times*, April 26, 2009, https://www.nytimes.com/2009/04/27/opinion/27taylor.html; Ann Kirschner, "Innovations in Higher Education? Hah!," *Chronicle of Higher Education*, April 8, 2012, https://www.chronicle.com/article/Innovations-in-Higher/131424; Richard A. DeMillo, *Abelard to Apple: The Fate of American Colleges and Universities* (Cambridge, Mass.: MIT Press, 2011).

40. Katy Murphy, "San Jose State to Offer Low-Cost, For-Credit Online Courses," *Mercury News*, January 15, 2013, https://www.mercurynews.com/2013/01/15/san-jose-state-to-offer-low-cost-for-credit-online-courses/.

41. Newfield, "MOOCs Have Become a Straight Business Play," *Remaking the University*, March 18, 2013, http://utotherescue.blogspot.com/2013/03/moocs-have-become-straight-business-play.html; Colleen Lye and James Vernon, "The Erosion of Faculty Rights," *Chronicle of Higher Education*, May 19, 2014, https://www.chronicle.com/blogs/conversation/2014/05/19/the-erosion-of-faculty-rights/; Porter, "A Smart Way to Skip College in Pursuit of a Job," *New York Times*, June 17, 2014, https://www.nytimes.com/2014/06/18/business/economy/udacity-att-nanodegree-offers-an-entry-level-approach-to-college.html.

42. For a discussion of the MOOC-based Theory X in higher education discussed earlier, see Newfield, "Quality Public Higher Ed: From Udacity to Theory Y," *Remaking the University*, June 6, 2012, http://utotherescue.blogspot.com/2012/06/quality-public-higher-ed-from-udacity.html.

43. Thomas L. Friedman, *The Lexus And the Olive Tree: Understanding Globalization*, updated and expanded ed. (New York: Random House, 2000).

44. Piya Chatterjee and Sunaina Maira, eds., *The Imperial University* (Minneapolis: University of Minnesota Press, 2014); Sabelo J. Ndlovu-Gatsheni and Siphamandla Zondi, *Decolonizing the University: Knowledge Systems and Disciplines in Africa* (Durham, N.C.: Carolina Academic Press, 2016); la paperson, *A Third University Is Possible* (Minneapolis: University of Minnesota Press, 2017); Gurminder K. Bhambra, Kerem Nisancioglu, and Delia Gebrial, eds., *Decolonizing the University* (Chicago: Pluto, 2018).

45. Michael Power, *The Audit Society: Rituals of Verification*, 2nd sub ed. (Oxford and New York: Oxford University Press, 1999). Power's incisive work, circulated as a *Demos* paper in the mid-1990s, helped inspire the large literature on New Public Management and the technology of audit as a mechanism of economic and institutional governance.

46. For a compact overview by two pioneer analysts of audit culture, see Cris Shore and Susan Wright, "Audit Culture Revisited: Rankings, Ratings, and the Reassembling of Society," *Current Anthropology* 56, no. 3 (June 1, 2015): 421–44, https://doi.org/10.1086/681534.

47. William Davies, "How Statistics Lost Their Power—and Why We Should Fear What Comes Next," *Guardian*, January 19, 2017, sec. Politics,

https://www.theguardian.com/politics/2017/jan/19/crisis-of-statistics-big-data-democracy.

48. William Davies, *Nervous States: Democracy and the Decline of Reason* (New York: W. W. Norton, 2019), 189.

49. See, for example, Colin Lecher, "How Amazon Automatically Tracks and Fires Warehouse Workers for 'Productivity,'" *Verge*, April 25, 2019, https://www.theverge.com/2019/4/25/18516004/amazon-warehouse-fulfillment-centers-productivity-firing-terminations. Amazon denies that it has automated the firing of workers through tracking data; Charlotte Jee, "Amazon's System for Tracking Its Warehouse Workers Can Automatically Fire Them," *MIT Technology Review*, April 26, 2019, https://www.technologyreview.com/f/613434/amazons-system-for-tracking-its-warehouse-workers-can-automatically-fire-them/.

50. For some foundational work on the importance of informal, craft-based employee know-how for production efficiency, see Herbert G. Gutman, *Work, Culture and Society in Industrializing America* (New York: Vintage, 1977).

51. Paul Erickson et al., *How Reason Almost Lost Its Mind: The Strange Career of Cold War Rationality* (Chicago and London: University of Chicago Press, 2013).

52. Dan Breznitz and Michael Murphree, *Run of the Red Queen: Government, Innovation, Globalization, and Economic Growth in China* (New Haven, Conn.: Yale University Press, 2011).

53. See, for example, Zach Horton and Newfield, *Whatever Happened to Solar Innovation?*, 1:24, https://vimeo.com/115560585.

54. Giovanni Arrighi, *Adam Smith in Beijing: Lineages of the Twenty-First Century* (London and New York: Verso, 2007).

55. Ibid., 331.

56. For a valuable accessible overview, see Robert Pollin, "Degrowth vs. A Green New Deal," *New Left Review* 112 (July–August 2018): 5–25.

57. For the related concept of fugitive interpretation, see Stefano Harney and Fred Moten, *The Undercommons: Fugitive Planning & Black Study* (Wivenhoe, UK: Autonomedia, 2013).

58. Ibid., 73.

59. Martha C. Nussbaum, *Not for Profit: Why Democracy Needs the Humanities*, 1st ed. (Princeton, N.J.: Princeton University Press, 2010); Doris Sommer, *The Work of Art in the World: Civic Agency and Public Humanities* (Durham, N.C.: Duke University Press, 2014); John Warner, *Why They Can't Write: Killing the Five-Paragraph Essay and Other Necessities* (Baltimore: Johns Hopkins University Press, 2018); Gayatri Chakravorty Spivak, *An Aesthetic Education in the Era of Globalization* (Cambridge, Mass.: Harvard University Press, 2012), 270; Arrighi, *Adam Smith in Beijing*, chapter 1.

60. Alain Badiou, "The Communist Hypothesis," *New Left Review* 2, no. 49 (2008): 29–42.

Absolute Capitalism

Étienne Balibar

Let's begin with the world, the "brave new world."[1]

Marx famously begins *Capital* with the sentence "The world in which the capitalist mode of production is dominant appears [*erscheint*] as a huge accumulation of commodities." Therefore, its "elementary" structures are relations of production and exchanges of commodities. Although the word "market" did exist at the time, it was not until Walras that the term acquired a formal theoretical function in economic theory, and so Marx himself had *scarce* use for it. Interestingly, however, the term did become important for Marx when it came to explaining how the *world* itself was the institutional space needed to realize the tendencies of capitalism. In its "concept" [*Begriff*], the market is therefore a world-market—that is, the place where the money-form finds its "adequate" expression. At the same time, Marx's analyses clearly referred to *market relations*, including the crucial dimension of the "labor market," where *force* or *power* is to be found for capitalist use.[2] Now it would seem that the *world* along with its "appearances" both *realizes* a tendency implicit in Marx's definition and vastly *exceeds* the limits within which he was circumscribing its "universality."

Financialization, Globalization, and the Limits of Commodification

The whole thing of course has to do with the correlation of two notions: *globalization* and *financialization*. We have come to acknowledge that their reciprocity generates the fact that *no place*, or almost no place in the world, remains "outside" the global constraints or is immune to the effects of financialization. Even if we do not adopt the hymns to the revolutionary effects of the "fusion" of internet communication that makes it possible to *delocalize* production with the quasi-instantaneous management of financial investments—in short, the new *liquidity* of capital—we must recognize that this is a qualitative leap, perhaps a change of civilization. Some bold minds compare it to the invention of agriculture or the "urban revolution" in prehistoric times. Less speculatively, Suzanne de Brunhoff spoke of entering *"l'heure du marché,"* or the times of the market, meaning that "absolute" or "unrestricted" competition has come with devastating consequences.[3] Human activities, production forces, relations of distribution of material and cultural goods among the classes, relations of power, alliances or antagonisms among nations and peoples, everyday habits and modes of life, travel, and settlement—all of these are increasingly determined by their *immediate* relationship to the global financialized market, which they confront *from the inside* with unequal powers and capacities to draw its benefits.

However true this picture must appear, in general, it nevertheless immediately calls for some caveats and qualifications. First, as every serious historian knows and as Marx had already emphasized, *globalization is not new*. Globalization both reveals and completes a long-term tendency. Capitalism, as opposed to every previous economic structure, has operated at a world level from the very beginning. According to some analysts, it was even from this wide range of commercial operations that it derived its capacity to commence a "primitive accumulation."[4] But the kind of globalization that existed between the so-called discovery of America (that is, the beginning of European colonization) and the end of the Cold War (after the formal decolonization process) relied on the fact that capital was *connecting* zones, or parts of the world, to one another—not on the fact that it was *incorporating* and *subsuming* them under a single logic.

But are things as simple as that? Incorporation into a single market or place, no doubt, is the tendency that overcomes the heterogeneity remaining from the previous stages of globalization. But there are more than mere *traces* of the old heterogeneity that are crucial to include in our picture of the new world. This is especially true for *the North-South divide*. For it is just as impossible to say that the North-South divide has been erased as it is to say that it has remained the same. Increasingly, from a territorial point of view, there is "North" in the South (where China is the emerging superpower), and there is "South" in the North (where migrants cross borders in increasing numbers). Both movements come with the statistical fact that "inequalities" measured by gross monetary income, or its "real" equivalent, have been *reduced* internationally and yet everywhere have *increased* nationally.[5] Even in the North, they border to the *exclusion* of whole populations. Financialization and globalization coincide with a new, more complex *polarization* that disturbs received descriptions of class and imperial domination.

Second, the advent of the Global Financial Market entails both extension and intensification. Put another way, market relations *expand* continuously and in two different directions. On the one hand, they seize new territories, erase boundaries, and merge or mix populations. But on the other, they also include new activities and services that either "commodify" preexisting needs and desires or *create* entirely new needs, which are linked to the use of technologies and the acquisition of commodities.

But there are also *limits* to that expansion, which it is both crucial and difficult to precisely identify, since they result from complicated tendencies, or relations of forces, which are *hidden* in the market relations themselves or in their consequences. The most obvious limits are resistances to globalization as deterritorialization, dilution of natural sovereignties, protections against opening of borders, and unrestricted competition, which range from neo-mercantilist state policies to "communitarian" defenses of traditional collective identities. Sometimes these appear as a form of resistance to cultural annihilation, sometimes as a form of xenophobic aggression against a cosmopolitanism "from below," and sometimes as an unstable and ambivalent combination of both.

More secretly perhaps, there are also obstacles to the *intensive* expansion of the market in the realm of our "forms of life." "Everything is marketable," but what is "everything"? Here I am not only thinking of the debate regarding the privatization of the *commons* (ancient commons and new commons, such as *knowledge*). I am also referring to the question of the marketization of desire, or the introduction of the logic of market value into the realm of intimacy, where some of the deepest roots of sociality, or human transindividuality, are located. Three-quarters of a century ago, Karl Polanyi famously argued that there were intrinsic cultural limits to the development of "fictitious commodities," which for him included *land*, *labor*, and *money* itself.[6] This is how he believed he could demonstrate that a *socialist* regulation of capitalism was inevitable and actually taking place before his eyes. Today we can see that commodification and marketization have transgressed these barriers. But a question remains about the kinds of contradiction (and therefore *violence*) that capitalism leads to when it develops a program of unlimited expansion of market relations on the *intensive* side as well.

And third, I want to refer to a specific aspect of globalization that calls for a dialectical analysis of opposite tendencies and a juxtaposition of heterogeneous experiences. This has to do with *contradictory patterns of mobility and immobility*. It is not true that mobility only forms the law of contemporary globalization. Rather, the law is differentiated mobility ranging from the extreme form represented by the "liquidity" of capital—which is closely followed by the circulation of commodities such that commodities now circulate as pure representatives of capital—to the other extreme that I call the *forced immobility* of populations.[7] By the latter I mean the reversal of sedentarity linked to work, dwelling, culture, genealogy, into a mechanism of constraint and a limitation of rights imposed on human collectivities. This is a very complex and conflictual situation, since the opposition of interests and perceptions of the world take place at the same time between the rich and the poor and between the poor (or the extremely poor) themselves.

So, as we proceed into a phenomenology of the new globalized and financialized world, we discover that it is no less complex than the one that preceded it, despite the overwhelming *power of simplification* that financial globalization entails, or rather *precisely because* of that power. This is what calls for theory—not just description, enthusiasm, or distress. But before I address my next topic I want to add a few other questions about the resources and obstacles that we find in Marx.

Withering Away of the Political?

First, I want to underscore the *political indeterminacy* of the globalized world, which of course is not a small reason for the chaotic and shifting nature of political commitments and ideological discourses in our situation, all of which clearly have entered a phase of rapid fluctuations between poles that classical political science considered antinomic, such as sovereignism and anarchism, nationalism and internationalism, "class" discourse and "theological" discourse. The difficulty here comes from the fact that anybody who raises this issue is caught in the indeterminacy herself and is not able to derive it from some given principle, especially not from the generalities about globalization that I just summarized. We must proceed through careful description of the *inversions* or *negations* of the political structures that we used to see as powers over our lives, but also as objects of our critique. This does not yield immediate results. Let me suggest two such "negations" that are offering themselves to our speculations. One has to do with *sovereignty*, the other with *antagonism*.

The problem with sovereignty is multifold. In modern times—the times of the Schmittian *Nomos of the Earth* that were also the times of the construction and destruction of colonial empires—sovereignty was mainly associated with the representation of national states: it should maintain an essential relation to the capacity of the state to represent a "people" or to secure its more or less permanent consent, often called "democratic legitimacy." This had a number of conditions, which formed the concrete substance of our national histories as exemplary *manifestations of the political*. The other side of the question was the existence of "hegemonic relations" among nations, with more or less acute conflicts, both between imperial nations and subjugated, colonized, or semi-colonized nations and among the imperial nations themselves. Globalization *cum* financialization seems to be undermining both types of structures. This is as true on the side of the articulation of *people* and *state* as it is on the side of "hegemonic" *relations of power* in the world.

On the side of the *people/state* binary, there are well-known phenomena of *métissage* (internationalization of culture from above and below) that make it increasingly difficult for people and state to maintain the kind of Hegelian process of "recognition" that allows them to see each other as *expressions of the same "spirit"* or the same national identity. But there are also more material phenomena. As Wolfgang Streeck has forcefully argued in his description of the transition from the state based on *taxes* (*Steuerstaat*) to the state based on *debt*—that is, borrowing from financial markets (*Schuldenstaat*), when the state becomes completely dependent on their "rating" of its policies, it must increasingly appear as an *intermediary* between the people and the financial institutions that are essentially transnational: something that is utterly destructive of national legitimacy without creating an alternative one.[8]

The same conclusion can be reached on the other side of the question of the *Nomos*: international hegemonies. We must be very careful here, not only because critical developments are arising fast, but because we Euro-Americans are perhaps *located in the wrong places* to perceive the dominant tendencies. A diagnosis of the declining hegemony of the U.S. empire in the world is on the table—and it has been for some time already—with contradictory elements. The U.S. largely escapes the financial *conundrum* of external debt, owing to its *seigniorage* privilege of emitting the quasi-global currency, but the mass of monetary reserves in dollars are owned by Asiatic states and banks. It remains the overwhelming military superpower, but the clear effect of thirty years of military interventions has been to demonstrate a growing incapacity to impose an American law and order anywhere in the world. The great difficulty seems to be the following: *supposing* that the U.S. hegemony is inexorably declining, with all the violent effects this may produce internally and externally, *what comes next?* Or what offers itself in terms of an alternative? The fact that China loudly denies trying to achieve a position of global hegemony is not sufficient proof that this is not ultimately its goal, but the fact that it could be its goal—using instruments and contractual forms (the "Silk Road") that would invent a new hegemonic style—is not sufficient proof that this is possible. Because the other phenomenon that we need to take into account is the quasi-sovereignty of the Global Financial Market (GFM) itself, which has national and multinational components and is not associated with a *state* construction. I say the quasi-sovereignty, but again this must be qualified: it makes sense only in a purely *negative* sense, because, by virtue of its capacity to impose economic policies on the States, the GFM finds itself de facto above the law, or above the "legitimate" power structures and structures of representation, which is the traditional definition of the absolute sovereign. On the other hand, the GFM is not a political institution in the strong sense; it is not *ruled* in a *centralized* manner, which at the same time makes its strength and its limitations when it comes to *governing the populations*. It "decides" nothing. It can be ambiguously perceived as manifestation of the new type of global politics that is emerging, something called "governance" instead of "politics," and, for the same reason, an extreme form of *depoliticization*.[9]

What is deeply disturbing, especially viewing things from the Left or a post-Marxian standpoint, is the fact that the other great *category of the political* in our modern tradition—namely, *antagonism*—is also fading into indeterminacy. And, with the joint decline in the capacity of sovereignty and antagonism to impose their rules and meanings, hence horizons and projects on our political experiences, it is the customary framework of debates over *democracy* that becomes shaky, on the side of popular sovereignty or on the side of emancipatory struggles. One might object: where do you see a decline of antagonism? Our experience within and across borders is full of *conflicts*, which become politicized in different languages, and these conflicts themselves are fought by millions of people who long for emancipation, crying for democracy, or rights that could be interpreted in a renewed democratic agenda. I don't deny that, but I claim that none of the great *dichotomies* that used to be invoked, in order to think "globally" the stakes and the historic horizons of the *political*, therefore infuse an *agency* that could be *universalized*, has survived the recent developments of globalization: neither the bourgeoisie-proletariat divide, nor the Global North vs Global South divide, nor the democracy vs. totalitarianism, nor the secularism vs. theocratic, nor the internationalism vs. nationalism divide. . . . We are left with a *multiplicity* of conflictual interests, which are all political in a sense, but cannot immediately become incorporated into a synthetic definition of *politics*.

The General Economy of Violence

It would be a much too easy step to bring in here the issue of *violence* as a simple counterpart of the previous "negations": *negation of the negation*, as it were, albeit not in the sense of reestablishing the positive, but as a *second degree* of the negative, an abyss of unfathomable negativity within the absence of the political itself. I do not believe that more or less uncontrollable violence: the individual and criminal gun-violence, the street-violence (often perpetrated by the police rather than by the youngsters), the terrorist violence (religious or not), the violence of mad politicians imposed on their peoples or outside, *logically derives* from the indeterminacy of politics, the destabilizing effects on our institutions and our imaginary of the withering away of traditional forms of sovereignty and antagonism. But I believe that a combination of the analysis of financial globalization *and* the crisis of the political is required to *approach* a correct evaluation of the function of violence in our contemporary world. However, I also think that this question must be treated in an autonomous manner. The fact that the current world is a world of "extreme violence" that escapes regulations (or produces regulations that, in fact, make it more violent) deserves special consideration. It is a challenge for theory per se, which requires a kind of critique that does not reduce it either to a simple instrument of other forces or a mediation between historical states of society where violence as such is kept under control.

One might object: what is new here? When was the world a peaceful one? Are you simply predicting the repetition of the critical situations that took place in the twentieth century when different types of conflicts and antagonisms merged into global armed confrontations? Not exactly, although I

exclude no fatal development. . . . I do not think that there exists any standard of measurement that would allow us to compare the amount of violence
waged in different societies and civilizations, either locally or globally, vis-
ibly or invisibly. I understand the argument that shows that capitalism as a
dominant social system since the very beginning was associated with extreme
violence aiming at dispossession and subjection, or developed itself "within
mud and blood," as Rosa Luxemburg famously wrote in her *Accumulation of
Capital*, but I am wary of the seemingly logical conclusion that, this world being now entirely dominated by capitalism, the society as such now lives in a
state of war, or a *state of exception*, where every rule, every law, is just a form of
civil or social war.[10] This seems to me to be a paranoid reasoning, and above
all it has the bad effect of *blurring distinctions* between forces and causes of
violence that must form a privileged object of reflection and intervention for
any citizenry that seeks to resist the neutralization of the political. *Distinctions
are crucial*, they are where we can bring in concepts, therefore intelligibility,
therefore agency.

This being said, I will acknowledge two aspects of the defining characteristics of violence in the global world that really challenge our theoretical instruments. One of them has to do with the capacity of extension of *zones of death*
into broader frames of time and space. The extended Middle East is the main
example here, ranging and expanding over parts of Asia, Africa, and the whole
Euro-Mediterranean space. The West identifies "terrorism," behind which
some ideologues name Islam as the root cause, as the main factor. Therefore,
they imagine the solution in terms of counterterrorism, waging a "war on
terror" whose designated target in fact is Islam. Part of the traditional anti-
imperialist Left identifies neocolonialism, the empire of oil, as the main factor, sometimes indulging in the idea that it is "Western civilization" as such
that generates the violence *from above*. In any case, we do not see the force, or
the strategy, that would reverse the course in any near future. This brings me
to the other aspect that I want to insist on.

In my 1996 Wellek Lectures at UC Irvine, I distinguished between two
modalities of extreme violence or cruelty, which I called "ultra-subjective violence" and "ultra-objective violence."[11] One has to do with the hysterization
of collective identities that seek to achieve an imaginary immunity through
the elimination of the *internal enemy* (who, for that purpose, must be isolated
from within the broad range of social differences). The other has to do with
the consequences of the capitalist use of humans as instruments of production
(which also includes the *elimination* of the instruments in excess or *disposable*

humans, as Bertrand Ogilvie called them, and whom Saskia Sassen also made the object of her remarkable analysis).[12] I keep using that distinction, which I find useful to acknowledge the *extremist* character of the violent situations in which most humans find themselves today directly or indirectly involved, while also avoiding reduction to a single cause or mechanism—particularly the mechanism of "global capital," as a good Marxist might be tempted to proceed, but which amounts to a tautology. However, I now make use of it with some additions.

For one, I am convinced that a central element in the delimitation of ultra-subjective violence—its mimetic effect on rival communities and its merging with phenomena of ultra-objective violence such as extreme mass poverty and overexploitation, eventually creating situations of *endemic war*—has to do with the repressive or *preventative annihilation of the emancipation of women*. There is a clear sexist dimension in the generalization of war (which makes, of course, the occasional intervention of women against war—as today in Turkey—all the more significant). Although there are other factors more directly linked to capitalism as such, such as the growing importance of weaponry in the market, there seems to be a point of no-return that has been reached in *the articulation of patriarchy and capitalism* that is an intrinsic part of the *economy of generalized extreme violence* where autonomous forms add themselves and, so to speak, constrain the political from two different sides. We will retrieve a symmetric problem in a moment when evoking the new articulation of "production" and "reproduction."

Externalities and the "Ecological Debt"

Similar remarks could be offered on a different side of the economy of violence (although I am not sure that they are totally separated) that I only mention here hoping to return to it in a different occasion: I mean the question of *violence against nature*. Marx famously wrote that capitalism continuously destroys "the original sources of all wealth, the land [soil] and the human labour power [worker]": this sentence is quoted again and again when people of good will want to show that Marxism and ecology can become a single discourse, adopt a single theoretical framework.[13] "Land" here could be taken as a metonymy for the environment or the planet. "Violence against nature" is a problematic formula if you do not want to "personalize" the environment; rather, it puts into question the "humanist" distinction between subject and object or human labor and material resources that, as we now acknowledge, is also part of what Marx *uncritically* inherited from classical political economy. In any case, it is becoming increasingly impossible to avoid the idea that the destruction of the environment is an *active* part of this generalized "economy" of violence I was talking about, both intensifying antagonisms between communities (particularly through migration of "climatic" refugees) and leading industrialization of agriculture and exploitation of wilderness into a savage race without rules: we are anxiously awaiting the crossing of the limit of irreversibility for global warming, if it is not already reached.

This is a reason, among others, that I regret not to have time to include a major point, which should be linked to any discussion of generalized valorization—namely, the "ecological debt." As we know, this category was introduced in a polemic manner by theorists like Martinez Alier, who argued that the development of the industrialized North (including its agriculture), would not have been possible over the centuries without a massive extraction and appropriation of natural resources, therefore a massive destruction of the environment in the South.[14] This remains true, of course, even if the *boundaries* between North and South are displaced. But there is another aspect, that global warming and the contamination of oceans dramatically bring to the fore: this is the *aggregate* "ecological debt" of human activities with respect to the planet, now often referred to as the "human footprint." A spectacular index of this debt—a debt that is clearly "unsustainable"—is given by the fact that the moment in the year when renewable planetary resources are exhausted by the economy (including production and individual consumption) increasingly arrives earlier. I believe it is now in August, meaning we consume almost "two planets" a year. It becomes therefore increasingly difficult to treat these distinctive effects as pure "externalities," which nobody has to pay for, as classical economics used to do. And for a long period, Marxism on its side was not really concerned, because of its one-sided interest in the function of *labor* (both "abstract" and "concrete") in processes of *valorization*. They probably should become integrated into a cost-benefit calculus at global scale that is expressed in "negative values."[15] But we also know that there is a *capitalist* exploitation of these externalities, therefore a valorization of the ecological debt, which includes everything from the green energies to the plans of investment in industries that will "repair the planet"—at least some parts of it—to the huge possibilities of exploitation of mineral resources or transportation routes, perhaps also military competition, that are opened by the melting of the Arctic and Antarctic ice. This shows, even very superficially, that the process of commodification and the question of its internal contradictions are very sensitive.

"Neoliberalism"?

The reference to ecological debt, even if we avoid any easy play on words, brings us back to the question of financialization, inasmuch as it is always based on credit, and the monetization of credit, that is the *exchange value* of debt, and the piling up of debts that are "hedged"—that is, transformed into options or securitized—and become profitable "industries" themselves.[16] If you see the operations of unlimited credit as a simple extension of debt beyond the possibility of repayment, there is an unsurmountable contradiction here; traditional theories of financial crises (including Marxist ones) presented this contradiction as a source of periodic catastrophes bearing enormous social costs, when the "fictitious" character of the accumulation was brought to the fore and the primacy of the "real" had to be forcefully restored. But if you see the inflation of credit operations as an anticipation of expanded commodification, even at the risk of intermediary losses (such as a collapsing of institutions who invest in subprimes), things are different. *The debts don't have to be repaid*: they generate a flow of interests, which are indefinitely paid by individuals, or by states (that is, by individuals by means of "their" state, as in Argentina or Greece). There must be an articulation between this structure and the fact that every new progress in the commodification of life, resources, and activities requires a huge *advance of money capital* provided by credit, just as the industrial revolution in the past mobilized and concentrated credit and made use of innovations in the bank industry and the international monetary system.[17]

A big controversy is now running among both Marxists and non-Marxists as to whether the "financial industry" is a *parasitic* industry that always runs the risk of *diverting* the funds, or the value, that it appropriates for the price of its services, away from productive uses. This was, in particular, the idea behind the Keynesian "liquidity trap" and behind the idea that the main form of accumulation today is not linked to *profits* whose maximization requires a capitalist organization of productive operations, globally and locally, but rather to financial *rents* that are essentially unproductive.[18] I tend to believe the opposite: financial capital is no longer external to the "productive" sphere; it has become an *"organizer" of production*, because it is making the strategic choices, allocating resources, and especially credit, according to a certain *logic*, however "invisible" or "aleatory" its anticipations must be. This logic has an absolute criterion: the shareholder's value, or "value to market" of a firm's shares, which is measured *daily* in real time, closely following the feedback effects of all sorts of commercial, cultural, political events. And, again, I submit that a major objective of that logic is not just quantitative growth (or the *rate of accumulation*) but the steady expansion of the realm of commodities. This could be considered analogous to *planning*, except that—contrary to certain indications by Marx in *Capital*, volume 3, which explained that banking and credit invented a kind of communist *simulacrum* or "communism within the limits of capitalism"[19]—this planning is not seeking a *balance* among different sectors of economic activity whose products must be exchanged against one another. It is seeking a *dynamic disequilibrium*, or at least an "imperfect equilibrium," where certain sectors, particularly innovative sectors, in the sense of new commodifications, draw a major part of the credit to maximize financial returns.[20] Perhaps we should call it "anti-planning."

This is indeed a form of extreme *competition*. Globalization, as I said with de Brunhoff, inaugurates *l'heure du marché*: the times of the "deregulated," and therefore ultra-competitive, market that expands across boundaries and social conditions. But this does not have only an *objective* or structural dimension. It also has a *subjective* face, or it involves processes of subjectivation. It is here, perhaps, what we can give some precise sense to the category "neoliberalism." In my view this is an ambiguous category, not only because there are *opposing trends within neoliberalism* that are diverging with respect to crucial questions of fiscal and monetary regulations (even if they share a motto of reducing the economic interventions of the state, above all its function of redistribution), but because the name "neoliberalism" itself oscillates between an ideological discourse and actual transformations of economic institutions and practices. There is a field, however, where the performativity of discourse immediately produces "real" effects out of ideology, and this is the field of the construction of subjectivities. Or should we rather say, the *destruction* of subjectivities? I follow here the work of the late Robert Castel, the interlocutor of Bourdieu and Foucault, who devoted the last part of his work to describing the emergence of "negative individualities" in the French *banlieues* and other places increasingly hosting *precarious work*, or the alternating of massive joblessness and unstable employment that he saw as a systematic dismantling of the *social* conditions and institutions without which there cannot be a "propriety in one's person" (self-ownership) in Lockean terms. Tendentially the social conditions of *positive individualism* had included wage labor itself, especially under the conditions of the modern welfare state ("société salariale").[21] *Possessive individualism* is decidedly not the same as "self-entrepreneurship," as advocated by capitalism in the age of neo-liberalism, or the extreme exposure to competition, which permeates every moment and every aspect of every single life. That leads us, which I admit is a short-circuit, to address the issues of stability and instability, crisis and historical "tendencies" inherent in this situation.

"Crisis" and "Historical Tendency"

Marxists are not unanimous, far from, about the "crisis" of contemporary capitalism. But *crisis* itself is a problematic concept, because it always involves choices regarding *which aspect* of the economy or *which part of the society* is in a critical situation. Since the origins in Ancient Medicine, where the term was applied "metaphorically" to the realm of politics, the question remains open whether a *crisis* names an interruption, a state of exception, or a moment of extreme danger—for indeed, crisis can also contaminate its opposite, so that *regimes* can exist that are in permanent critical state, or that derive their strength from the crisis itself, or its continuous deferral. This is how Machiavelli or Max Weber saw *democracy* as a "political regime" and also probably how Marx initially viewed capitalism itself as an institutionalized form of antagonism that is unsustainable by nature—a view that did not prevent him from trying to *conceptualize* the "crises of capitalism," whether cyclical or temporary, even "final."

These problems remain involved in current debates concerning the interpretation of *financialization* as a central feature of the globalization process, its factor of acceleration and intensification: the form that, for example, through the proliferation of debt, makes it impossible for anyone—individual or state—to escape the quasi-sovereignty of the GFM in his daily life. It seems to me that Marxists are dividing themselves along two lines on this point.

First, there is a division that concerns the periodic return of phases of financialization in the history of capitalism, characterized by a growing importance of interest with respect to profit or speculation and the "preference for liquidity" with respect to commercial and industrial investments. Giovanni Arrighi features a theorist for whom financialization is a recurrent phenomenon, to be located in the *intermediary moments* between regimes of accumulation that are also characterized by the relative stability of the hege-monic political power.[22] The current "excess" of financialization would have to be linked to the demise in the position of the U.S. dollar and the declining hegemony of America. But others would insist that *there is something new* in its current form: precisely the fact that today financialization is not purely speculative, but has acquired a capacity to organize *production*, generating some sort of "anti-planning," inaugurating an era in the history of capitalism *structurally* defined by the fact that financial operations, the management of "liquidity," are central and not peripheral.[23]

The second controversy opposes those theorists for whom these are the symptoms of the *general crisis*—a final crisis of the "capitalist world system" that entered a phase of "chaotic oscillations" toward the end of the Cold War whose result is unpredictable but cannot become indefinitely deferred—and others for whom this change itself is a feature of "post-capitalism"—that is, a new regime that is still "capitalist," albeit not resting on the same productive basis as before.[24]

It might seem, certainly, that my own evocation of "total subsumption" goes rather in that second direction.[25] In a different manner, Wolfgang Streeck recently brought to the fore the idea of the "end of capitalism" as something that has not already taken place, but is approaching.[26] My goal, ultimately, is to try and displace such alternatives. . . . Beyond the discussion of "facts" (which are always impossible to entirely isolate from interpretations) it seems to me that, for a Marxist or a post-Marxist, such questions involve a return to the obscurities and tensions involved in the way Marx conceptualized what he called, in the singular, *the* historical *tendency* of capitalist accumulation, from which the historical pattern of development, of crises, and the eventual collapsing of capitalism could be derived. This is typically what I call after David Harvey a *point of "stress" in Marx's* theory:[27] it is located in the immedi-ate vicinity of what is central in his discovery—namely, the articulation of *social relation, contradiction,* and *process* as a structural transformation. What is at stake is how we understand a "historical" tendency and, conversely, how we explain history or bring *intelligibility* into its empirical development through the definition of "tendencies."

We remember the way in which, in the final sections of *Capital,* volume 1, Marx would articulate the idea of a "law of accumulation" of capitalism with a series of related *cumulative* processes. On the one side, we have the fact that capitalist social relations (wage labor, valorization, commodification) cannot feature a *simple reproduction*: they must undergo an *enlarged reproduction* or reproduction on ever larger scale. On the other side, we have a rising "organic composition of capital," therefore increasing productivity of labor, inexorable *concentration* of capitalist property, and a structural "law of population" that creates a permanent "industrial reserve army" or a relative overpopulation. This is part of a fundamental effort by Marx to *historicize* the categories of political economy, which means that they do not have *eternal* validity. Above all, it means that social relations that have historically emerged and are historically determined also *transform* their own conditions, therefore involve a historical *negativity*. But this is also where the difficulties begin. A careful reading of Marx's text that includes all its internal variations, and therefore treats it as an essentially *open, unfinished* piece of theory, clearly shows that— except sometimes for militant purposes—Marx never wanted to eliminate the political contingency and describe a single, linear path of development; the main line of his argument nevertheless is *evolutionist* and therefore contains an *eschatological* dimension inasmuch as the question of the "essential" transformation of capitalism is at stake. This means that, for Marx, a "tendency" is not only a *tendency of* certain forces or processes to produce certain effects, but it is also a tendency *toward* a certain "final" situation in the time of history, or perhaps a "final" dilemma (capitalism *or* communism). Although Marx included in his description a reference to *counter-tendencies*—so that the result would contain an overdetermination that could even affect the understanding of the postcapitalist state to come—this is not sufficient to neutralize the fact that, in such a representation, actual history is *subjected to* the definition of the tendency or appears as its progressive realization. In fact, it is "subsumed" under the tendency.

This illustrates the paradoxically *ahistorical* character of Marx's radical *historicism*, or what calls for a *surplus of historicity*: a kind of "historicization" of Marx's concept of history and historical time itself. And, in fact, the most creative Marxists in the past devoted their efforts to achieving just that: introducing and integrating a *deeper* form of historicity into Marx's theory of capitalism. This deeper form of historicity tentatively rectified the "evolutionist" character without eliminating the dynamic element that was involved in the notion of a (contradictory) tendency—that is, the idea that there is an *immanent* capacity of transformation in the very form of the capitalist social relation. Interestingly (also because these efforts were linked to revolutionary moments in given situations), this always meant a *politicization* of Marx's concept of history; these projects restored as an organic component certain *political* elements that Marx had first marginalized or "postponed," such as the geography of imperialist domination, the global determinations of the population law, the role of the state (therefore the nation) in the class struggles. . . . Tronti's *operaismo* and Wallerstein's *world-system analysis* are examples of neo-Marxist elaborations that, relying on different experiences, go into opposite directions to "rectify" the evolutionist conception of the articulation between *history* and *tendency* in Marx's theory. And I would give more recent discussions about "anthropocene" or "capitalocene" as a very different manner of thinking historicity beyond Marx, *oltre Marx*, as Negri would say. It is a very paradoxical attempt, following the standards of classical historicism, because it forces us to identify *a surplus of historicity* with an element of "naturalization" of the economy—or perhaps rather, a highly conflictual dialectic of naturalization and denaturalization, "natural constraints," and "second nature" that I am ready to integrate into a notion of *absolute capitalism*.

Absolute vs. Historical Capitalism

Let me, then, clarify my use of the term.[28] I would like to submit that contemporary capitalism, globalized and financialized, is *not* just one more "stage" in the historical development of capitalism or *another cycle* of accumulation and hegemony in the history of the capitalist world-system. But it is also not the "end" of capitalism, at least not *qualitatively*, in the sense that it would be based on forces and norms that make it more or less immediately "impossible." Such prophecies have been frequent in the Marxist tradition. Ours is a capitalism that keeps accumulating, in fact, on a broader basis, having achieved a form of "global transformation" of all dimensions of life under the law of the valorization process (for which "private" property is just a legal instrument, however indispensable), but whose "rules" are very different from the rules of yesteryear—a very long yesteryear indeed, since it covers at least five centuries of transformations. The core of the proposal, which is also the crux of the difficulty, lies in the idea that such capitalism does not only *come after* a certain (long-term) history, but radically modifies the social formations, the typical conflicts, and the hierarchy of institutions of that history. By twisting Wallerstein's terminology, I will say that this capitalism *overcomes the "historical capitalism"* that emerged from the Great Discoveries and was reborn successively through the "bourgeois revolutions" (democratic and industrial) and the "passive revolution" of the interwar period (in Gramsci's terminology). This will explain why I borrow the concept of an "absolute spirit" (in this case capitalism is itself the material spirit), since "absolute" in Hegel is what takes us beyond the *historical* in the first degree, which he calls "objective spirit."[29] Allow me to insist very schematically on three aspects of this overcoming of historical capitalism that involve a deep change in our representation of historicity:

1. The typical "social formations" (or institutional "masses," as Hegel would say) of historical capitalism are *classes* defined in terms of property, distribution of revenues, therefore inequalities, sources of income, professional status, etc., and *nations* (emerging primarily in the center, therefore indissociable from empires, then extended progressively to the whole world, together with the institutions of *boundaries*, through the processes of liberation and decolonization). "History" in that sense, with the periodic climaxes of wars and revolutions, is a *political* combination of class struggles and confrontation (wars) between nations that enhance the "sovereign" function of the state. I am not saying that nothing remains of nations and classes in today's world, but they have been devalued as formations of the collective, dissolved into more complex patterns of social inequalities and solidarities.

2. The development of "historical capitalism" can thus be seen as a *Great Transformation* itself, stretching over several centuries, that is now more or less completely achieved everywhere in the world. This is Polanyi's category, of course, giving its title to the book published in 1944.[30] For Polanyi, the Great Transformation taking place in the twentieth century was the constitution of the Welfare State in Western social-democratic countries. As an institution the Welfare State *reversed* the tendencies of liberal capitalism after the industrial revolution when society became aware of the *internal limit* that cannot be abolished through the creation of "fictitious commodities," because the process of endless commodification is becoming destructive. In my representation, this is only the penultimate episode of the transition. The Great Transformation in fact is coextensive with four or five centuries of historical capitalism, a process in which valorization has seized one domain of life and human agency after the other, and particularly *reproduction* after *production*.[31] Throughout historical capitalism, the labor force needed to be reproduced *outside* capitalist social relations in the strict sense, whereas in "absolute capitalism" the reproduction takes place *within such relations*, or it is "totally subsumed." More generally, the Great Transformation covers the long period in which capitalism coexists with many other modes of production and consumption that are more or less subjugated, but without whose *heterogeneity* it could not work.

3. And finally, of course, absolute capitalism is *postcolonial*, just as globalization and financialization are: they were made possible by decolonization, and they exploited decolonization particularly in terms of the expansion of credit and debt to ex-colonial, independent countries, making them servants of the expansion of financial capital and the emergence of new active poles of accumulation in the ex-Third World. Of course, this doesn't mean that relations of dependency and domination—the radical inequality among territories—of populations and states no longer exist. We observe that postcolonial geography and demography have nothing to do with an equalization or a homogenization of the human condition across the world. But the distribution of those inequalities is no longer a proper colonial one, opposing center and periphery, and it is also not a simple North/South distinction, except in a metaphoric sense. This is why I find so important the kind of "population law" exposed in Sunder Rajan's work on *pharmocracy*, which describes the *unequal distribution*—between India, on the one side, and the U.S., on the other—of experimentation (testing) and production-prescription of those drugs and biotechnologies that generate surplus-value in the form of *surplus-health*.[32] But I should also mention, foremost, the fluxes of migrations and the new function of borders that interrupt and violently "regulate" these fluxes.[33] And I should turn once again toward the fact that, instead of withering away in a new cosmopolitanism, the racial antagonisms, or cultural, ethnic, and religious differences turned into racial antagonisms, prevail and will prevail in "absolute capitalism."

To these three main characteristics of Absolute Capitalism one aspect remains to be added, at least from my point of view: the fact that absolute capitalism must become understood as *postsocialism*. This is empirically true in the sense that it comes after the cycle of socialist "revolutions" in the twentieth century—attempts at creating socialist states and socialist economies—had been completed. The more or less advanced *transition from capitalism to socialism*, advocated by Marxists, has been succeeded by a *transition from socialism to capitalism*, which in some sense allows us to understand what "socialism" was about: an amazing effect of the "cunning of history." More essentially, it is true in the sense that contemporary capitalism is based on the systematic deconstruction, therefore also the *use*, of the institutions to be listed under the name "socialism" directly or indirectly. And this is what, in a sense, the name "neoliberalism" best expresses, if we insist on the idea that "neoliberalism" is not a *continuation* of classical liberalism, but an imaginary restoration of liberalism—the absolute rule of free trade and private property—*beyond* the socialist experiences and the social and economic transformations they had produced.

Now, we must indeed understand "socialism" here in a very broad sense, including what Marx would call "bourgeois socialism" (that is, ranging from social-democratic Welfare State to Soviet-type planning, from Keynesian economics and Fordist social policies to developmental programs in the Third World), as combining different degrees of *state interventions* with different forms of "mixed economics" in which *collective interests*, which can remain class interests, are combined with competition and entrepreneurship. This is precisely what in 1944 Hayek had named "serfdom," putting together *all* the forms and degrees of public regulation of the economy in a single "adversarial field."[34] What remains of socialism in its antithetic forms today is just that, and we see something very strange happening. On the one hand, neoliberalism systematically *destroys* the commons or abolishes the limits of commodification that "socialism," the Welfare State, the Keynesian ("New Deal") social contract, and developmental national policies had instituted in the form of protections or institutional solidarities with greater or lesser inequalities and loopholes.

But of course, neoliberalism could not do this if there were nothing to destroy, nothing that is to expropriate, appropriate, or *dispossess*, as Harvey says. For example, you could not privatize Medicare and education if public social policies (socialism of the "care," if you like) had not created a base of mass education and general medicine on the background of one century of class struggles. More than that, while neoliberal policies *commodify* services and appropriate life in new manners, they realize that they still *need* to conceive and make use of something that comes from socialism: Trump needs to keep something of Obamacare, even if all his party does not want to understand that. Banks need the state not only as a police apparatus but as a financial lender in the last resort, if the phrase "Too Big to Fail" is to mean something effective—just as the global institutions such as IMF need the state in the debtor countries to levy the taxes through which the interests will be restructured indefinitely. It remains to be seen to which extremities you can go in cutting the social services while keeping the fiscal resources. So, the *appearance* is a monolinear trend toward the minimal state, but the *reality* is a much more conflictual situation, in which absolute capitalism *needs* to make use of the very public structures and social functions that it seeks to delegitimize and undermine. It must keep alive (even if starving) what it destroys continuously. I would connect this to the idea that—contrary to a simple logic of *succession*, in which ideologies become reified as "stages" in the history of capitalism—neoliberalism is now *dominant*, but socialism is a *latent* or *repressed* element of internal contradiction. This is linked to what Egidius Berns aptly called the "porous" relationship between economy and politics in neoliberalism.[35] Absolute capitalism, therefore, is not a *stable* social and economic system. It is highly unstable, both because it is extremely violent and because an immediate *reversibility* of the economic and the political, rather than a "neutralization of the political," is its structural defining characteristic.

Notes

1. This chapter is drawn from particular sections of three lectures I delivered at the University of California, Irvine (Critical Theory Emphasis) on April 17–21, 2017. Other sections from those lectures appear in Étienne Balibar, "Towards a New Critique of Political Economy," in *Capitalism: Concept & Idea; The Philosophy and Politics of Marx's "Capital" Today*, ed. Peter Osborne, Eric Alliez and Eric-John Russell (London: CRMEP, Kingston University, 2019). The two pieces are complementary but can be read separately.

2. See in particular *Capital*, vol. 1, chapter 3: "It is in the world market that money first functions to its full extent as the commodity whose natural form is also the directly social form of realization of human labour in the abstract. Its mode of existence becomes adequate to its concept"; and chapter 6: "Why this free worker confronts him in the sphere of circulation is a question which does not interest the owner of money, for he finds the labour-market in existence as a particular branch of the commodity-market"; Karl Marx, *Capital*, vol. 1, introduction by Ernest Mandel, trans. Ben Fowkes (New York: Vintage, 1977), 241, 273.

3. Suzanne de Brunhoff, *L'heure du marché* (Paris: Presses Universitaires de France, 1986).

4. This is of course the position that has been powerfully advocated by Immanuel Wallerstein in his series of volumes on *The Modern World-System* (1974; repr. New York: Academic Press, 2014). More generally it belongs to all modern continuators of the pioneering work by Rosa Luxemburg, *The Accumulation of Capital* (1913), ed. Dr. W. Stark (London: Routledge and Kegan Paul, 1951).

5. See Pierre-Noel Giraud, *La mondialisation: Emergences et fragmentations* (Paris: Sciences Humaines, 2012).

6. Karl Polanyi, *The Great Transformation: The Political and Economic Origins of Our Time*, foreword by Joseph E. Stiglitz, introduction by Fred Block (1944; repr. Boston: Beacon Press, 2001).

7. See Balibar, "The New Law of Population of Absolute Capitalism," presented at the 19th Nordic Migration Research Conference, Norrköping (Sweden), August 2018, publication forthcoming.

8. Wolfgang Streeck, *Buying Time: The Delayed Crisis of Democratic Capitalism* (London: Verso 2017).

9. The category "governance" was apparently invented in the early 1990s by experts from the World Bank; see the historical and epistemological dossier published in Italian by Parolechiave (Rome: Carocci editore, 2017), n. 56.

10. A position that, with significant nuances, is today shared by such authors as Giorgio Agamben, Eric Alliez, Maurizio Lazzarato, Anselm Jappe, and others.

11. Balibar, *Violence and Civility: On the Limits of Political Philosophy*, trans. Michael Goshgarian (New York: Columbia University Press, 2015).

12. Saskia Sassen, *Expulsions: Brutality and Complexity in the Global Economy* (Cambridge, Mass.: Harvard University Press, 2014).

13. Karl Marx, *Capital*, 1:638. See the special dossier on *Marxism, Environmental Studies, Global Approaches: New Critical Horizons*, ed. Paul Gillibert and Stephane Haber, in *Actuel Marx* 61, no. 1 (2017).

14. Joan Martinez-Alier, *The Environmentalism of the Poor: A Study of Ecological Conflicts and Valuation* (Northhampton, Mass.: Edward Elgar, 2002).

15. This very interesting idea, which confers a new algebraic dimension to the Marxian "theory of value," is offered by David Harvey, *Marx, Capital, and the Madness of Economic Reason* (New York: Oxford University Press, 2017).

16. I find the work of Robert Meister very useful here, even if I do not really share the idea that the "democratization" of the financial market through pension funds and hedge funds opens a possibility of blocking the system analogous to a general strike; see Meister, "Liquidity," in *Derivatives and the Wealth of Societies*, ed. Benjamin Lee and Randy Martin (Chicago: Chicago University Press, 2016).

17. See Balibar, "Politics of the Debt," in *Postmodern Culture* 23, no. 3 (May 2013).

18. See in particular Michael Hardt and Antonio Negri, *Commonwealth* (Cambridge, Mass.: Harvard University Press 2009).

19. Karl Marx, *Capital*, vol. 3, *The Role of Credit in Capitalist Production* (New York: Penguin Classics, 1991), 569.

20. A fascinating critique of neo-classical theories of partial and general equilibrium with its bearing on Marxism is provided by Yahya Madra, *Late Neoclassical Economics: The Restoration of Theoretical Humanism in Contemporary Economic Theory* (New York: Routledge 2016).

21. Robert Castel, *From Manual Workers to Wage Laborers: Transformation of the Social Question*, trans. Richard Boyd (New Brunswick, N.J.: Transaction, 2002).

22. Giovanni Arrighi, *Adam Smith in Beijing: Lineages of the Twenty-First Century* (London: Verso, 2007).

23. See Meister, "Liquidity," and John Milios, with Dimitris P. Sotiropoulos and Spyros Lapatsioras, *A Political Economy of Contemporary Capitalism and Its Crisis: Demystifying Finance* (London and New York: Routledge, 2013).

24. See Paul Mason, *Postcapitalism: A Guide to Our Future* (New York: Farrar, Straus and Giroux, 2016).

25. See Balibar, "Towards a New Critique of Political Economy."

26. He argues in a rather traditional way through the combination of declining profit rates and increasing inequalities that undermine the global consumption, but also integrate the environmental crisis and the exhaustion of natural resources; Wolfgang Streeck, *How Will Capitalism End? Essays on a Failing System* (London: Verso, 2017).

27. Harvey, *A Companion to Marx's Capital*, vol. 2 (London: Verso, 2013).

28. The concept of "absolute capitalism" has been in use for some years now, albeit with different meanings, in post-Marxist works like those of Franco Berardi, Jacques Rancière, Ingmar Granstedt, and Bertrand Ogilvie.

29. The distinction is elaborated by Hegel mainly in the *Encyclopaedia* (1817–27) and the *Logic* (1812–16).

30. The same year, incidentally, as the political and philosophical manifesto of what would come to be known as "neo-liberalism"; see Friedrich von Hayek, *The Road to Serfdom*.

31. See Melinda Cooper, *Family Values: Between Neoliberalism and the New Social Conservatism* (New York: Zone Books, 2017).

32. Kaushik Sunder Rajan, *Pharmocracy: Value, Politics, and Knowledge in Global Biomedicine* (Durham, N.C.: Duke University Press, 2017).

33. See Sandro Mezzadra and Brett Neilson, *Border as Method, or, The Multiplication of Labor* (Durham, N.C.: Duke University Press, 2013); Wendy Brown, *Walled States, Waning Sovereignty* (New York: Zone Books, 2013); and Balibar, "Strangers as Enemies: Further Reflections on Trans-National Citizenship," (Hamilton, Canada: McMaster University, 2006, http://www.globalautonomy .ca/global1/article.jsp?index=RA_Balibar_Strangers.xml.

34. A category used by Foucault in his genealogy of neoliberalism; see Michel Foucault, *The Birth of Biopolitics: Lectures at the Collège de France, 1978–1979* (New York: Palgrave Macmillan, 2008).

35. Egidius Berns, "Gouvernance, souveraineté, globalisation," in *Décider avec les parties prenantes*, sous la direction de Maria Bonnafous-Boucher et Yvon Pesqueux (Paris: La Découverte 2006).

ÉTIENNE BALIBAR is Professor Emeritus of Moral and Political Philosophy at Université de Paris X–Nanterre and Anniversary Chair of Contemporary European Philosophy at Kingston University. He is author of *Reading Capital* (with Louis Althusser [Verso, 1965]), and his most recent books include *Equaliberty* (Duke University Press, 2014), *Violence and Civility* (Columbia University Press, 2015), *Citizen Subject: Foundations for Philosophical Anthropology* (Fordham University Press, 2016), and *Secularism and Cosmopolitanism: Critical Hypotheses on Religion and Politics* (Columbia University Press, 2018).

SÖREN BRANDES is a research fellow at the International Max Planck Research School (IMPRS) for Moral Economies of Modern Societies at the Max Planck Institute for Human Development in Berlin and a Ph.D. candidate at the Free University Berlin. He is coeditor of a special issue on "Practices of Capitalism" in *Mittelweg 36* and has published on the history of neoliberalism and mass media in the United States and the United Kingdom.

WENDY BROWN is Class of 1936 First Professor of Political Science at the University of California, Berkeley, where she is also affiliated with the Program in Critical Theory. Among her many book titles are *Regulating Aversion: Tolerance in the Age of Empire and Identity* (Princeton University Press, 2006), *Walled States, Waning Sovereignty* (Zone Books, 2010), *Undoing the Demos: Neoliberalism's Stealth Revolution* (Zone Books, 2015), and *In the Ruins of Neoliberalism: The Rise of Anti-Democratic Politics in the West* (Columbia University Press, 2019).

MELINDA COOPER is Associate Professor in the School of Social and Political Science at the University of Sydney, Australia. Her research focuses on the broad areas of social studies of finance, biomedical economies, neoliberalism, and new social conservatisms. She is author of *Life as Surplus: Biotechnology and Capitalism in the Neoliberal Era* (University of Washington Press, 2008) and *Family Values: Between Neoliberalism and the New Social Conservatism* (Zone Books, 2017). She is coeditor, with Martijn Konings, of the Stanford University Press book series Currencies: New Thinking for Financial Times.

JULIA ELYACHAR is an Associate Professor of Anthropology at Princeton University and a member of Princeton's Institute for International and Regional Studies. She is an anthropologist broadly trained in economics, social theory, the history of political and economic thought, Middle Eastern Studies, and the Arabic language. She is author of *Markets of Dispossession: NGOs, Economic Development, and the State in Cairo* (Duke University Press, 2005), which won the American Ethnological Association's Sharon Stephens First Book Prize in 2007.

MICHEL FEHER is a philosopher, a founding editor of Zone Books, and the cofounder and president of Cette France-là, Paris, a monitoring group on French immigration policy. He is currently a visiting professor at Goldsmiths, University of London. His publications include *Powerless by Design: The Age of the International Community* (Duke University Press, 2000), *Nongovernmental Politics* (Zone Books, 2007), *Xénophobie d'en haut: Le choix d'une droite éhontée* (La Découverte, 2012), "Europe at a Crossroads" (Near Futures Online, 2016), and *Rated Agency: Investee Politics for a Speculative Age* (Zone Books, 2018).

MEGAN MOODIE is Associate Professor of Anthropology and Affiliated Faculty in Feminist Studies at the University of California, Santa Cruz. Her research focuses on feminist political and legal anthropology, kinship and reproduction, and experimental ethnographic writing in South Asia, East Europe, and the United States. She is author of *We Were Adivasis: Aspiration in an Indian Scheduled Tribe* (University of Chicago Press, 2015). She is also the curator and editor of the Margaret Mead Journalism Project, a popular-media public anthropology initiative housed at the UCSC Center for Emerging Worlds.

CHRISTOPHER NEWFIELD is Professor of English and American Studies at the University of California, Santa Barbara. His current areas of research span innovation theory, race relations, science studies, the future of solar energy, humanities-based approaches to economics, and Critical University Studies, a field that he helped found. His most recent books include *Ivy and Industry: Business and the Making of the American University, 1880–1980* (Duke University Press, 2003), *Unmaking the Public University: The*

Forty-Year Assault on the Middle Class (Harvard University Press, 2008), and *The Great Mistake: How We Wrecked Public Universities and How We Can Fix Them* (Johns Hopkins University Press, 2016).

DIETER PLEHWE is a Senior Research Fellow in the Department of Inequality and Social Policy at the Berlin Social Science Research Center (WZB). His recent books include *Neoliberal Hegemony: A Global Critique* (with Walpen, Routledge, 2006); *The Road from Mont Pèlerin: The Making of the Neoliberal Thought Collective* (with Mirowski, Harvard University Press, 2009); and *Liberalism and the Welfare State: Economists and Arguments for the Welfare State* (with Backhouse, Bateman, and Nishizawa, Oxford University Press, 2017). His research in the WZB project "Modes of Economic Governance" focuses on European interest groups, think tank networks, and the transformation of transnational governance. He is currently working on an edited volume on neoliberalism with Quinn Slobodian and Philip Mirowski.

LISA ROFEL is Professor of Anthropology at the University of California, Santa Cruz. Her publications include *Other Modernities: Gendered Yearnings in China after Socialism* (University of California Press, 1999) and *Desiring China: Experiments in Neoliberalism, Sexuality, and Public Culture* (Duke University Press, 2007). Her most recent work, with Sylvia Yanagisako, *Fabricating Transnational Capitalism: A Collaborative Ethnography of Italian-Chinese Global Fashion* (Duke University Press, 2019) offers an innovative approach to studying the commodity chains of transnational capitalism.

LESLIE SALZINGER is Associate Professor of Gender and Women's Studies at the University of California, Berkeley. She is a sociologist and ethnographer who focuses on Latin America, and her research is concerned with gender, capitalism, globalization, and economic sociology. She is the author of the award-winning book *Genders in Production: Making Workers in Mexico's Global Factories* (University of California Press, 2003), and is currently working on a book provisionally entitled *Model Markets: Peso Dollar Exchange as a Site of Neoliberal Incorporation*.

QUINN SLOBODIAN is Associate Professor of History at Wellesley College. His books include *Foreign Front: Third World Politics in Sixties West Germany* (Duke University Press, 2012), *Comrades of Color: East Germany in the Cold War World* (Berghahn, 2015), and *Globalists: The End of Empire and the Birth of Neoliberalism* (Harvard University Press, 2018). He is currently coediting a volume on neoliberalism with Dieter Plehwe and Philip Mirowski.

WILLIAM CALLISON is Visiting Assistant Professor of Government and Law at Lafayette College. He holds a Ph.D. in Political Science with a Designated Emphasis in Critical Theory from the University of California, Berkeley, and an M.A. in Philosophy from the Humboldt University of Berlin. He is editor of "Rethinking Sovereignty and Capitalism" (*Qui Parle*) and coeditor of "Europe at a Crossroads" (*Near Futures Online*, Zone Books).

ZACHARY MANFREDI is an Equal Justice Works Fellow at the Asylum Seeker Advocacy Project. He received his J.D. from Yale Law School and is a Ph.D. candidate in the Rhetoric Department at U.C. Berkeley. He also holds an M.Phil. in Political Theory from Oxford University, where he studied as a Rhodes Scholar. His recent work has appeared or is forthcoming in *Humanity*, the *New York University Law Review*, the *Texas Journal of International Law*, and *Critical Times*.

www.ingramcontent.com/pod-product-compliance
Lightning Source LLC
Chambersburg PA
CBHW022139020426
42334CB00015B/966